CLASSIC TEXTS SERIES

THE ELEMENTS OF STATICS AND DYNAMICS

PART 1 STATICS

SL LONEY

arihant
SUCCESS AND NOTHING LESS

PO No. : TXT-59-T064127-03-25

arihant
SUCCESS AND NOTHING LESS

ARIHANT PRAKASHAN (Series), MEERUT

Administrative & Production Offices

Regd. Office

'Ramchhaya' 4577/15, Agarwal Road, Darya Ganj, New Delhi -110002
Tele: 011- 47630600, 43518550

Head Office

Kalindi, TP Nagar, Meerut (UP) - 250002
Tel: 0121-7156203, 7156204

Sales & Support Offices

Agra, Ahmedabad, Bengaluru, Bareilly, Chennai, Delhi, Guwahati, Hyderabad, Jaipur, Jhansi, Kolkata, Lucknow, Nagpur & Pune.

PRICE ₹245.00

PO No. : TXT-59-T069711-3-26

Published by Arihant Publications (India) Ltd.

For further information about the books published by Arihant, log on to www.arihantbooks.com or e-mail at info@arihantbooks.com

Follow us on

PREFACE

TO PART I

In the following work I have aimed at writing a working textbook on Statics for the use of Junior Students.

Throughout the book will be found a large number of examples; most of them, with the exception of many of those at the end of the chapter on friction and the Miscellaneous Examples at the end of the volume, are of an easy type.

I have tried to make the book complete as far as it goes; it is suggested, however, that the student should, on the first reading of the subject, omit everything marked with an asterisk.

I must express my obligations to my friend Mr HC Robson, MA, Fellow and Lecturer of Sidney Sussex College, Cambridge, for his kindness in reading through the proof-sheets, and for many suggestions that he has made to me.

Any corrections of errors, or hints for improvement will be thankfully received.

SL LONEY

BARNES,SW

PREFACE

FIFTH EDITION

The book has been somewhat altered, and I hope improved, for this edition, and the type entirely re-set. Graphic solutions have been introduced much earlier, and more use has been made of graphic methods throughout the book. More experimental work has also been introduced.

The chapter on Work has been placed earlier, and much greater stress has been laid upon the Principle of Work.

Sundry somewhat long analytical proofs have been relegated to the last chapter, and here I have not scrupled to introduce alternative proofs involving the use of the Differential Calculus.

For ten of the new figures in this book I am much indebted to the kindness and courtesy of Dr RT Glaze book, who allowed me to use the blocks prepared for his Statics. Most of these figures have the additional merit of having been drawn from actual apparatus in use at the Cavendish Laboratory at Cambridge.

SL LONEY

CONTENTS

1 Introduction

1. A **Body** is a portion of matter limited in every direction.

2. Force is anything which changes, or tends to change, the state of rest, or uniform motion, of a body.

3. Rest. A body is said to be at rest when it does not change its position with respect to surrounding objects.

4. Statics is the science which treats of the action of forces on bodies, the forces being so arranged that the bodies are at rest.

The science which treats of the action of force on bodies in motion is called **Dynamics.**

In the more modern system of nomenclature which is gradually gaining general acceptance, the science which treats of the action of force on bodies is called Dynamics, and it has two subdivisions, Statics and Kinetics, treating of the action of forces on bodies which are at rest and in motion respectively.

5. A **Particle** is a portion of matter which is indefinitely small in size, or which, for the purpose of our investigations, is so small that the distances between its different parts may be neglected.

A body may be regarded as an indefinitely large number of indefinitely small portions, or as a conglomeration of particles.

6. A **Rigid Body** is a body whose parts always preserve an invariable position with respect to one another.

This conception, like that of a particle, is idealistic. In nature no body is perfectly rigid. Every body yields, perhaps only very slightly, if force be applied to it. If a rod, made of wood, have one end firmly fixed and the other end be pulled, the wood stretches slightly; if the rod be made of iron the deformation is very much less.

To simplify our enquiry we shall assume that all the bodies with which we have to deal are prefectly rigid.

7. Equal Forces. Two forces are said to be equal when, if they act on a particle in opposite directions, the particle remains at rest.

8. Mass. The mass of a body is the quantity of matter in the body. In most of the countries, the theoretical unit of mass used is gramme and is defined to be the one-thousandth part of a lump of platinum-iridium, called a kilogramme. In England, the theoretical unit of mass hitherto used is a pound and is defined to be the mass of a certain piece of platinum kept in the Exchequer office. Accordingly, the mass of a body is two, three, four... etc. lb, when it contains two, three, four... times as much matter as the standard lump of platinum and also, the mass of a body is two, three, four ... gm, when it contains twice, thrice ...... of the one-thousandth part of a lump of platinum-iridium. A kilogramme which is a practical unit is equal to about 2.2046 lb.

9. Weight. The idea of weight is one with which everyone is familiar. We all know that a certain amount of exertion is required to prevent any body from falling to the ground. The earth attracts every body to itself with a force which, as we shall see in Dynamics, is proportional to the mass of the body.

The force with which the earth attracts any body to itself is called the weight of the body.

10. *Measurement of Force.* We shall choose, as our unit of force in Statics, the weight of one pound or of one gramme. The unit of force is therefore equal to the force which would just support a mass of one pound or of one gramme when hanging freely.

We shall find in Dynamics that the weight of one gramme is not quite the same at different points of the earth's surface.

In Statics, however, we shall not have to compare forces at different points of the earth's surface, so that this variation in the weight of a pound or of a gramme is of no practical importance ; we shall therefore neglect this variation and assume the weight of a pound or of a gramme to be constant.

Two systems of measurement. There are two principal systems of units, to measure physical quantities.

(i) The C.G.S. (centimetre-gramme-seconds or French [Metric] system) ; and

(ii) The F.P.S. System (the foot-pound-second) or British System.

We have already defined earlier (vide Art. 8) what are meant by 'unit gramme' and 'unit pound'. Now, in both the systems the unit of time is second, rather mean solar second, which is the $1/24 \times 60 \times 60$th or 1/86400th part of a solar day, which is the average value, for one year, of the solar day or the time which elapses between two consecutive transits of the Sun across the Meridian, at any place on the Earth's surface.

The unit of length in C.G.S. system is centimetre, which is the one-hundredth part of a metre, which is the distance between two lines engraved upon a platinum-iridium bar kept in Paris, the temperature being kept at 0° C.

The unit of length in F.P.S. system is foot, which is one-third the distance between two transverse lines, at 62° F on two gold plugs in a platinum-iridium bar kept in London.

In addition to these systems of units, there is a comparatively new system very much similar to the C.G.S. system, in which the units of length, mass and time are the Metre , the Kilogramme, and the Second respectively. This system is known as M.K.S. system.

11. In practice the expression 'weight of one pound' is, in Statics, often shortened into 'one pound'. The student will therefore understand that

'a force of 10lb' means 'a force equal to the weight of 10 lb'. Similarly, 'a force of 10 g' means 'a force equal to the weight of 10 g'.

12. *Forces represented by straight lines.* A force will be completely known when we know (i) its magnitude, (ii) its direction, and (iii) its point of application, *i.e.* the point of the body at which the force acts.

Hence we can conveniently represent a force by a straight line drawn through its point of application; for a straight line has both magnitude and direction.

Thus suppose a straight line *OA* represents a force, equal to 10 kg weight, acting at a point *O*. A force of 5 kg weight acting in the same direction would be represented by *OB*, where *B* bisects the distance *OA*, whilst a force, equal to 20 kg weight, would be represented by *OC*, where *OA* is produced till *AC* equals *OA*.

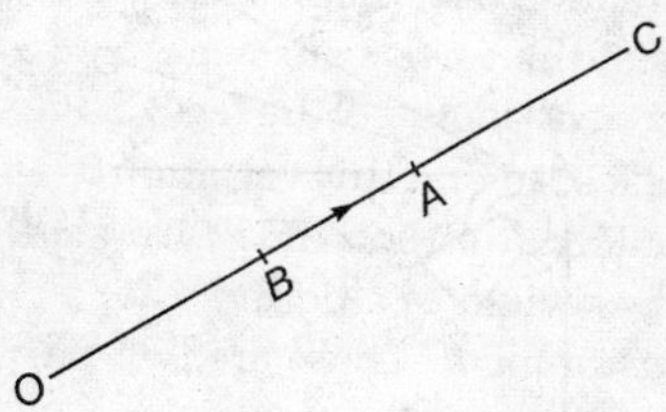

An arrowhead is often used to denote the direction in which a force acts.

13. *Subdivisions of Force.* There are three different forms under which a force may appear when applied to a mass, *viz.* as (i) an attraction, (ii) a tension, and (iii) a reaction.

14. *Attraction.* An attraction is a force exerted by one body on another without the intervention of any visible instrument and without the bodies being necessarily in contact. The only example we shall have in this book is the attraction which the earth has for every body; this attraction is (Art. 9) called its weight.

15. *Tension.* If we tie one end of a string to any point of a body and pull at the other end of the string, we exert a force on the body ; such a force, exerted by means of a string or rod, is called a **tension**.

If the string is light [*i.e.* one whose weight is so small that it may be neglected] the force exerted by the string is the same throughout its length.

For example, if a weight *W* is supported by means of a light string passing over the smooth edge of a table it is found that the same force must be applied to the string whatever is the point, *e.g.* *A*, *B*, or *C* of the string at which the force is applied.

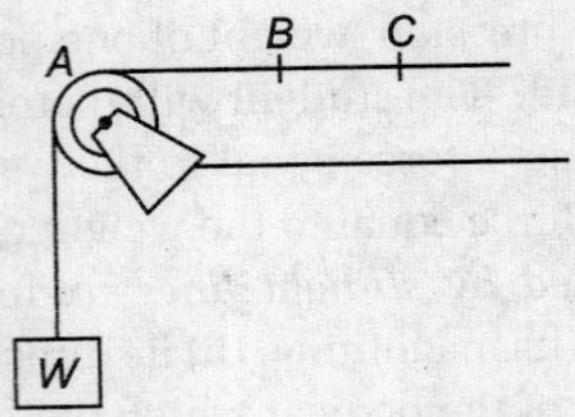

Now the force at A required to support the weight is the same in each case; hence it is clear that the effect at A is the same at whatever point of the string the tension is applied and that the tension of the string is therefore the same throughout its length.

Again, if the weight W is supported by a light string passing round a smooth peg A, it is found that the same force must be exerted at the other end of the string whatever be the direction (AB, AC, or AD) in which the string is pulled and that this force is equal to the weight W.

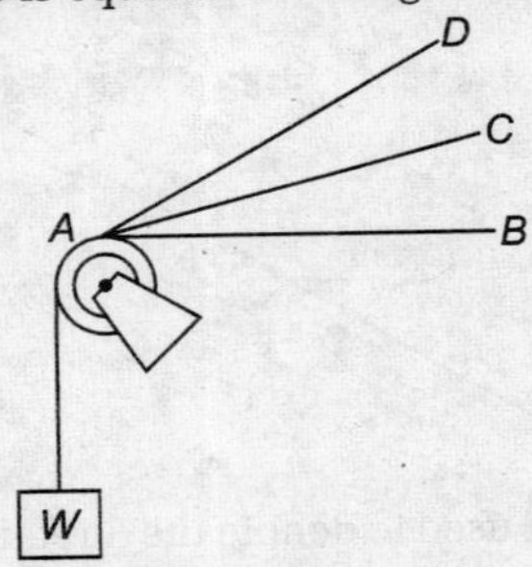

[These forces may be measured by attaching the free end of the string to a spring-balance.]

Hence *the tension of a light string passing round a smooth peg is the same throughout its length.*

If two or more strings be knotted together the tensions are not necessarily the same in each string.

The student must carefully notice that the tension of a string is not proportional to its length. It is a common error to suppose that the longer a string the greater is its tension ; it is true that we can often apply our force more advantageously if we use a longer piece of string, and hence a beginner often assumes that, other things being equal, the longer string has the greater tension.

16. *Reaction.* If one body leans, or is pressed, against another body, each body experiences a force at the point of contact ; such a force is called a reaction.

The force, or action, that one body exerts on a second body is equal and opposite to the force, or reaction, that the second body exerts on the first.

The idea of the "magnitude and direction of the reaction can well be understood from Newton's Third Law of Motion which states that 'To every action, there is an equal and opposite reaction'."

Examples. If a ladder leans against a wall the force exerted by the end of the ladder upon the wall is equal and opposite to that exerted by the wall upon the end of the ladder.

If a cube of wood is placed upon a table the force which it exerts upon the table is equal and opposite to the force which the table exerts on it.

17. Equilibrium. When two or more forces act upon a body and are so arranged that the body remains at rest, the forces are said to be in equilibrium.

18. *Introduction, or removal, of equal and opposite forces.* We shall assume that if at any point of a rigid body we apply two equal and opposite forces, they will have no effect on the equilibrium of the body ; similarly, that if at any point of a body two equal and opposite forces are acting they may be removed.

19. *Principle of the Transmissibility of Force. If a force acts at any point of a rigid body, it may be considered to act at any other point in its line of action provided that this latter point is rigidly connected with the body.*

Let a force F act at a point A of a body in a direction AX. Take any point B in AX and at B introduce two equal and opposite forces, each equal to F, acting in the directions BA and BX; these will have no effect on the equilibrium of the body.

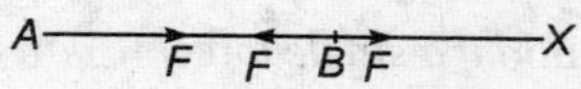

The forces F acting at A in the direction AB, and F at B in the direction BA are equal and opposite; we shall assume that they neutralise one another and hence that they may be removed.

We have thus left the force F at B acting in the direction BX and its effect is the same as that of the original force F at A.

The internal forces in the above body would be different according as the force F is supposed applied at A or B; of the internal forces, however, we do not treat in the present book.

20. *Smooth bodies.* If we place a piece of smooth polished wood, having a plane face, upon a table whose top is made as smooth as possible we shall find that, if we attempt to move the block along the surface of the table some resistance is experienced. There is always some force, however small, between the wood and the surface of the table.

If the bodies were perfectly smooth there would be no force, parallel to the surface of the table, between the block and the table ; the only force between them would be perpendicular to the table.

Def. When two bodies, which are in contact, are perfectly smooth the force, or reaction, between them is perpendicular to their common surface at the point of contact.

2

Composition and Resolution of Forces

21. SUPPOSE a flat piece of wood is resting on a smooth table and that it is pulled by means of three strings attached to three of its corners, the forces exerted by the strings being horizontal ; if the tensions of the strings are so adjusted that the wood remains at rest it follows that the three forces are in equilibrium.

Hence two of the forces must together exert a force equal and opposite to the third. This force, equal and opposite to the third, is called the resultant of the first two.

22. Resultant. Def. *If two or more forces P, Q, S ... act upon a rigid body and if a single force, R, can be found whose effect upon the body is the same as that of the forces P, Q, S ... this single force R is called the resultant of the other forces and the forces P, Q, S ... are called the components of R.*

It follows from the definition that if a force is applied to the body equal and opposite to the force R, then the forces acting on the body will balance and the body be in equilibrium; conversely, if the forces acting on a body balance then either of them is equal and opposite to the resultant of the others.

23. *Resultant of forces acting in the same straight line.* If two forces act on a body in the same direction their resultant is clearly equal to their sum ; thus two forces acting in the same direction, equal to 5 and 7 kg weight respectively, are equivalent to a force of 12 kg weight acting in the same direction as the two forces.

If two forces act on a body in opposite directions their resultant is equal to their difference and acts in the direction of the greater; thus two forces acting in opposite directions and equal to 9 and 4 kg weight respectively are equivalent to a force of 5 kg weight acting in the direction of the first of the two forces.

24. When two forces act at a point of a rigid body in different directions their resultant may be obtained by means of the following.

Theorem. Parallelogram of Forces. *If two forces, acting at a point, are represented in magnitude and direction by the two sides of a parallelogram drawn from one of its angular points, their resultant is represented both in magnitude and direction by the diagonal of the parallelogram passing through that angular point.*

This fundamental theorem of Statics, or rather another form of it, *viz.* the Triangle of Forces (Art. 36), was first enunciated by Stevinus of Bruges in the year 1586. Before his time the science of Statics rested on the Principle of the Lever as its basis.

In the following article we shall give an experimental proof; a more formal proof will be found in the last chapter.

In Art. 72 of Part II of this boog will be found a proof founded on Newton's Laws of Motion.

25. Experimental proof. Let F and G be two light pulleys attached to a fixed support ; over them let there pass two light strings tied together at O, and carrying scale-pans L and M at their other ends.

A second string is knotted at O and carries a third scale-pan N.

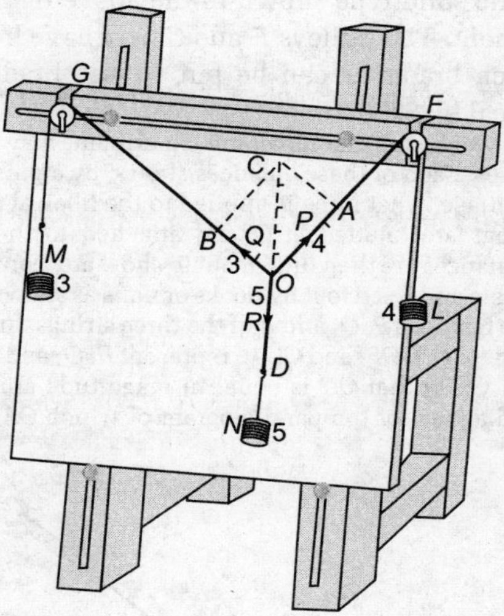

Into these scale-pans are placed known weights, and the whole system is allowed to take up a position of equilibrium. Let the weights in the scale-pans, together with the weights of the scale-pans themselves, be P, Q and R kg.

On a blackboard, or a piece of paper, conveniently placed behind the system draw the lines OF, OG, ON as in the figure.

Taking some convenient scale (say three cm, or less, per kg) mark off OA, OB, and OD to represent P, Q, and R lb. Complete the parallelogram $OACB$. Then OC will be found to be equal in length, and opposite in direction, to OD.

But, since P, Q, and R balance, therefore R must be equal and opposite to the resultant of P and Q.

Therefore the resultant of P and Q is represented by OC, *i.e.* by the diagonal of the parallelogram whose sides represent P and Q.

This will be found to be true whatever is the relative magnitudes of P, Q, and R, provided only that one of them is not greater than the sum of the other two.

In the figure P, Q, and R are taken respectively to be 4, 3, and 5 kg. In this case, since $5^2 = 4^2 + 3^2$, the angle AOB is a right angle.

When the experiment is performed, it will probably be found that the point O may be moved into one of several positions close to one another. The reason for this is that we cannot wholly get rid of the friction on the pivots of the pulleys. The effect of this friction will be minimised, in this and similar statical experiments, if the pulleys are of fairly large diameter ; aluminium pulleys are suitable because they can be made of comparatively large size and yet be of small weight.

Apparatus of the solid type shown in the above figure is not necessary for a rough experiment. The pulleys F and G may have holes bored through them through which bradawls can be put ; these bradawls may then be pushed into a vertical blackboard.

The pulleys and weights of the foregoing experiment may be replaced by three Salter's Spring Balances. Each of these balances shows, by a pointer which travels up and down a graduated face, what force is applied to the hook at its end.

Three light strings are knotted at O and attached to the ends of the spring balances. The three balances are then drawn out to show any convenient tensions, and laid on a horizontal table and fixed to it by hooks or nails as shown. The readings of the balances then give the tensions P, Q, and R of the three strings. Just as in the preceding experiment we draw lines OA, OB, and OC to represent P, Q, and R on any scale that is convenient, and then verify that OC is equal in magnitude and exactly opposite in direction to OD, the diagonal of the parallelogram of which OA and OB are adjacent sides.

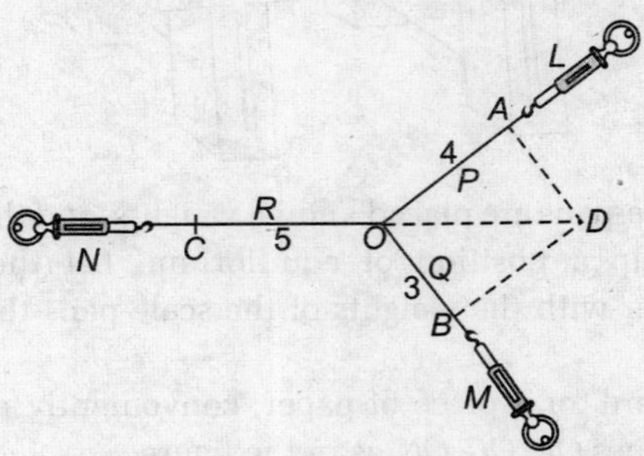

26. To find the direction and magnitude of the resultant of two forces, we have to find the direction and magnitude of the diagonal of a parallelogram of which the two sides represent the forces.

Ex. 1. *Find the resultant of forces equal to* 12 *and* 5 kg *weight respectively acting at right angles.*

(*Note* : The force unit 'kg weight' is now replaced by the unit kgf (kg force). 1 kg weight = 1kgf.)

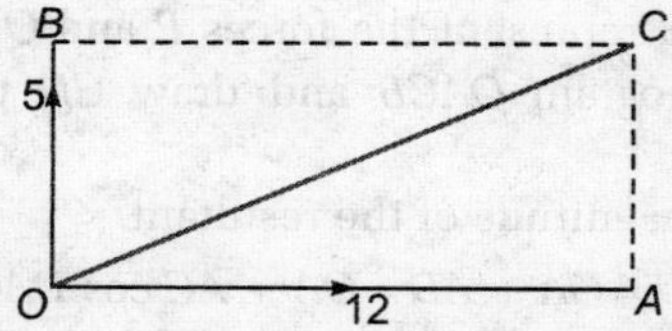

Let OA and OB represent the forces so that OA is 12 units of length and OB is 5 units of length ; complete the rectangle $OACB$.

Then $\quad OC^2 = OA^2 + AC^2 = 12^2 + 5^2 = 169 \qquad \therefore \quad OC = 13.$

Also $$\tan COA = \frac{AC}{OA} = \frac{5}{12}.$$

Hence the resultant is a force equal to 13 kg force making with the first force an angle whose tangent is $\frac{5}{12}$, *i.e.* about 22°37′.

Ex. 2. *Find the resultant of forces equal to the weights of* 5 *and* 3 *kg respectively acting at an angle of* 60°.

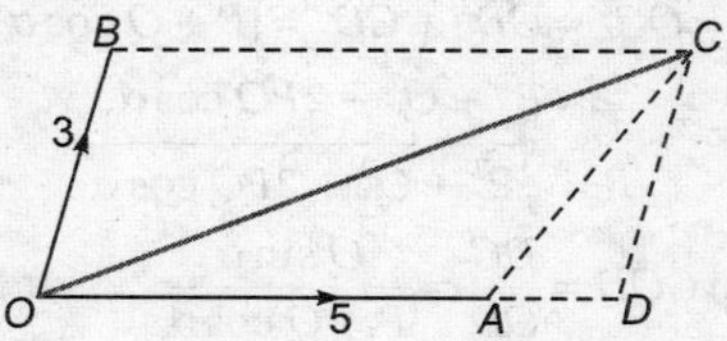

Let OA and OB represent the forces, so that OA is 5 units and OB 3 units of length ; also let the angle AOB be 60°.

Complete the parallelogram $OACB$ and draw CD perpendicular to OA. Then OC represents the required resultant.

Now $\quad AD = AC \cos CAD = 3 \cos 60° = \frac{3}{2}; \qquad \therefore \quad OD = \frac{13}{2}.$

Also $$DC = AC \sin 60° = 3\frac{\sqrt{3}}{2}.$$

$$\therefore \qquad OC = \sqrt{OD^2 + DC^2} = \sqrt{\frac{169}{4} + \frac{27}{4}} = \sqrt{49} = 7,$$

and $$\tan COD = \frac{DC}{OD} = \frac{3\sqrt{3}}{13} = .3997.$$

Hence the resultant is a force equal to 7 kg force in a direction making with OD an angle whose tangent is .3997.

On reference to a table of natural tangents this angle is easily seen to be about 21°47′.

27. The resultant, R, of two forces P and Q acting at an angle α may be easily obtained by trigonometry.

For let OA and OB represent the forces P and Q acting at an angle α. Complete the parallelogram $OACB$ and draw CD perpendicular to OA, produced if necessary.

Let R denote the magnitude of the resultant.

Then $$OD = OA + AD = OA + AC \cos DAC$$
$$= P + Q \cos BOD + Q \cos \alpha.$$

[If D falls between O and A, as in the second figure, we have
$$OD = OA - DA = OA - AC \cos DAC$$
$$= P - Q \cos (180° - \alpha) = P + Q \cos \alpha.]$$

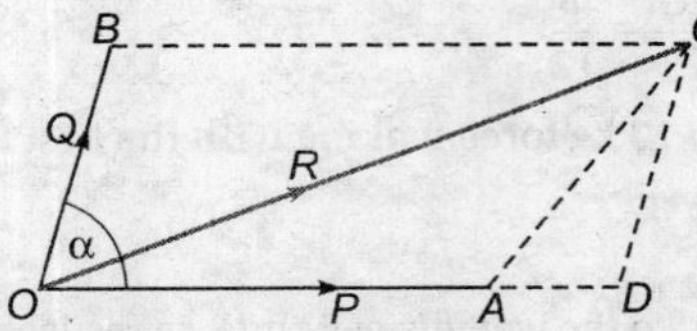

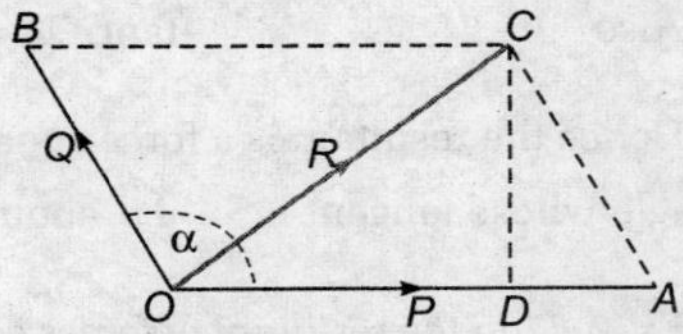

Also $$DC = AC \sin DAC = Q \sin \alpha.$$

$\therefore$ $$R^2 = OC^2 = OD^2 + CD^2 = (P + Q \cos \alpha)^2 + (Q \sin \alpha)^2$$
$$= P^2 + Q^2 + 2PQ \cos \alpha.$$

$\therefore$ $$R = \sqrt{P^2 + Q^2 + 2PQ \cos \alpha} \qquad \text{...(i).}$$

Also $$\tan COD = \frac{DC}{OD} = \frac{Q \sin \alpha}{P + Q \cos \alpha} \qquad \text{...(ii).}$$

These two equations give the required magnitude and direction of the resultant.

Cor. 1. If the forces are at right angles, we have $\alpha = 90°$, so that $R = \sqrt{P^2 + Q^2}$, and $\tan COA = \frac{Q}{P}$.

Cor. 2. If the forces are each equal to P, we have
$$r = \sqrt{P^2 (1 + 1 + 2 \cos \alpha)}$$
$$= P\sqrt{2 (1 + \cos \alpha)}$$
$$= P \sqrt{2.2 \cos^2 \frac{\alpha}{2}} = 2P \cos \frac{\alpha}{2},$$

and $$\tan COA = \frac{P \sin \alpha}{P + P \cos \alpha} = \frac{2 \sin \frac{\alpha}{2} \cos \frac{\alpha}{2}}{2 \cos^2 \frac{\alpha}{2}} = \tan \frac{\alpha}{2},$$

so that the resultant of two equal forces, bisects the angle between them ; this is obvious also from first principles.

Examples I

1. In the following seven examples P and Q denote two component forces acting at an angle α and R denotes their resultant. [The results should also be verified by a graph and measurement.]
   (i). If $P = 24; Q = 7; \alpha = 90°$; find R.
   (ii). If $P = 13; R = 14; \alpha = 90°$; find Q.
   (iii). If $P = 7; Q = 8; \alpha = 60°$; find R.
   (iv). If $P = 5; Q = 9; \alpha = 120°$; find R.
   (v). If $P = 3; Q = 5; R = 7$; find α.
   (vi). If $P = 13; Q = 14; \alpha = \sin^{-1}\frac{12}{13}$; find R
   (vii) If $P = 5; R = 7; \alpha = 60°$; find Q.
2. Find the greatest and least resultants of two forces whose magnitudes are 12 and 8 g force respectively.
3. Forces equal respectively to 3, 4, 5 and 6 g force act on a particle in directions respectively north, south, east, and west ; find the direction and magnitude of their resultant.
4. Forces of 84 and 187 kg force act at right angles ; find their resultant.
5. Two forces whose magnitudes are P and $P\sqrt{2}$ g force act on a particle in directions inclined at an angle of 135° to each other ; find the magnitude and direction of the resultant.
6. Two forces acting at an angle of 60° have a resultant equal to $2\sqrt{3}$ g force; if one of the forces is 2 g force, find the other force.
7. Find the resultant of two forces equal to the weights of 13 and 11 g acting at an angle whose tangent is $\frac{12}{5}$. Verify by a drawing.
8. Find the resultant of two forces equal to the weights of 10 and 9 g acting at an angle whose tangent is $\frac{4}{3}$. Verify by a drawing.
9. Two equal forces act on a particle ; find the angle between them when the square of their resultant is equal to three times their product.
10. Find the magnitude of two forces such that, if they act as right angles, their resultant is $\sqrt{10}$ kg force, whilst when they act at an angle of 60° their resultant is $\sqrt{13}$ kg force.
11. Find the angle between two equal forces P when their resultant is (1) equal to P, (2) equal to $\frac{P}{2}$.
12. At what angle do forces, equal to $(A + B)$ and $(A - B)$, act so that the resultant may be $\sqrt{A^2 + B^2}$?
13. Two given forces act on a particle ; find in what direction a third force of given magnitude must act so that the resultant of the three may be as great as possible.
14. By drawing along solve the following :
   (i) If $P = 10; Q = 15; \alpha = 37°$; find R.
   (ii) If $P = 9; Q = 7; \alpha = 133°$; find R.
   (iii) If $P = 7; Q = 5; R = 10$; find α.
   (iv) If $P = 7.3; R = 8.7; \alpha = 65°$; find Q

15. If the resultant of two forces acting on a particle be at right angles to one of them, and its magnitude be $\frac{1}{3}$rd of the other, show that the ratio of the longer force to the smaller is $3 : 2\sqrt{2}$.

16. Two forces acting at a point have got their resultant 10 when acting at right angles, and this resultant is 2. Find the greatest resultant, and also the resultant when they act at an angle of 60°.

28. Two forces, given in magnitude and direction, have only one resultant ; for only one parallelogram can be constructed having two lines *OA* and *OB* (Fig. Art. 27) as adjacent sides.

29. A force may be resolved into two components in an infinite number of ways ; for an infinite number of parallelograms can be constructed having *OC* as a diagonal and each of these parallelograms would give a pair of such components.

30. The most important case of the resolution of forces occurs when we resolve a force into two components **at right angles** to one another.

Suppose we wish to resolve a force *F*, represented by *OC*, into two components, one of which is in the direction *OA* and the other is perpendicular to *OA*.

Draw *CM* perpendicular to *OA* and complete the parallelogram *OMCN*. The forces represented by *OM* and *ON* have as their resultant the force *OC*, so that *OM* and *ON* are the required components.

Let the angle *AOC* be α.

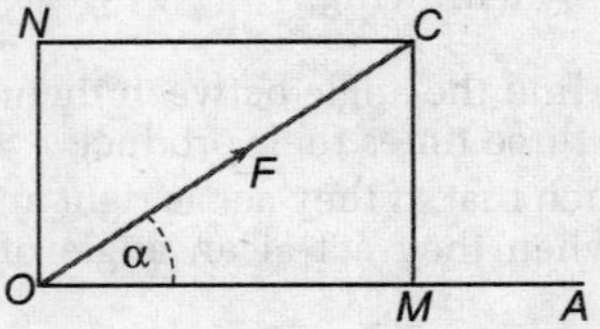

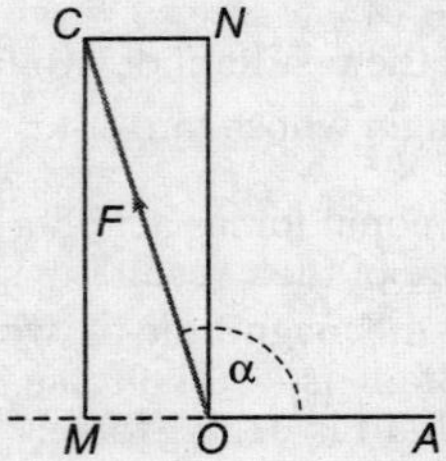

Then $\qquad OM = OC \cos\alpha = F \cos\alpha,$

and $\qquad ON = MC = OC \sin\alpha = F \sin\alpha.$

[If the point *M* lies in *OA* produced backwards, as in the second figure, the component of *F* in the direction *OA*

$$= -OM = -OC \cos COM = -OC \cos(180° - \alpha)$$

$$= OC \cos\alpha = F \cos\alpha.$$

Also the component perpendicular to *OA*

$$= ON = MC = OC \sin COM = F \sin\alpha.]$$

Hence, in each case, the required components are

$$F \cos\alpha \quad \text{and} \quad F \sin\alpha.$$

Thus a force equal to 10 kg force acting at an angle of 60° with the horizontal is equivalent to $10 \cos 60° \left(= 10 \times \frac{1}{2} = 5 \text{ kg force}\right)$ in a horizontal direction, and $10 \sin 60°$ $(= 10 \times \frac{\sqrt{3}}{2} = 5 \times 1.732 = 8.66$ kg force) in a vertical direction.

31. Def. The resolved part of a given force in a given direction is the component in the given direction which, with a component in a direction perpendicular to the given direction, is equivalent to the given force.

Thus in the previous article the resolved part of the force F in the direction OA is $F \cos \alpha$. Hence.

The resolved part of a given force in a given direction is obtained by multiplying the given force by the cosine of the angle between the given force and the given direction.

32. A force cannot produce any effect in a direction perpendicular to its own line of action. For (Fig. Art. 30) there is no reason why the force ON should have any tendency to make a particle at O move in the direction OA rather than to make it move in the direction AO produced ; hence, the force ON cannot have any tendency to make the particle move in either the direction OA or AO produced.

For example, if a railway carriage is standing at rest on a railway line it cannot be made to move along the rails by any force which is acting horizontally and in a direction perpendicular to the rails.

33. The resolved part of a given force in a given direction represents the *whole effect* of the force in the given direction. For (Fig. Art. 30) to force OC is completely represented by the forces ON and OM. But the force ON has no effect in the direction OA. Hence, the whole effect of the force F in the direction OA is represented by OM, *i.e.* by the resolved part of the force in the direction OA.

34. A force may be resolved into two components in any two assigned directions. Let the components of a force F, represented by OC, in the directions OA and OB be required and let the angles AOC and COB be α and β respectively.

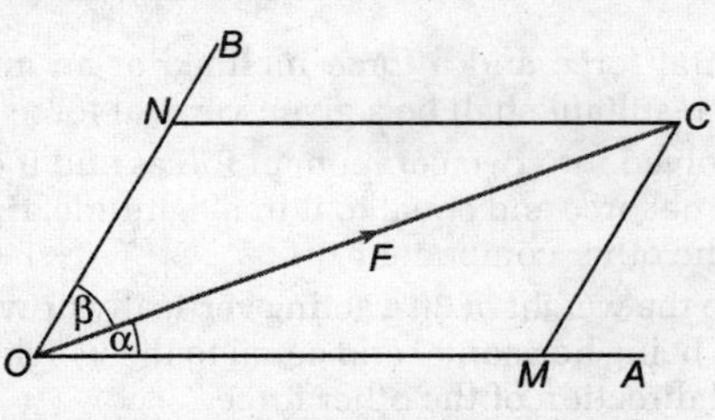

Draw OM parallel to OB to meet OA in M and complete the parallelogram $OMCN$. Then OM and ON are the required components.

Since, MC and ON are parallel, we have

$OCM = \beta$; also $OMC = 180° - CMA = 180° - (\alpha + \beta)$

Since, the sides of the triangle OMC are proportional to the sines of the opposite angles, we have

$$\frac{OM}{\sin OCM} = \frac{MC}{\sin MOC} = \frac{OC}{\sin OMC}.$$

$$\therefore \quad \frac{OM}{\sin\beta} = \frac{MC}{\sin\alpha} = \frac{F}{\sin(\alpha+\beta)}.$$

Hence the required components are

$$F\frac{\sin\beta}{\sin(\alpha+\beta)} \text{ and } F\frac{\sin\alpha}{\sin(\alpha+\beta)}.$$

35. The student must carefully notice that the components of a force in two assigned directions are not the same as the resolved parts of the forces in these directions. For example, the resolved part of F in the direction OA is, by Art. 30, $F\cos\alpha$.

Examples II

1. A force equal to 10 kg force is inclined at an angle of 30° to the horizontal; find its resolved parts in a horizontal and vertical direction.

2. Find the resolved part of a force P in a direction making (1) an angle of 45°, (2) an angle equal to $\cos^{-1}\left(\frac{12}{13}\right)$ with its direction.

3. A truck is at rest on a railway line and is pulled by a horizontal force equal to the weight of 100 kg in a direction making an angle of 60° with the direction of the rails ; what is the force tending to urge the truck forwards ?

4. Resolve a force of 100 g force into two equal forces acting at an angle of 60° to each other. Verify by a graph and measurement.

5. Resolve a force of 50 g force into two forces making angles of 60° and 45° with it on opposite sides. Verify by a graph and measurement.

6. Find the components of a force P along two directions making angles of 30° and 45° with P on opposite sides.

7. If a force P is resolved into two forces making angles of 45° and 15° with its direction, show that the latter force is $\frac{\sqrt{6}}{3}P$.

8. Find a horizontal force and a force inclined at an angle of 60° with the vertical whose resultant shall be a given vertical force F.

9. If a force is resolved into two component forces and if one component is at right angles to the force and equal to it in magnitude, find the direction and magnitude of the other component.

10. A force equal to the weight of 20 g acting vertically upwards is resolved into two forces, one being horizontal and equal to the weight of 10 g ; what is the magnitude and direction of the other force ?

11. By a graphic construction and measurement resolve a force equal to 35 kgf into components making angles of 98° and 40° with it on opposite sides.

36. Triangle of Forces. *If three forces, acting at a point, are represented in magnitude and direction by the sides of a triangle, taken in order, they will be in equilibrium.*

Let the forces, P, Q, and R acting at the point O be represented in magnitude and direction by the sides AB, BC, and CA of the triangle ABC; they shall be in equilibrium.

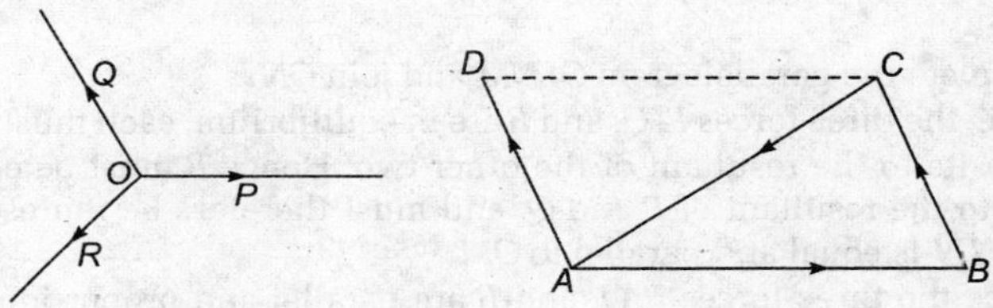

Complete the parallelogram $ABCD$.

The forces represented by BC and AD are the same, since BC and AD are equal and parallel.

Now the resultant of the forces AB and AD, is, by the parallelogram of forces, represented by AC.

Hence the resultant of AB, BC, and CA is equal to the resultant of forces AC and CA, and is therefore zero.

Hence the three forces P, Q, and R are in equilibrium.

Cor. Since forces represented by AB, BC, and CA are in equilibrium, and since, when three forces are in equilibrium, each is equal and opposite to the resultant of the other two, it follows that the resultant of AB and BC is equal and opposite to CA *i.e.* their resultant is represented by AC.

Hence the resultant of two forces, acting at a point and represented by the sides AB and BC of a triangle, is represented by the third side AC.

37. In the Triangle of Forces the student must carefully note that the forces must be parallel to the sides of a triangle *taken in order, i.e., taken the same way round.*

For example, if the first force acts in the direction AB, the second must act in the direction BC, and the third in the direction CA; if the second force were in the direction CB, instead of BC, the forces would not be in equilibrium.

The three forces must also act *at a point*; if the lines of action of the forces were BC, CA, and AB they would not be in equilibrium ; for the forces AB and BC would have a resultant, acting at B, equal and parallel to AC. The system of forces would then reduce to two equal and parallel forces acting in opposite directions, and, as we shall see in a later chapter, such a pair of forces could not be in equilibrium.

38. The converse of the Triangle of Forces is also true, *viz*, that *If three forces acting at a point are in equilibrium they can be represented in magnitude and direction by the sides of any triangle which is drawn so as to have its sides respectively parallel to the directions of the forces.*

Let the three forces P, Q, and R, acting at a point O, be in equilibrium. Measure off lengths OL and OM along the directions of P and Q to represent these forces respectively.

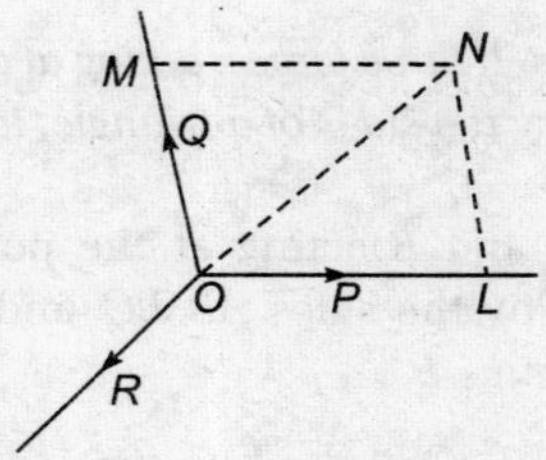

Complete the parallelogram *OLNM* and join *ON*.

Since, the three forces *P*, *Q*, and *R* are in equilibrium, each must be equal and opposite to the resultant of the other two. Hence *R* must be equal and opposite to the resultant of *P* and *Q*, and must therefore be represented by *NO*. Also *LN* is equal and parallel to *OM*.

Hence the three forces *P*, *Q*, and *R* are parallel and proportional to the sides *OL*, *LN*, and *NO* of the triangle *OLN*.

Any other triangle, whose sides are parallel to those of the triangle *OLN*, will have its sides proportional to those of *OLN* and therefore proportional to the forces.

Again, any triangle, whose sides are respectively perpendicular to those of the triangle *OLN*, will have its sides proportional to the sides of *OLN* and therefore proportional to the forces.

39. The proposition of the last article gives an easy graphical method of determining the relative directions of three forces which are in equilibrium and whose magnitudes are known. We have to construct a triangle whose sides are proportional to the forces, and this can always be done unless two of the forces added together are less than the third.

40. Lami's Theorem. *If three forces acting on a particle keep it in equilibrium, each is proportional to the sine of the angle between the other two.*

Taking Fig., Art. 38, let the forces *P*, *Q*, and *R* be in equilibrium. As before, measure off lengths *OL* and *OM* to represent the forces *P* and *Q*, and complete the parallelogram *OLNM*. Then *NO* represents *R*.

Since the sides of the triangle *OLN* are proportional to the sines of the opposite angles, we have

$$\frac{OL}{\sin LNO} = \frac{LN}{\sin LON} = \frac{NO}{\sin OLN}.$$

But

$$\sin LNO = \sin NOM = \sin(180° - QOR) = \sin QOR,$$

$$\sin LON = \sin(180° - LOR) = \sin ROP,$$

and $\sin OLN = \sin(180° - POQ) = \sin POQ.$

Also $LN = OM.$

Hence $$\frac{OL}{\sin QOR} = \frac{OM}{\sin ROP} = \frac{NO}{\sin POQ},$$

i.e. $$\frac{P}{\sin QOR} = \frac{Q}{\sin ROP} = \frac{R}{\sin POQ}.$$

41. Polygon of Forces. *If any number of forces, acting on a particle, be represented, in magnitude and direction, by the sides of polygon, taken in order, the forces will be in equilibrium.*

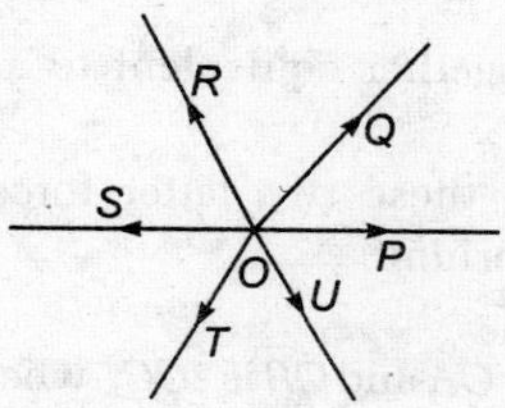

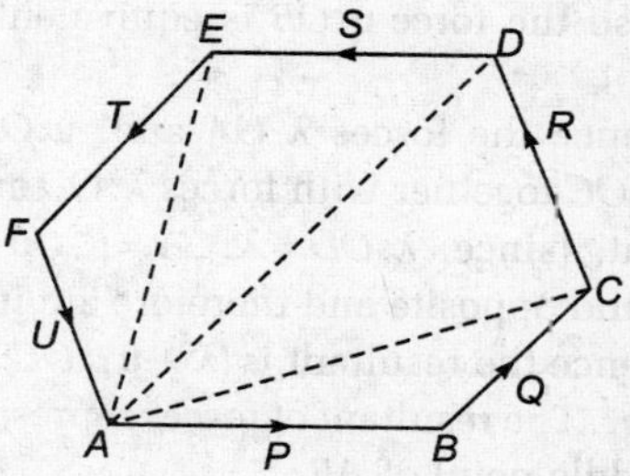

Let the sides AB, BC, CD, DE, EF, and FA of the polygon $ABCDEF$ represent the forces acting on a particle O. Join AC, AD, and AE.

By the corollary to Art. 36, the resultant of forces AB and BC is represented by AC.

Similarly the resultant of forces AC and CD is represented by AD ; the resultant of forces AD and DE by AE; and the resultant of forces AE and EF by AF.

Hence the resultant of all the forces is equal to the resultant of AF and FA, *i.e.* the resultant vanishes.

Hence the forces are in equilibrium.

A similar method of proof will apply whatever the number of forces. It is also clear from the proof that the sides of the polygon need not be in the same plane.

The converse of the Polygon of Forces is not true ; for the ratios of the sides of a polygon are not known when the directions of the sides are known. For example, in the above figure, we might take any point A' on AB and draw $A'F'$ parallel to AF to meet EF in F' ; the new polygon $A'BCDEF'$ has its sides respectively parallel to those of the polygon $ABCDEF$ but the corresponding sides are clearly not proportional.

42. *The resultant of two forces, acting at a point O in directions OA and OB are represented in magnitude by* $\lambda . OA$ *and* $\mu . OB$ *is represented by* $(\lambda + \mu) . OC$, *where C is a point in AB such that* $\lambda \cdot CA = \mu \cdot CB$.

For let C divide the line AB, such that

$$\lambda \cdot CA = \mu \cdot CB.$$

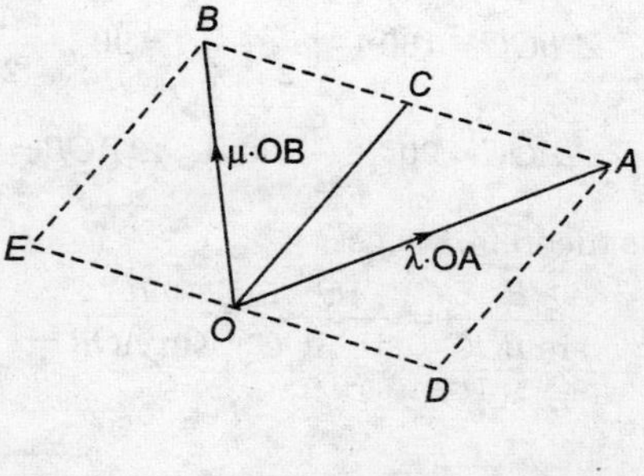

Complete the parallelograms $OCAD$ and $OCBE$.

By the parallelogram of forces the force $\lambda.OA$ is equivalent to forces represented by $\lambda.OC$ and $\lambda.OD$.

Also the force $\mu.OB$ is equivalent to forces represented by $\mu.OC$ and $\mu.OE$.

Hence the forces $\lambda.OA$ and $\mu.OB$ are together equivalent to a force $(\lambda + \mu)\,OC$ together with forces $\lambda.OD$ and $\mu.OE$.

But, (since, $\lambda.OD = \lambda.CA = \mu.CB = \mu.OE$) these two latter forces are equal and opposite and therefore are in equilibrium.

Hence the resultant is $(\lambda + \mu).OC$.

Cor. The resultant of forces represented by OA and OB is $2OC$, where C is the middle point of AB.

This is also clear from the fact that OC is half the diagonal OD of the parallelogram of which OA and OB are adjacent sides.

Ex. 1 *A particle is placed at the centre of a circle and is acted on by three forces, P, Q, and R tending towards the angular points A, B, and C of a circumscribed triangle. Prove that when the forces are in equilibrium.*

$$\frac{P}{\cos\frac{A}{2}} = \frac{Q}{\cos\frac{B}{2}} = \frac{R}{\cos\frac{C}{2}}$$

where A, B, and C are the angles of the triangle.

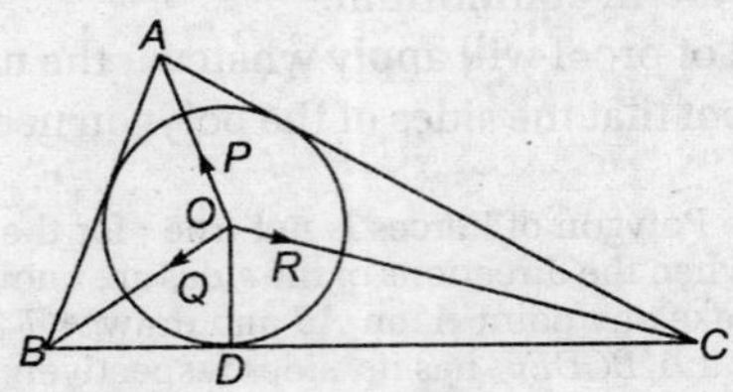

Let O be the centre of the circle.

OD is drawn perpendicular to BC.

$$\angle DOC = 90° - \angle OCD = 90° - \frac{C}{2}$$

Also, $$\angle BOD = 90° - \angle OBD = 90° - \frac{B}{2}$$

Hence, $$\angle BOC = 180° - \left(\frac{C}{2} + \frac{B}{2}\right) = 90° + \frac{A}{2}$$

Similarly, $$\angle AOC = 90° + \frac{B}{2} \quad \text{and} \quad \angle AOB = 90° + \frac{C}{2}$$

Applying Lami's theorem, we get

$$\frac{P}{\sin BOC} = \frac{Q}{\sin AOC} = \frac{R}{\sin AOB}$$

i.e. $$\frac{P}{\sin\left(90° + \frac{A}{2}\right)} = \frac{Q}{\sin\left(90° + \frac{B}{2}\right)} = \frac{R}{\sin\left(90° + \frac{C}{2}\right)}$$

hence, $$\frac{P}{\cos\frac{A}{2}} = \frac{Q}{\cos\frac{B}{2}} = \frac{R}{\cos\frac{C}{2}}.$$

Ex. 2. *A bead of weight W can slide on a smooth circular wire in a vertical plane. The bead is attached by a light thread to the highest point of the wire, and in equilibrium the thread is taut and makes an angle θ with the vertical. Find the tension of the thread and the reaction of the wire on the bead.*

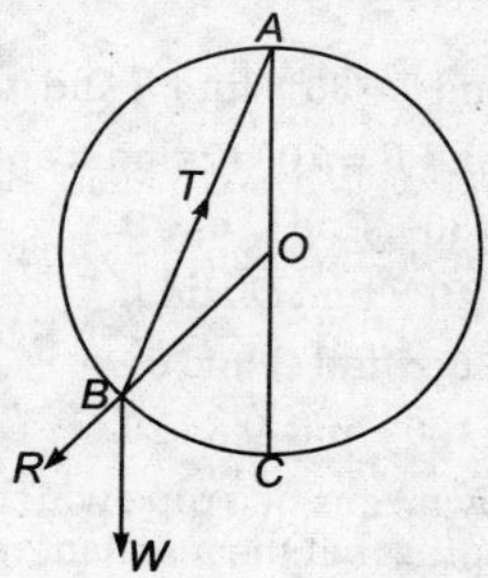

BAO is a triangle whose sides are parallel to the forces, so that

$$\frac{T}{BA} = \frac{R}{OB} = \frac{W}{AO}$$

Hence, $$T = W \cdot \frac{BA}{AO} = W \cdot \frac{2AO \cdot \cos\theta}{AO} = 2W\cos\theta.$$

Also $$R = W, \qquad (\because AO = OB)$$

Examples III

1. Three forces acting at a point are in equilibrium; if they make angles of 120° with one another, show that they are equal.
   If the angles are 60°, 150°, and 150°, in what proportions are the forces ?
2. Three forces acting on a particle are in equilibrium ; the angle between the first and second is 90° and that between the second and third is 120°; find the ratios of the forces.
3. Forces equal to $7P$, $5P$, and $8P$ acting on a particle are in equilibrium; find, by geometric construction and by calculation, the angle between the latter pair of forces.
4. Forces equal to $5P$, $12P$, and $13P$ acting on a particle are in equilibrium; find, by geometric construction and by calculation, the angles between their directions.
5. Construct geometrically the directions of two forces $2P$ and $3P$ which are in equilibrium with a force of $4P$ whose direction is given.

6. The sides AB and AC of a triangle ABC are bisected at D and E ; show that the resultant of forces represented by BE and DC is represented in magnitude and direction by $\frac{3}{2}$ BC.
7. P is a particle acted on by forces represented by λ. AP and λ. PB where A and B are two fixed points ; show that their resultant is constant in magnitude and direction wherever the point P is.
8. $ABCD$ is a parallelogram; a particle P is attracted towards A and C by forces which are proportional to PA and PC respectively and repelled from B and D by forces proportional to PB and PD ; show that P is in equilibrium wherever it is situated.

The following are to be solved by **geometric construction**. In each case P and Q are two forces inclined at an angle α and R is their resultant making an angle θ with P.

9. $P = 25$ kgf, $Q = 20$ kgf and $\theta = 35°$; find R and α.
10. $P = 50$ kgf, $Q = 60$ kgf and $R = 70$ kf ; find α and θ.
11. $P = 30$, $R = 40$ and $\alpha = 130°$; find Q and θ.
12. $P = 60$, $\alpha = 75°$ and $\theta = 40°$; find Q and R.
13. $P = 60$, $R = 40$ and $\theta = 50°$; find Q and α.
14. $P = 80$, $\alpha = 55°$ and $R = 100$; find Q and θ.
15. A boat is being towed by means of a rope which makes an angle of 20° with the boat's length ; assuming that the resultant reaction R of the water on the boat is inclined at 40° to the boat's length and that the tension of the rope is equal to 280 kgf, find, by drawing, the resultant force on the boat, supposing it to be in the direction of the boat's length.

Examples IV

1. Two forces act at an angle of 120°. The greater is represented by 80 and the resultant is at right angles to the smaller. Find the latter.
2. If one of two forces is double the other and the resultant is equal to the greater force, find the angle between the forces.
3. Two forces acting on a particle are at right angles and are balanced by a third force making an angle of 150° with one of them. The greater of the two forces being 3 kg force, what must be the values of the other two ?
4. The resultant of two forces acting at an angle equal to $\frac{5}{3}$ of a right angle is perpendicular to the smaller component. The greater being equal to 30 kg force, find the other component and the resultant.
5. The magnitudes of two forces are as 3 : 5, and the direction of the resultant is at right angles to that of the smaller force; compare the magnitudes of the larger force and of the resultant.
6. The sum of two forces is 18, and the resultant, whose direction is perpendicular to the lesser of the two forces, is 12; find the magnitude of the forces.
7. If two forces P and Q act at such an angle that $R = P$, show that, if P is doubled, the new resultant is at right angles to Q.

8. The resultant of two forces P and Q is equal to $\sqrt{3}Q$ and makes an angle of 30° with the direction of P ; show that P is either equal to, or is double, Q.

9. Two forces equal to $2P$ and P respectively act on a particle; if the first is doubled and the second increased by 12 kg force the direction of the resultant is unaltered ; find the values of P.

10. The resultant of two forces P and Q acting at an angle θ is equal to $(2m+1)\sqrt{P^2+Q^2}$; when they act at an angle $90° - \theta$, the resultant is $(2m-1)\sqrt{P^2+Q^2}$; prove that

$$\tan\theta = \frac{m-1}{m+1}.$$

11. The resultant of forces P and Q is R ; if Q is doubled R is doubled whilst, if Q be reversed, R is again doubled ; show that

$$P : Q : R :: \sqrt{2} : \sqrt{3} : \sqrt{2}.$$

12. If the resultant, R, of two forces P and Q, inclined to one another at any given angle, make an angle θ with the direction of P, show that the resultant of forces $(P+R)$ and Q, acting at the same given angle, will make an angle $\frac{\theta}{2}$ with the direction of $(P+R)$.

13. Three given forces acting at a point are in equilibrium. If one of them is turned about its point of application through a given angle, find by a simple construction the resultant of the three, and, if the inclination of the force continues to alter, show that the inclination of the resultant alters by half the amount.

14. Decompose a force, whose magnitude and line of action are given, into two equal forces passing through two given points, giving a geometrical construction, (1) when the two points are on the same side of the force, (2) when they are on opposite sides.

15. Two given forces act at two given points of a body ; if they are turned round those points in the same direction through any two equal angles, show that their resultant will always pass through a fixed point.

16. A, B and C are three fixed points, and P is a point such that the resultant of forces PA and PB always passes through C ; show that the locus of P is a straight line.

17. A given force acting at a given point in a given direction is resolved into two components. If for all directions of the components one remains of invariable magnitude, show that the extremity of the line representing the other lies on a definite circle.

18. Show that the system of forces represented by the lines joining any point to the angular points of a triangle is equivalent to the system represented by straight lines drawn from the same point to the middle points of the sides of the triangle.

19. Find a point within a quadrilateral such that, if it is acted on by forces represented by the lines joining it to the angular points of the quadrilateral, it will be in equilibrium.

20. Four forces act along and are proportional to the sides of the quadrilateral $ABCD$; three act in the directions AB, BC, and CD and the fourth acts from A to D ; find the magnitude and direction of their resultant, and determine the point in which it meets CD.

21. The sides BC and DA of a quadrilateral $ABCD$ are bisected in F, and H respectively; show that if two forces parallel and equal to AB and DC act on a particle, then the resultant is parallel to HF and equal to $2 \cdot HF$.

22. The sides AB, BC, CD, and DA of a quadrilateral $ABCD$ are bisected at E, F, G, and H respectively. Show that the resultant of the forces acting at a point which are represented in magnitude and direction by EG, and HF is represented in magnitude and direction by AC.

23. From a point, P, within a circle whose centre is fixed, straight lines PA_1, PA_2, PA_3, and PA_4 are drawn to meet the circumference, all being equally inclined to the radius through P ; show that, if these lines represent forces radiating from P, their resultant is independent of the magnitude of the radius of the circle.

24. Forces P, Q, and E acting along OA, OB, and OC where O is the circumcentre of the triangle ADC, are in equilibrium. Show that

$$\frac{P}{a^2(b^2+c^2-a^2)} = \frac{Q}{b^2\,(c^2+a^2-b^2)} = \frac{R}{c^2\,(a^2+b^2-c^2)}$$

25. If the resultant of two forces P and $Q\,(P > Q)$ is a mean proportional between the greatest and least values, show that the angle between P and Q is $\cos^{-1}\left(-\frac{Q}{P}\right)$.

26. The angle of inclination between two forces P and Q is θ. If P and Q are interchanged in position, show that the resultant will be turned through an angle ϕ, where

$$\tan\frac{\phi}{2} = \frac{P-Q}{P+Q}\tan\frac{\theta}{2}.$$

27. ABC is a triangle with a right angle at A. AD is perpendicular to BC. Prove that the resultant of the forces $\frac{1}{AB}$ acting along AB and $\frac{1}{AC}$ acting along AC is $\frac{1}{AD}$ acting along AD.

28. Two forces $P + Q, P - Q$ make an angle 2α with one another and their resultant makes an angle θ with the bisector of the angle between them. Show that $P\tan\theta = Q\tan\alpha$.

29. When two equal forces are inclined at an angle 2α, their resultant is twice as great as when they act at angle 2β. Show that $\cos\alpha = 2\cos\beta$.

3

Composition and Resolution of Forces *(Continued)*

43. *The sum of the resolved parts of two forces in a given direction is equal to the resolved part of their resultant in the same direction.*

Let OA and OB represent the two forces P and Q, and OC their resultant R, so that $OACB$ is a parallelogram.

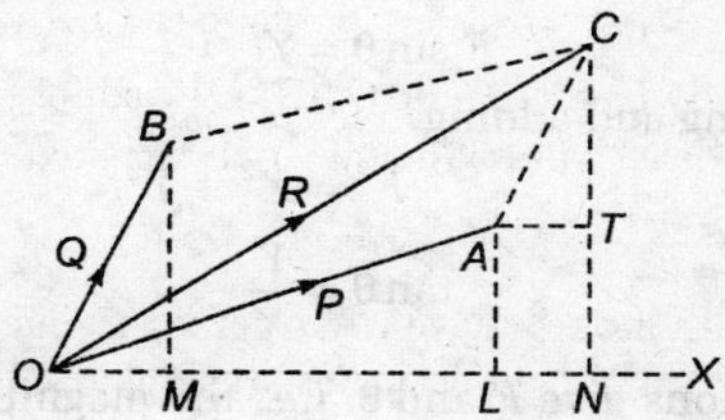

Let OX be the given direction ; draw AL, BM, and CN perpendicular to OX and AT perpendicular to CN.

The sides of the two triangles OBM, ACT are respectively parallel, and OB is equal to AC in magnitude ;

$\therefore$ $$OM = AT = LN.$$

Hence $$ON = OL + LN = OL + OM.$$

But OL, OM, and ON represent respectively the resolved parts of P, Q, and R in the direction OX.

Hence the theorem is proved.

The theorem may easily be extended to the resultant of any number of forces acting at a point.

44. *To find the resultant of any number of forces in one plane acting upon a particle.*

Let the forces $P, Q, R \ldots$ act upon a particle at O.

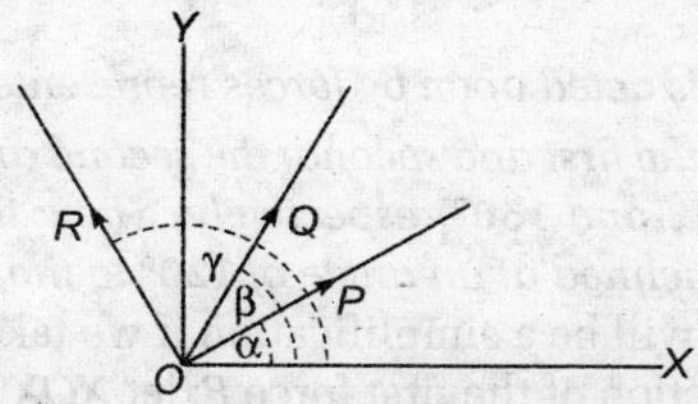

Through O draw a fixed line OX and a line OY at right angles to OX.

Let the forces $P, Q, R, \ldots$ make angles $\alpha, \beta, \gamma, \ldots$ with OX.

The components of the force P in the directions OX and OY are, by Art. 30, $P\cos\alpha$ and $P\sin\alpha$ respectively ; similarly, the components of Q are $Q\cos\beta$ and $Q\sin\beta$; similarly for the other forces.

Hence the forces are equivalent to a component,

$$P\cos\alpha + Q\cos\beta + R\cos\gamma \ldots \text{ along } OX,$$

and a component,

$$P\sin\alpha + Q\sin\beta + R\sin\gamma \ldots \text{along } OY.$$

Let these components be X and Y respectively, and let F be their resultant inclined at an angle θ to OX.

Since F is equivalent to $F\cos\theta$ along OX, and $F\sin\theta$ along OY, we have, by the previous article,

$$F\cos\theta = X \qquad \ldots(1),$$

and

$$F\sin\theta = Y \qquad \ldots(2).$$

Hence, by squaring and adding,

$$F^2 = X^2 + Y^2.$$

Also, by division,

$$\tan\theta = \frac{Y}{X}.$$

These two equations give F and θ, *i.e.*, the magnitude and direction of the required resultant.

Ex. 1. *A particle is acted upon by three forces, in one plane, equal to 2, $2\sqrt{2}$ and 1 kg force respectively; the first is horizontal, the second acts at 45° to the horizontal, and the third is vertical ; find their resultant.*

Here

$$X = 2 + 2\sqrt{2}\cos 45° + 0 = 2 + 2\sqrt{2}\cdot\frac{1}{\sqrt{2}} = 4,$$

$$Y = 0 + 2\sqrt{2}\sin 45° + 1 = 2\sqrt{2}\cdot\frac{1}{\sqrt{2}} + 1 = 3.$$

Hence,

$$F\cos\theta = 4; F\sin\theta = 3;$$

$$\therefore \quad F = \sqrt{4^2 + 3^2} = 5, \text{ and } \tan\theta = \frac{3}{4}.$$

The resultant is therefore a force equal to 5 kg force acting at an angle with the horizontal whose tangent is $\frac{3}{4}$, *i.e.* 36° 52′.

Ex. 2. *A particle is acted upon by forces represented by $P, 2P, 3\sqrt{3}P$, and $4P$; the angles between the first and second, the second and third, and the third and fourth are 60°, 90°, and 150° respectively, Show that the resultant is a force P in a direction inclined at an angle of 120° to that of the first force.*

In this example it will be a simplification if we take the fixed line OX to coincide with the direction of the first force P; let XOX' and YOY' be the two fixed lines at right angles.

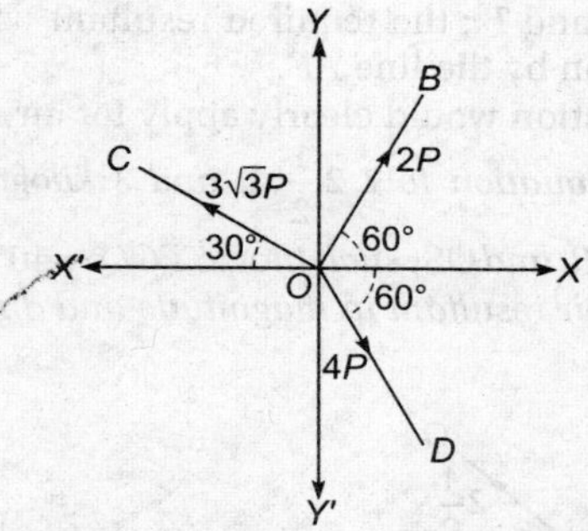

The second, third, and fourth forces are respectively in the first, second, and fourth quadrants, and we have clearly

$$BOX = 60°; \quad COX' = 30°; \quad \text{and} \quad DOX = 60°.$$

The first force has no component along OY.

The second force is equivalent to components $2P\cos 60°$ and $2P\sin 60°$ along OX and OY respectively.

The third force is equivalent to forces

$$3\sqrt{3}P\cos 30° \quad \text{and} \quad 3\sqrt{3}P\sin 30°$$

along OX' and OY respectively,
i.e. to forces $-3\sqrt{3}P\cos 30°$ and $3\sqrt{3}P\sin 30°$ along OX and OY.

So the fourth force is equivalent to $4P\cos 60°$ and $4P\sin 60°$ along OX and OY', *i.e.* to $4P\cos 60°$ and $-4P\sin 60°$ along OX and OY.

Hence $$X = P + 2P\cos 60° - 3\sqrt{3}P\cos 30° + 4P\cos 60°$$

$$= P + P - \frac{9P}{2} + 2P = -\frac{P}{2},$$

and $$Y = 0 + 2P\sin 60° + 3\sqrt{3}P\sin 30° - 4P\sin 60°$$

$$= P\sqrt{3} + \frac{3\sqrt{3}}{2}P - 4P\cdot\frac{\sqrt{3}}{2} = \frac{\sqrt{3}}{2}P.$$

Hence, if F is the resultant at an angle θ with OX, we have

$$F = \sqrt{X^2 + Y^2} = P,s$$

and $$\tan\theta = \frac{Y}{X} = -\sqrt{3} = \tan 120°,$$

so, that the resultant is a force P at an angle of 120° with the first force.

45. Graphical Construction. The resultant of a system of forces acting at a point may also be obtained by means of the Polygon of Forces. For, (Fig. Art. 41), forces acting at a point O and represented in magnitude and direction by the sides of the polygon $ABCDEF$ are in equilibrium. Hence the resultant of forces represented by AB, BC, CD, DE, and EF must be equal and opposite to the remaining forces FA, *i.e.*, the resultant must be represented by AF.

It follows that the resultant of forces P, Q, R, S, and T acting on a particle may be obtained thus ; take a point A and draw AB parallel and proportional to P, and in succession BC, CD, DE, and EF parallel and proportional respectively to Q, R, S, and T; the required resultant will be represented in magnitude and direction by the line AF.

The same construction would clearly apply for any number of forces.

Ex. *Four forces equation to* $2, 2\frac{1}{2}, 1$, *and* 3 *kilogramme wt act along straight lines* OP, OQ, OR, *and* OS, *such that* $\angle POQ = 40°$, $\angle QOR = 100°$, *and* $\angle ROS = 125°$; *find their resultant in magnitude and direction.*

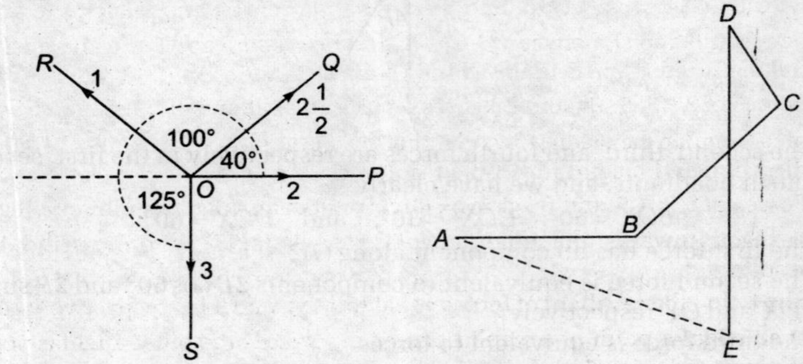

Draw AB parallel to OP and equal to 4 cm; through B draw BC parallel to OQ and equal to 5 cm, and then CD parallel to OR and equal to 2 cm, and finally DE parallel to OS and equal to 6 cm. On measurement we have AE equal to 5.98 cm and $\angle BAE$ equal to a little over 14°.

Hence, the resultant is 2.99 kilogramme wt acting at 14° to OP.

Examples V

[*Questions* 2, 3, 4, 5, *and* 8 *are suitable for graphic solutions.*]

1. Forces of 1, 2, and $\sqrt{3}$ g weight act at a point A in directions AP, AQ, and AR, the angle PAQ being 60° and PAR a right angle; find their resultant.
2. A particle is acted on by forces of 5 and 3 kg force which are at right angles and by a force of 4 kg force bisecting the angle between them ; find the force that will keep it at rest.
3. Three equal forces, P, diverge from a point, the middle one being inclined at an angle of 60° to each of the others. Find the resultant of the three.
4. Three forces $5P$, $10P$, and $13P$ act in one plane on a particle, the angle between any two of their directions being 120°. Find the magnitude and direction of their resultant.
5. Forces $2P$, $3P$, and $4P$ act at a point in directions parallel to the sides of an equilateral triangle taken in order; find the magnitude and line of action of the resultant.
6. Forces P_1, P_2, P_3, and P_4 act on a particle O at the centre of a square $ABCD$; P_1 and P_2 act along the diagonals OA and OB, and P_3 and P_4 perpendicular to the sides AB and BC. If

$$P_1 : P_2 : P_3 : P_4 :: 4 : 6 : 5 : 1,$$

find the magnitude and direction of their resultant.

7. *ABCD* is a square; forces of 1 kgf, 6 kgf, and 9 kgf act in the directions *AB*, *AC*, and *AD* respectively ; find the magnitude of their resultant correct to two places of decimals.
8. Five forces, acting at a point, are in equilibrium; four of them, whose respective magnitudes are 4, 4, 1, and 3 kg force make, in succession, angles of 60° with one another. Find the magnitude of the fifth force. Verify by a drawing and measurement.
9. Four equal forces *P*, *Q*, *R*, and *S* act on a particle in one plane ; the angles between *P* and *Q*, between *Q* and *R*, and between *R* and *S* are all equal and that between *P* and *S* is 108°. Find their resultant.
10. Forces of 2, $\sqrt{3}$, 5, $\sqrt{3}$, and 2 kgf respectively act at one of the angular points of a regular hexagon towards the five other angular points; find the direction and magnitude of the resultant.
11. Forces of 2, 3, 4, 5 and 6 kgf respectively act at an angular point of a regular hexagon towards the other angular points taken in order; find their resultant.
12. Show that the resultant of forces equal to 7, 1, 1, and 3 kgf respectively acting at an angular point of a regular pentagon towards the other angular points, taken in order is $\sqrt{71}$ kgf. Verify by a drawing and measurement.
13. Equal forces *P* act on an angular point of an octagon towards each of the other angular points; find their resultant.

By the use of trigonometrical Tables, or by a graphic construction find the magnitude (to two places of decimals) and the direction (to the nearest minute by calculation, and to the nearest degree by drawing) of the resultant of

14. **Three forces equal to 11, 7, and 8 kg force, making angles of 18°18′, 74°50′ and 130°20′ with a fixed line.**
15. **Four forces equal to 4, 3, 2, and 1 g force, making angles of 20°, 40°, 60°, and 80° with a fixed line.**
16. **Four forces equal to 8, 12, 15 and 20 kg force, making angles of 30°, 70°, 120°15′, and 155° with a fixed line.**
17. **Three forces equal to 85, 47, and 63 kgf acting along lines *OA*, *OB*, and *OC*, where ∠ *AOB* = 78° and ∠ *BOC* = 125°.**
18. **Forces *P*, and *Q*, whose resultant is *R*, act at a point *O*; a transversal is drawn meeting these directions at *L*, *M* and *N* respectively show that.**

$$\frac{P}{OL} + \frac{Q}{OM} = \frac{R}{ON}.$$

19. **Forces P_1, P_2, and P_3 act on a particle and are parallel to the sides of an equilateral triangle taken in order ; show that their resultant is**

$$\sqrt{(P_1^2 + P_2^2 + P_3^2 - P_2P_3 - P_3P_1 - P_1P_2)}.$$

20. Three forces *P*, *Q*, and *R* acting at *O*, the ortho-centre of the triangle *ABC*, along *OA*, *OB*, and *OC* are in equilibrium. Show that

$$P : Q : R = BC : CA : AB.$$

46. *To find the conditions of equilibrium of any number of forces acting upon a particle.*

Let the force act upon a particle O as in Art. 44.

If the forces balance one another the resultant must vanish, *i.e.* F must be zero.

Hence $$X^2 + Y^2 = 0.$$

Now, the sum of the squares of two real quantities cannot be zero unless each quantity is separately zero;

$$\therefore \quad X = 0, \quad \text{and} \quad Y = 0.$$

Hence, if the forces acting on a particle are in equilibrium, the algebraic sum of their resolved parts in two directions at right angles are separately zero.

Conversely, if the sum of their resolved parts in two directions at right angles separately vanish, the forces are in equilibrium.

For, in this case, both X and Y are zero, and therefore F is also zero.

Hence, since the resultant of the forces vanishes, the forces are in equilibrium.

47. When there are only three forces acting on a particle the conditions of equilibrium are often most easily found by applying Lami's Theorem (Art. 40).

48. Ex. 1. *A body of* 65 *kg force is suspended by two strings of lengths* 5 *and* 12 *metres attached to two points in the same horizontal line whose distance apart is* 13 *metres ; find the tensions of the strings.*

Let AC and BC be the two strings, so that

$$AC = 5 \text{ metres}, \ BC = 12 \text{ metres, and } \ AB = 13 \text{ metres}.$$

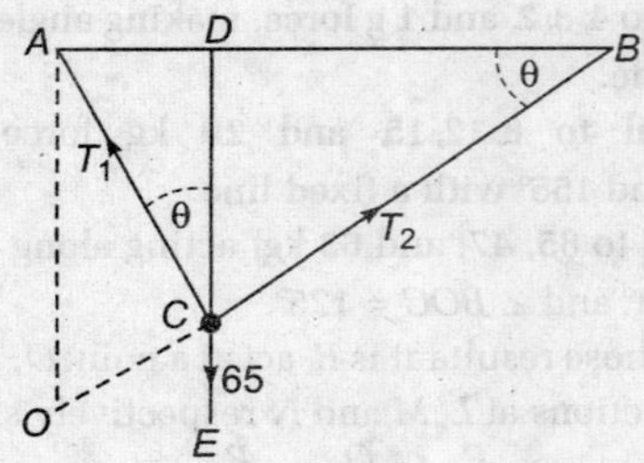

Since $13^2 = 12^2 + 5^2$, the angle ACB is a right angle.

Let the direction CE of the weight be produced to meet AB in D; also let the angle CBA be θ, so that

$$\angle ACD = 90° - \angle BCD = \angle CBD = \theta.$$

Let T_1 and T_2 be the tensions of the strings. By Lami's theorem we have

$$\frac{T_1}{\sin ECB} = \frac{T_2}{\sin ECA} = \frac{65}{\sin ACB};$$

$$\therefore \quad \frac{T_1}{\sin BCD} = \frac{T_2}{\sin\theta} = \frac{65}{\sin 90^\circ};$$

$$\therefore \quad T_1 = 65\cos\theta, \quad \text{and} \quad T_2 = 65\sin\theta.$$

But $\qquad \cos\theta = \dfrac{BC}{BA} = \dfrac{12}{13}, \quad \text{and} \quad \sin\theta = \dfrac{AC}{AB} = \dfrac{5}{13};$

$$\therefore \quad T_1 = 60, \quad \text{and} \quad T_2 = 25 \text{ kgf}.$$

Otherwise thus; The triangle ACB has its sides respectively perpendicular to the directions of the forces T_1, T_2, and 65;

$$\therefore \quad \frac{T_1}{BC} = \frac{T_2}{CA} = \frac{65}{AB};$$

$$\therefore \quad T_1 = 65\frac{BC}{AB} = 60, \quad \text{and} \quad T_2 = 65\frac{AC}{AB} = 25.$$

Graphically ; Produce BC to meet a vertical line through A in O. Then ACO is a triangle having its sides parallel to the three forces T_1, T_2, and W. Hence it is the triangle of forces, and

$$\therefore \quad \frac{T_1}{AC} = \frac{T_2}{CO} = \frac{W}{OA}.$$

Ex. 2. *A string ABCD, attached to two fixed points A and D, has two equal weights, W, knotted to it at B and C and rests with the portions AB and CD inclined at angles of* 30° *and* 60° *respectively to the vertical. Find the tensions of the portions of the string and the inclination of BC to the vertical.*

Let the tension in the strings be T_1, T_2, and T_3 respectively and let BC be inclined at an angle θ to be the vertical.

[N.B. The string BC pulls B towards C and pulls C towards B, the tension being the same throughout its length.]

Since B is in equilibrium the vertical components and the horizontal components of the forces acting on it must both vanish (Art. 46).

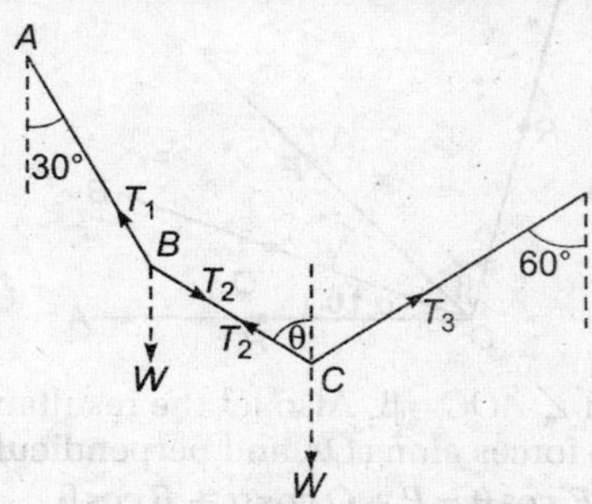

Hence $\qquad T_1\cos 30^\circ - T_2\cos\theta = W \qquad \ldots(1),$

and $\qquad T_1\sin 30^\circ - T_2\sin\theta = 0 \qquad \ldots(2).$

Similarly, since C is in equilibrium,

$\qquad T_3\cos 60^\circ + T_2\cos\theta = W \qquad \ldots(3),$

and $\qquad T_3\sin 60^\circ - T_2\sin\theta = 0 \qquad \ldots(4).$

From (1) and (2), substituting for T_1, we have

$$W = T_2[\cot 30° \sin\theta - \cos\theta] = T_2[\sqrt{3}\sin\theta - \cos\theta] \quad \ldots(5).$$

So, from (3) and (4), substituting for T_3, we have

$$W = T_2[\cot 60° \sin\theta + \cos\theta] = T_2\left[\frac{1}{\sqrt{3}}\sin\theta + \cos\theta\right] \quad \ldots(6);$$

therefore from (5) and (6),

$$\sqrt{3}\sin\theta - \cos\theta = \frac{1}{\sqrt{3}}\sin\theta + \cos\theta;$$

$$\therefore \qquad 2\sin\theta = 2\sqrt{3}\cos\theta;$$

$$\therefore \qquad \tan\theta = \sqrt{3}, \quad \text{and} \quad \text{hence, } \theta = 60°.$$

Substituting this value in (5), we have

$$W = T_2\left[\sqrt{3}\cdot\frac{\sqrt{3}}{2} - \frac{1}{\sqrt{2}}\right] = T_2.$$

Hence, from (2), we have

$$T_1 = T_2\frac{\sin 60°}{\sin 30°} = W\cdot\sqrt{3},$$

and from (4) $$T_3 = T_2\frac{\sin\theta}{\sin 60°} = T_2 = W.$$

Hence, the inclination of BC to the vertical is 60°, and the tensions of the portions AB, BC, and CD are $W\sqrt{3}$, W, and W respectively.

Ex. 3. Three forces P, Q, and R act along the coplanar straight line OA, OB, and OC respectively, and F is the magnitude of their resultant. Prove that

$$F^2 = P^2 + Q^2 + R^2 + 2QR\cos BOC + 2RP\cos COA + 2PQ\cos AOB.$$

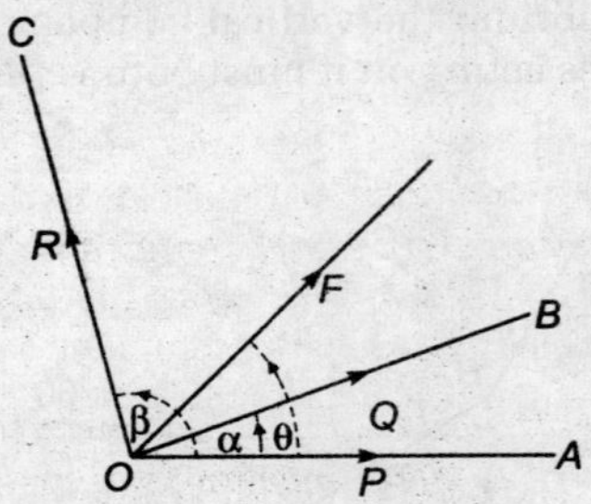

Let $\angle AOB = \alpha$ and $\angle AOC = \beta$. Also let the resultant F make an angle θ with OA. Resolving the forces along OA and perpendicular to OA, we get,

$$F\cos\theta = P + Q\cos\alpha + R\cos\beta$$

$$F\sin\theta = Q\sin\alpha + R\sin\beta.$$

Squaring and adding, we have

$$F^2 = P^2 + Q^2 + R^2 + 2PQ\cos\alpha + 2QR(\cos\alpha\cos\beta + \sin\alpha\sin\beta) + 2PR\cos\beta.$$

$$= P^2 + Q^2 + R^2 + 2PQ\cos\alpha + 2QR\cos(\beta - \alpha) + 2PR\cos\beta.$$

$$= P^2 + Q^2 + R^2 + 2PQ\cos AOB + 2QR\cos BOC + 2PR\cos AOC.$$

Examples VI

1. Two men carry a weight W between them by means of two ropes fixed to the weight; one rope is inclined at 45° to the vertical and the other at 30°; find the tension of each rope.
2. A body, of mass 2 kg, is fastened to a fixed point by means of a string of length 25 cm ; it is acted on by a horizontal force F and rests of a distance of 20 cm from the vertical line through the fixed point; find the value of F and the tension of the string.
3. A body, of mass 65 kg, is suspended from a horizontal beam by strings, whose lengths are respectively 40 cm and 157.5 cm, the strings being fastened to the beam at two points 162.5 cm apart. What are the tensions of the strings ?
4. A body, of mass 70 kg, is suspended by strings, whose lengths are 6 and 8 metres respectively, from two points in a horizontal line whose distance apart is 10 metres; find the tensions of the strings.
5. A mass of 60 kg is suspended by two strings of lengths 9 and 12 metres respectively, the other ends of the strings being attached to two points in a horizontal line at a distance of 15 metres apart; find the tensions of the strings.
6. A string suspended from a ceiling supports three bodies, each of mass 4 kg, one at its lowest point and each of the others at equal distances from its extremities; find the tensions of the parts into which the string is divided.
7. Two equal masses, of weight W, are attached to the extremities of a thin string which passes over 3 tacks in a wall arranged in the form of an isosceles triangle, with the base horizontal and with a vertical angle of 120°; find the pressure on each tack.
8. A stream is 32 m wide and a boat is dragged down the middle of the stream by two men on opposite banks, each of whom pulls with a force equal to 45 kgf wt; if the ropes are attached to the same point of the boat and each is of length 20 m, find the resultant force on the boat.
9. A string passing over two smooth parallel bars in the same horizontal plane has two equal weights fastened to its ends and another equal weight is fastened to a point of the string between the bars ; find the position of equilibrium of the system and the thrust upon each bar.
10. A string is tied to two points in a horizontal plane; a ring of weight 27 kg can slide freely along the string and is pulled by a horizontal force equal to the weight of P kg. If in the position of equilibrium the portions of the string be inclined at angles of 45° and 75° to the vertical, find the value of P.
11. Two weightless rings slide on a smooth vertical circle and through the rings passes a string which carries weights at the two ends and at a point between the rings. If equilibrium exist when the rings are at points distance 30° from the highest point of the circle, find the relation between the three weights.
12. Two masses, each equal to 50 kg, are joined by a string which passes over two small smooth pegs, A and B, in the same horizontal plane ; if a mass of 2.5 kg is attached to the string halfway between A and B, find in cm the depth to which it will descend below the level of AB, supposing AB to be 3.2 m. What would happen if the small mass were attached to any other point of the string ?

13. A body of mass 5 kg, is suspended by two strings, 17.5 and 60 cm long, their other ends being fastened to the extremities of a rod of length 62.5 cm. If the rod is held so that the body hangs immediately below its middle point, find the tensions of the string.

14. A heavy chain has weights of 10 and 16 kg attached to its ends and hangs in equilibrium over a smooth pulley; if the greatest tension of the chain be 20 kgf, find the weight of the chain.

15. A heavy chain, of length 2.45 m and weighing 7 kgf, has a weight of 3.4 kg attached to one end and is in equilibrium hanging over a smooth peg. What length of the chain is on each side ?

16. A body is free to slide on a smooth vertical circular wire and is connected by a string, equal in length to the radius of the circle, to the highest point of the circle; find the tension of the string and the reaction of the circle.

17. A uniform plane lamina in the form of a rhombus, one of whose angles is 120°, is supported by two forces applied at the centre in the directions of the diagonals so that one side of the rhombus is horizontal; show that, if P and Q are the forces and P is the greater, then

$$P^2 = 3Q^2.$$

18. The ends of a driving rein are passed through two smooth rings which are fastened, one to each side of the bit. They are then doubled back and tied to fixed points in the headpiece one on each side of the horse's head. Find the pressure produced by the bit on the horse's tongue by a given pull P of the driver.

19. Three equal strings, of negligible weight, are knotted together to form an equilateral triangle ABC and a weight W is suspended from A. If the triangle and weight are supported, with BC horizontal, by means of two strings at B and C, each at the angle of 135° with BC, show that the tension in BC is

$$\frac{W}{6}(3 - \sqrt{3}).$$

20. Three weightless strings AC, BC, and AB are knotted together to form an isosceles triangle whose vertex is C. If a weight W is suspended from C and the whole is supported, with AB horizontal, by two forces bisecting the angles at A and B, find the tension of the string AB.

21. A weightless string is suspended from two points not in the name horizontal line and passes through a small smooth heavy ring which is free to slide on the string; find the position of equilibrium of the string.

If the ring, instead of being free to move on the string, is tied to a given point of it, find equations to give the ratio of the tensions of the two portions of the string.

22. Four pegs are fixed in a wall at the four highest points of a regular hexagon (the two lowest points of the hexagon being in a horizontal straight line) and over these is thrown a loop supporting a weight W; the loop is of such a length that the angles formed by it at the lowest pegs are right angles. Find the tension of the string and the pressures on the pegs.

23. Explain how the force of the current may be used to urge a ferry-boat across the river, assuming that the centre of the boat is attached by a long rope to a fixed point in the middle of the stream.

24. *Explain how a vessel is enabled to sail in a direction nearly opposite to that of the wind.*

Show also that the sails of the vessel should be set so as to bisect the angle between the keel and the apparent direction of the wind in order that the force to urge the vessel forward may be as great as possible.

[Let AB be the direction of the keel and therefore that of the ship's motion, and OA the apparent direction of the wind, the angle OAB being acute and equal to α. Let AC be the direction of the sail, AC being between OA and AB and the angle BAC being θ.

Let P be the force of the wind on the sail; resolve it in directions along and perpendicular to the sail. The component $(KA) = P\cos(\alpha - \theta)$ along the sail has no effect. The component $(LA) = P\sin(\alpha - \theta)$ perpendicular to the sail may again be resolved into two, *viz.* $(NA) = P\sin(\alpha - \theta)\cos\theta$ perpendicular to AB and $(MA) = P\sin(\alpha - \theta)\sin\theta$ along AB.

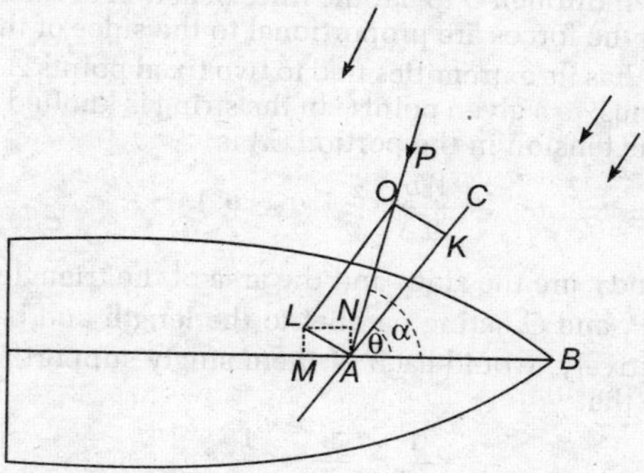

The former component produces motion sideways *i.e.* in a direction perpendicular to the length of the ship. This is called ice-way and is considerably lessened by the shape of the keel which is so designed as to give the greatest possible resistance to this motion.

The latter component, $P\sin(\alpha - \theta)\sin\theta$, along AB is never zero unless the sail is set in either the direction of the keel or of the wind, or unless α is zero in which case the wind is directly opposite to the direction of the ship. Thus there is always the force to make the ship move forward ; but the rudder has to be continually applied to counteract the tendency of the wind to turn the boat about.

This force $= \frac{1}{2}P[\cos(\alpha - 2\theta) - \cos\alpha]$ and it is therefore greatest when $\cos(\alpha - 2\theta)$ is greatest, *i.e.* when $\alpha - 2\theta = 0$, *i.e.* when $\theta = \frac{\alpha}{2}$, *i.e.* when the direction of the sail bisects the angle between the keel and the apparent direction of the wind.]

25. Two forces R and S act at a point along two straight lines inclined at an angle θ, and F is their resultant. Two other forces R and S' acting along the same lines have a resultant F'. If ϕ is the angle between the lines of action of F and F', prove that

$$(1 - \cos\phi)(1 + \cos\phi) = (R^2S'^2 - 2RR'SS' + R'^2S^2)\cdot\frac{(1 - \cos\theta)(1 + \cos\theta)}{F^2F'^2}.$$

26. Forces act through the angular points of a triangle ABC perpendicular to the opposite sides, and are measured by the cosines of the corresponding angles; show that their resultant is

$$\sqrt{(1 - 8 \cos A \cos B \cos C)}.$$

27. Three force acting at a point are each equal to F and parallel to the sides of a triangle ABC in order; show that their resultant is

$$F\sqrt{(3 - 2 \cos A - 2 \cos B - 2 \cos C)}.$$

28. Forces P, and Q whose resultant is R, act at a point O. A transversal is drawn meeting these directions in L, M, and N respectively.

Show that $$\frac{P}{OL} + \frac{Q}{OM} = \frac{R}{ON}.$$

29. Three forces act in given directions at a point O and are in equilibrium. If a circle is drawn through O to cut the lines of action of the forces in A, B, and C, prove that the forces are proportional to the sides of the triangle ABC.

30. A string ACB has its extremities tied to two fixed points A and B in the same horizontal lines; to a given point C in the string is knotted a given weight W. Prove that the tension in the portion CA is

$$\frac{Wb}{4c\Delta}(c^2 + a^2 - b^2)$$

where a, b, and c are the sides and the area of the triangle ABC.

31. Two forces P, and Q acting parallel to the length and base of an inclined plane respectively, would each of them singly support a weight W on the plane; prove that

$$\frac{1}{P^2} - \frac{1}{Q^2} = \frac{1}{W^2}.$$

32. A weight is supported on a smooth plane of inclination α to the horizon by a string inclined to the vertical at an angle γ. If the slope of the plane be increased to β and the slope of the string unaltered, the tension of the string is doubled to support the weight. Prove that

$$\cot\alpha - \cot\gamma = 2 \cot\beta.$$

49. Examples of graphical solution. Many problems which would be difficult or, at any rate, very laborious, to solve by analytical methods are comparatively easy to solve graphically.

These questions are of common occurrence in engineering and other practical work. There is generally little else involved besides the use of the Triangle of Forces and Polygon of Forces.

The instruments chiefly used are compasses, rulers, scales and diagonal scales, and protractors for measuring angles.

The results obtained are of course not mathematically accurate; but, if the student is careful, and skilful in the use of his instruments, the answer ought to be reliable, in general, to the first place of decimals.

In the following worked out examples the figures are reduced from the original drawings; the student is recommended to re-draw them for himself on the scale mentioned in each example.

50. Ex. 1. *ACDB is a string whose ends are attached to two points, A and B, which are in a horizontal line and are 2.10 m apart. The length of*

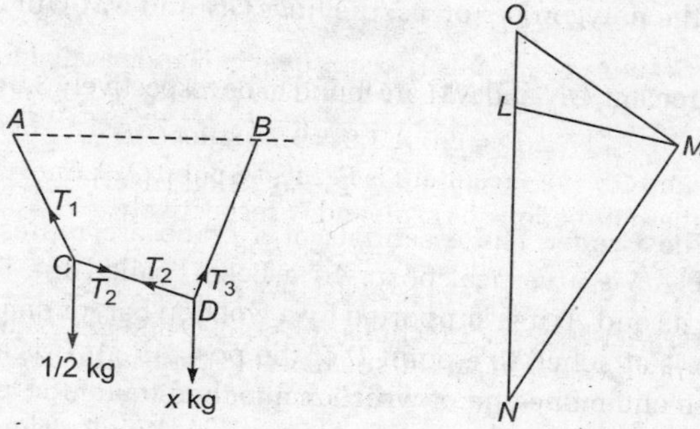

AC, CD, and DB are 1.05, 0.90, and 1.20 m respectively, and at C is attached $\frac{1}{2}$ kg weight. An unknown weight is attached to D of such a magnitude that, in the position of equilibrium, CDB is a right angle. Find the magnitude of this weight and the tensions of the strings.

Let T_1, T_2, and T_3 be the required tensions and let x kg be the weight at D.

Take a vertical line OL, one cm in length, to represent the weight, $\frac{1}{2}$ kgf, at C. Through O draw OM parallel to AC, and through L draw LM parallel to CD.

By the triangle of forces OM represents T_1, and LM represents T_2. Produce OL vertically downwards and through M draw MN parallel to BD.

Then, since LM represents T_2, it follows that T_3 is represented by MN, and x by LN.

By actual measurement, we have

$$OM = 2.8 \text{ cm}, \quad LM = 2.2 \text{ cm}, \quad MN = 5.0 \text{ cm},$$

and

$$NL = 5.45 \text{ cm}.$$

Hence the weight at D is 2.72 kgf and the tensions are respectively 1.4, 1.1, and 2.5 kgf.

Ex. 2. *A and B are two points in a horizontal line at a distance of 4.80 m apart ; AO and OB are two strings of lengths 1.80 and 3.60 m carrying, at O, a body of weight 10 kg; a third string, attached to the body at O, passes over a small smooth pulley at the middle point, C, of AB and is attached to a body of weight 2.5 kg; find the tensions of the string AO and OB.*

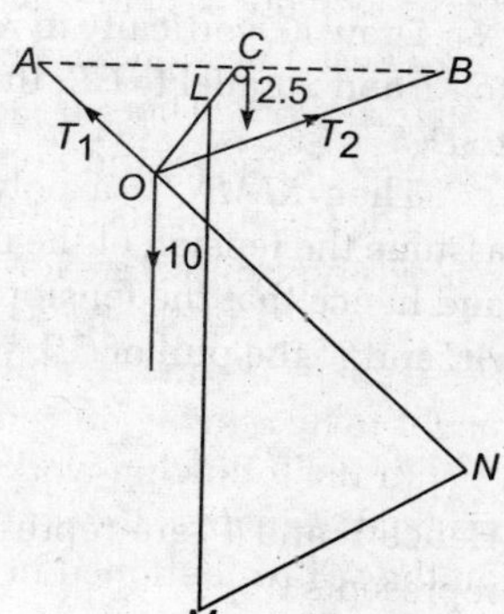

Let T_1 and T_2 be the required tensions. On OC mark off OL, equal to one cm, to represent the tension 2.5 kgf, of the string OC.

Draw *LM* vertical and equal to 4 cm. Through *M* draw *MN*, parallel to *OB*, to meet *AO* produced in *N*.

Then, by the polygon of Forces, the lines *ON* and *NM* will represent the tensions T_1 and T_2.

On measurement, *ON* and *NM* are found to be respectively 3.9 and 2.45 cm.

Hence $\qquad T_1 = 2.5 \times 3.9 = 9.75$ kgf,

and $\qquad T_2 = 2.5 \times 2.45 = 6.13$ kgf (nearly).

Ex. 3. The Crane. The essentials of a crane are represented in the below figures. *AB* is a vertical post; *AC* a beam, called the jib capable of turning about its end *A*; it is supported by a wooden bar, or chain, *CD*, called the tie, which is attached to a point *D* of the post *AB*. At *C* is a pulley, over which passes a chain one end of which is attached to a

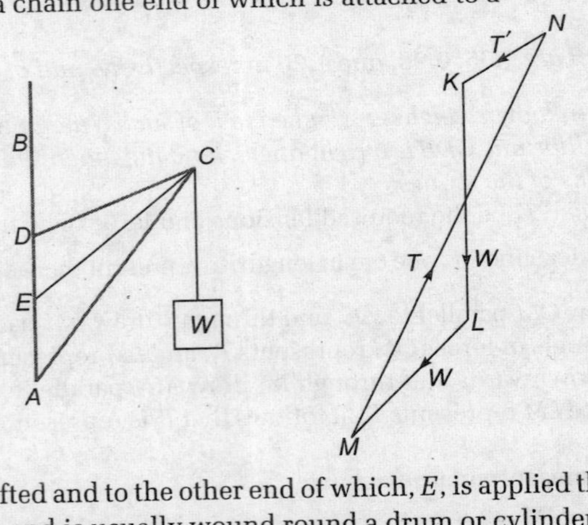

weight to be lifted and to the other end of which, *E*, is applied the force which raises *W*. This end is usually wound round a drum or cylinder. The tie *CD* is sometimes horizontal, and often the direction of the chain *CE* coincides with it. In the above crane the actions in the jib and tie may be determined graphically as follows.

Draw *KL* vertically to represent *W* on any scale, and then draw *LM* equal to *KL* and parallel to *CE*; through *M* draw *MN* parallel to *AC* and *KN* parallel to *DC*.

Then *KLMN* is a polygon of forces for the equilibrium of *C*; for we assume the tension of the chain to be unaltered in passing over the pulley *C*, and hence that the tensions of *CE* is equal to *W*. Hence, if *T* be the thrust of *AC* and *T′* the pull of *CD*, we have

$$\frac{T}{MN} = \frac{T'}{NK} = \frac{W}{KL}.$$

Hence *T* and *T′* are represented by *MN* and *NK* on the same scale that *KL* represents *W*.

Examples VII

[*The following examples are to be solved by geometric construction.*]

1. A boat is towed along a river by means of two ropes, attached to the same point, which are pulled by two men who keep at opposite points of the bank 50 metres apart ; one rope is 30 metres long and is pulled with a force equal to the weight of 35 kg, and the other rope is 45 metres long; the boat is in this way made to move uniformly in a straight line; find the resistance offered to the boat by the stream and the tension of the second rope.

2. The jib of a crane is 3 m long, and the tie-rod is horizontal and attached to a point 1.8 m vertically above the foot of the jib; find the tension of the tie-rod, and the thrust on the jib, when the crane supports a mass of 1000 kg.

3. A and B are two fixed points, B being below A, and the horizontal and vertical distances between them are 1.2 m and .3 m respectively; AC and BC are strings of length 1.5 and 1.2 m respectively, and at C is tied a body of weight 50 kg; find the tensions of the strings.

4. $ABCD$ is a light string attached to two points A and D, in the same horizontal line, and at the points B and C are attached weights. In the position of equilibrium the distances of the points B and C below the line AD are respectively 4 and 6 metres. If the lengths of AB and CD are respectively 6 and 8 metres and the distance AD is 14 metres, find the weight at C, the magnitude of the weight at B being 4 kg.

5. A framework ABC is kept in a vertical plane with AB horizontal by supports at A and B ; if the lengths AB, BC, and CA are 3, 2.1, and 2.7 m respectively, and a weight of 500 kg is placed at C, find the reactions at A and B and the forces exerted by the different portions of the framework.

6. A framework ABC is supported at A and B so that it is in a vertical plane with AB horizontal, and a weight of 200 kg is hung on at C; if $AB = 5$ metres, $BC = 4$ metres and $AC = 3$ metres, find the tensions or thrusts in AC and CB, and the reactions at A and B.

7. The jib of a crane is 6 m long, the tie 4.8 m, and the post 3 m. A load of 50 kg is hung at the end of a chain which passes over a pulley at the end of the jib and then along the tie. Find the thrust in the jib and the pull in the tie.

8. In the figure of Ex. 3, Art. 50, the tie DC is horizontal and the chain coincides with it; if $W = 500$ kg, $AC = 3.3$ m, and $DC = 1.5$m, find the actions along DC and AC.

9. In the figure of Ex. 3, Art. 50, the angle $CDB = 45°$, and the angle $ACD = 15°$; the chain EC coincides with DC; if W is one metric ton, find the forces exerted by the parts AC, CD.

10. In the figure of Ex. 3, Art. 50, $DA = 4.5$ m, $DC = 6$ m and $AC = 9$ m, and a weight of one metric ton is suspended from C, find the thrusts or tensions produced in AC, CD, and DA when the chain coincides with

(1) the jib CA,

(2) the tie CD.

11. In the figure of Ex. 3, Art. 50, the jib AC is 7.5 m long, the tie CD is 5.4 m, $AD = 3.6$ m and $AE = 2.4$ m; find the tensions or thrusts in AC and CD, when a weight of 2 metric tons is suspended from the ends of the chain.

12. *ABCD* is a frame-work of four weightless rods, loosely jointed together, *AB* and *AD* being each of length 4 metres and *BC* and *CD* of length 2 metres. The hinge *C* is connected with *A* by means of a fine string of length 5 metres. Weights of 100 kg each are attached to *B* and *D* and the whole is suspended from *A*. Show that the tension in *AC* is 52 kg force.
13. In the preceding question, instead of the string *AC* a weightless rod *BD* of length 3 metres is used to stiffen the frame; a weight of 100 kg is attached to *C* and nothing at *B* and *D*. Show that the thrust in the rod *BD* is about 77 kg force.
14. In question 12 there are no weights attached to *B* and *D* and the whole framework is placed on a smooth horizontal table; the hinges *B* and *D* are pressed toward one another by two forces each equal to the weight of 25 kg in the straight line *BD*. Show that the tension of the string is about 3.16 kg force.
15. *ABCD* is a rhombus formed by four weightless rods loosely jointed together, and the figure is stiffened by a weightless rod, of one-half the length of each of the four rods, joined to the middle points of *AB* and *AD*. If this frame is suspended from *A* and a weight of 100 kg be attached to it at *C*, show that the thrust of the cross rod is about 115.5 kg force.

4

Parallel Forces

51. IN Chapters II and III we have shown how to find the resultant of forces which meet at a point. In the present chapter we shall consider the composition of parallel forces.

In the ordinary statical problems of every-day life parallel forces are of constant occurrence.

Two parallel forces are said to be **like** when they act in the same direction ; when they act in opposite parallel directions they are said to be **unlike**.

52. *To find the resultant of two parallel forces acting upon a rigid body.*

Case I. *Let the forces be* **like**.

Let P and Q be the forces acting at points A and B of the body, and let them be represented by the lines AL and BM.

Join AB and at A and B apply two equal and opposite forces, each equal to S, and acting in the directions BA and AB. Let these forces be represented by AD and BE: These two forces balance one another and have no effect upon the equilibrium of the body.

Complete the parallelograms $ALFD$ and $BMGE$; let the diagonals FA and GB be produced to meet in O. Draw OC parallel to AL or BM to meet AB in C.

The forces P and S at A have a resultant P_1, represented by AF. Let its point of application be removed to O.

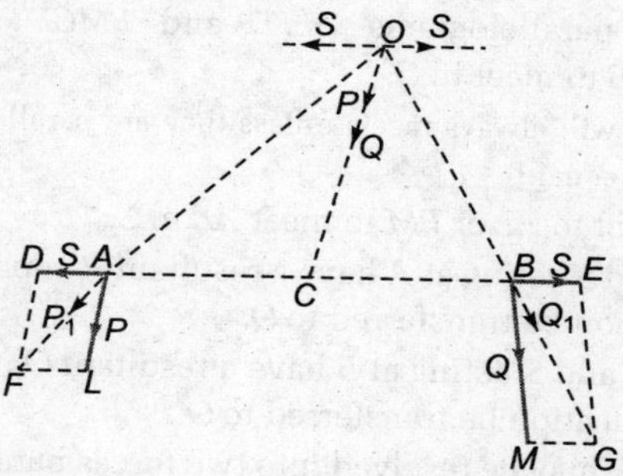

So the forces Q and S at B have a resultant Q_1 represented by BG. Let its point of application be transferred to O.

The force P_1 at O may be resolved into two forces, S parallel to AD, and P in the direction OC.

So, the forces Q_1 at O may be resolved into two forces S parallel to BE and Q in the direction OC.

Also these two forces S acting at O are in equilibrium.

Hence, the original forces P and Q are equivalent to a force $(P + Q)$ acting along OC *i.e.*, acting at C parallel to the original direction of P and Q.

To determine the position of the point C. The triangle OCA is, by construction, similar to the triangle ALF;

$$\therefore \qquad \frac{OC}{CA} = \frac{AL}{LF} = \frac{P}{S},$$

so that
$$P \cdot CA = S \cdot OC \qquad \ldots(1)$$

So, since the triangles OCB and BMG are similar, we have

$$\frac{OC}{CB} = \frac{BM}{MG} = \frac{Q}{S},$$

so that
$$Q \cdot CB = S \cdot OC \qquad \ldots(2)$$

Hence, from (1) and (2), we have

$$P \cdot CA = Q\,CB$$

so that
$$\frac{CA}{CB} = \frac{Q}{P}$$

i.e. C divides the line AB *internally* in the inverse ratio of the forces.

Case II. *Let the forces be* **unlike.**

Let P, Q be the forces (P being the greater) acting at points A and B of the body, and let them be represented by the lines AL and BM.

Join AB, and at A and B apply two equal and opposite forces, each equal to S, and acting in the direction BA and AB respectively. Let these forces be represented by AD and BE respectively; they balance one another and have no effect on the equilibrium of the body.

Complete the parallelograms $ALFD$ and $BMGE$ and produce the diagonals AF and GB to meet in O.

[These diagonals will always meets unless they are parallel, in which case the forces P and Q will be equal.]

Draw OC parallel to AL or BM to meet AB in C.

The forces P and S acting at A have a resultant P_1 represented by AF. Let its point of application be transferred to O.

So the forces Q and S acting at B have a resultant Q_1 represented by BG. Let its point of application be transferred to O.

The force P_1 at O may be resolved into two forces parallel to AD, and P in the direction CO produced.

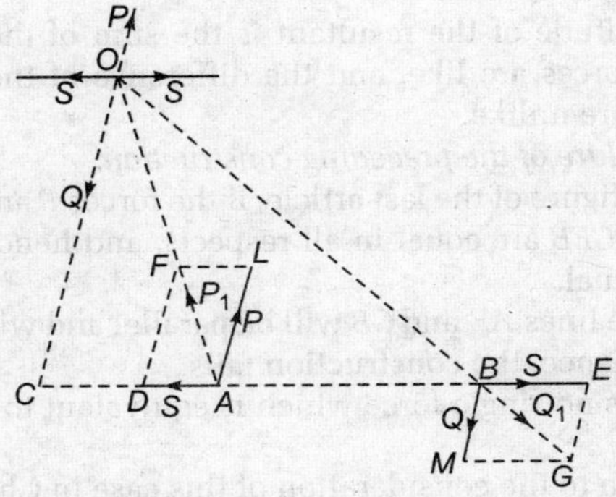

So the forces Q_1 at O may be resolved into two forces, S parallel to BE, and Q in the direction OC.

Also these two forces S acting at O are in equilibrium.

Hence the original forces P and Q are equivalent to a force $P - Q$ acting in the direction CO produced.

i.e. acting at C in a direction parallel to that of P.

To determine the position of the point C. The triangle OCA is, by construction, similar to the triangle FDA ;

$$\therefore \qquad \frac{OC}{CA} = \frac{FD}{DA} = \frac{AL}{AD} = \frac{P}{S},$$

so that

$$P \cdot CA = S \cdot OC \qquad ...(1).$$

Also, since the triangles OCB and BMG are similar, we have

$$\frac{OC}{CB} = \frac{BM}{MG} = \frac{Q}{S},$$

that

$$Q \cdot CB = S \cdot OC \qquad ...(2).$$

Hence, from (1) and (2),

$$P \cdot CA = Q \cdot CB.$$

Hence, $\frac{CA}{CB} = \frac{Q}{P}$, *i.e.* C divides the line AB *externally* in the inverse ratio of the forces.

To sum up; If two parallel forces, P and Q, act at points A and B of a rigid body,

(i) their resultant is a force whose line of action is parallel to the lines of action of the component forces; also, when the component forces are like, its direction is the same as that of the two forces, and, when the forces are unlike, its direction is the same as that of the greater component.

(ii) the point of application is a point C in AB such that

$$P \cdot AC = Q \cdot BC.$$

(iii) the magnitude of the resultant is the sum of the two component forces when the forces are like, and the difference of the two component forces when they are unlike.

53. *Case of failure of the preceding construction.*

In the second figure of the last article, if the forces P and Q are equal, the triangles FDA and GEB are equal in all respects, and hence the angles DAF and EBG will be equal.

In this case the lines AF and GB will be parallel and will not meet in any such points as O; hence, the construction fails.

Hence, there is no single force which is equivalent to two equal unlike parallel forces.

We shall return to the consideration of this case in Chapter VI.

54. If we have a number of like parallel forces acting on a rigid body we can find their resultant by successive applications of Art. 53. We must find the resultant of the first and second, and then the resultant of this resultant and the third, and so on.

The magnitude of the final resultant is the sum of the forces.

If the parallel forces be not all like, the magnitude of the resultant will be found to be the algebraic sum of the forces each with its proper sign prefixed.

Later on (see Art. 114) will be found formulae for calculating the centre of a system of parallel forces, *i.e.* the point at which the resultant of the system acts.

55. *Resultant of two parallel forces. Experimental verification.*

Take a uniform rectangular bar of wood about 3 feet long, whose cross-section is a square of side an inch or rather more. A face of this bar should be graduated, say in inches or centimetres, as in the figure.

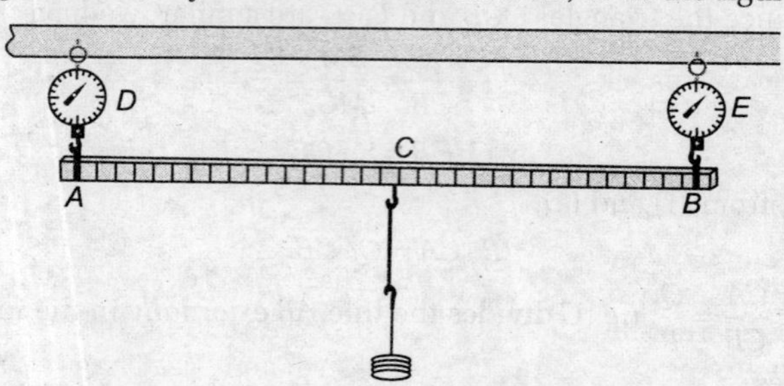

Let the ends A and B be supported by spring balances which are attached firmly to a support. For this purpose a Salter's circular balance is the more convenient form as it drops much less than the ordinary form when it is stretched. On the bar AB let there be a movable loop C carrying a hook from which weights can be suspended; this loop can be moved into any position along the bar.

Before putting on any weights, and when C is at the middle points of AB, let the readings of the balances D and E be taken. The bar being uniform, these readings should be the same and equal to R (say).

Now hang known weights, amounting in all to W, on to C, and move C into any position C_1 on the bar. Observe the new readings of the balances D and E, and let them be P and Q respectively.

Then $P - R (= P_1)$ and $Q - R (= Q_1)$ are the additional readings due to the weight W, and therefore P_1 and Q_1 are the forces at D and E which balance the force W at C_1.

It will be found that the sum of

$$P_1 \text{ and } Q_1 \text{ is equal to } W \qquad \ldots(1).$$

Again measure carefully the distances AC_1 and BC_1.

It will be found that

$$P_1 \times AC_1 = Q_1 \cdot BC_1. \qquad \ldots(2).$$

In other words *the resultant of forces P_1 and Q_1 at A and B is equal to $P_1 + Q_1$ acting at C_1, where*

$$P_1 \cdot AC_1 = Q_1 \cdot BC_1.$$

But this is the result given by the theoretical investigation of Art. 52 (Case I).

Perform the experiment again by shifting the position of C_1, keeping W the same; the values of P_1 and Q_1 will alter, but their sum will still be W, and the new value of $P_1 \cdot AC_1$ will be found to be equal to the new value of $Q_1 BC_1$.

Similarly the theorem of Art. 52 will be found to be true for any position of C_1 and any value of W.

Numerical illustration. Suppose the weight of the beam and the attached apparatus (without any weights) to be 2 kg. Then the original reading, R, of the balances will be each 1 kg. Put on a weight of 4 kg at C and move C to C_1 until the readings of the balances A and B are respectively 4 and 2 kg.

Then a force 4 kg at C_1 is balanced by a force 3 kg (= 4 – 1) at A and 1 kg (= 2 – 1) at B.

Measure the distances AC_1 and BC_1; they will be found to be 22.5 cm and 67.5 cm respectively (assuming the length AB to be 90 cm).

We thus have $\qquad P_1 \cdot AC_1 = 3 \times 22.5,$

and $\qquad Q_1 \cdot BC_1 = 1 \times 67.5,$

and these are equal.

Hence the truth of Art. 52 (Case I) for this case.

Unlike parallel forces.

In the last experiment the forces P_1, W and Q_1 at A, C_1, and B are in equilibrium, so that the resultant of P_1 upwards and W downwards is equal and opposite to Q_1. Measure the distances AB and C_1B. Then it will be found that

$$Q_1 = W - P,$$

and $\qquad P_1 \cdot AB = W \cdot C_1B.$

Hence, the truth of Art. 52 (Case II) is verified.

56. Ex. *A horizontal rod,* 1.8 *m long, whose weight may be neglected rests on two supports at its extremities; a body. of weight* 300 *kg, is suspended from the rod at a distance of* 0.75 *m from one end; find the reaction at each point of support. If one support could only bear a thrust equal to the weight of*

50 kg, what is the greatest distance from the other support at which the body could be suspended ?

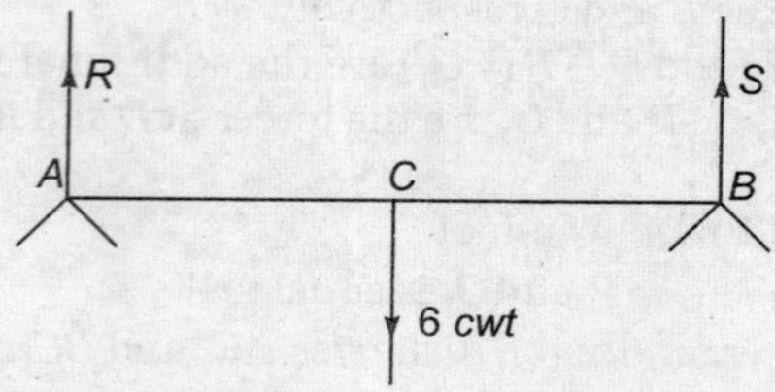

Let AB be the rod and R and S the reactions at the points of support. Let C be the point at which the body is suspended so that $AC = 1.05$ and $CB = 0.75$ m. For equilibrium the resultant of R and S must balance 300 kgf. Hence, by Art. 52,

$$R + S = 300 \qquad \text{...(1)},$$

and
$$\frac{R}{S} = \frac{BC}{AC} = \frac{0.75}{1.05} = \frac{5}{7} \qquad \text{...(2)}.$$

Solving (1) and (2), we have $R = \frac{5}{2}$, and $S = \frac{1}{2}$. Hence the reactions are 125 and 175 kgf respectively.

If the reaction at A can only be equal to 50 kgf, S must be 250 kgf. Hence, if AC is x, we have

$$\frac{1}{5} = \frac{BC}{AC} = \frac{1.8 - x}{x}.$$

$$\therefore \qquad x = 1.5 \text{ m}.$$

Hence BC is 30 cm.

Examples VIII

In the four following examples A and B denote the points of application of parallel forces P and Q, and C is the point in which their resultant R meets AB.

1. Find the magnitude and position of the resultant (the forces being like) when
(i) $P = 4$; $Q = 7$; $AB = 22$ cm;
(ii) $P = 11$; $Q = 19$; $AB = 75$ cm;
(iii) $P = 5$; $Q = 5$; $AB = 90$ cm.

2. Find the magnitude and position of the resultant (the forces being unlike) when
(i) $P = 17$; $Q = 25$; $AB = 20$ cm;
(ii) $P = 23$; $Q = 15$; $AB = 100$ cm;
(iii) $P = 26$; $Q = 9$; $AB = 90$ cm.

3. The forces being like,
(i) if $P = 8$; $R = 17$; $AC = 9$ cm ; find Q and AB;
(ii) if $Q = 11$; $AC = 14$ cm ; $AB = 17\frac{1}{2}$ cm ; find P and R ;
(iii) if $P = 6$; $AC = 18$ cm ; $CB = 16$ cm ; find Q and Rs.

4. The forces being unlike,
(i) if $P = 8$; $R = 17$; $AC = 9$ cm ; find Q and AB ;

(ii) if $Q = 11$; $AC = -14$ cm ; $AB = 17\frac{1}{2}$ cm; find P and R ;

(iii) if $P = 6$; $AC = -18$ cm ; $AB = 24$ cm ; find Q and R.

5. Find two like parallel forces acting at a distance of 2 metres apart, which are equivalent to a given force of 20 kgf, the line of action of one being at a distance of 50 cm from the given force.

6. Find two unlike parallel forces acting at a distance of 18 cm apart which are equivalent to a force of 30 kgf, the greater of the two forces being at a distance of 8 cm from the given force.

7. Two parallel forces, P and Q, act at given points of a body, if Q is changed to $\frac{P^2}{Q}$, show that the line of action of the resultant is the same as it would be if the forces were simply interchanged.

8. Two men carry a heavy cask of weight 75 kg, which hangs from a light pole, of length 1.8 m, each end of which rests on a shoulder of one of the men. The point from which the cask is hung is 30 cm nearer to one man than to the other. What is the pressure on each shoulder?

9. Two men, one stronger than the other, have to remove a block of stone weighing 270 kg by means of a light plank whose length is 6 metres; the stronger man is able to carry 180 kg; how must the block be placed so as to allow him that share of the weight?

10. A uniform rod, 12 metres long and weighing 17 kg, can turn freely about a point in it and the rod is in equilibrium when a weight of 7 kg is hung at one end; how far from the end is the point about which it can turn?
N.B. *The weight of a uniform rod may be taken to act at its middle point.*

11. A straight uniform rod is 3 metres long; when a load of 5 kg is placed at one end it balances about a point 25 cm from that end; find the weight of the rod.

12. A uniform bar, of weight 3 kg and length 4 metres, passes over a prop and is supported in a horizontal position by a force equal to 1 kg wt acting vertically upwards at the other end, find the distance of the prop from the centre of the beem.

13. A heavy uniform rod, 4 metres long, rests horizontally on two pegs which are one metre apart; a weight of 10 kg suspended from one end, or a weight of 4 kg suspended from the other end, will just tilt the rod up; find the weight of the rod and the distances of the pegs from the centre of the rod.

14. A uniform iron rod, 75 cm long and of weight 4 kg is placed on two rails fixed at two points. A and B, in a vertical wall AB is horizontal and 12.5 cm long; find the distances at which the ends of the rod extend beyond the rails if the difference of the thrusts on the rails be 3 kgf.

15. A uniform beam, 4 metres long, is supported in a horizontal position by two props, which are 3 metres apart, so that the beam projects one metre beyond one of the props; show that the force on one prop is double that on the other.

16. A straight weightless rod, 48 cm in length, rests in a horizontal position between two pegs placed at a distance of 6 cm apart, one peg being at one end of the rod, and a weight of 2 kg is suspended from the other end; find the pressure on the pegs.

17. One end of a heavy uniform rod, of weight W, rests on a smooth horizontal plane, and a string tied to the other end of the rod is fastened to a fixed point above the plane; find the tension of the string.

18. A man carries a bundle at the end of a stick which is placed over his shoulder; if the distance between his hand and his shoulder is changed how does the pressure on his shoulder change?
19. A man carries a weight of 50 kg at the end of a stick, 3 metres long, resting on his shoulder. He regulates the stick so that the length between his shoulder and his hands is (i) 100, (ii) 150 and (iii) 200 cm; how great are the forces exerted by his hand and the pressures on his shoulder in each case?
20. Three parallel forces act on a horizontal bar. Each is equal to 1 kg wt, the right-hand one acting vertically upward and the other two vertically down at distances of 2 metres and 3 metres respectively from the first; find the magnitude and position of their resultant.
21. A portmanteau, of length 90 cm and height 60 cm and whose centre of gravity is at its centre of figure, is carried upstairs by two men who hold it by the front and back edges of its lower face. If this is inclined at an angle of 30° to the horizontal, and the weight of the portmanteau is 50 kg, find how much of the weight each supports.
22. P and Q are two like parallel forces acting at A and B respectively. Show that if they interchange positions the point of application of the resultant is displaced along AB through a distance d where

$$d = \frac{P-Q}{P+Q} \cdot AB.$$

23. P and Q are like parallel forces. If P is moved parallel to itself through a distance x, show that the resultant of P and Q moves through a distance $\frac{Px}{P+Q}$.
24. Like parallel forces act at the vertices A, B, and C of a triangle and are proportional to the lengths BC, CA, and AB respectively. Prove that the in-centre of the triangle is the centre of the forces.
25. Three like parallel forces P, Q, and R act at the corners of a triangle ABC. If the line of action of their resultant passes through
    (i) the centroid, show that $P = Q = R$;
    (ii) the incentre, show that $\frac{P}{a} = \frac{Q}{b} = \frac{R}{c}$;
    (iii) the circumcentre, show that $\frac{P}{\sin 2A} = \frac{Q}{\sin 2B} = \frac{R}{\sin 2C}$,

    where a, b, c are the sides of the triangle.
26. Show that if each of the two unlike forces P, and Q $(P > Q)$ acting at a distance d apart, be increased by S, their resultant will not be altered in magnitude, but its point of application will be moved through a distance $\frac{S \cdot d}{(P-Q)}$.

5 Moments

57. Def. *The moment of a force about a given point is the product of the force and the perpendicular distance from the given point to the line of action of the force.*

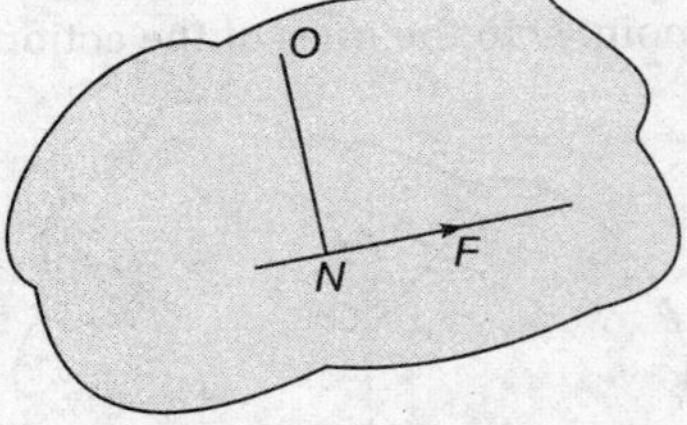

Thus the moment of a force F about a given point O is $F \times ON$, where ON is the perpendicular drawn from O to the line of action of F.

It will be noted that the moment of a force F about a given point O never vanishes, unless either the force vanishes or the force passes through the point about which the moment is taken.

58. *Geometrical representation of a moment.*

Suppose the force F is represented in magnitude, direction, and line of action by the line AB. Let O be any given point and ON the perpendicular from O to AB or AB produced.

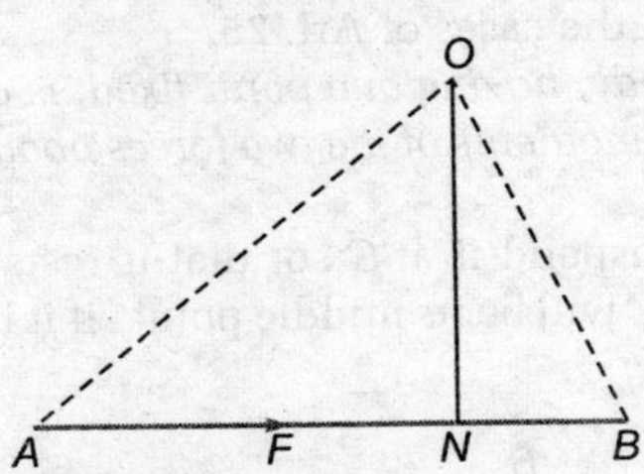

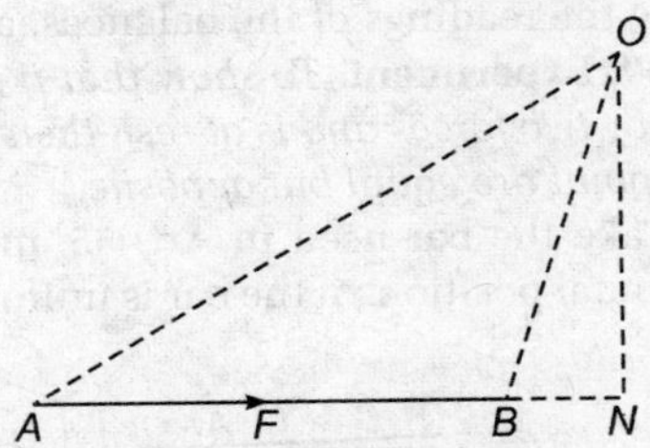

Join OA and OB.

By definition the moment of F about O is $F \times ON$, *i.e.* $AB \times ON$. But $AB \times ON$ is equal to twice the area of the triangle OAB [for it is equal to the area of a rectangle whose base is AB and whose height is ON]. Hence the moment of the force F about the point O is represented by twice the area of the triangle OAB, *i.e. by twice the area of the triangle whose base is the line representing the force and whose vertex is the point about the moment is taken.*

59. *Physical meaning of the moment of a force about a point.*

Suppose the body in the figure of Art. 57 to be a plane lamina [*i.e.* a body of very small thickness, such as a piece of sheet-tin or a thin piece of board] resting on a smooth table and suppose the point O of the body to be fixed. The effect of a force F acting on the body would be to cause it to turn about the point O as a centre, and this effect would not be zero unless (1) the force F were zero, or (2) the force F passed through O, in which case the distance ON would vanish. Hence the product $F \times ON$ would seem to be a fitting measure of the tendency of F to turn the body about O. This may be experimentally verified as follows ;

Let the lamina be at rest under the action of two strings whose tensions are F and F_1, which are tied to fixed points of the lamina and whose lines of action lie in the plane of the lamina. Let ON and ON_1 be the perpendiculars drawn from the fixed point O to the lines of the action of F and F_1.

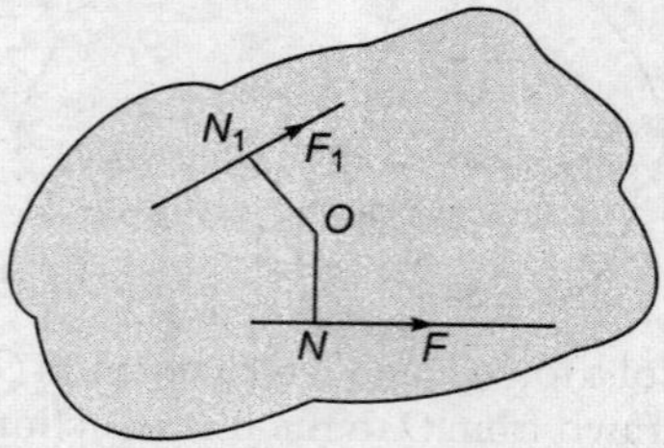

If we measure the lengths ON and ON_1 and also the forces F and F_1, it will be found that the product $F . ON$ is always equal to the product $F_1 \cdot ON_1$.

Hence the two force, F and F_1, will have equal but opposite tendencies to turn the body about O if their moments about O have the same magnitude.

These forces F and F_1 may be measured by carrying the strings over light smooth pulleys and hanging weights at their ends sufficient to give equilibrium ; or by tying the strings to the hooks of two spring balances and noting the readings of the balances, as in the cases of Art. 25.

60. Experiment. *To show that if a body, having one point fixed, is acted upon by two forces and is at rest, then the moments of the two forces about the fixed point are equal but opposite.*

Take the bar used in Art. 55 and suspend it at C so, that it rests in a horizontal position ; if the bar is uniform C will be its middle point ; if it is not

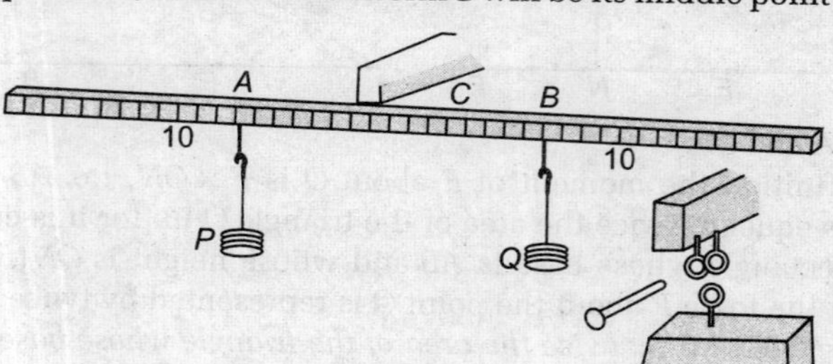

uniform, then C will be its centre of gravity [Chapter IX]. The beam must be so suspended that it turns easily and freely about C.

When the forces are parallel. From any two points A, B of the bar suspend carriers on which place weights until the beam again balances in a horizontal position.

Let P be the total weight, including that of the carrier at A, and Q the total weight similarly at B. Measure carefully the distances AC and BC.

Then it will be found that the products $P \cdot AC$ and $Q \cdot BC$ are equal.

The theorem can be verified for more than two forces by placing several such carriers on the bar and putting weights on them such it is in equilibrium.

In every such case it will be found that the sum of the moments of the weights on one side of C is equal to the sum of the moments of those on the other side.

When the forces are not parallel. Arrange the bar as before but let light strings be attached at A and B which after passing over light pulleys support carriers at their other ends. Let these carriers have weights put upon them until the beam balances in a horizontal position.

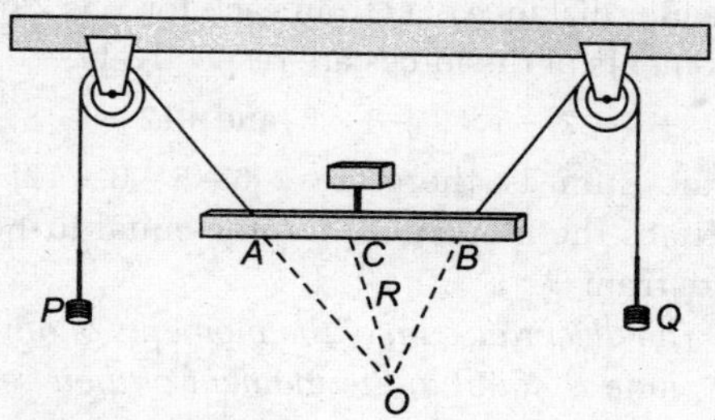

Let P and Q be the total weights on the carriers including the weights of the carriers themselves ; these will be the tensions of the strings at A and B.

Measure the perpendicular distances, p and q, from C to OA and OB respectively.

Then it will be found that

$$P \cdot p = Q \cdot q.$$

61. *Positive and negative moments.* In Art. 57 the force F would, if it were the only force acting on the lamina, make it turn in a direction opposite to that in which the hands of a watch move, when the watch is laid on the table with its face upwards.

The force F_1 would, if it were the only force acting on the lamina, make it turn in the same direction as that in which the hands of the watch move.

The moment of F about O, *i.e.* in a direction ↶, is said to be *positive*, and the moment of F_1 about O, *i.e.* in a direction ↷, is said to be *negative*.

Algebraic sum of moments. The algebraic sum of the moments of a set of forces about a given point is the sum of the moments of the forces, each moment having its proper sign prefixed to it.

Ex. *ABCD is a square ; along the sides AB, CB, DC, and DA forces act equal respectively to 6, 5, 8, and 12 kgf. Find the algebraic sum of their moments about the centre, O, of the square, if the side of the square is 4 metres.*

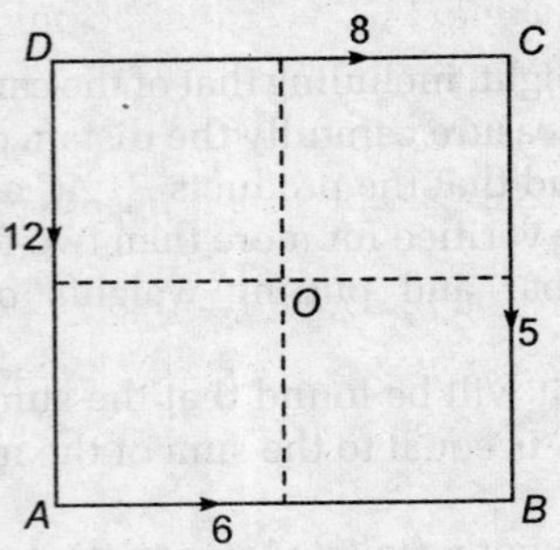

The forces along *DA* and *AB* tend to turn the square about *O* in the positive direction, whilst the forces along the sides *DC* and *CB* tend to turn it in the negative direction.

The perpendicular distance of *O* from each force is 2 metres.

Hence, the moments of the forces are respectively

$$+6 \times 2, -5 \times 2, -8 \times 2, \text{ and } +12 \times 2.$$

Their algebraic sum is therefore $2[6 - 5 - 8 + 12]$ or 10 units of moment, *i.e.*, 10 times the moment of a force equal to 1 kgf acting at the distance of 1 metre from *O*.

62. Theorem. *The algebraic sum of the moments of any two forces about any point in their plane is equal to the moment of their resultant about the same point.*

Case I. *Let the forces meet in a point.*

Let *P* and *Q* acting at the point *A* be the two forces and *O* the point about which the moments are taken. Draw *OC* parallel to the direction of *P* to meet the line of action of *Q* in the point *C*.

Let *AC* represents *Q* in magnitude and on the same scale let *AB* represents *P* ; complete the parallelogram *ABDC*, and join *OA* and *OB*.

Then *AD* represents the resultant, *R*, of *P* and *Q*.

(α) If *O* is outside the angle *DAC*, as in the first figure, we have to show that

$$2\,\Delta\,OAB + 2\,\Delta\,OAC = 2\,\Delta\,OAD.$$

[For the moments of *P* and *Q* about *O* are in the same direction.]

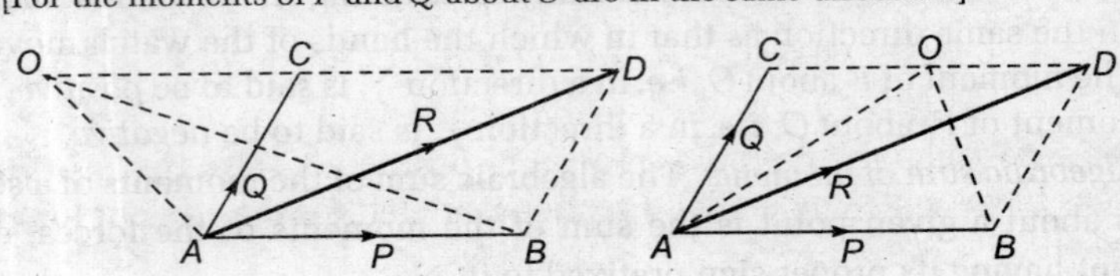

Since AB and OD are parallel, we have

$$\Delta\, OAB = \Delta\, DAB = \Delta\, ACD.$$

$$\therefore \quad 2\,\Delta\, OAB + 2\,\Delta\, OAC = 2\,\Delta\, ACD + 2\,\Delta\, OAC = 2\,\Delta\, OAD.$$

(β) If O is within the angle CAD, as in the second figure, we have to show that

$$2\,\Delta AOB - 2\,\Delta\, AOC = 2\,\Delta\, AOD.$$

[For the moments of P and Q about O are in opposite directions.]
As in (α), we have

$$\Delta AOB = \Delta DAB = \Delta ACD.$$

$$\therefore \quad 2\,\Delta\, AOB - 2\,\Delta\, AOC = 2\,\Delta\, ACD - 2\,\Delta\, OAC = 2\,\Delta\, OAD.$$

Case II. *Let the forces be parallel.*

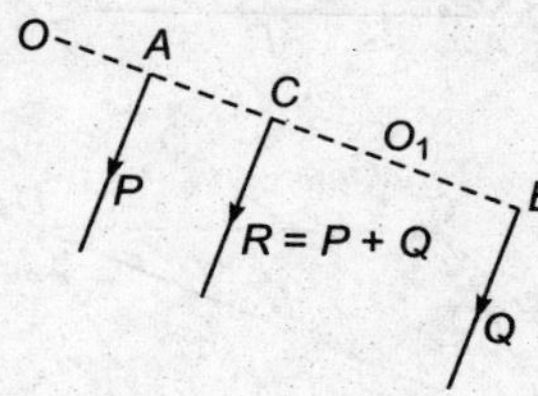

Let P and Q be two parallel forces and $R\,(= P + Q)$ their resultant.

From any point O in their plane draw $OACB$ perpendicular to the forces to meet them in $A, C,$ and B respectively.

By Art. 52 we have $\qquad P \cdot AC = Q \cdot CB \qquad$ ...(1);

$\therefore$ the sum of the moments of P and Q about O

$$= Q \cdot OB + P \cdot OA$$
$$= Q\,(OC + CB) + P\,(OC - AC)$$
$$= (P + Q)\,OC + Q \cdot CB - P \cdot AC$$
$$= (P + Q) \cdot OC, \text{ by equation (1),}$$
$$= \text{moment of the resultant about } O.$$

If the points about which the moments arc taken is between the forces, as O_1, the moments of P and Q have opposite signs.

In this case we have

Algebraic sum of moments of P and Q about O_1

$$= P \cdot O_1A - Q \cdot O_1B$$
$$= P(O_1C + CA) - Q\,(CB - O_1C)$$
$$= (P + Q) \cdot O_1C + P \cdot CA - Q \cdot CB$$
$$= (P + Q) \cdot O_1C, \text{ by equation (1).}$$

The case when the point has any other position, as also the case when the forces have opposite parallel directions, are left for the student to prove for himself.

63. Case I of the preceding proposition may be otherwise proved as follows :

Let the two forces, P and Q, be represented by AB and AC respectively and let AD represent the resultant R so that $ABDC$ is a parallelogram.

Let O be any point in the plane of the forces. Join OA and draw BL and CM, parallel to OA, to meet AD in L and M respectively.

Since the sides of the triangle ACM are respectively parallel to the sides of the triangle DBL, and since AC is equal to BD,

$$\therefore \quad AM = LD,$$

$$\therefore \quad \Delta\, OAM = \Delta\, OLD.$$

First, let O fall outside the angle CAD, as in the first figure.

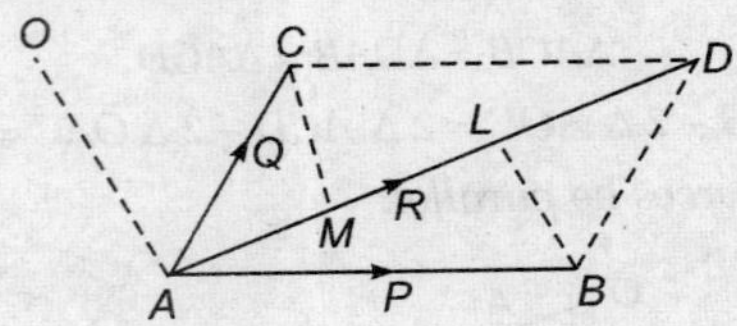

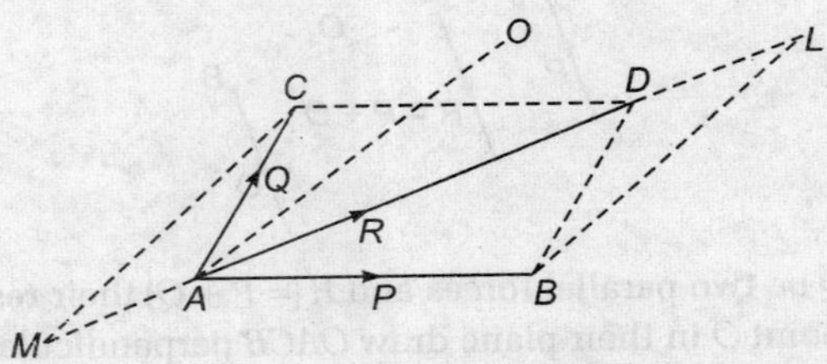

Then
$$2\,\Delta\, OAB + 2\,\Delta\, OAC$$
$$= 2\,\Delta\, OAL + 2\,\Delta\, OAM$$
$$= 2\,\Delta\, OAL + 2\,\Delta\, OLD$$
$$= 2\,\Delta\, OAD.$$

Hence, the sum of the moments of P and Q is equal to that of R.

Secondly, let O fall within the angle CAD, as in the second figure.

The algebraic sum of the moments of P and Q about O
$$= 2\,\Delta\, OAB - 2\,\Delta OAC$$
$$= 2\,\Delta\, OAL - 2\,\Delta\, OAM$$
$$= 2\,\Delta\, OAL - 2\,\Delta\, OLD$$
$$= 2\,\Delta\, OAD$$
$$= \text{moment of } R \text{ about } O.$$

64. If the point O about which the moments are taken lies on the resultant, the moment of the resultant about the point vanishes. In this case the algebraic sum of the moments of the component forces about the given point vanishes, *i.e. The moments of two forces about any point on the line of action of their resultant are equal and of opposite sign.*

The student will easily be able to prove this theorem independently from a figure; for, in Art. 62, the point O will be found to coincide with the point D and we have only to show that the triangles ACO and ABO are now equal, and this is obviously true.

65. Generalised theorem of moments. *If any number of forces in one plane acting on a rigid body have a resultant, the algebraic sum of their moments about any point in their plane is equal to the moment of their resultant.*

For let the forces be $P, Q, R, S, \ldots$, and let O be the point about which the moments are taken.

Let P_1 be the resultant of P and Q,

P_2 be the resultant of P_1 and R,

P_3 be the resultant of P_2 and S,

and so on till the final resultant is obtained.

Then the moment of P_1 about O = sum of the moments of P and Q (Art. 62);

Also the moment of P_2 about O = sum of the moments of P_1 and R

= sum of the moments of P, Q, and R.

So the moment of P_3 about O

= sum of the moments of P_2 and S

= sum of the moments of P, Q, R, and S,

and so on until all the forces have been taken.

Hence, the moment of the final resultant

= algebraic sum of the moments of the component forces.

Cor. It follows, as in Art. 64, that the algebraic sum of the moments of any number of forces about a point on the line of action of their resultant is zero ; so, conversely, if the algebraic sum of the moments of any number of forces about any point in their plane vanishes, then, *either* their resultant is zero (in which case the forces are in equilibrium), *or* the resultant passes through the point about which the moments are taken.

66. The theorem of the previous article enables us to find points on the line of action of the resultant of a system of forces. For we have only to find a point about which the algebraic sum of the moments of the system of forces vanishes, and then the resultant must pass through that point. This principle is exemplified in examples 2 and 3 of the following article.

If we have a system of parallel forces the resultant is known both in magnitude and direction when one such point is known.

66 (a). Moment about an axis.

Let F be the force and PP' the axis. We want to find the moment about PP'. Let OO' be the shortest distance between the axis PP' and OF, the line of action of F. Through O, let us draw QOQ' parallel to the axis PP' making with OF an angle θ. Take the plane containing QOQ' and F.

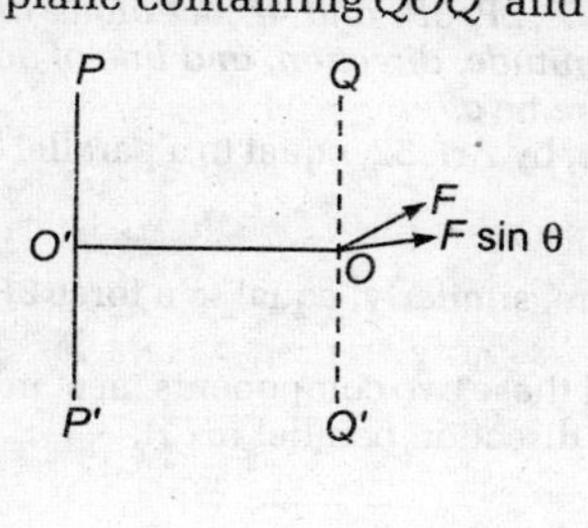

Let $(F \cos\theta, F \sin\theta)$ be the components of F along the axis *i.e.* along OQ and perpendicular to the axis, *i.e.* along OO' respectively. $F \cos\theta$ cannot have any turning effect about PP' (which is parallel to it), while the turning effect of $F \sin\theta \times OO' = F \sin\theta \times m = Mm$, say, where M represents the resolved part of perpendicular to the axis and m the shortest distance between the axis and the line of action of the force F.

Def. The moment of a force about an axis in the product of the resolved part of the force in a direction perpendicular to the axis (the other component being parallel to the axis and the shortest distance between the axis and the line of the force.

67. Ex. 1. *A rod, 5 metres long, supported by two vertical strings attached to its ends, has weight of 4, 6, 8, and 10 kg hung from the rod at distances of 1, 2, 3, and 4 metres from one end. If the weight of the rod is 2 kg, what are the tensions of the strings ?*

Let AF be the rod, B, C, D, and E the points at which the weights are hung;

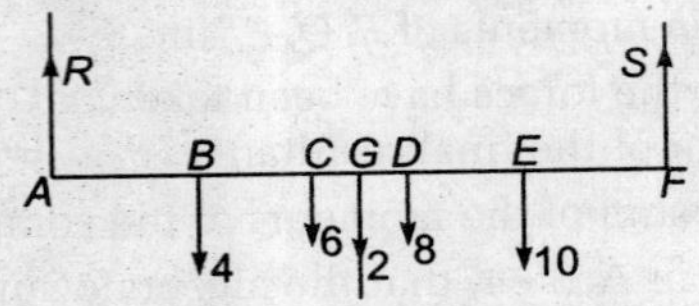

let G be the middle point; we shall assume that the weight of the rod acts here.

Let R and S be the tensions of the strings. Since the resultant of the forces is zero, its moment about A must be zero.

Hence, by Art. 65, the algebraic sum of the moments about A must vanish.

Therefore, $$4 \times 1 + 6 \times 2 + 2 \times 2\frac{1}{2} + 8 \times 3 + 10 \times 4 - S \times 5 = 0$$

$$\therefore \quad 5S = 4 + 12 + 5 + 24 + 40 = 85,$$

$$\therefore \quad S = 17.$$

Similarly, taking moments about F, we have

$$5R = 10 \times 1 + 8 \times 2 + 2 \times 2\frac{1}{2} + 6 \times 3 + 4 \times 4 = 65,$$

$$\therefore \quad R = 13.$$

The tension R may be otherwise obtained. For the resultant of the weights is a weight equal to 30 kg and that of R and S is a force equal to $R + S$. But these resultants balance one another.

$$\therefore \quad R + S = 30;$$

$$\therefore \quad R = 30 - S = 30 - 17 = 13.$$

Ex. 2. *Forces equal to P, 2P, 3P, and 4P act along the sides of a square ABCD taken in order ; find the magnitude, direction, and line of action of the resultant*

Let the side of the square be a.

The forces P and $3P$ are, by Art. 52, equal to a parallel force $2P$ acting at E, where DE is $\frac{a}{2}$.

The forces $4P$ and $2P$ are, similarly, equal to a force $2P$ acting at a point F on CD where DF is a.

Let the lines of action of these two components meet in O. Then the final resultant is equal to $2P\sqrt{2}$ acting in a direction parallel to CA.

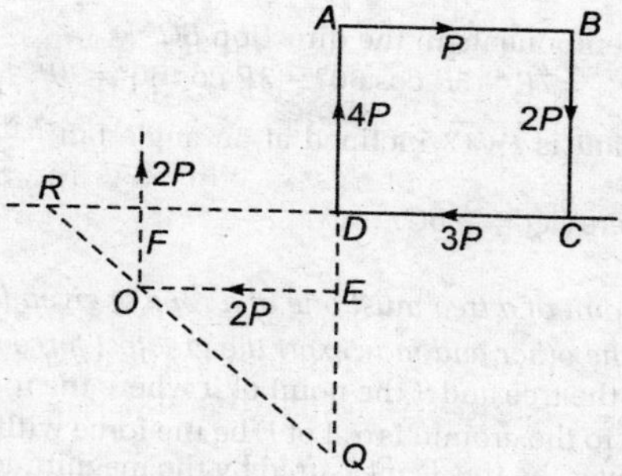

Otherwise thus; without making any geometric construction (which is often tedious) the line of action of the resultant force can be easily obtained by using the theorem of Art. 65.

Let the line of action meet *AD* and *CD* in *Q* and *R*.

Since *Q* is a point on the line of action of the resultant the algebraic sum of the moments of the four forces about *Q* must be zero ;

$$\therefore \qquad P\,(DQ + a) + 2P\,(a) = 3P \cdot DQ\,;$$

$$\therefore \qquad dQ = \frac{3a}{2}.$$

So for the point *R* we have

$$P \cdot a + 2P = (RD + a)\,4P \cdot RD;$$

$$\therefore \qquad RD = \frac{3a}{2}.$$

Also the components of the forces perpendicular to *CD* are $4P - 2P$ *i.e.* $2P$, and the components parallel to *CD* are $3P - P$, *i.e.* $2P$. Hence, the magnitude of the resultant is$2\sqrt{2}P$.

Ex. 3. *Forces equal to* $3P, 7P$, *and* $5P$ *act along the sides AB, BC, and CA of an equilateral triangle ABC; find the magnitude, direction, and line of action of the resultant.*

Let the side of the triangle be a, and let the resultant force meet the side *BC* in *Q*. Then, by Art. 65, the moments of the forces about *Q* vanish.

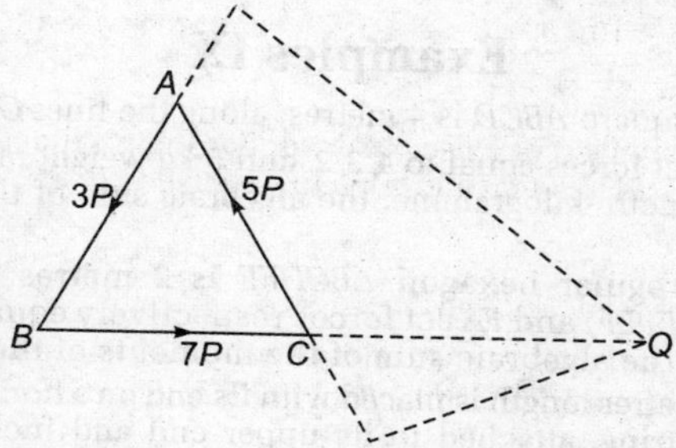

$$\therefore \qquad 3P \times (QC + a) \sin 60° = 5P \times QC \sin 60°.$$

$$\therefore \qquad QC = \frac{3a}{2}.$$

The sum of the components of the forces perpendicular to *BC*

$$= 5P \sin 60° - 3P \sin 60° = P\sqrt{3}.$$

Also the sum of components in the direction BC

$$= 7P - 5P \cos 60° - 3P \cos 60° = 3P.$$

Hence, the resultant is $P\sqrt{12}$ inclined at an angle $\tan^{-1}\frac{\sqrt{3}}{3}$, *i.e.* 30°, to BC and passing through Q where $CQ = \frac{3}{2} BC$.

Ex. 4. *At what point of a tree must one of a rope of given length a be attached so that a man pulling at the other end may exert the greatest force to pull it over ?*

Solution : PQ is the tree and S the point of it where the rope RS is attached. The inclination of the rope to the ground is α. Let F be the force with which the man pulls. The tendency to pull over the tree is measured by the magnitude of the moment of the force F along RS about P.

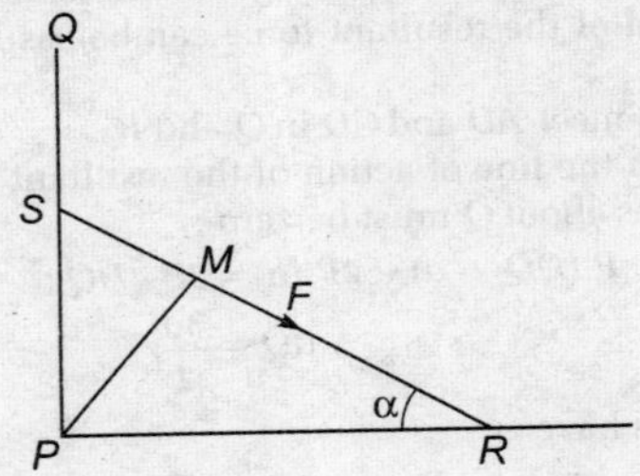

Now, this moment

$$= F \cdot f = F \times PR \sin\alpha = F \times RS \sin\alpha \cos\alpha$$

$$= \frac{1}{2} \cdot F \cdot a \sin 2\alpha$$

The maximum value of $\sin 2\alpha$ is 1

i.e. $\sin 2\alpha = 1 = \sin 90°$

so that $\alpha = 45°$

$\therefore$ $PS = a \sin 45° = \frac{a}{\sqrt{2}}$

Examples IX

1. The side of a square $ABCD$ is 4 metres; along the lines CB, BA, DA, and DB, respectively act forces equal to 4, 3, 2, and 5 kg weight ; find, to the nearest decimal of a metre-kilogramme, the algebraic sum of the moments of the forces about C.
2. The side of regular hexagon $ABCDEF$ is 2 metres ; along the sides AB, CB, DC, DE, EF, and FA act forces respectively equal to 1, 2, 3, 4, 5 and 6 kg-wt; find the algebraic sum of the moments of the forces about A.
3. A pole of 20 metres length is placed with its end on a horizontal plane and is pulled by a string, attached to its upper end and inclined at 30° to the horizon, whose tension is equal to 30 kgf-wt; find the horizontal force which applied at a point 4 metres above the ground will keep the pole in a vertical position.
4. A uniform iron rod is of length 6 metres and mass 9 kg, and from its extremities are suspended masses of 6 and 12 kg respectively ; from what point must the rod be suspended so that it may remain in a horizontal position ?

5. A uniform beam is of length 12 metres and weight 50 kg, and from its ends are suspended bodies of weights 20 and 30 kg respectively ; at what point must the beam be supported so that it may remain in equilibrium ?
6. Masses of 1 kg, 2 kg, 3 kg, and 4 kg are suspended from a uniform rod, of length 5 metres, at distances of 1 metre, 2 metres, 3 metres, and 4 metres respectively from one end. If the mass of the rod is 4 kg, find the position of the point about which it will balance.
7. A uniform rod, 4 metres in length and weighing 2 kg, turns freely about a point distant one metre from one end and from that end a weight of 10 kg is suspended. What weight must be placed at the other end to produce equilibrium ?
8. A heavy uniform beam, 10 metres long, whose mass is 10 kg, is supported at a point 4 metres from one end; at this end a mass of 6 kg is placed ; find the mass which, placed at the other end, would give equilibrium.
9. The horizontal roadway of a bridge is 9 m long, weighs 6 tonnes, and rests on similar supports at its ends. What is the thrust borne by each support when a carriage, of weight 2 tonnes, is (1) halfway across, (2) two-thirds of the way across ?
10. A light rod, AB, 20 cm long, rests on two pegs whose distance apart is 10 cm. How must it be placed so that the reactions of the pegs may be equal when weights of $2W$ and $3W$ respectively are suspended from A and B ?
11. A light rod, of length 72 cm, has equal weights attached to it, one at 18 cm from one end and the other at 30 cm from the other end; if it be supported by two vertical strings attached to its ends and if the strings cannot support a tension greater than due weight of 50 kg, what is the greatest magnitude of the equal weights ?
12. A heavy uniform beam, whose mass is 40 kg, is suspended in a horizontal position by two vertical strings each of which can sustain a tension of 35 kg weight. How far from the centre of the beam must a body, of mass 20 kg, be placed so that one of the strings may just break ?
13. A uniform bar, AB, 10 metres long and of mass 50 kg, rests on the ground. If a mass of 100 kg is laid on it at a point, distant 3 metres from B, find what vertical force applied to the end A will just begin to lift that end.
14. A rod, 16 cm long, rests on two pegs, 9 cm apart, with its centre midway between them. The greatest masses that can be suspended in succession from the two ends without disturbing the equilibrium are 4 kg and 5 kg respectively. Find the weight of the rod and the position of the point at which its weight acts.
15. A straight rod, 60 cm long, is movable about a hinge at one end and is kept in a horizontal position by a thin vertical string attached to the rod at a distance of 20 cm from the hinge and fastened to a fixed point above the rod; if the string can just support a mass of 270 g without breaking, find the greatest mass that can be suspended from the other end of the rod, neglecting the weight of the rod.
16. A tricycle, weighing 37 kg, has a small wheel symmetrically placed 72 cm behind two large wheels which are 72 cm apart ; if the centre of gravity of the machine is at a horizontal distance of 18 cm behind the front wheels and that of the rider, whose weight is 63 kg, is 6 cm behind the front wheels, find the thrusts on the ground of the different wheels.

17. A tricycle, of weight 42 kg, has a small wheel symmetrically placed 105 cm front of the line joining the two large wheels which are 90 cm apart ; if the centre of gravity of the machine is distant horizontally 30 cm in front of the hind wheels and that of the rider, whose weight is 77 kg, is 15 cm in front of the hind wheels, find how the weight is distributed on the different wheels.
18. A dog-cart, loaded with 200 kg, exerts a force on the horse's back equal to 5 kgf; find the position of the centre of gravity of the load if the distance between the pad and the axle is 1.8 m.
19. Forces of 3, 4, 5 and 6 kgf respectively act along the sides of a square *ABCD* taken in order; find the magnitude, direction, and line of action of their resultant.
20. *ABCD* is a square ; along *AB*, *CB*, *AD*, and *DC* equal forces, *P*, act ; find their resultant.
21. *ABCD* is a square the length of whose side is 30 cm ; along *AB*, *BC*, *DC*, and *AD* act forces proportional to 1, 2, 4, and 3 respectively ; show that the resultant is parallel to diagonal of the square and find where it cuts the sides of the square.
22. *ABCD* is a rectangle of which adjacent sides *AB* and *BC* are equal to 3 and 4 metres respectively; along *AB*, *BC*, and *CD* forces of 30, 40, and 50 kgf act; find the resultant.
23. Three forces *P*, 2*P*, and 3*P* act along the sides *AB*, *BC*, and *CA* of a given equilateral triangle *ABC*; find the magnitude and direction of their resultant, and find also the point in which its line of action meets the side *BC*.
24. *ABC* is an isosceles triangle whose angle *A* is 120° and forces of magnitude 1, 1, and $\sqrt{3}$ kgf act along *AB*, *AC*, and *BC*; show that the resultant bisects *BC* and is parallel to one of the other sides of the triangle.
25. Forces proportional to *AB*, *BC* and 2*CA* act along the sides of a triangle *ABC* taken in order; show that the resultant is represented in magnitude and direction by *CA* and that its line of action meets *BC* at a point *X* where *CX* is equal to *BC*.
26. *ABC* is a triangle and *D*, *E*, and *F* are the middle points of the sides; forces represented by *AD*, $\frac{2}{3}$ *BE*, and $\frac{1}{3}$*CF* act on a particle at the point where *AD* and *BE* meet; show that the resultant is represented in magnitude and direction by $\frac{1}{2}$ *AC* and that its line of action divides *BC* in the ratio 2 : 1.
27. Three forces act along the sides of a triangle ; show that, if the sum of two of the forces is equal in magnitude but opposite in sense to the third force, then the resultant of the three forces passes through the centre of the inscribed circle of the triangle.
28. The wire passing round a telegraph pole is horizontal and the two portions attached to the pole are inclined at an angle of 60° to one another. The pole is supported by a wire attached to the middle point of the pole and inclined at 60° to the horizon; show that the tension of this wire is $4\sqrt{3}$ times that of the telegraph wire.
29. At what height from the base of a pillar must the end of a rope of given length be fixed so that a man standing on the ground and pulling at its other end with a given force may have the greatest tendency to make the pillar overturn ?

30. The magnitude of a force is known and also its moments about two given points A and B. Find, by a geometrical construction, its line of action.

31. Find the locus of all points in a plane such that two forces given in magnitude and position shall have equal moments, in the same sense, round any one of these points.

32. AB is a diameter of a circle and BP and BQ are chords at right angles to one another; show that the moments of forces represented by BP and BQ about A are equal.

33. A cyclist, whose weight is 75 kg, puts all his weight upon one pedal of his bicycle when the crank is horizontal and the bicycle is prevented from moving forwards. If the length of the crank is 15 cm and the radius of the chain-wheel is 10 cm, find the tension of the chain.

34. A heavy non-uniform beam AB, of length l, rests across a fixed peg P and carries equal loads W_1 hung from each end. In the equilibrium position with the beam horizontal the distance AP is X_1. For another pair of equal loads, W_2, the corresponding distance AP is X_2. Prove that the weight of the beam W is given by

$$(X_1 - X_2)\,W = (W_1 - W_2)\,l - 2W_1X_1 + 2W_2X_2.$$

35. OX and OY are two straight lines at right angles, and a force acting in their plane at O has moments G and G' about the two points whose co-ordinates are (X, Y) and (X', Y') respectively with the lines OX and OY as axes of co-ordinates. If $(XY' - X'Y)$ is not zero, prove that the magnitude R of the force and the angle θ between its line of action and OX are given by

$$R^2 = \frac{(XG' - X'G)^2 + (YG' - Y'G)^2}{(XY' - X'Y)^2} \text{ and } \tan\theta = \frac{YG' - Y'G}{XG' - X'G}.$$

36. A heavy carriage wheel of weight W and radius r is to be dragged over an obstacle of height h by a horizontal force P applied to the centre of the wheel. Show that P must be greater than

$$\frac{W\sqrt{2rh - h^2}}{t - h}.$$

37. Forces P, Q, R, and S acting along AB, CB, CD, and AD of a quadrilateral $ABCD$ are in equilibrium. Show that

$$\frac{P}{AB} : \frac{Q}{CB} = \frac{S}{AD} : \frac{R}{CD}.$$

38. The algebraic sums of the moments of a system of co-planar forces about points whose co-ordinates are (1, 0), (0, 2) and (2, 3) referred to rectangular axes, are G_1, G_2, G_3 respectively. If θ is the angle which the direction of the resultant force makes with the axis of X, show that

$$\tan\theta = \frac{G_1 - 3G_2 + 2G_3}{2G_1 - G_2 - G_3}.$$

6

Couples

68. Def. Two equal unlike parallel forces whose lines of action are not the same, form a couple.

The arm of a couple is the perpendicular distance between the lines of action of the two forces which form the couple *i.e.*, the perpendicular drawn from any point lying on the line of action of one of the forces upon the line of action of the other. Thus the arm of the couple (P, P) is the length AB.

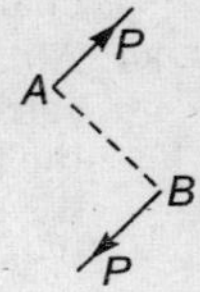

The moment of a couple is the product of one of the forces forming the couple and the arm of the couple.

In the figure the moment of the couple is $P \times AB$.

Examples of a couple are the forces applied to the handle of a screw-press or to the key of a clock in winding it up or by the hands to the handle of a door in opening it.

A couple is sometimes called a torque; the word torque is also used to denote the moment of the couple.

69. Theorem. *The algebraic sum of the moments of the two forces forming a couple about any point in their plane is constant, and equal to the moment of the couple.*

Let the couple consists of two forces, each equal to P, and let O be any point in their plane.

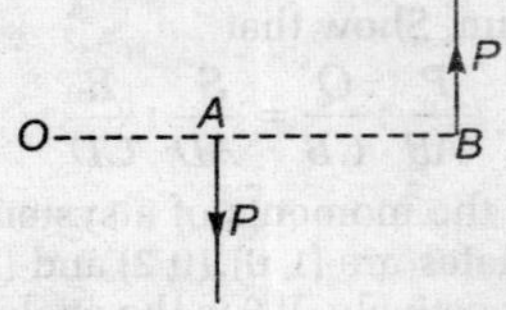

Draw OAB perpendicular to the lines of action of the forces to meet them in A and B respectively.

The algebraic sum of the moments of the forces about O.

$$= P \cdot OB - P \cdot OA = P\,(OB - OA) = P \cdot AB$$

= the moment of the couple, and is therefore the same whatever the point O about which the moments are taken.

70. Theorem. *Two couples, acting in one plane upon a rigid body, whose moments are equal and opposite balance one another.*

Let one couple consist of two forces (P, P), acting at the ends of an arm p, and let the other couple consist of two forces (Q, Q) acting at the ends of an arm q.

Case I. Let one of the forces P meet one of the forces Q in a point O, and let the other two forces meet in O'. From O' draw perpendiculars, $O'M$ and $O'N$, upon the forces which do not pass through O', so that the lengths of these perpendiculars are p and q respectively.

Since the moments of the couples are equal in magnitude, we have

$$P \cdot p = Q \cdot q$$

i.e.

$$P \cdot O'M = Q \cdot O'N.$$

Hence, (Art. 64) O' is on the line of action of the resultant of P and Q acting at O, so that OO' is the direction of this resultant.

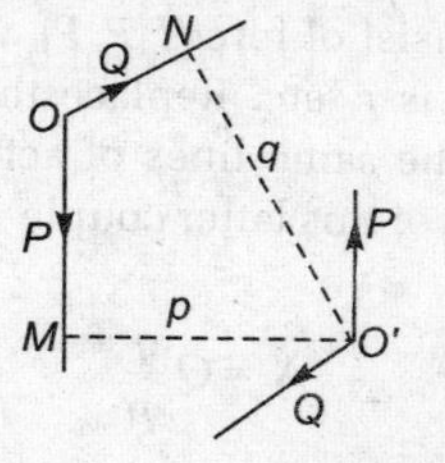

Similarly, the resultant of P and Q at O' is in the direction $O'O$.

Also these resultants are equal in magnitude; for the forces at O are respectively equal to, and act at the same angles as, the forces at O'.

Hence, these two resultant destroy one another, and therefore the four forces composing the two couples are in equilibrium.

Case II. Let the forces composing the couples be all parallel, and let any straight line perpendicular to their directions meet them in the points A, B, C and D, as in the figure, so that, since the moments are equal, we have

$$P \cdot AB = Q \cdot CD \quad \text{...(i)}$$

Let L be the point of application of the resultant of Q at C and P at B so that

$$P \cdot BL = Q \cdot CL \quad \text{(Art. 52) ...(ii)}$$

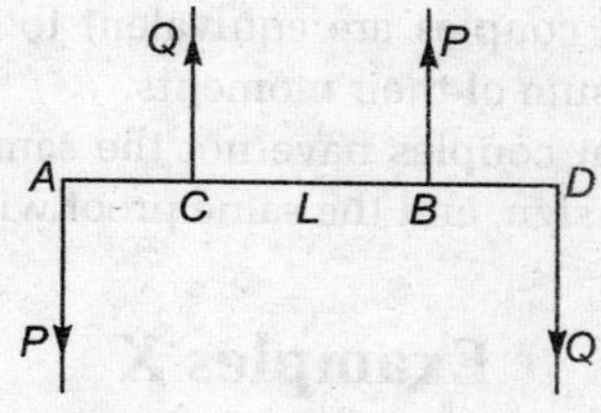

By subtracting (ii) from (i), we have

$$P \cdot AL = Q \cdot LD,$$

so that L is the point of application of the resultant of P at A, and Q at D.

But the magnitude of each of these resultant is $(P+Q)$, and they have opposite directions; hence they are in equilibrium.

Therefore the four forces composing the two couples balance.

71. Since two couples in the same plane, of equal but opposite moment, balance, it follows, by reversing the directions of the forces composing one of the couples, that

Any two couples of equal moment in the same plane are equivalent.

It follows also that two like couples of equal moment are equivalent to a couple of double the moment.

72. Theorem. *Any number of couples in the same plane acting on a rigid body are equivalent to a single couple, whose moment is equal to the algebraic sum of the moments of the couples.*

For let the couples consist of forces (P, P) whose arm is p, (Q, Q) whose arm is q, (R, R) whose arm is r, etc. Replace the couple (Q, Q) by a couple whose components have the same lines of action as the forces (P, P). The magnitude of each of forces of this latter couple will be X, where $X \cdot p = Q \cdot q$, (Art. 71),

so that $$X = Q\frac{q}{p}.$$

So let the couple (R, R) be replaced by a couple $\left(R\frac{r}{p}, R\frac{r}{p}\right)$, whose forces act in the same lines as the forces (P, P).

Similarly for the other couples.

Hence all the couples are equivalent to a couple, each of whose forces is $P + Q\frac{q}{p} + R\frac{r}{p} + \ldots$ acting at an arm p.

The moment of this couple is

$$\left(P + Q\frac{q}{p} + R\frac{r}{p} + \ldots\right)p,$$

i.e., $$P \cdot p + Q \cdot q + R \cdot r + \ldots$$

Hence, the original couples are equivalent to a single couple, whose moment is equal to the sum of their moments.

If all the component couples have not the same sign we must give to each moment its proper sign, and the same proof will apply.

Examples X

1. *ABCD* is a square whose side is 2 metres ; along *AB, BC, CD* and *DA* act forces equal to 1, 2, 8 and 5 kg-wt, and along *AC* and *DB* forces equal to $5\sqrt{2}$ and $2\sqrt{2}$ kg-wt ; show that they are equivalent to a couple whose moment is equal to 16 metre-kilogramme weight.

2. Along the sides *AB* and *CD* of a square *ABCD* act forces each equal to 2 kg weight, whilst along the sides *AD* and *CB* act forces each equal to 5 kg weight ; if the side of the squares is 3 metres, find the moment of the couple that will give equilibrium.
3. *ABCDEF* is a regular hexagon; along the sides *AB*, *CB*, *DE* and *FE* act forces respectively equal to 5, 11, 5 and 11 kg weight, and along *CD* and *FA* act forces each equal to *x* kg weight. Find *x*, if the forces are in equilibrium.
4. A horizontal bar *AB*, without weight, is acted upon by a vertical downward force of 1 kg weight at *A*, a vertical upward force of 1 kg weight at *B*, and a downward force of 5 kg weight at a given point *C* inclined to the bar at an angle of 30°. Find at what point of the bar a force must be applied to balance these and find also its magnitude and direction.

---

73. Theorem. *The effect of a couple upon a rigid body is unaltered if it is transferred to any plane parallel to its own, the arm remaining parallel to its original position.*

Let the couple consist of two forces (*P*, *P*), whose arm is *AB* and let their lines of action be *AC* and *BD*.

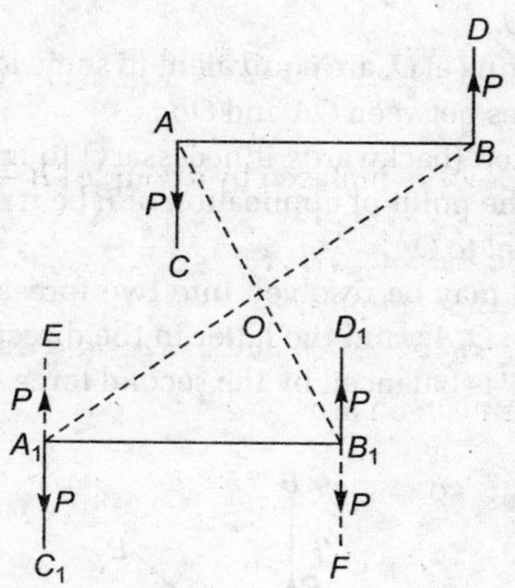

Let A_1B_1 be any line equal and parallel to *AB*.

Draw A_1C_1 and B_1D_1 parallel to *AC* and *BD* respectively.

At A_1 introduce two equal and opposite forces, each equal to *P*, acting in the direction A_1C_1 and the opposite direction A_1E.

At B_1 introduce, similarly, two equal and opposite forces, each equal to *P*, acting in the direction B_1D_1 and the opposite direction B_1F.

These forces will have no effect on the equilibrium of the body.

Join AB_1 and A_1B, and let them meet in *O*; then *O* is the middle point of both AB_1 and A_1B.

The forces *P* at *B* and *P* acting along A_1E have a resultant $2P$ acting at *O* parallel to *BD*.

The forces *P* at *A* and *P* acting along B_1F have a resultant $2P$ acting at *O* parallel to *AC*.

These two resultants are equal and opposite, and therefore balance. Hence we have left the two forces (P, P) at A_1 and B_1 acting in the directions A_1C_1 and B_1D_1 *i.e.* parallel to the direction of the forces of the original couple.

Also the plane through A_1C_1 and B_1D_1 is parallel to the plane through AC and BD.

Hence, the theorem is proved.

Cor. From this proposition and Art. 71 we conclude that a *couple may be replaced by any other couple acting in a parallel plane, provided that the moments of the two couples are the same.*

74. Theorem. *A single force and a couple acting in the same plane upon a rigid body cannot produce equilibrium, but are equivalent to the single force acting in a direction parallel to its original directions.*

Let the couple consist of two forces, each equal to P, their lines of action being OB and O_1C respectively.

Let the single force be Q.

Case I. If Q is not parallel to the forces of the couple, let it be produced to meet one of them in O.

Then P and Q, acting at O, are equivalent to some force R, acting in some direction OL which lies between OA and OB.

Let OL be produced (backwards if necessary) to meet the other force of the couple in O_1, let the point of application of R be transferred to O_1.

Draw O_1A_1 parallel to OA.

Then the force R may be resolved into two forces Q and P, the former acting in the direction O_1A_1, and the latter in the direction opposite to O_1C.

This latter force P is balanced by the second force P of the couple acting in the direction O_1C.

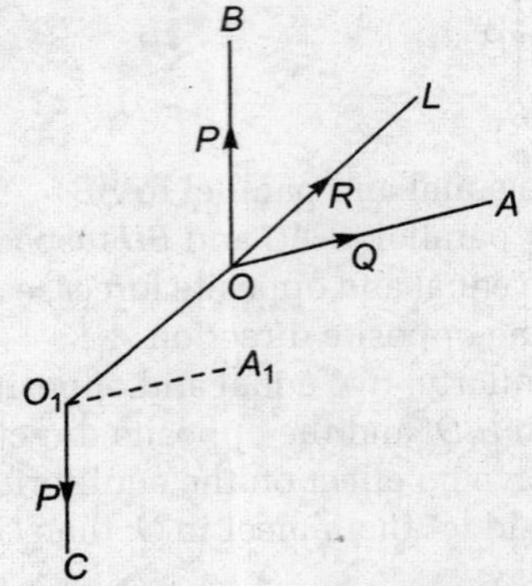

Hence, we have left as the resultant of the system a force Q acting in the direction O_1A_1 parallel to its original direction OA.

Case II. Let the force Q be the parallel to one of the forces of the couple.

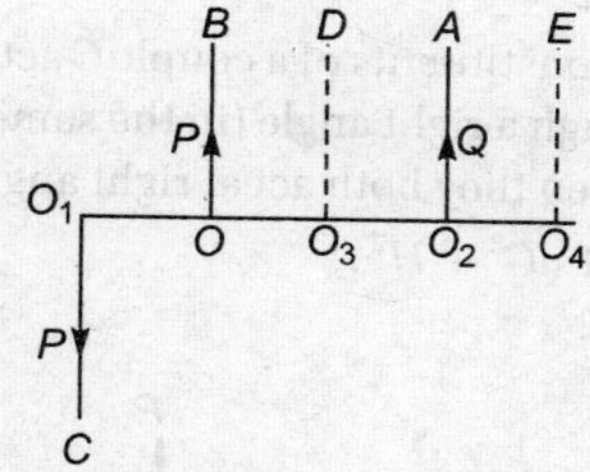

Let O_1O meet the force Q in O_2.

The parallel forces P at O and Q at O_2 are by Art. 52, equivalent to a force $(P + Q)$ acting at some point O_3 in a direction parallel to OB. The unlike parallel forces $(P + Q)$ at O_3 and P at O_1 are similarly, equivalent to a force Q acting at some point O_4 in a direction parallel to O_3D.

Hence, the resultant of the system is equal to the single force Q acting in a direction parallel to its original direction.

75. *If three forces, acting upon a rigid body, are represented in magnitude, direction, and line of action by the sides of a triangle taken in order, they are equivalent to a couple whose moment is represented by twice the area of the triangle.*

Let ABC be the triangle and P, Q, and R the forces, so that P, Q, and R are represented by the sides BC, CA, and AB of the triangle.

Through B draw LBM parallel to the side AC, and introduce two equal and opposite forces, equal and opposite forces equal to Q, at B acting in the directions BL and BM respectively. By the triangle of forces (Art. 36) the forces P, R and Q acting in the straight line BL, are in equilibrium.

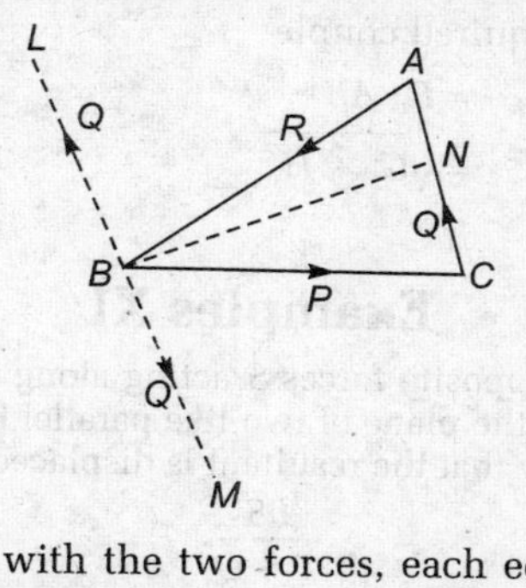

Hence, we are left with the two forces, each equal to Q acting in the directions CA and BM respectively.

These form a couple whose moment is $Q \times BN$, when BN is drawn perpendicular to CA.

Also $Q \times BN = CA \times BN =$ twice the area of the triangle ABC.

Cor. In a similar manner it may be shown that if a system of forces acting on one plane on a rigid body is represented in magnitude, direction, and line of action by the sides of the polygon, they are equivalent to couple whose moment is represented by twice the area of the polygon.

75. (a). Ex. 1. The constituents of a couple C act at A and B; if their lines of action are turned through a right angle (in the same sense) they will form a couple of moment H. When they both act at right angles to AB show that they form a couple of moment $\sqrt{G^2 + H^2}$.

From the diagram,

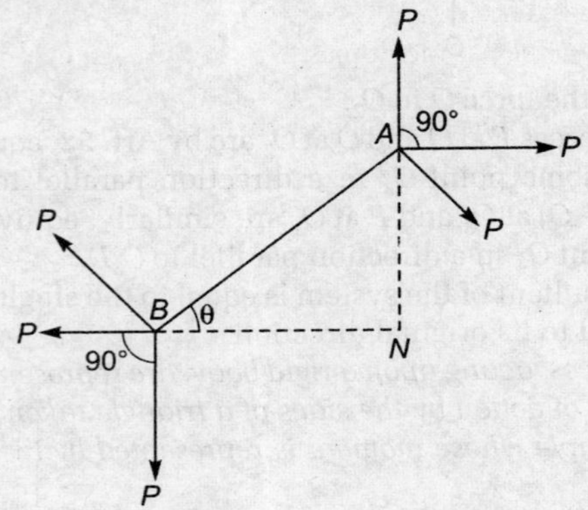

$$G = +P \cdot AN \qquad \ldots(1)$$

and
$$H = P \cdot BN \qquad \ldots(2)$$

squaring and adding (1) and (2) we have

$$G^2 + H^2 = P^2(AN^2 + BN^2) = P^2 AB^2 \qquad \ldots(3)$$

∴ moment of the required couple

$$= P \cdot AB$$

$$= \sqrt{G^2 + H^2} \qquad \text{(from (3))}$$

Examples XI

1. If two equal and opposite forces S acting along any two parallel lines a distance b apart in the plane of two like parallel forces, P, Q are combined with P and Q, show that the resultant is displaced a distance
$$\frac{bS}{P + Q}.$$
2. If three forces P, Q and R acting at the angular points of a triangle ABC along the tangents (in the same sense) to the circumcircle, are equivalent to a couple, show that
$$P : Q : R = \sin 2A : \sin 2B : \sin 2C.$$
3. $ABCD$ is a square whose side is 2 units in length. Forces a, b, c and d act along the sides AB, BC, CD and DA taken in order, and forces $p\sqrt{2}, q\sqrt{2}$ act along AC and BD respectively. Show that, if $p + q = c - a$ and $p - q = d - b$, the forces are equivalent to a couple of moment $a + b + c + d$.

4. Four forces are represented completely by the sides AD, and BC and the diagonals CA, and DB of a quardrilateral $ABCD$. Show that they are equivalent to a couple of moment $AB \cdot CD \sin\theta$, where θ is the angles between AB and CD.
5. Forces P, Q, P, Q act along the sides AB, BC, CD, DA respectively of a square. If these four forces and a fifth force R in the same plane have a resultant which passes through the centre of the square, prove that the line of action of R touches a fixed circle.
6. P and Q are two like parallel forces. If a couple each of which forces is F, and whose arm is a in the plane of P and Q, is combined with them. Show that the resultant is displaced through a distance

$$\frac{Fa}{(P+Q)}.$$

7

Equilibrium of a Rigid Body Acted on By Three Forces in a Plane

76. IN the present chapter we shall discuss some simple cases of the equilibrium of a rigid body acted upon by three forces lying in a plane.

By the help of the theorem of the next article we shall find that the conditions of equilibrium reduce to those of a single particle.

77. Theorem. *If three forces, acting in one plane upon a rigid body, keep it in equilibrium, they must either meet in a point or be parallel.*

If the forces are not all parallel at least two of them must meet ; let these two be P and Q, and let their direction meet in O.

The third force R shall then pass through the point O.

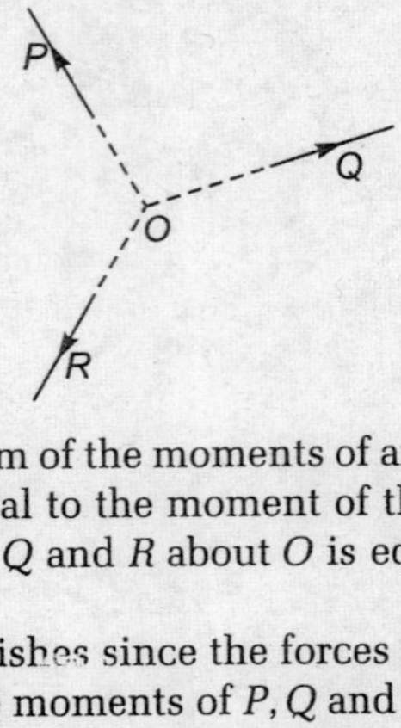

Since the algebraic sum of the moments of any number of forces about a point in their plane is equal to the moment of their resultant, therefore the sum of the moments of P, Q and R about O is equal to the moment of their resultant.

But this resultant vanishes since the forces are in equilibrium.

Hence, the sum of the moments of P, Q and R about O is zero.

But, since P and Q both pass through O, their moments about O vanish.

Hence, the moment of R about O vanishes.

Hence, by Art. 57, since R is not zero, its line of action must pass through O.

Hence, the forces meet in a point.

Otherwise. The resultant of P and Q must be some force passing through O.

But, since the forces P, Q and R are in equilibrium, this resultant must balance R.

But two forces cannot balance unless they have the same line of action.

Hence, the line of action of R must pass through O.

78. By the preceding theorem we see that the conditions for equilibrium of three forces, acting in one plane are easily obtained. For the three forces must meet in a point ; and by using Lami's Theorem, (Art. 40), or by resolving the forces in two directions at right angles. (Art. 46), or by a graphic construction, we can obtain the required conditions.

Ex. 1. *A heavy uniform rod AB is hinged at A to a fixed point, and rests in a position inclined at* 60° *to the horizontal being acted upon by a horizontal force F applied at the lower end B; find the action of the hinge and the magnitude of F.*

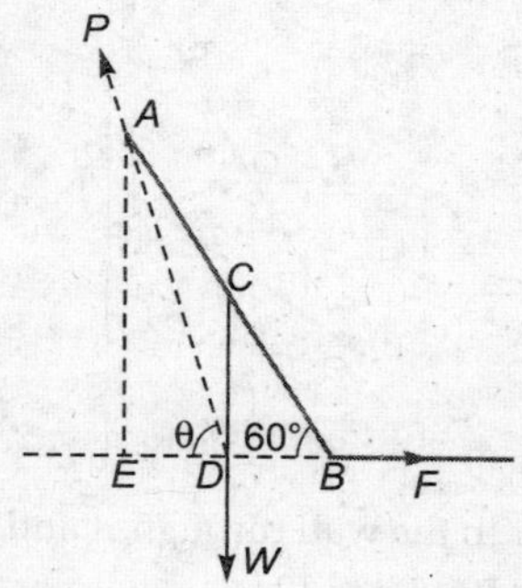

Let the vertical through *C*, the middle point of the rod meet the horizontal line through *B* in the point *D* and let the weight of the rod be *W*.

There are only three forces acting on the rod, *viz*, the force *F*, the weight *W*, and the unknown reaction, *P*, of the hinge.

These three forces must therefore meet in a point.

Now *F* and *W* meet at *D*; hence the direction of the action at the hinge must be the line *DA*.

Draw *AE* perpendicular to *EB*, and let the angle *ADE* be θ.

Then $$\tan\theta = \frac{AE}{ED} = \frac{2AE}{EB} = 2\tan 60° = 2\sqrt{3}.$$

Also, by Lami's Theorem

$$\frac{F}{\sin WDA} = \frac{W}{\sin ADB} = \frac{P}{\sin WDB},$$

i.e., $$\frac{F}{\sin(90° + \theta)} = \frac{W}{\sin(180° - \theta)} = \frac{P}{\sin 90°},$$

∴ $$F = W\frac{\cos\theta}{\sin\theta} = W\cot\theta = \frac{W}{2\sqrt{3}} = \frac{W}{6}\sqrt{3},$$

and $$P = W\frac{1}{\sin\theta} = W\sqrt{1 + \cot^2\theta} = W\sqrt{\frac{13}{12}}.$$

Otherwise ; *ADE* is a triangle of forces, since its sides are parallel to the force. Hence, θ can be measured, and

$$\frac{P}{AD} = \frac{F}{ED} = \frac{W}{AE}.$$

Ex. 2. *A uniform rod, AB, is inclined at an angle of 60° to the vertical with one end A resting against a smooth vertical wall, being supported by a string attached to a point C of the rod, distant 30 cm from B, and also to a ring in the wall vertically above A; if the length of the rod is 1.20 m, find the position of the ring and the inclination and tension of the string.*

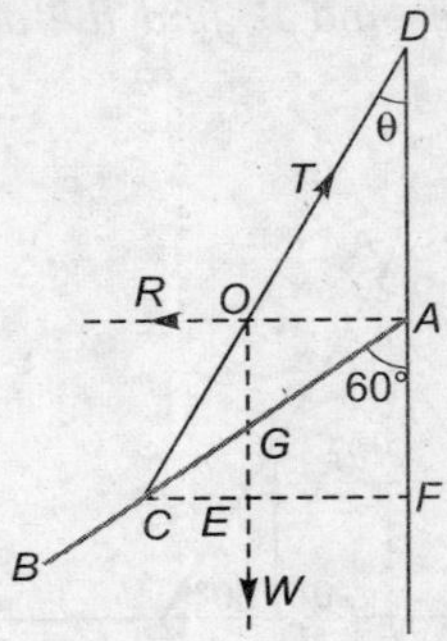

Let the perpendicular to the wall through A and the vertical line through the middle point G, of the rod meet in O.

The third force, the tension T of the string must therefore pass through O. Hence, CO produced must pass through D, the position of the ring.

Let the angle CDA be θ, and draw CEF horizontal to meet OG in E and the wall in F.

Then $$\tan\theta = \tan COE = \frac{CE}{OE} = \frac{CG \sin CGE}{AF}$$

$$= \frac{30° \cdot \sin 60°}{90° \cdot \cos 60°} = \frac{1}{\sqrt{3}}$$

$\therefore$ $$\theta = 30°$$

$\therefore$ $$ACD = 60° - \theta = 30°.$$

Hence, $AD = AC = 90$ cm, giving the position of the ring.

If R is the reaction of the wall, and W is the weight of the beam, we have, since the forces are proportional to the sides of the triangle AOD,

$$\frac{T}{OD} = \frac{R}{AO} = \frac{W}{DA}$$

$\therefore$ $$T = W\frac{OD}{DA} = \frac{W}{\cos 30°} = W \cdot \frac{2}{\sqrt{3}},$$

and $$R = W\frac{AO}{DA} = W \tan 30° = W \cdot \frac{1}{\sqrt{3}}.$$

Ex. 3. *A rod whose centre of gravity divides it into two portions, whose lengths are a and b, has a string, of length l, tied to its two ends and the string is slung over a small smooth peg; find the position of equilibrium of the rod, in which it is not vertical.*

[N.B. *The centre of gravity of a body is the point at which its weight may be assumed to act.*]

Let AB be the rod and C its centre of gravity ; let O be the peg and let the lengths of the portions AO and OB of the string be x and y respectively.

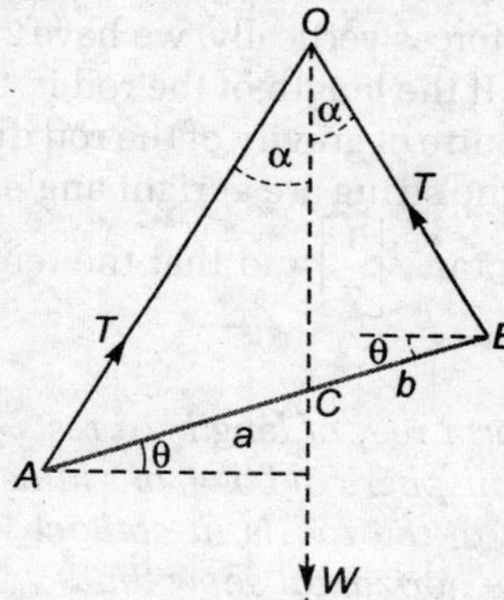

Since, there are only three forces acting on the body they must meet in a point.

But the two tensions pass through O; hence, the line of action of the weight W must pass through O, and hence, the line CO must be vertical.

Now the tension T of the string is not altered, since the string passes round a smooth peg; hence, since W balances the resultant of two *equal* forces, it must bisect the angle between them.

$$\therefore \qquad \angle AOC = \angle BOC = \alpha \text{ (say)}$$

Hence, by geometry $\dfrac{x}{y} = \dfrac{AC}{CB} = \dfrac{a}{b}$

Also, $x + y = l.$

∴ Solving these equations, we have

$$\frac{x}{a} = \frac{y}{b} = \frac{l}{a+b} \qquad \text{...(i)}$$

Also, from the triangle AOB, we have

$$(a+b)^2 = x^2 + y^2 - 2xy\cos 2\alpha = (x+y)^2 - 2xy(1+\cos 2\alpha)$$

$$= (x+y)^2 - 4xy\cos^2\alpha = l^2 - 4\frac{l^2 ab}{(a+b)^2}\cos^2\alpha.$$

$$\therefore \qquad \cos^2\alpha = \frac{l^2 - (a+b^2)}{4l^2}\frac{(a+b)^2}{ab} \qquad \text{...(ii)}$$

This equation gives α.

Let θ be the inclination of the rod to the horizon, so that

$$OCA = 90° + \theta.$$

From the triangle ACO we have

$$\frac{\sin(90° + \theta)}{\sin\alpha} = \frac{AO}{AC} = \frac{x}{a} = \frac{l}{a+b}, \text{ by (i)}$$

$$\therefore \qquad \cos\theta = \frac{l \sin\alpha}{a+b}, \text{ giving } \theta.$$

Also, by resolving the forces vertically, we have $2T\cos\alpha = W$, giving T.

Numerical Example. If the length of the rod is 150 cm, the length of the string 210 cm, and if the centre of gravity of the rod divides it in the ratio 4 : 3, show that the portions of the string are at right angles, that the inclination of the rod to be horizontal is $\tan^{-1}\left[\frac{1}{7}\right]$ and that the tension of the string to the weight of the rod as $\sqrt{2} : 2$.

Ex. 4. *A heavy uniform rod, of length 2a rests partly within and partly without a fixed smooth hemispherical bowl, of radius r ; the rim of the bowl is horizontal, and one point of the rod is in contact with the rim ; if θ is the inclination of the rod to the horizontal show that*

$$2r\cos 2\theta = a\cos\theta.$$

Let the figure represents that vertical section of the hemisphere which passes through the rod.

Let AB be the rod, G its centre of gravity, and C the point where the rod meets the edge of the bowl.

The reaction at A is along the line to the centre O, of the bowl for AO is the only line through A which is perpendicular to the surface of the bowl at A.

Also the reaction at O is perpendicular to the rod : for this is the only direction that is perpendicular to both the rod and the rim of the bowl.

These two reactions meet in a point D ; also by Euc. m 31. D must lie on the geometrical sphere of which the bowl is a portion.

Hence the vertical line through G, the middle point of the rod must pass through D.

Through A draw AE horizontal to meet DG in E and join OC.

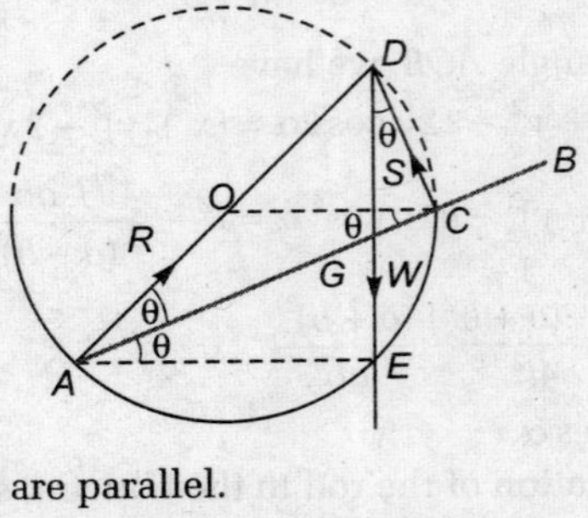

Since OC and AE are parallel.

$$\therefore \qquad \angle OCA = \angle CAE = \theta.$$

Since, $\qquad OC = OA,$

$\therefore$ $$\angle OAC = \angle OCA = \theta.$$

Also, $$\angle GDC = 90° - \angle DGC = \theta.$$

Now, $$AE = AG\cos\theta = a\cos\theta.$$

and $$AE = AD\cos 2\theta = 2r\cos 2\theta.$$

$\therefore$ $$2r\cos 2\theta = a\cos\theta, \text{ giving } \theta$$

Also, by Lami's Theorem, if R and S are the reactions at A and C, we have

$$\frac{R}{\sin\theta} = \frac{S}{\sin ADG} = \frac{W}{\sin ADC},$$

i.e., $$\frac{R}{\sin\theta} = \frac{S}{\cos 2\theta} = \frac{W}{\cos\theta}$$

Numerical Examples. If $r = \frac{\sqrt{3}}{2}a$, then we have $\theta = 30°$, and

$$R = S = W\frac{\sqrt{3}}{3}.$$

Ex. 5. *A beam whose centre of gravity it into two portions, a and b is placed inside a smooth sphere; show that, if θ is its inclination to the horizontal in the position of equilibrium and 2a is the angle subtended by the beam of the beam of the centre of the sphere, then*

$$\tan\theta = \frac{b-a}{b+a}\tan\alpha$$

In this case both the reactions, R and S, at the ends of the rod pass through the centre O, of the sphere. Hence, the centre of gravity G, of the rod must be vertically below O.

Let OG meet the horizontal line through A in N.

Draw OD perpendicular to AB.

Then $$\angle AOD = \angle BOD = \alpha$$

and $$\angle DOG = 90° - \angle DGO = \angle DAN = \theta.$$

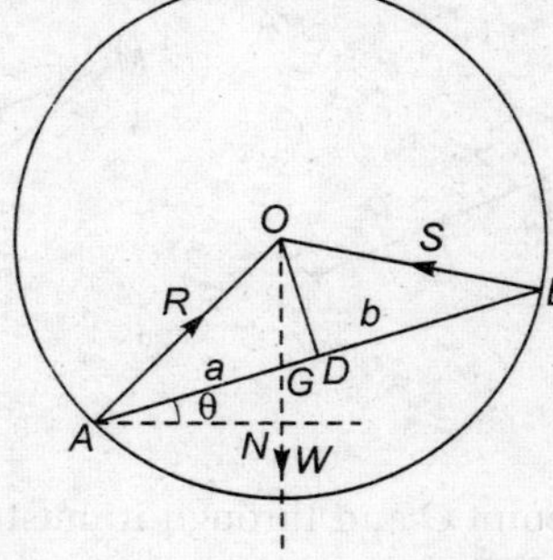

Hence, $$\frac{a}{b} = \frac{AG}{GB} = \frac{AD - GD}{BD + GD} = \frac{OD\tan AOD - OD\tan GOD}{OD\tan BOD + OD\tan GOD}$$

$$= \frac{\tan\alpha - \tan\theta}{\tan\alpha + \tan\theta}.$$

$$\therefore \qquad \tan\theta = \frac{b-a}{b+a}\tan\alpha.$$

This equation gives θ.

Also, by Lami's theorem,

$$\frac{R}{\sin BOG} = \frac{S}{\sin AOG} = \frac{W}{\sin AOB}.$$

$$\therefore \qquad \frac{R}{\sin(\alpha+\theta)} = \frac{S}{(\alpha-\theta)} = \frac{W}{\sin 2\alpha},$$

giving the reactions.

Numerical Examples. If the rod is of weight 40 kg and subtends a right angle at the centre of the sphere, and if its centre of gravity divides it in the ratio 1 : 2, show that its inclination to the horizontal is $\tan^{-1}\left[\frac{1}{2}\right]$, and that the reaction are $8\sqrt{5}$ and $16\sqrt{5}$ kg weight respectively.

Ex. 6. *Show how the forces act on a kite maintain it in equilibrium, proving that the perpendicular to the kite must lie between the direction of the string and the vertical.*

Let *AB* be the middle line of the kite, *B* being the point at which the tail is attached ; the plane of the kite is perpendicular to the plane of the paper. Let *G* be the centre of gravity of the kite including its tail.

The action of the wind may be resolved at each point of the kite into two components, one perpendicular to the kite and the other along its surface. The latter components have no effect on it and may be neglected. The former components compound into a single force *R* perpendicular to the kite which acts at a point *H* which is short distance above *G*.

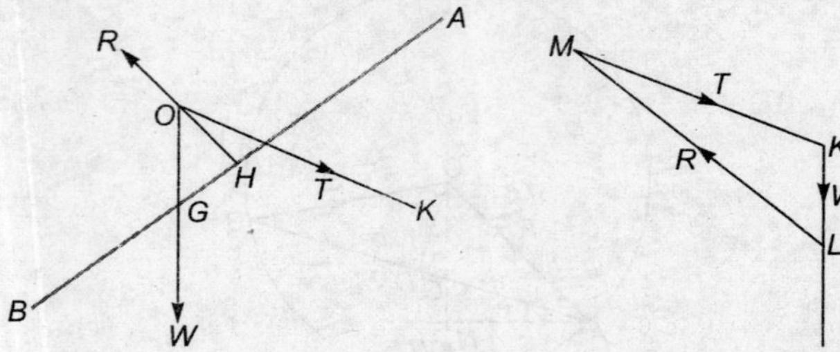

R and *W* meet at a point *O* and through it must pass the direction the third force, *viz*, the tension *T* of the string.

Draw *KL* vertically to represent the weight *W*, and *LM* parallel to *HO* to represent *R*.

Then, by the triangle of forces, MK must represent the tension T of the string.

It is clear from the figure that the line MK must make a greater angle with the vertical LK than the line LM,

i.e. the perpendicular to the kite must lie between the vertical and the direction of the string.

From the triangle of forces it is clear that both T and W must be smaller than the force R exerted by the wind.

Ex. 7. *A solid cone, of height h and semi-vertical angle α, is placed with its base against a smooth vertical wall and is supported by a string attached to its vertex and to a point in the wall; show that the greatest possible length of the string is*

$$h\sqrt{1+\frac{16}{9}\tan^2\alpha}$$

Solution : Since the three forces are in equilibrium, W, the weight acting vertically downwards through G, the reaction perpendicular to the wall CD and the tension T along FC, the string will meet at O.

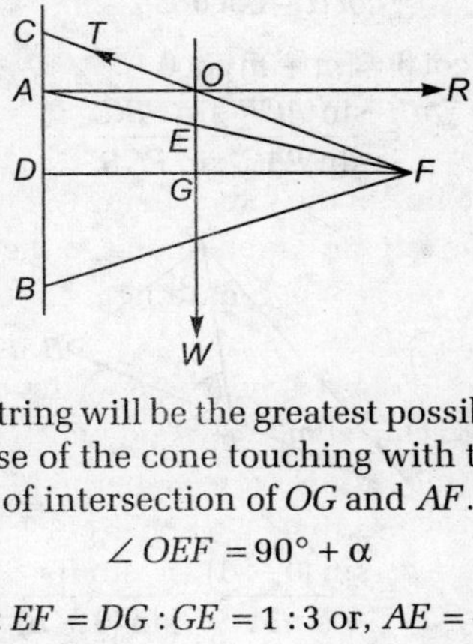

The length of the string will be the greatest possible when R acts at A, the highest point of the base of the cone touching with the wall.

Let E be the point of intersection of OG and AF.

Then, $\angle OEF = 90° + \alpha$

Now, $AE : EF = DG : GE = 1 : 3$ or, $AE = \frac{1}{4} AF$ and $EF = \frac{3}{4} AF$.

Further, $(AE + EF)\cot(90° + \alpha) = AE \cot AOE - EF \cot EOF$

$$-AF\tan\alpha = \frac{1}{4} AF \cot 90° - \frac{3}{4}\cot\theta.$$

gives $4\tan\alpha = 3\cot\theta$

Therefore, $\operatorname{cosec}\theta = \sqrt{1+\cot^2\theta} = \sqrt{1+\frac{16}{9}\tan^2\alpha}.$

Hence, the length of the string $= CF = DF \operatorname{cosec}\theta$

$$= h\operatorname{cosec}\theta$$

$$= h\sqrt{1+\frac{16}{9}\tan^2\alpha}.$$

79. Trigonometrical Theorems. There are two trigonometrical theorem which are useful in statical problems, *viz. If P is any point in the base AB of a triangle ABC, and if CP divides AB into two parts m and n, and the angle C into two parts α and β, and if the angle CPB is θ, then*

$$(m + n) \cot \theta = m \cot \alpha - n \cot \beta \qquad \ldots(1)$$

and

$$(m + n) \cot \theta = n \cot A - m \cot B \qquad \ldots(2)$$

For

$$\frac{m}{n} = \frac{AP}{PB} = \frac{AP}{PC} \cdot \frac{PC}{PB} = \frac{\sin ACP}{\sin PAC} \cdot \frac{\sin PBC}{\sin PCB}$$

$$= \frac{\sin \alpha}{\sin (\theta - \alpha)} \cdot \frac{(\sin (\theta + \beta)}{\sin \beta},$$

since $\angle PBC = 180° - (\beta + \theta)$

$$= \frac{\sin \alpha (\sin \theta \cos \beta + \cos \theta \sin \beta)}{\sin \beta (\sin \theta \cos \alpha - \cos \theta \sin \alpha)}$$

$$= \frac{\cot \beta + \cot \theta}{\cot \alpha - \cot \theta}$$

$\therefore \qquad m \cot \alpha - n \cot \beta = (m + n) \cot \theta$

Again,

$$\frac{m}{n} = \frac{\sin ACP}{\sin PAC} \frac{\sin PBC}{\sin PCB}$$

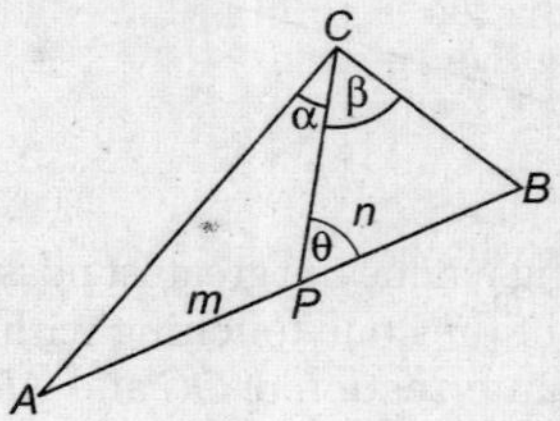

$$= \frac{\sin (\theta - A)}{\sin A} \cdot \frac{\sin B}{\sin (\theta + B)}$$

$$= \frac{(\sin \theta \cos A - \cos \theta \sin A) \sin B}{\sin A (\sin \theta \cos B + \cos \theta \sin B)}$$

$$= \frac{\cot A - \cot \theta}{\cot B + \cot \theta}$$

$\therefore \qquad (m + n) \cot \theta = n \cot A - m \cot B.$

As an illustration of the use of these formulae take Ex. 5 of Art. 78.
Here. formula (2) gives

$$(a + b) \cot OGB = b \cot OAB - a \cot OBA,$$

i.e.,

$$(a + b) \tan \theta = b \tan \alpha - a \tan \alpha$$

Other illustration of their use be found later on in this book.

Examples XII

1. A uniform rod, AB, of weight W, is movable in a vertical plane about a hinge at A, and is sustained in equilibrium by a weight P attached to a string BCP passing over a smooth peg C, AC being vertical; if AC is equal to AB, show that $P = W \cos ACB$.
2. A uniform rod can turn freely about one of its ends, and is pulled aside from the vertical by a horizontal force acting at the other end of the rod and equal to half its weight; at what inclination to the vertical will the rod rest ?
3. A rod AB, hinged at A, is suspended in a horizontal position by a string BC, making an angle of 45° with the rod, and the rod has a mass of 10 kg suspended from B. Neglecting the weight of the rod, find the tension of the string and the action at the hinge.
4. A uniform heavy rod AB has the end A in contact with a smooth vertical wall, and one end of a string is fastened to the rod at a point C, such that $AC = \frac{1}{4} AB$, and the other end of the string is fastened to the wall ; find the length of the string, if the rod rests in a position inclined at an angle to the vertical.
5. ABC is a uniform rod, of weight W ; it is supported (B being uppermost) with its end A against a smooth vertical wall AD by means of a string CD, DB being horizontal and CD inclined to the wall at an angle of 30°. Find the tension of the string and the reaction of the wall, and prove that $AC = \frac{1}{2} AB$.
6. A uniform rod AB, resting with one end A against a smooth vertical wall is supported by a string BC which is tied to a point C vertically above A and to the other end B of the rod. Draw a diagram showing the lines of action of the forces which keep the rod in equilibrium and show that the tension of the string is greater than the weight of the rod.
7. A uniform beam AB, of given length is supported with it extremity, A in contact with a smooth wall by means of a string CD fastened to a known point C of the beam and to a point D of the wall ; if the inclination of the beam to the wall is given show how to find by geometrical construction the length of the string CD and the height of D above A.

   For the problem to be possible, show that the given angle BAD must be acute or obtuse according as AC is less or greater than $\frac{1}{2} AB$.
8. A uniform rod, of length a, hangs against a smooth vertical wall being supported by means of a string, of length l, tied to one end of the rod, the other end of the string being attached to a point in the wall ; show that the rod can rest inclined to the wall at an angle θ given by $\cos^2\theta = \frac{l^2 - a^2}{3a^2}$. What are the limits of the ratio of $a : l$ for which equilibrium is possible ?
9. Equal weights P and P are attached to two strings ACP and BCP passing over a smooth peg C. AB is a heavy beam, of weight W, whose centre of gravity is a cm from A and b cm from B ; show that AB is inclined to the horizontal at an angle
$$\tan^{-1}\left[\frac{a-b}{a+b}\tan\left(\sin^{-1}\frac{W}{2P}\right)\right].$$
10. A heavy uniform beam is hung from a fixed point by two strings attached to its extremities ; if the lengths of the strings and beam are as 2 : 3 : 4, show that the tensions of the strings and the weight of the beam are as $2 : 3 : \sqrt{10}$.

11. A heavy uniform rod, 15 cm long, is suspended from a fixed point by strings fastened to its ends, their lengths being 9 and 12 cm ; if θ is the angle at which the rod is inclined to the vertical, show that

$$25 \sin\theta = 24.$$

12. A straight uniform rod, of weight 3 kg, is suspended from a peg by two strings, attached at one end to the peg and at the other to the extremities of the rod ; the angle between the strings is a right angle and one is twice as long as the other ; find their tensions.

13. Two equal heavy spheres of 1 cm radius, are in equilibrium within a smooth spherical cup of 3 cm radius. Show that the action between the cup and one sphere is double that between the two spheres.

14. A sphere, of given weight W, rests between two smooth planes one vertical and the other inclined at a given angle α to the vertical find the reaction of the planes.

15. A solid sphere rests upon two parallel bars which are in the same horizontal plane, the distance between the bars being equal to the radius of the sphere ; find the reaction of each bar.

16. A smooth sphere is supported in contact with a smooth vertical wall by a string fastened to a point on its surface, the other end being attached to a point in the wall ; if the length of the string is equal to the radius of the sphere, find the inclination of the string to the vertical, the tension of the string, and the reaction of the wall.

17. A picture of given weight, hanging vertically against a smooth wall is supported by a string passing over a smooth peg driven into the wall; the ends of the string are fastened to two points in the upper rim of the frame which are equidistant from the centre of the rim and the angle at the peg is 60° ; compare the tension in this case with what it will be when the string is shortened to two-thirds of its length.

18. A picture of 40 kgf, is hung with its upper and lower edges horizontal, by a cord fastened to the two upper corners and passing over a nail, so that the parts of the cord at two sides of the nail are inclined to one another at an angle of 60°. Find the tension of the cord in kg weight.

19. A picture hangs symmetrically be means of a string passing over a nail and attached to two rings in the picture ; what is the tension of the string when the picture weights 5 kg, if the string is 120 cm long and the nail distant 45 cm from the horizontal line joining the rings ?

20. A picture frame, rectangular in shape, rests against a smooth vertical wall, from two point in which it is suspended by parallel strings attached to two points in the upper edge of the back of the frame, the length of each string being equal to the height of the frame. Show that, if the centre of gravity of the frame coincides with the centre of the figure, the picture will hang against the wall at an angle $\tan^{-1} \dfrac{b}{3a}$ to the vertical, where a is the height and b the thickness of the picture.

21. It is required to hang a picture on a vertical wall so that it may rest at a given inclination, a, to the wall and be supported by a cord attached to a point in the wall at a given height h above the lowest edge of the picture ; determine, by a geometrical construction the point on the back of the picture to which the cord is to be attached and find the length of the cord that will be required.

22. A rod rests wholly within a smooth hemispherical bowl, of radius r, its centre of gravity dividing the rod into two portions of lengths a and b. Show that, if θ is the inclination of the rod to the horizontal in the position of equilibrium, then $\sin\theta = \dfrac{b-a}{2\sqrt{r^2-ab}}$, and find the reactions between the rod and the bowl.

23. In a smooth hemispherical cup is placed a heavy rod, equal in length to the radius of the cup, the centre of gravity of the rod being one third of its length from one end; show that the angle made by the rod with the vertical is $\tan^{-1}(3\sqrt{3})$.

24. A uniform rod, 8 cm in length, is placed with one end inside a smooth hemispherical bowl, of which the axis is vertical and the radius $2\sqrt{3}$ cm; show that a quarter of the rod will project over the edge of the bowl. Prove also that the shortest rod that will thus rest is of length $4\sqrt{2}$ cm.

25. A sphere of radius r and weight W rests against a smooth vertical wall, to which is attached a string of length l fastened to a point on its surface. Show that the tension of the string is

$$W(l+r)/\sqrt{l^2+2lr}.$$

26. A smooth rod of length $2a$, has one end resting on a plane of inclination to the horizon and is supported by a horizontal rail which is parallel to the plane and at a distance c from it. Show that he inclination θ of the rod to the inclined plane is given by the equation.

$$c\sin\alpha = a\sin^2\theta\cos(\theta-\alpha)$$

27. The altitude of a cone is h and the radius of the base is r ; a string is fastened to the vertex and to a point on the circumference of the circular base and is then put over a smooth peg ; if the cone rests in equilibrium with its axis horizontal, show that the length of the string must be $\sqrt{h^2+4r^2}$.

The following examples are to be solved graphically.

28. A heavy beam, AB, 10 metres long. is supported, A uppermost, by two ropes attached to it at A and B which are respectively inclined at 55° to 50° the horizontal ; if AB be inclined at 20° to the horizontal, find at what distance from A its centre of gravity is. Also, if its weight is 200 kg, find the tensions of the two ropes.

29. A light rod AB, of length 2 metres, is smoothly jointed to a fixed support at A and rests horizontally ; at D, where AD = 75cm, it carries a weight of 10 kg, being supported by a light rod CB, where C is exactly underneath A and AC = 50 cm ; find the thrust in the rod CB.

30. AB is a uniform beam turning on a pivot at C and kept in equilibrium by a light string AD attached to the highest point A and to a point D vertically below C. If AB = 90 cm, AC = 30 cm, CD = 60 cm and DA = 81 cm, and the weight of the beam is 5 kg, find the tension of the string and the reaction of the pivot.

31. A cantilever consists of a horizontal rod AB hinged to a fixed supports at A, and a rod DC hinged at a point C of AB and also hinged to a fixed point D vertically below A. A weight of 50 kg is attached at B ; find the actions of A and C, given that AB = 1.8 cm, AC = 60 cm, and AD = 90 cm, the weights of the rods being neglected.

32. The plane of a kite is inclined at 50° to the horizontal, and its weight is 5 kg. The resultant thrust of the air on it acts at a point 16 cm above its centre of gravity, and the string is tied at a point 20 cm above it. Find the tension of the string and the thrust of the air.

8

General Conditions of Equilibrium of a Body Acted on by Forces in One Plane

80. Theorem. *Any system of forces, acting in one plane upon a rigid body, can be reduced to either a single force or a single couple.*

By the parallelogram of forces any two forces, whose directions meet, can be compounded into one force; also, by Art. 52, two parallel forces can be compounded into one force provided they are not equal and unlike.

First compound together all the parallel forces, or sets of parallel forces, of the given system.

Of the resulting system take any two forces, not forming a couple, and find their resultant R_1; next find the resultant R_2 of R_1 and a suitable third force of the system; then determine the resultant of R_2 and a suitable fourth force of the system; and so on until all the forces have been exhausted.

Finally, we must either arrive at a single force, or we shall have two equal parallel unlike forces forming a couple.

81. Theorem. *If a system of forces acts in one plane upon a rigid body, and if the algebraic sum of their moments about each of three points in the plane (not lying in the same straight line) vanish separately, the system of forces is in equilibrium.*

For any such system of forces, by the last article, reduces to either a single force or a single couple.

In our case they cannot reduce to a single couple ; for if they did, the sum of their moments about any point in their plane would, by Art. 69, be equal to a constant which is *not* zero, and this is contrary to our hypothesis.

Hence, the system of forces cannot reduce to a single couple.

The system must therefore either be in equilibrium or reduce to a single force F.

Let the three points about which the moments are taken be A, B and C.

Since the algebraic sum of the moments of a system of forces is equal to that of their resultant (Art. 62), therefore the moment of F about the point A must be zero.

Hence F is either zero, or passes through A.

Similarly, since the moment of F about B vanishes, F must be either zero or must pass through B,

i.e., F is either zero or acts in the line AB.

Finally, since the moment about C vanishes, F must be either zero or pass through C.

But (since the points A, B, C are *not* in the same straight line] the force cannot act along AB and also pass through C.

Hence the only admissible case is that F should be zero, *i.e.*, that the forces should be in equilibrium.

The system will also be in equilibrium if (1) the sum of the moments about each of two points, A and B, separately vanishes, and if (2) the sum of the forces resolved along AB is zero. For, if (1) holds, the resultant, by the foregoing article, is either zero or acts along AB. Also, if (2) is true there is no resultant in the direction AB; hence the resultant force is zero. Also, as in the foregoing article, there is no resultant couple. Hence the system is in equilibrium.

82. Theorem. *A system of forces, acting in one plane upon a rigid body, is in equilibrium, if the sum of their components parallel to each of two lines in their plane is zero, and if the algebraic sum of their moments about any point is also zero.*

For any such system of forces, by Art. 80, can be reduced to either a single force or a single couple.

In out case they cannot reduce to a single force.

For, since the sums of the components of the forces parallel to two lines in their plane are separately zero, therefore the components of their resultant force parallel to these two lines are zero also, and therefore the resultant force vanishes.

Neither can the forces reduce to a single couple ; for, if they did, the moment of this couple about any point in its plane would be equal to a constant which is *not* zero; this, however, is contrary to our hypothesis.

Hence, the system of forces must be in equilibrium.

83. It will be noted that in the enunciation of the last article nothing is said about the directions in which we are to resolve. In practice, however, it is almost always desirable to resolve along two directions at right angles.

Hence, the conditions for equilibrium of any system of forces, acting in one plane upon a rigid body, may be obtained as follows ;

I. Equate to zero the algebraic sum of the resolved parts of all the forces in some fixed direction.

II. Equate to zero the algebraic sum of the resolved parts of all the forces in a perpendicular direction.

III. Equate to zero the algebraic sum of the moments of the forces about any points in their plane.

I and II ensure that there shall be no motion of the body as a whole ; III ensures that there shall be no motion of rotation about any point.

The three statical relations above, together with the geometrical relations holding between the component portions of a system, will, in general, be sufficient to determine the equilibrium of any system acted on by forces which are in one plane.

In applying the preceding conditions of equilibrium to any particular case, great simplifications can often be introduced into the equations by properly choosing the directions along which we resolve. In general, the horizontal and vertical directions are the most suitable.

Again, the position of the point about which we take moments is important ; it should be chosen so that as few of the forces as possible are introduced into the equation of moments.

84. We have shown that the conditions given in the previous article are sufficient for the equilibrium of the system of forces ; they are also necessary.

Suppose we knew only that the first two conditions were satisfied. The system of forces might them reduce to a single couple ; for the forces of this couple, being equal and opposite, are such that their components in any direction would vanish. Hence, resolving in any third direction would give us no additional condition. In this case the forces would not be in equilibrium unless the third condition were satisfied.

Suppose, again, that we knew only that the components of the system along one given line vanished and that the moments about a given point vanished also ; in this case the forces might reduce to a single force through the given point perpendicular to the given line; hence, we see that it is necessary to have the sum of the components parallel to another line zero also.

85. We shall now give some examples of application of the general conditions of equilibrium. In solving any statical problem the student should proceed as follows :

(1) Draw the figure according to the conditions given.

(2) Mark all the forces acting on the body or bodies, taking care to assume an unknown reaction (to be determined) wherever one body presses against another, and to mark a tension along any supporting string, and to assume a reaction wherever the body is hinged to any other body or fixed point.

(3) For each body, or system of bodies, involved in the problem, equate to zero the forces acting on it resolved along two convenient perpendicular directions (generally horizontal and vertical).

(4) Also equate to zero the moments of the forces about any convenient point.

(5) Write down any geometrical relations connecting the lengths or angles involved in the figure.

Ex. 1. *A heavy uniform beam rests with one end upon a horizontal plane, and the other end upon a given inclined plane; it is kept in equilibrium by a string which is attached to the end resting on the horizontal plane and to the intersection of the inclined and horizontal planes ; given that the inclination (α) of the beam to the horizontal is one-half that of the inclined plane, find the tension of the string and the reactions of the planes.*

Let AB be the beam, AO the horizontal, and OB the inclined plane.

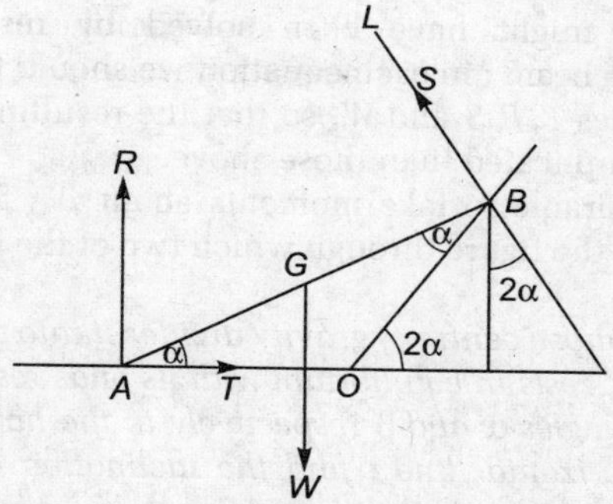

Let T be the tension of the string AO, W the weight of the body, R and S the reactions at A and B respectively vertical and perpendicular to OB.

Resolving horizontally and vertically we have

$$T = S \sin 2\alpha \quad \ldots(1),$$

$$W = R + S \cos 2\alpha \quad \ldots(2).$$

Also, taking moments about A, we have

$$W \cdot a \cos \alpha = S \cdot AB \sin ABL = S \cdot 2a \cos \alpha \quad \ldots(3),$$

where $2a$ is the length of the beam.

These three equations are sufficient for equilibrium.

From (3), we have $$S = \frac{1}{2} W.$$

$$\therefore \text{ from (2), } \quad R = W - \frac{1}{2} W \cos 2\alpha = W\left(1 - \frac{1}{2}\cos 2\alpha\right).$$

Also, from (1),

$$T = \frac{W}{2} \sin 2\alpha.$$

Hence the reactions and the tension of the string are determined. Suppose that, instead of the inclination of the beam to the horizon being given, the length of the string were given ($= l$ say).

Let us assume the inclination of the beam to the horizon to be θ.

The equations (1) and (2) remain the same as before.

The equation of moments would be, however,

$$W \cdot a \cos \theta = S \cdot AB \sin ABL = S \cdot 2a \cos ABO$$
$$= S \cdot 2a \cos (2\alpha - \theta) \quad \ldots(4),$$

We should have a geometrical equation to determine θ, *viz*,

$$\frac{l}{2a} = \frac{OA}{AB} = \frac{\sin ABO}{\sin AOB} = \frac{\sin (2\alpha - \theta)}{\sin 2\alpha} \quad \ldots(5).$$

The latter equation determines θ, and then the equations (1), (2) and (4) would give T, R and S.

This question might have been solved by resolving along and perpendicular to the beam ; in each equation we should then have involved each of the quantities T, R, S and W, so that the resulting equations would have been more complicated than those above.

It was also desirable to take moments about A ; for this is the only convenient point in the figure through which two of the forces which act on the body pass.

Ex. 2. *A beam whose centre of gravity divides it into portions, of lengths a and b respectively, rests in equilibrium with its ends resting on two smooth planes inclined at angles α and β respectively to the horizontal, the planes intersecting in a horizontal line ; find the inclination of the beam to the horizontal and the reactions of the planes.*

Let the planes be OA and OB and let AB be the rod, whose centre of gravity is G, so that GA and GB are a and b respectively.

Let R and S be the reactions at A and B perpendicular to the inclined planes and let θ be the inclination of the beam to the horizontal.

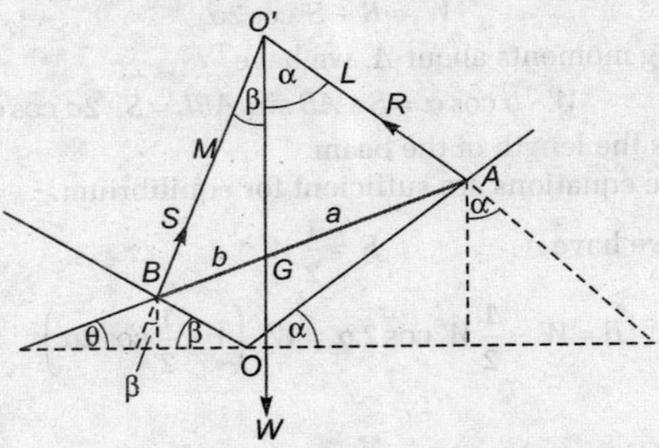

Resolving vertically and horizontally, we have

$$R\cos\alpha + S\cos\beta = W \quad \ldots(1)$$

$$R\sin\alpha = S\sin\beta \quad \ldots(2)$$

Also, by taking moments about G, we have

$$R \cdot GA \sin GAL = S \cdot GB \sin GBM$$

Now, $\angle GAL = 90° - BAO = 90° - (\alpha - \theta)$,

and $\angle GBM = 90° - ABO = 90° - (\beta + \theta)$.

Hence the equation of moments becomes

$$R \cdot a\cos(\alpha - \theta) = S \cdot b\cos(\beta + \theta) \quad \ldots(3)$$

From (2), we have

$$\frac{R}{\sin\beta} = \frac{S}{\sin\alpha} = \frac{R\cos\alpha + S\cos\beta}{\sin\beta\cos\alpha + \sin\alpha\cos\beta} = \frac{W}{\sin(\alpha+\beta)}, \text{ by (1).}$$

These equations give R and S, also substituting for R and S in (3) we have

$$\alpha\sin\beta\cos(\alpha - \theta) = b\sin\alpha\cos(\beta + \theta);$$

$\therefore a \sin\beta\,(\cos\alpha\cos\theta + \sin\alpha\sin\theta) = b\sin\alpha\,(\cos\beta\cos\theta - \sin\beta\sin\theta)$;

$\therefore \qquad (a+b)\sin\alpha\sin\beta\sin\theta = \cos\theta\,(b\sin\alpha\cos\beta - a\cos\alpha\sin\beta)$;

$$\therefore \qquad (a+b)\tan\theta = b\cot\beta - a\cot\alpha \qquad \ldots(4),$$

giving the value of θ.

Otherwise thus ; Since there are only three forces acting on the body this question might have been solved by the methods of the last chapter.

For the three forces R, S, and W, must meet in a point O'.

The theorem of Art. 79 then gives

$$(a+b)\cot O'GA = b\cot\beta - a\cot\alpha,$$

i.e.,

$$(a+b)\tan\theta = b\cot\beta - a\cot\alpha.$$

which is equation (4),

Also Lami's Theorem (Art. 40) gives

$$\frac{R}{\sin BO'G} = \frac{S}{\sin AO'G} = \frac{W}{\sin AO'B},$$

i.e.,

$$\frac{R}{\sin\beta} = \frac{S}{\sin\alpha} = \frac{W}{\sin(\alpha+\beta)}.$$

Ex. 3. *A ladder, whose weight is 96 kg and whose length is 7.5 m rests with one end against a smooth vertical wall and with the other end upon the ground; if it is prevented from slipping by a peg at its lowest point, and if the lowest point is distant 2.1 m from the wall, find the reactions of the peg the ground, and the wall.*

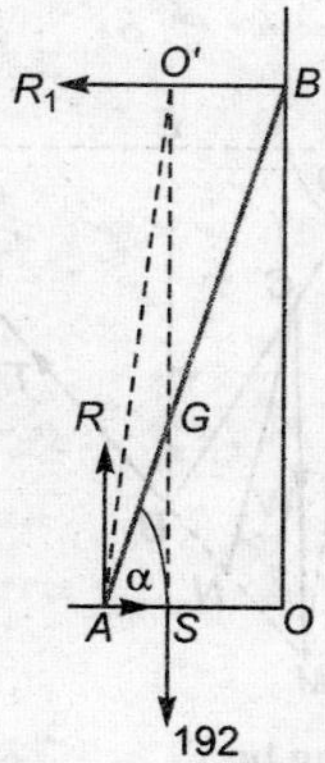

Let AB be the rod and G its middle point ; let R and R_1 be the reactions of the ground and wall, and S the horizontal reaction of the peg. Let the angle GAO be α, so that

$$\cos\alpha = \frac{AO}{AB} = \frac{2\cdot 1}{7\cdot 5} = \frac{7}{25}.$$

and hence

$$\sin\alpha = \sqrt{1 - \frac{49}{625}} = \sqrt{\frac{576}{625}} = \frac{24}{25}.$$

Equating to zero the horizontal and vertical components of the forces acting on the rod, we have.

$$R - 96 = 0 \qquad \ldots(1),$$

and

$$R_1 - S = 0 \qquad \ldots(2),$$

Also, taking moments about A, we have

$$96 \times AG \cos\alpha = R_1 \times AB \sin\alpha \qquad \ldots(3).$$

$$\therefore \quad R_1 = 96 \times \frac{1}{2} \cot\alpha = 48 \times \frac{7}{24} = 14.$$

Hence, from (1) and (2),

$$R = 96 \quad \text{and} \quad S = 14.$$

The required reactions are therefore 14, 96, and 14 kg weight respectively.

The resultant of R and S must by the last chapter pass through O' the point of intersection of the weight and R_1.

Ex. 4. *One end of a uniform rod is attached to a hinge, and the other end is supported by a string attached to the extremity of the rod, and the rod and string are inclined at the same angle* θ, *to the horizontal ; if* W *is the weight of the rod, show that the action of the hinge is* $\frac{W}{4}\sqrt{8 + \operatorname{cosec}^2\theta}$.

Let AB be the rod, C its middle point, and BD the string meeting the horizontal line through A in D.

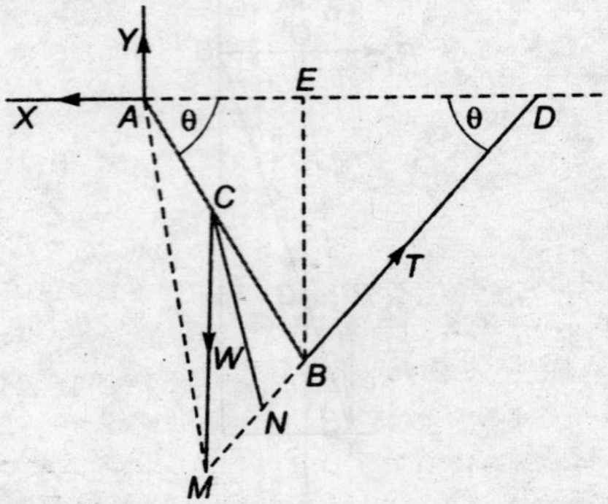

Let the tension of the string be T.

The action at the hinge is unknown both in magnitude and direction. Let the horizontal and vertical components of this action be X and Y, as marked in the figure. Draw BE perpendicular to AD. Then $AD = 2AE = 2AB\cos\theta$.

Resolving horizontally and vertically, we have

$$X = T\cos\theta \qquad \ldots(1),$$

$$Y + T\sin\theta = W \qquad \ldots(2).$$

Also, taking moment about A, we have

$$W \cdot AC\cos\theta = T \cdot AD\sin\theta = T \cdot 2AB\cos\theta\sin\theta \qquad \ldots(3).$$

From (3), $$T = W\frac{AC}{2AB\sin\theta} = \frac{W}{4\sin\theta}$$

Hence, by (1) and (2),

$$X = \frac{W}{4}\cot\theta, \quad \text{and} \quad Y = W - \frac{W}{4} = \frac{3W}{4}.$$

Therefore, the action at the hinge $= \sqrt{X^2 + Y^2}$

$$= \frac{W}{4}\sqrt{9 + \cot^2\theta} = \frac{W}{4}\sqrt{8 + \operatorname{cosec}^2\theta}.$$

If DB meets the direction of W in M, then, by the last chapter, AM is the direction of the action at A. Hence, if CN is parallel to AM, then CMN is a triangle of forces.

Ex. 5. *A uniform heavy rod can turn freely about one end, which is fixed to this end is attached a string which supports a sphere of radius a. If the length of the rod is 4 a, the length of the string a, and the weight of the sphere and rod each W, find the inclination of the rod and string to the vertical and the tension of the string.*

Let OA be the rod, OC the string, B the centre of the sphere, and D the point in which the rod touches the sphere.

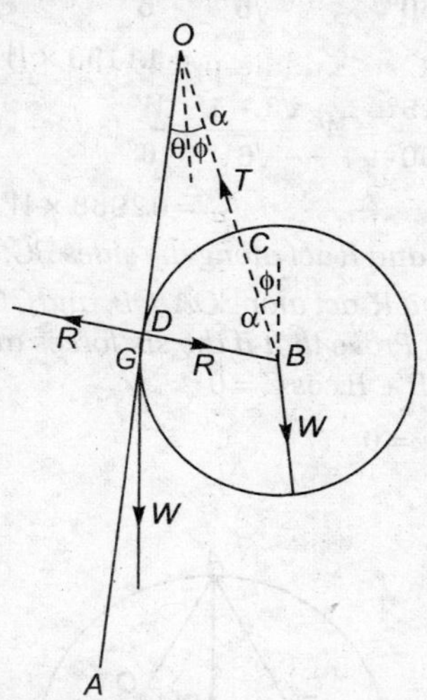

Between the sphere and the rod at D there is a reaction, R, perpendicular to OD, acting in opposite directions on the two bodies.

The forces which act on the sphere only must be in equilibrium; and so also must the forces which act on the rod.

Since there are only three forces acting on the sphere they must meet in a point, *viz*, the centre of the sphere.

Hence, OCB is a straight line.

Let θ and ϕ be the inclination of the rod and string to the vertical .

Then $$\sin(\theta + \phi) = \frac{DB}{OB} = \frac{a}{2a} = \frac{1}{2},$$

so that $$\theta + \phi = 30° \qquad ...(1).$$

The forces acting on the rod are the reaction at D, the weight of the rod , and the action at the hinge O.

If we take moments about O we shall avoid this action, and we have

$$W \cdot 2a \sin\theta = R \cdot OD = R \cdot 2a \cos 20° \qquad ...(2).$$

From the conditions of equilibrium of the sphere,

$$\frac{T}{\sin(\phi + 60°)} = \frac{R}{\sin\phi} = \frac{W}{\sin 60°} \qquad ...(3).$$

Therefore, from (2) and (3)

$$\frac{\sin\theta}{\cos 30°} = \frac{R}{W} = \frac{\sin\phi}{\sin 60°}.$$

$\therefore \phi = \theta$, and hence, from (1)

$$\theta = \phi = 15°.$$

Substituting in (3), we have

$$T = W\frac{\sin 75°}{\sin 60°} = W\frac{\sqrt{3}+1}{\sqrt{6}} = \frac{W}{6}(3\sqrt{2} + \sqrt{6})$$

$$= 1.1153 \times W,$$

and $$R = W\frac{\sin 15°}{\sin 60°} = W\frac{\sqrt{3}-1}{\sqrt{6}} = \frac{W}{6}(3\sqrt{2} - \sqrt{6})$$

$$= 0.2988 \times W.$$

Ex. 6. *Forces P, Q, and R act along the sides BC, CA, and AB of a triangle ABC and forces P′, Q′, and R′ act along OA, OB, and OC where O is the centre of the circumscribed circle. Prove that if the six forces are in equilibrium.*

(1) $P\cos A + Q\cos B + R\cos C = 0$

(2) $\dfrac{PP'}{a} + \dfrac{QQ'}{b} + \dfrac{RR'}{c} = 0$

Solution.

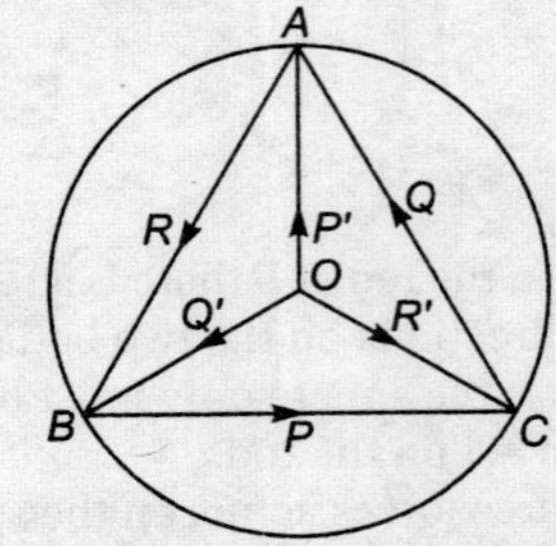

Let X be the circum-radius, then the perpendicular distances of BC, CA and AB from O are respectively $X\cos A$, $X\cos B$ and $X\cos C$.

Taking moment about O, we have

so that $P \cdot X \cos A + Q \cdot X \cos B + R \cdot X \cos C = 0,$

Again, taking moments about A,

$$P \times \frac{2\,\Delta\,ABC}{BC} - Q' \times \frac{2\,\Delta\,OAB}{OB} + R' \times \frac{2\,\Delta\,AOC}{OC} = 0 \qquad \ldots(1).$$

Taking moments about B and C, we get

$$Q \times \frac{2\,\Delta\,ABC}{CA} + P' \times \frac{2\,\Delta\,BOA}{OA} - R \times \frac{2\,\Delta\,BOC}{OC} = 0 \qquad \ldots(2),$$

$$R \times \frac{2\,\Delta\,ABC}{AB} + Q' \times \frac{2\,\Delta\,COB}{OB} - P' \times \frac{2\,\Delta\,COA}{OA} = 0 \qquad \ldots(3).$$

Multiplying (1), (2), (3) by P', Q', R' in order and adding, we get.

$$\frac{PP'}{a} + \frac{QQ'}{b} + \frac{RR'}{c} = 0.$$

Examples XIII

1. A uniform beam, AB, whose weight is W, rests with one end, A, on a smooth horizontal plane AC. The other end, B, rests on a plane CB inclined to the former at an angle 60°. If a string CA equal to CB, prevents motion, find its tension.
2. A ladder, of weight W, rests with one end against a smooth vertical wall and with the other resting on a smooth floor; if the inclination of the ladder to the horizon is 60°, find by calculation graphically, the horizontal force that must be applied to the lower end to prevent the ladder from sliding down.
3. A beam, of weight W, is divided by its centre of gravity C into two portions AC and BC, whose lengths are a and b respectively. The beam rests in a vertical plane on a smooth floor AD and against a smooth vertical wall DB. A string is attached to a hook at D and to the beam at a point P. If T is the tension of the string and θ and ϕ are the inclinations of the beam and string respectively to the horizon, show that
$$T = W \frac{a \cos\theta}{(a+b)\sin(\theta - \phi)}.$$
4. A ladder rest at an angle α to the horizon, with the ends resting on a smooth floor and against a smooth vertical wall, the lower end being attached by a string to the junction of the wall and floor ; find the tension of the string. Find also the tension of the string when a man, whose weight is one-half that of the ladder, has ascended the ladder two thirds of its length.
5. One end of a uniform beam, of weight W, is placed on a smooth horizontal plane; the other end, to which a string is fastened rests against another smooth plane inclined at an angle α to the horizon ; the string, passing over a pulley at the top of the inclined plane, hangs vertically, and supports a weight P ; show that the beam will rest in all positions if $2P = W \sin\alpha$.
6. A heavy uniform beam rest with its extremities on two smooth inclined planes, which meet in a horizontal line, and whose inclinations to the horizontal are α and β ; find its inclination to the horizontal in the position of equilibrium, and the reactions of the planes.

7. A uniform beam rests with a smooth end against the junction of the ground and a vertical wall, and is supported by a string fastened to the other end of the beam and to a staple in the wall. Find the tension of the string, and show that it will be one-half the weight of the beam if the length of the string is equal to the height of the staple above the ground.
8. A uniform rod BC, of weight 2 kg, can turn freely about B and is supported by a string AC, 8 cm long, attached to a point A in the same horizontal line as B, the distance AB being 10 cm. If the rod is 6 cm long, find the tension of the string. Verify by a drawing and measurement.
9. A uniform rod has its upper end fixed to a hinge and its other end attached by a string to a fixed point in the same horizontal plane as the hinge, the length of the string being equal to the distance between the fixed point and the hinge. If the tension of the string is equal to the weight W of the rod, show that the rod is inclined to the horizontal at an angle $\tan^{-1}\left[\frac{1}{2}\right]$, and that the action of the hinge is equal to a force $\frac{W}{5}\sqrt{10}$ inclined at an angle $\tan^{-1}\left[\frac{1}{3}\right]$ to the horizontal.
10. A rod is movable in a vertical plane about a hinge at one end, and at the other end is fastened a weight equal to half the weight of the rod; this end is fastened by a string, of length l, to a point at a height c vertically over the hinge. Show that the tension of the string is $\frac{lW}{c}$, where W is the weight of the rod.
11. AB is a uniform rod, of length $8a$, which can turn freely about the end A, which is fixed ; C is a smooth ring, whose weight is twice that of the rod, which can slide on the rod, and is attached by a string CD to a point D in the same horizontal plane as the point A ; if AD and CD are each of length a, find the position of the ring and the tension of the string when the system is in equilibrium.
Show also that the action on the rod at the fixed end A is a horizontal force equal to $\sqrt{3}W$, where W is the weight of the rod.
12. A rigid wire, without weight, in the form of the arc of a circle subtending an angle α at its centre, and having two weights P and Q at its extremities, rests with its convexity downwards upon a horizontal plane ; show that, if θ is the inclination to the vertical of the radius to the end at which P is suspended, then

$$\tan\theta = \frac{Q\sin\alpha}{P + Q\cos\alpha}.$$

13. A smooth hemispherical bowl, of diameter a, is placed so that its edge touches a smooth vertical wall ; a heavy uniform rod is in equilibrium inclined at 60° to the horizontal, with one end resting on the inner surface of the bowl, and the other end resting against the wall ; show that the length of the rod must be $a + \frac{a}{\sqrt{13}}$.
14. A cylindrical vessel, of height 8 cm and diameter 6 cm, stands upon a horizontal plane, and a smooth uniform rod, 18 cm long, is placed within it resting against the edge. Find the actions between the rod and the vessel, the weight of the former being 16 g.

15. A thin ring, of radius R and weight W, is placed round a vertical cylinder of radius r and prevented from falling by a nail projecting horizontally from the cylinder. Find the horizontal reactions between the cylinder and the ring.

16. A heavy carriage wheel, of weight W and radius r, is to be dragged over an obstacle, of height h, by a horizontal force F applied to the centre of the wheel ; show that F must be slightly greater than

$$W \frac{\sqrt{2rh - h^2}}{r - h}.$$

17. A uniform beam, of length $2a$, rests in equilibrium, with one end resting against a smooth vertical wall and with a point of its length resting upon a smooth horizontal rod, which is parallel to the wall and at a distance b from it ; show that the inclination of the beam to the vertical is

$$\sin^{-1}\left(\frac{b}{a}\right)^{\frac{1}{3}}.$$

18. A circular disc, BCD, of radius a and weight W, is supported by a smooth band, of inappreciable weight and thickness, which surrounds the disc along the arc BCD and is fastened at its extremities to the point A in a vertical wall, the portion AD touching the wall and the plane of the disc being at right angles to the wall. If the length of the band not in contact with the disc is $2b$, show that the tension of the band is $\frac{W}{2}\frac{a^2 + b^2}{b^2}$, and find the reaction at D.

19. Two equal uniform heavy straight rods are connected at one extremity by a string and rest upon two smooth pegs in the same horizontal line, one rod upon one peg and the other upon the other ; if the distance between the pegs is equal to the length of each rod and the length of the string is half that, show that the rods rest at an angle θ to the horizontal given by $2 \cos^3 \theta = 1$.

20. A uniform rod, whose weight is W, is supported by two fine strings, one attached to each end, which, after passing over small fixed smooth pulleys, carry weights w_1 and w_2 respectively at the other ends. Show that the rod is inclined to the horizontal at an angle

$$\sin^{-1} \frac{w_1^2 - w_2^2}{W\sqrt{2(w_1^2 + w_2^2) - W^2}}.$$

21. A uniform rod, of weight W, is supported in equilibrium by a string of length $2l$, attached to its ends and passing over a smooth peg. If a weight W' is now attached to one end of the rod, show that it can be placed in another position of equilibrium by sliding a length $\frac{lW'}{W + W'}$, of the string over the peg.

22. AB is a straight rod, of length $2a$ and weight λW, with the lower end A on the ground at the foot of a vertical wall AC, B and C being at the same vertical height $2b$ above A ; a heavy ring, of weight W, is free to move along a string, of length $2l$, which joins B and C. If the system is in equilibrium with the ring at the middle point of the string, show that

$$l^2 = a^2 - b^2 \frac{\lambda(\lambda + 2)}{(\lambda + 1)^2}.$$

23. A given square board $ABCD$, of side b, is supported horizontally by two given loops of string $OACO$ and $OBDO$ passing under opposite corners and hung over a fixed hook O ; find the tension of the strings, if the height of O above the board is b.

24. A gate weighing 100 kg is hung on two hinges, 3 decimetres apart, in a vertical line which is distant 4 decimetres from the centre of gravity of the gate. Find the magnitude of the reactions at each hinge on the assumption that the whole of the weight of the gate is borne by the lower hinge.

25. A triangle, formed of three rods, is fixed in a horizontal position and a homogeneous sphere rests on it ; show that the reaction on each rod is proportional to its length.

26. A light triangular frame ABC stands in a vertical plane, C being uppermost, on two supports, A and B, in the same horizontal line and a mass of 9 kg weight is suspended from C. If $AB = AC = 540$ cm, and $BC = 150$ cm, find the reactions of the supports.

27. The sides of a triangular framework are 13, 20 and 21 cm in length ; the longest side rests on a horizontal smooth table and a weight of 63 kg is suspended from the opposite angle. Find the tension in the side on the table. Verify by a drawing and measurement.

28. A bowl is formed from a hollow sphere, of radius a, and is so placed that the radius of the sphere drawn to each point in the rim makes an angle α with the vertical, whilst the radius drawn to a point A of the bowl makes an angle β with the vertical ; if a smooth uniform rod remains at rest with one end at A and a point of its length in contact with the rim, show that the length of the rod is

$$4a \sin\beta \sec \frac{\alpha - \beta}{2}.$$

29. Moments of the resultant R of a system of coplanar forces about three points O, A, and B lying in the plane of the forces are G, $G + f_1$, and $G + f_2$ respectively. If referred to O as origin, the polar co-ordinates of A and B be (r_1, θ_1) and (r_2, θ_2), show that

$$R^2 \sin^2(\theta_1 - \theta_2) = \frac{f_1^2}{r_1^2} + \frac{f_2^2}{r_2^2} - \frac{2f_1f_2 \cos(\theta_1 - \theta_2)}{r_1r_2}$$

30. Inside a fixed hollow cylinder of radius R, whose generators are horizontal there are placed two equal cylinders each of radius r ; a third cylinder equal to each of the latter is placed symmetrically on them ; show that equilibrium cannot exist unless $R < r\,(1 + 2\sqrt{7})$.

31. If a system of forces in one plane reduces to a couple of moment G and when each force is turned round its point of application through a right angle, it reduces to a couple H ; prove that when each force is turned through an angle α, the system is equivalent to a couple whose moment is $G \cos\alpha + H \sin\alpha$.

86. In the following articles the conditions of equilibrium enunciated in Art. 83 will be obtained in a slightly different manner.

***87. Theorem.** *Any system of forces, acting in one plane upon a rigid body, is equivalent to a force acting at an arbitrary point of the body together with a couple.*

Let P be any force of the system acting at a point A of the body, and let O be any arbitrary point. At O introduce two equal and opposite forces, the magnitude of each being P, and let their line of action be parallel to that of P. These do not alter the state of equilibrium of the body.

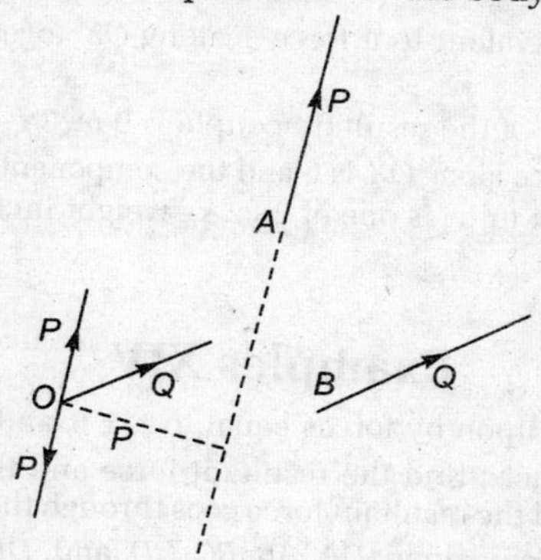

The force P at A and the opposite parallel force P at O form a couple of moment $P \cdot p$ where p, is the perpendicular from O upon the line of action of the original force P.

Hence the force P at A is equivalent to a parallel force P at O and a couple of moment $P \cdot p$.

So the force Q at B is equivalent to a parallel force Q at O and to a couple of moment $Q \cdot q$, where q is the perpendicular from O on the line of action of Q.

The same holds for each of the system of forces.

Hence the original system of forces is equivalent to forces P, Q, R ... acting at O, parallel to their original directions, and a number of couples ; these are equivalent to a single resultant force at O, and a single resultant couple of moment

$$P \cdot p + Q \cdot q + \ldots$$

***88.** By Art. 74 a force and a couple cannot balance unless each is zero.

Hence the resultant of P, Q, R ... at O must be zero, and therefore, by Art. 46, *the sum of their resolved parts in two directions must separately vanish.*

Also the moment $Pp + Qq + \ldots$ must be zero, *i.e. he algebraic sum of the moments of the forces about an arbitrary point O must vanish also.*

***89. Ex.** *ABCD is a square; along the sides AB, BC, DC, and DA act forces equal to 1, 9, 5, and 3 kg weight ; find the force, passing through the centre of the square, and the couple which are together equivalent to the given system.*

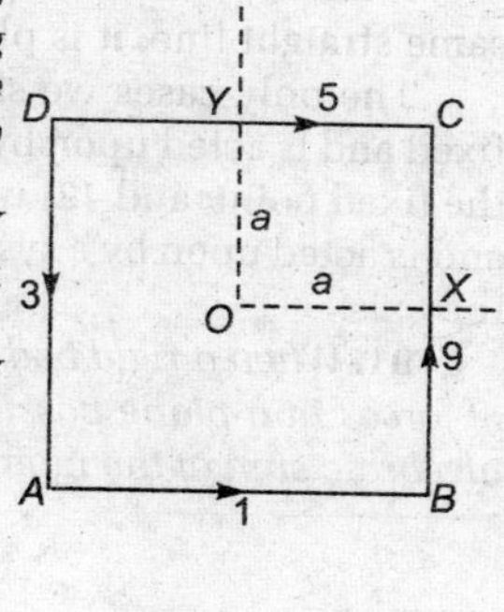

Let O be the centre of the square and let OX and OY be perpendicular to the sides BC, CD respectively. Let the side of the square be $2a$.

The force 9 is equivalent to a force 9 along OY together with a couple of moment $9 \cdot a$.

The force 3 is equivalent to a force –3 along *OY* together with a couple of moment $3 \cdot a$.

The force 5 is equivalent to a force 5 along *OX* together with a couple of moment $-5 \cdot a$.

The force 1 is equivalent to a force 1 along *OX* together with a couple of moment $1 \cdot a$.

Hence the moment of the resultant couple is $9a + 3a - 5a + 1 \cdot a$, *i.e.*, $8 \cdot a$.

The component force along *OX* is 6 and the component along *OY* is 6.

Hence the resultant force is one of $6\sqrt{2}$ kg weight inclined at 45° to the side *AB*.

Examples XIV

1. A square is acted upon by forces equal to 2, 4, 6, and 8 kg weight along its sides taken in order ; find the resultant force and the resultant couple of these forces, when the resultant force goes through the centre of the square.
2. *ABCD* is a square ; along *DA*, *AB*, *BC*, *CD* and *DB* act forces equal to *P*, 3*P*, 5*P*, 7*P*, and $9\sqrt{2}P$; find the force, passing through *A*, and the couple which are together equivalent to the system.
3. Forces equal to 1, 2, 3, 4, 5 and 6 kg weight respectively act along the sides *AB*, *BC*, *CD*, *DE*, *EF* and *FA* of a regular hexagon; find the force, passing through *A*, and the couple, which are together equivalent to the system.
4. Given in position a force equal to 10 kg weight and a couple consisting of two forces, equal to 4 kg weight, at a distance apart of 8 cm, draw the equivalent single force.

Constrained body

90. *A body is said to be constrained when one or more points of the body are fixed. For example, a rod attached to a wall by a ball-socket has one point fixed and is constrained.*

If a rigid body have two points *A* and *B* fixed, all the points of the body in the line *AB* are fixed , and the only way in which the body can move is by turning round *AB* as an axis. For example, a door attached to the door post by two hinges can only turn about the line joining the hinges.

If a body has three points in it fixed, the three points not being in the same straight line, it is plainly immovable.

The only cases we shall consider are (1) when the body has one point fixed and is acted upon by a system of forces lying in a plane passing through the fixed point, and (2) when the body can only move about a fixed axis in it and is acted upon by a system of forces whose directions are perpendicular to the axis.

91. *When a rigid body has one point fixed, and is acted upon by a system of forces in a plane passing through the point, it will be in equilibrium if the algebraic sum of the moments of the forces about the fixed point vanishes.*

When a body has one point A fixed (as in the case of Ex. 4 Art. 85), there must be exerted at the point some force of constraint, F, which together with the given system of forces is in equilibrium. Hence the conditions of equilibrium of Art. 83 must apply.

If we resolve along two directions at right angles, we shall have two equations to determine the magnitude and direction of the force F.

If we take moments about A for all the forces, the force F (since it passes through A) does not appear in our equation, and hence the equation of moments of Art. 83 will become an equation expressing the fact that the algebraic sum of the moments of the given system of forces about A is zero.

Hence for the equilibrium of the body (unless we wish to find the force of constraint F) we have only to express that the algebraic sum of the moments of the forces about the fixed point A is zero.

92. Ex. *A rod AB has one end A fixed, and is kept in a horizontal position by a force equal to 10 kg weight acting at B in a direction inclined at 30° to the rod; if the rod is homogeneous, and of length 4 metres, find its weight.*

The moment of the weight about A must be equal to the moment of the force about A.

If W is the weight, the former moment is $W \times 2$, and the latter is $10 \times 4 \sin 30°$.

$$\therefore \quad 2W = 10 \times 4 \sin 30° = 20,$$

$$\therefore \quad W = 10 \text{ kgf}.$$

93. *When a rigid body has an axis fixed, and is acted upon by forces, whose directions are perpendicular to this axis, it will be in equilibrium if the algebraic sum of the moments of the forces about the fixed axis vanishes.*

[If a force is perpendicular to a given axis and does not meet it, its moment about the axis is the product of the force and the perpendicular distance between the axis and the force.]

Suppose AB to be the fixed axis in the body, and let the body be acted on by forces $P, Q \ldots$; these forces need not be parallel but their directions must be perpendicular to the axis.

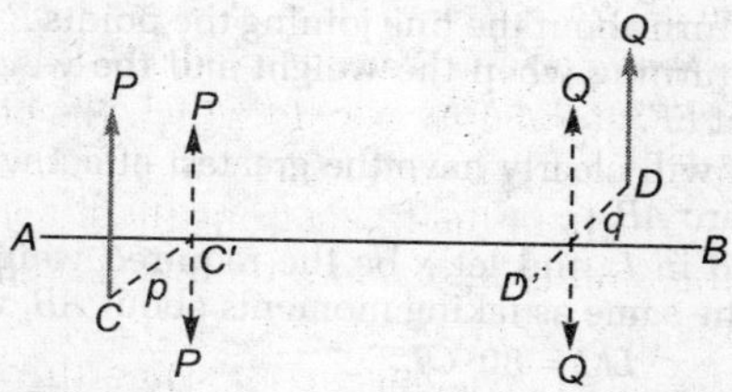

Draw CC' perpendicular to both the axis and P, and DD' perpendicular to the axis and Q; let their lengths be p and q.

At C' introduce two equal and opposite forces, each equal to P, one of these being parallel to the original force P.

The force P at C and the two forces (P, P) at C' are equivalent to a force P, parallel to the original P, and a couple of moment $P \cdot p$.

Similarly, the force Q at D is equivalent to a force Q at D' and a couple of moment $Q \cdot q$.

Similarly for the other forces.

The forces, since they intersect the axis, can have no effect in turning the body about the axis and are balanced by the forces of constraint applied to the axis.

The couples are, by Arts. 72 and 73, equivalent to a couple of moment $P \cdot p + Q \cdot q + \ldots$ in a plane perpendicular to the axis.

Hence the body will be in equilibrium if

$$P \cdot p + Q \cdot q + \ldots \text{is zero;}$$

also the latter expression is the algebraic sum of the moments of the forces about the axis.

Hence the theorem is true.

94. Ex. *A circular uniform table, of weight 80 kg, rests on four equal legs placed symmetrically round its edge ; find the least weight which hung upon the edge of the table will just overturn it.*

Let *AE* and *BF* be two of the legs of the table whose centre is *O*; the weight of the table will act through the point *O*.

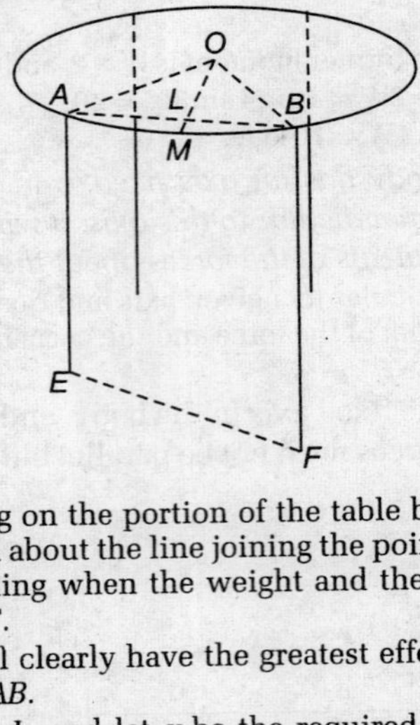

If the weight is hung on the portion of the table between *A* and *B* the table will, if it turns at all, turn about the line joining the points *E* and *F*. Also it will be just on the point of turning when the weight and the weight of the table have equal moments about *EF*.

Now the weight will clearly have the greatest effect when placed at *M*, the middle point of the arc *AB*.

Let *OM* meet *AB* in *L*, and let *x* be the required weight. Taking moments about *EF*, which is the same as taking moments about *AB*, we have

$$x \cdot LM = 80 \cdot OL.$$

But
$$LM = OM - OL = OA - OA\cos 45^\circ$$
$$= OA\left(1 - \frac{1}{\sqrt{2}}\right).$$

$\therefore$
$$x\left(1 - \frac{1}{\sqrt{2}}\right)OA = 80 \cdot OL = 80 \cdot \frac{1}{\sqrt{2}} \cdot OA,$$

and
$$x = \frac{80}{\sqrt{2}-1} = (\sqrt{2}+1)$$
$$= 193.1 \text{ kgf.}$$

95. Theorem. *If three forces acting on a body keep it in equilibrium, they must lie in a plane.*

Let the three forces be P, Q, and R.

Let P_1 and Q_1 be *any* two points on the lines of action of P and Q respectively.

Since the forces are in equilibrium, they can, taken together, have no effect to turn the body about the line P_1Q_1. But the forces P and Q meet this line, and therefore separately have no effect to turn the body about P_1Q_1. Hence the third force R can have no effect to turn the body about P_1Q_1.

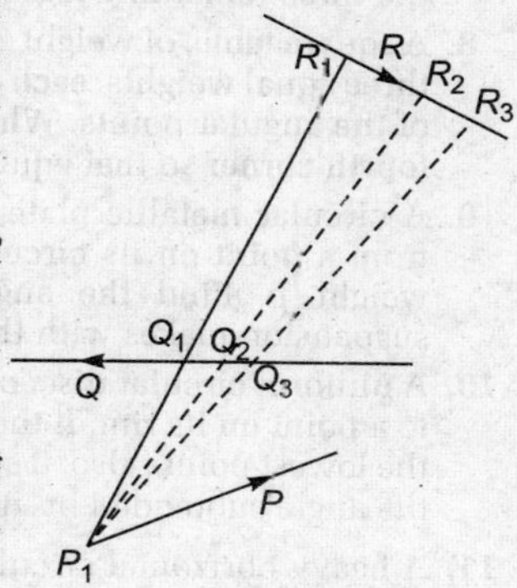

Therefore the line P_1Q_1 must meet R Similarly, if $Q_2, Q_3, \ldots$ are other points on the line of action of Q, the lines $P_1Q_2, P_1Q_3, \ldots$ must meet R.

Hence R must lie in the plane through P_1 and the line of action of Q, *i.e.*, the lines of action of Q, and R must be in a plane which passes through P_1.

But P_1 is *any* point on the line of action of P ; and hence the above plane passes through *any* point on the line of action of P,

i.e., it contains the line of action of P.

Cor. From Art. 77 it now follows that the three forces must also meet in a point or be parallel.

Examples XV

1. A square uniform plate is suspended at one of its vertices, and a weight, equal to half that of the plate, is suspended from the adjacent vertex of the square. Find the position of equilibrium of the plate.
2. A hollow vertical cylinder, or radius $2a$ and height $3a$ rests on a horizontal table, and a uniform rod is placed within it with its lower end resting on the circumference of the base ; if the weight of the rod is equal to that of the cylinder, how long must the rod be so that it may just cause the cylinder to topple over ?
3. A cylinder, whose length is b and the diameter of whose base is c is open at the top and rests on a horizental plane; a uniform rod rests partly within the cylinder and in contact with it at its upper and lower edges ; supposing the weight of the cylinder to be n times that of the rod, find the length of the rod when the cylinder is on the point of falling over.
4. A square table stands on four legs placed respectively at the middle points of its sides ; find the greatest weights that can be put at one of the corners without upsetting the table.
5. A round table stands upon three equidistant weightless legs at its edge, and a man sits upon its edge opposite a leg. It just upsets and falls upon its edge and two legs. He then sits upon its highest point and just tips it up again. Show that the radius of the table is $\sqrt{2}$ times the length of a leg.

6. A circular table, whose weight is 10 kg, is provided with three vertical legs attached to three points in the circumference equidistant from one another; find the least weight which hung from any point in the edge of the table will just cause it to overturn.
7. A square four-legged table has lost one leg; where on the table should a weight, equal to the weight of the table, be placed, so that the pressures on the three remaining legs of the table may be equal ?
8. A square table, of weight 20 kg, has legs at the middle points of its sides, and three equal weights, each equal to the weight of the table, are placed at three of the angular points. What is the greatest weight that can be placed at the fourth corner so that equilibrium may be preserved ?
9. A circular metallic plate, of uniform thickness and of weight w, is hung from a point on its circumference. A string wound on its edge, carries a weight p. Find the angle which the diameter through the point of suspension makes with the vertical.
10. A uniform circular disc, of weight nW, has a particle, of weight W, attached to a point on its rim. If the disc is suspended from a point A on its rim, B is the lowest point; also, if suspended from B, A is the lowest point. Show that the angle subtended by AB at the centre of the disc is $2 \sec^{-1} 2(n + 1)$.
11. A heavy horizontal circular ring rests on three supports at the points A, B, and C of its circumference. Given its weight and the sides and angles of the triangle ABC, find the reactions of the supports.

9

Centre of Gravity

96. Every particle of matter is attracted to the centre of the Earth, and the force with which the Earth attracts any particle to itself is, we shall see in Dynamics, proportional to the mass of the particle.

Any body may be considered as an agglomeration of particles.

If the body is small, compared with the Earth, the lines joining its component particles to the centre of the Earth will be very approximately parallel, and within the limits of this book , we shall consider them to be absolutely parallel.

On every particle, therefore, of a rigid body there is acting a force vertically downwards which we call its weight.

These forces may by the process of compounding parallel forces, Art. 52, be compounded into a single force, equal to the sum of the weights of the particles, acting at some definite point of the body. Such a point is called the centre of gravity of the body.

Centre of gravity. Def. *The centre of gravity of a body, or system of particles rigidly connected together, is that point through which the line of action of the weight of the body always passes in whatever position the body is placed.*

97. *Every body, or system of particles rigidly connected together, has a centre of gravity.*

Let $A, B, C, D \ldots$ be system of particles whose weights are $w_1, w_2, w_3, \ldots$

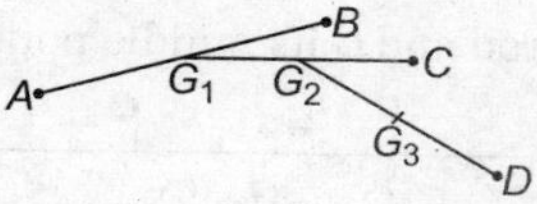

Join AB, and divide it at G_1 so that

$$AG_1 : G_1B :: w_2 : w_1.$$

Then parallel forces $w_1$and w_2 acting at A and B, are, by Art. 52, equivalent to a force $(w_1 + w_2)$ acting at G_1.

Join G_1C, and divide it at G_2 so that

$$G_1G_2 : G_2C :: w_3 : w_1 + w_2.$$

Then parallel forces , $(w_1 + w_2)$ at G_1 and w_2 at C, are equivalent to a force $(w_1 + w_2 + w_3)$ at G_2.

Hence the forces w_1, w_2, and $w_3$may be supposed to be applied at G_2 without altering their effect.

Similarly, dividing G_2D in G_3 so that

$$G_2G_3 : G_3D :: w_4 : w_1 + w_2 + w_3,$$

we see that the resultant of the four weights at A, B, C and D is equivalent to a vertical force, $w_1 + w_2 + w_3 + w_4$ acting at G_3.

Proceeding in this way, we see that the weights of any number of particles composing any body may be supposed to be applied at some point of the body without altering their effect.

98. Since the construction for the position of the resultant of parallel forces depends *only* on the point of application and magnitude, and *not* on the direction of the forces, the point we finally arrive at is the same if the body is turned through any angle; for the weights of the portions of the body are still parallel, although they do not have the same direction, relative to the body, in the two positions.

We can hence show that a body can only have one centre of gravity. For, if possible, let it have two centres of gravity G and G_1. Let the body be turned, if necessary, until GG_1 is horizontal. We shall then have the resultant of a system of vertical forces acting both through G and through G_1. But the resultant force, being itself necessarily vertical, cannot act in the horizontal line GG_1.

Hence there can be only one centre of gravity.

99. If the body is not so small that the weights of its component parts may all be considered to be approximately parallel, it has not necessarily a centre of gravity.

In any case, the point of the body at which we arrive by the construction of Art. 97, has, however, very important properties and is called its Centre of Mass, or Centre of Inertia. If the body is of uniform density its centre of mass coincides with its Centroid.

100. We shall now proceed to the determination of the centre of gravity of some bodies of simple forms.

I. A uniform rod.

Let AB be a uniform rod and G its middle point.

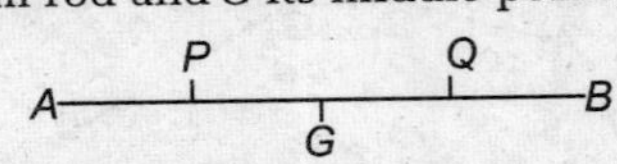

Take any point P of the rod between G and A, and a point Q in GB, such that

$$GQ = GP.$$

The centre of gravity of equal particles at P and Q is clearly G; also, for every particle between G and A, there is an equal particle at an equal distance from G, lying between G and B.

The centre of gravity of each of these pairs of particles is at G; therefore the centre of gravity of the whole rod is at G.

101. II. A uniform parallelogram

Let $ABCD$ be a parallelogram, and let E and F be the middle points of AD and BC.

Divide the parallelogram into a very large number of strips, by means of lines parallel to *AD*, of which *PR* and *QS* are any consecutive pair. Then *PQRS* may be considered to the a uniform straight line, whose centre of gravity is at its middle point G_1.

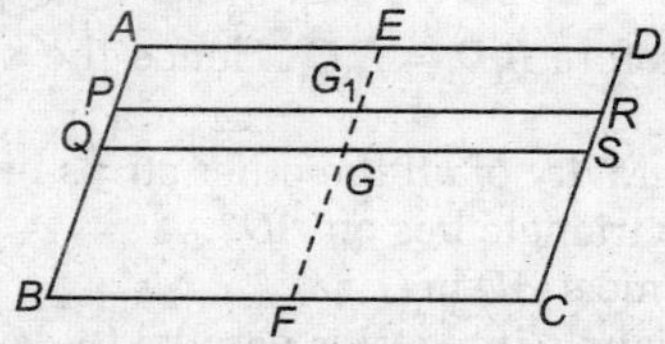

So the centre of gravity of all the other strips lies on *EF*, and hence the centre of gravity of the whole figure lies on *EF*.

So, by dividing the parallelogram by lines parallel to *AB*, we see that the centre of gravity lies on the line joining the middle points of the sides *AB* and *CD*.

Hence the centre of gravity is at *G* the point of intersection of these two lines.

G is clearly also the point of intersection of the diagonals of the parallelogram.

102. It is clear from the method of the two previous articles that, if in a uniform body we can find a point *G* such that the body can be divided into pairs of particles balancing about it, then *G* must be the centre of gravity of the body.

The centre of gravity of a uniform circle, or uniform sphere, is therefore its centre.

It is also clear that if we can divide a lamina into strips, the centre of gravity of which all lie on a straight line, then the centre of gravity of the lamina must lie on that line.

Similarly, if a body can be divided into portions, the centres of gravity of which lie in a plane, the centre of gravity of the whole must lie in that plane.

103. III. Uniform triangular lamina.

Let *ABC* be the triangular lamina and let *D* and *E* be the middle points of the sides *BC* and *CA*.Join *AD* and *BE*, and let them meet in *G*. Then *G* shall be the centre of gravity of the triangle.

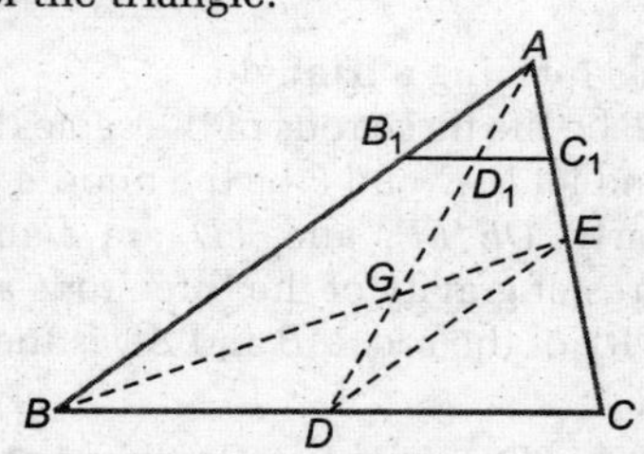

Let B_1C_1 be *any* line parallel to the base *BC* meeting *AD* in D_1.

As in the case of the parallelogram, the triangle may be considered to be made up of a very large number of strips, such as B_1C_1, all parallel to the base *BC*.

Since B_1C_1 and BC are parallel, the triangles AB_1D_1 and ABD are similar; so also the triangles AD_1C_1 and ADC are similar.

Hence, $$\frac{B_1D_1}{BD} = \frac{AD_1}{AD} = \frac{D_1C_1}{DC}.$$

But $BD = DC$; therefore $B_1D_1 = D_1C_1$. Hence the centre of gravity of the strip B_1C_1 lies on AD.

So the centres of gravity of all the other strips lie on AD, and hence the centre of gravity of the triangle lies on AD.

Join BE, and let it meet AD in G.

By dividing the triangle into strips parallel to AC we see, similarly, that the centre of gravity lies on BE.

Hence the required centre of gravity must be at G.

Since D is the middle point of BC and E is the middle point of CA, therefore DE is parallel to AB.

Hence the triangles GDE and GAB are similar,

$$\therefore \quad \frac{GD}{GA} = \frac{DE}{AB} = \frac{CE}{CA} = \frac{1}{2},$$

so that $$2GD = GA,$$

and $$3GD = GA + GD = AD.$$

$$\therefore \quad GD = \frac{1}{3} AD.$$

Hence the centre of gravity of a triangle is on the line joining the middle point of any side to the opposite vertex at a distance equal to one-third the distance of the vertex from that side.

104. *The centre of gravity of any uniform triangular lamina is the same as that of three equal particles placed at the vertices of the triangle.*

Taking the figure of Art. 103, the centre of gravity of two equal particles, each equal to w, at B and C, is at D the middle point of BC, also the centre of gravity of $2w$ at D and w at A divides the line DA in the ratio of $1:2$. But G, the centre of gravity of the lamina, divides DA in the ratio of $1:2$.

Hence the centre of gravity of the three particles is the same as that of the lamina.

105. IV. Three rods forming a triangle.

Let BC, CA, and AB be the three rods of the same thickness and material, forming the triangle, and let D, E, and F be the middle points of the rods. Join DE, EF, and FD. Clearly DE, EF, and FD are half of AB, BC, and CA respectively. The centres of gravity of the three rods are D, E and F.

The centre of gravity of the rods AB and AC is therefore a point L on EF such that

$$EL : LF :: \text{weight at } F : \text{weight at } E$$
$$:: AB : AC$$
$$:: DE : DF,$$

so that, by geometry , DL bisects the angle FDE.

Also the centre of gravity of the three rods must lie on *DL*.

Similarly the centre of gravity must lie on *EM* which bisects the angle *DEF*.

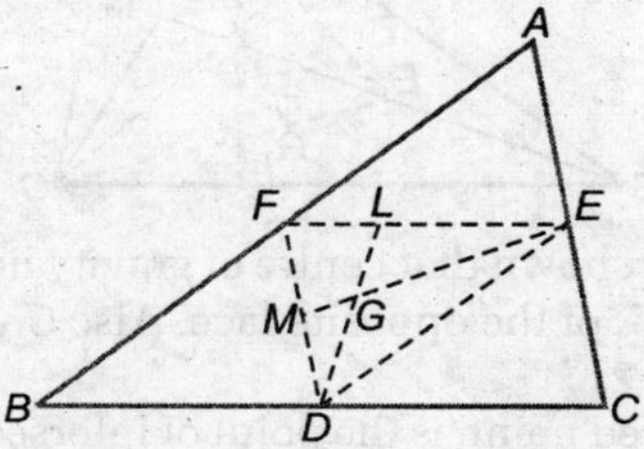

Hence the required point is the point at which *EM* and *DL* meet, and is therefore the centre of the circle inscribed in the triangle *DEF*,

i.e., the centre of the circle inscribed in the triangle formed by joining the middle points of the rods.

106. V. Tetrahedron.

Let *ABCD* be the tetrahedron, *E* the middle point of *AB*, and G_1 the centre of gravity of the base *ABC*.

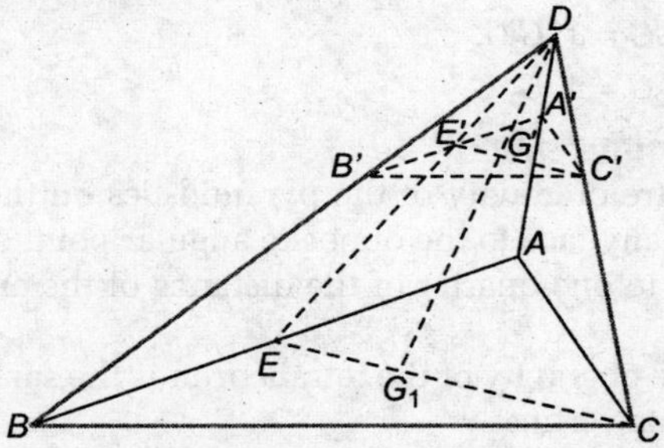

Take *any* section $A'B'C'$ of the tetrahedron which is parallel to *ABC*; let *DE* meets $A'B'$ in E' and let DG_1 meets $E'C'$ in G'.

Then

$$\frac{E'G'}{EG_1} = \frac{DG'}{DG_1}, \text{ by similar } \Delta\text{s } DE'G',\ DEG_1,$$

$$= \frac{C'G'}{CG_1}, \text{ by similar } \Delta\text{s } DG'C',\ DG_1C,$$

$$\therefore \quad \frac{E'G'}{C'G'} = \frac{EG_1}{CG_1} = \frac{1}{2}.$$

Hence G' is the centre of gravity of the section $A'B'C'$.

By considering the tetrahedron as built up of triangles parallel to the base *ABC*, it follows, since the centre of gravity of each triangle is in the line DG_1, that the centre of gravity of the whole lies in DG_1.

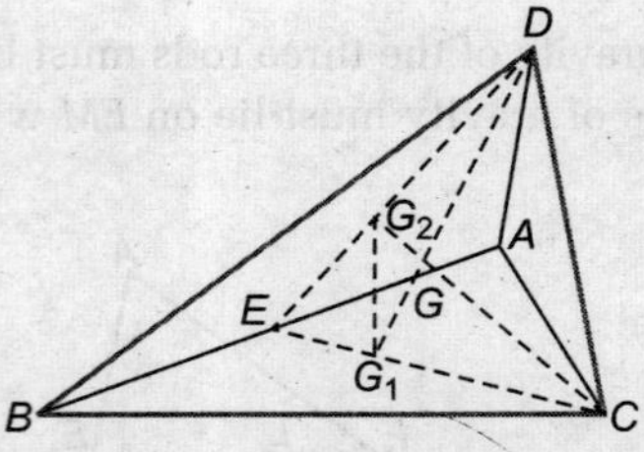

Similarly, it may be shown that centre of gravity lies on the line joining C to the centre of gravity G_2 of the opposite face. Also G_2 lies in the line ED and divides it in the ratio 1 : 2.

Hence G, The required point, is the point of intersection of CG_2 and DG_1.

Join G_1G_2.

Then

$$\frac{G_2G}{GC} = \frac{G_2G_1}{DC}, \text{by similar } \Delta s\ GG_2G_1 \text{ and } GCD,$$

$$= \frac{EG_1}{EC}, \text{ by similar } \Delta s\ EG_1C_2 \text{ and } ECD,$$

$$= \frac{1}{3}.$$

$\therefore \quad GC = 3 \,.\, G_2G,$

$\therefore \quad G_2C = 4 \,.\, G_2\,G.$

Similarly $\quad G_1D = 4G_1G.$

Hence the centre of gravity of the pyramid lies on the line joining the centre of gravity of any face to the opposite angular point of the tetrahedron at a distance equal to one quarter of the distance of the angular point from that face.

Cor. The centre of gravity of the tetrahedron is the same as that of equal particles placed at its vertices.

For equal weights w placed at the angular points ABC of a triangle are equivalent, by Art. 104, to a weight $3w$ placed at G_1, the centre of gravity of ABC. Also $3w$ at G_1 and w at D are equivalent to $4w$ at G, since G divides G_1D in the ratio 1 : 3.

107. VI. Pyramid on any base. Solid Cone.

If the base of the pyramid in the previous article, instead of being a triangle, is any plane figure $ABCLMN$... whose centre of gravity is G_1, it may be shown, by a similar method of proof, that the centre of gravity must lie on the line joining D to G_1.

Also by drawing the planes DAG_1, DBG_1,... the whole pyramid may be split into a number of pyramids on triangular bases, the centres of gravity of which all lie on a plane parallel to $ABCL$... and at a distance from D of three-quarters that of the latter plane.

Hence the centre of gravity of the whole lies on the line G_1D, and divides it in the ratio 1 : 3.

Let now the sides of the plane base form a regular polygon, and let their number be indefinitely increased. Ultimately the plane base becomes a circle,and the pyramid becomes a solid cone having D as its vertex; also the point G_1 is now the centre of the circular base.

Hence the centre of gravity of a solid right circular cone is on the line joining the centre of the base to the vertex at a distance equal to one-quarter of the distance of the vertex from the base.

108. VII. Surface of a hollow cone.

Since the surface of a cone can be divided into an infinite number of triangular laminas, by joining the vertex of the cone to points on the circular base indefinitely close to one another, and since their centres of gravity all lie in a plane parallel to the base of the cone at a distance from the vertex equal to two-thirds of that of the base, the centre of the gravity of the whole cone must lie in that plane.

But, by symmetry, the centre of gravity must lie on the axis of the cone.

Hence the required point is the point in which the above plane meets the axis, and therefore is on the axis at a point distance from the base one-third the height of the cone.

Examples XVI

1. An isosceles triangular lamina has its equal sides of length 5 cm and its base of length 6 cm; find the distance of the centre of gravity from each of its sides.
2. The sides of a triangular lamina are 6, 8, and 10 cm in length; find the distance of the centre of gravity from each of the sides.
3. The base of an isosceles triangular lamina is 4 cm and the equal sides are each 7 cm in length; find the distances of its centre of gravity from the angular points of the triangle.
4. D is the middle point of the base BC of a triangle ABC; show that the distance between the centres of gravity of the triangles ABD and ACD is $\frac{1}{3} BC$.
5. A heavy triangular plate ABC lies on the ground; if a vertical force applied at the point A is just great enough to begin to lift that vertex from the ground, show that the same force will suffice, if applied at B or C.
6. Three men carry a weight, W, by putting it on a smooth triangular board, of weight w, and supporting the system on their shoulders placed respectively at the angular points; find the weight that each man supports.
7. The base of a triangle is fixed, and its vertex moves on a given straight line; show that the centre of gravity also moves on a straight line.
8. The base of a triangle is fixed, and it has a given vertical angle; show that the centre of gravity of the triangle moves on an arc of a certain circle.
9. A given weight is placed anywhere on a triangle; show that the centre of gravity of the system lies within a certain triangle.
10. A uniform equilateral triangular plate is suspended by a string attached to a point in one of its sides, which divides the side in the ratio 2:1; find the inclination of this side to the vertical.

11. A uniform lamina in the shape of a right-angled triangle, and such that one of the sides containing the right angle is three times the other, is suspended by a string attached to the right angle; in the position of equilibrium, show that the hypotenuse is inclined at an angle $\sin^{-1}\frac{3}{5}$ to the vertical.

12. A uniform triangular lamina, whose sides are 3, 4, and 5 cm, is suspended by a string from the middle point of the longest side; find the inclination of this side to the vertical.

---

109. General formulae for the determination of the centre of gravity.

In the following articles formulae will be obtained giving the position of the centre of gravity of any system of particles, whose position and weights are known.

Theorem. *If a system of particles whose weights $w_1, w_2, \ldots w_n$ are on a straight line, and if their distances measured from a fixed point O in the line are*

$$x_1, x_2, \ldots x_n,$$

the distance, $\bar{x}$, of their centre of gravity from the fixed point is given by

$$\bar{x} = \frac{w_1x_1 + w_2x_2 + \ldots + w_nx_n}{w_1 + w_2 + \ldots + w_n}.$$

Let $A, B, C, D \ldots$ be the particles and let the centre of gravity of w_1 and w_2 at A and B be G_1; let the centre of gravity of $(w_1 + w_2)$ at G_1 and w_3 at C be G_2, and so for the other particles of the system.

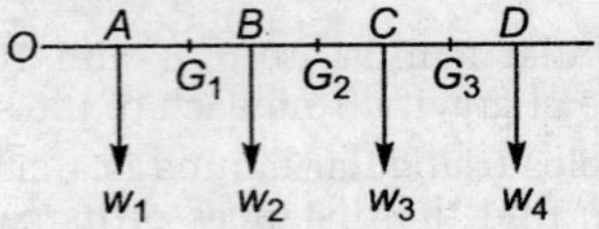

By Art. 97, we have $\quad w_1 \cdot AG_1 = w_2 \cdot G_1B;$

$\therefore \quad w_1(OG_1 - OA) = w_2(OB - OG_1).$

Hence $\quad (w_1 + w_2) \cdot OG_1 = w_1 \cdot OA + w_2 \cdot OB,$

i.e., $$OG_1 = \frac{w_1x_1 + w_2x_2}{w_1 + w_2} \qquad \ldots(1).$$

Similarly, since G_2 is the centre of gravity of $(w_1 + w_2)$ at G_1 and w_3 at C, we have

$$OG_2 = \frac{(w_1 + w_2) \cdot OG_1 + w_3 \cdot OC}{(w_1 + w_2) + w_3}$$

$$= \frac{w_1x_1 + w_2x_2 + w_3x_3}{w_1 + w_2 + w_3}, \text{ by (1).}$$

So $$OG_3 = \frac{(w_1 + w_2 + w_3) \cdot OG_2 + w_4 \cdot OD}{(w_1 + w_2 + w_3) + w_4}$$

$$= \frac{w_1x_1 + w_2x_2 + w_3x_3 + w_4x_4}{w_1 + w_2 + w_3 + w_4}.$$

Proceeding in this manner we easily have

$$\overline{x} = \frac{w_1x_1 + w_2x_2 + ... + w_nx_n}{w_1 + w_2 + ... + w_n},$$

whatever the number of the particles in the system.

Otherwise. The above formula may be obtained by the use of Article 65. For the weights of the particles form a system of parallel forces whose resultant is equal to their sum, *viz.* $w_1 + w_2 + ... w_n$. Also the sum of the moments of these forces about any point in their plane is the same as the moment of their resultant. But the sum of the moments of the forces about the fixed point O is

$$w_1x_1 + w_2x_2 + ... + w_nx_n.$$

Also, if $\overline{x}$ is the distance of the centre of gravity from O, the moment of the resultant is

$$(w_1 + w_2 ... + w_n) \times \overline{x}.$$

Hence $\quad \overline{x}\,(w_1 + w_2 ... + w_n) = w_1x_1 + w_2x_2 + ... + w_nx_n;$

i.e.,

$$\overline{x} = \frac{w_1x_1 + w_2x_2 + ... + w_nx_n}{w_1 + w_2 + ... + w_n}.$$

110. Ex. 1. *A rod AB, 60 cm in length, and of weight 2.5 kg, is bisected in the points C and D, and at the points A, C, D, and B are placed particles of* $\frac{1}{2}, 1, 1\frac{1}{2}$, *and* 2 *kg weight respectively; find what point of the rod must be supported so that the rod may rest in any position, i.e., find the centre of gravity of the system.*

Let G be the middle point of the rod and let the fixed point O of the previous article be taken to coincide with the end A of the rod. The quantities $x_1, x_2, x_3, x_4,$ and x_5 are in this case 0, 20, 30, 40, and 60 cm respectively.

Hence, if X is the point required, we have

$$AX = \frac{0.5 \times 0 + 1 \times 20 + 2.5 \times 30 + 1.5 \times 40 + 2 \times 60}{0.5 + 1 + 2.5 + 1.5 + 2}$$

$$= \frac{275}{7.5} = 36\frac{2}{3} \text{ cm}.$$

Ex. 2. *If, in the previous question, the body at B is removed and another body be substituted, find the weight of this unknown body so that the new centre of gravity may be at the middle point of the rod.*

Let λ lb be the required weight.

Since the distance of the new centre of gravity from A is to be 30 cm, we have

$$30 = \frac{0.5 \times 0 + 1 \times 20 + 2.5 \times 30 + 1.5 \times 40 + \lambda.60}{0.5 + 1 + 2.5 + 1.5 + \lambda} = \frac{155 + 60\lambda}{5.5 + \lambda}.$$

$$\therefore \quad 165 + 30\lambda = 155 + 60\lambda.$$

$$\therefore \quad \lambda = \frac{1}{3} \text{ kg}.$$

Ex. 3. *To the end of a rod, whose length is* 60 *cm and whose weight is* 1.5 *kg, is attached a sphere of radius* 5 *cm and weight* 5 *kg; find the position of the centre of gravity of the compound body.*

Let OA be the rod, G_1 its middle point, G_2 the centre of the sphere, and G the required point.

Then $$OG = \frac{1.5OG_1 + 5OG_2}{1.5+5}.$$

But $$OG_1 = 30 \text{ cm}; OG_2 = 65 \text{ cm}.$$

$$\therefore \quad OG = \frac{1.5 \times 30 + 5 \times 65}{1.5+5}$$

$$= \frac{740}{13} = 56.9 \text{cm nearly.}$$

Examples XVII

1. A straight rod, 1 foot in length and of mass 1 ounce, has an ounce of lead fastened to it at one end, and another ounce fastened to it at a distance from the other and equal to one-third of its length; find the centre of the system.

2. A uniform bar, 90 cm in length and of mass 180 g, has 3 rings, each of mass 90 g, at distances $7\frac{1}{2}, 37\frac{1}{2}$, and $52\frac{1}{2}$ cm from the one end. About what point of the bar will the system balance?

3. A uniform rod AB is four decimetres long and weight 3 kg. One kg is attached at A,2 kg at a point distant 1 decimetre from A, 3 kg at 2 decimetres from A, 4 kg at 3 disimetres from A, and 5 kg at B. Find the distance from A of the centre of gravity of the system.

4. A telescope consists of 3 tubes, each 10 cm in length, one within the other, and of weights 8, 7, and 6 g. Find the position of the centre of gravity when the tubes are drawn out at full length.

5. Twelve heavy particles at equal intervals of one cm along a straight rod weigh 1,2,3,...12 g respectively; find their centre of gravity, neglecting the weight of the rod.

6. Weights proportional to 1, 4, 9, and 16 are placed in a straight line so that the distances between them are equal; find the position of their centre of gravity.

7. A rod, of uniform thickness, has one-half of its length composed of one metal and the other half composed of a different metal, and the rod balances about a point distant one-third of its whole length from one end; compare the weights of equal quantities of the metal.

8. An inclined plane, with an angle of inclination of 60°,is 90 cm long; masses of 210, 150, 120, and 240 g are placed on the plane in order at distances of 1 cm, the latter being the highest; find the distance of their centre of gravity from the base of the inclined plane.

9. AB is a uniform rod, of length n cm and weight $(n + 1)W$. To the rod masses of weight $W, 2W, 3W, \ldots nW$ are attached at distances, 1, 2, 3, ...n cm respectively from A. Find the distance from A of the centre of gravity of the rod and weights.

10. A rod, 12 cm long, has a mas of 1 kg suspended from one end and, when 15 kg is suspended from the other end, it balances about a point distant 3 cm from that end; if 8 kg is suspended there, it balances about a point 4 cm from that end. Find the weight of the rod and the position of its centre of gravity.

111. Theorem. *If a system of particles, whose weights are $w_1, w_2, .. w_n$, lie in a plane, and if OX and OY are two fixed straight lines in the plane at right angles, and if the distances of the particles from OX are $y_1, y_2, ... y_n$, and the distance of their centre of gravity is $\bar{y}$, then*

$$\bar{y} = \frac{w_1y_1 + w_2y_2 + .. + w_ny_n}{w_1 + w_2 + ... + w_n}.$$

Similarly, if the distances of the particles from OY be $x_1, x_2, ... x_n$, and that of their centre of gravity is $\bar{x}$, then

$$\bar{x} = \frac{w_1x_1 + w_2x_2 + ... + w_nx_n}{w_1 + w_2 + ... + w_n}.$$

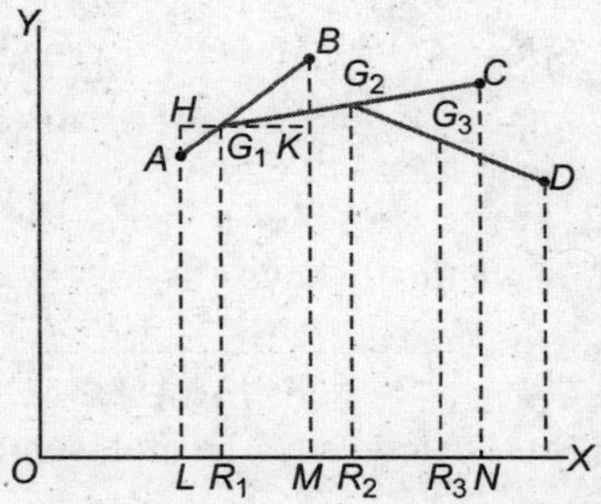

Let $A, B, C, ...$ be the particles, and $AL, BM, CN ...$ the perpendiculars on OX.

Let G_1 be the centre of gravity of w_1 and w_2, G_2 the centre of gravity of $(w_1 + w_2)$ at G_1 and w_3 at C, and so on.

Draw $G_1R_1, G_2R_2, ...$ perpendicular to OX, and through G_1 draw HG_1K parallel to OX to meet AL and BN in H and K.

Since G_1 is the centre of gravity of w_1 and w_2, we have

$$\frac{AG_1}{G_1B} = \frac{w_2}{w_1}. \text{(Art. 97).}$$

Now AG_1H and BG_1K are similar triangles,

$$\therefore \quad \frac{HA}{BK} = \frac{AG_1}{G_1B} = \frac{w_2}{w_1}.$$

But $\quad HA = HL - AL = G_1R_1 - y_1,$

and $\quad BK = BM - KM = y_2 - G_1R_1;$

$$\therefore \quad \frac{G_1R_1 - y_1}{y_2 - G_1R_1} = \frac{w_2}{w_1}.$$

Hence $\quad w_1(G_1R_1 - y_1) = w_2(y_2 - G_1R_1);$

$$\therefore \quad G_1R_1 = \frac{w_1y_1 + w_2y_2}{w_1 + w_2} \quad ...(1)$$

Similarly, since G_2 is the centre of gravity of $(w_1 + w_2)$ at G_1 and w_3 at C, we have

$$G_2R_2 = \frac{(w_1 + w_2) \cdot G_1R_1 + w_3y_3}{w_1 + w_2 + w_3} = \frac{w_1y_1 + w_2y_2 + w_3y_3}{w_1 + w_2 + w_3}, \text{by (1)}.$$

Proceeding in this way we easily obtain

$$\bar{y} = \frac{w_1y_1 + w_2y_2 + \ldots + w_ny_n}{w_1 + w_2 + \ldots + w_n}.$$

Again, since the triangles AG_1H and BG_1K are similar, we have

$$\frac{HG_1}{G_1K} = \frac{AG_1}{G_1B} = \frac{w_2}{w_1}.$$

But $\qquad HG_1 = LR_1 = OR_1 - OL = OR_1 - x_1,$

and $\qquad G_1K = R_1M = OM - OR_1 = x_2 - OR_1.$

$\therefore \qquad w_1(OR_1 - x_1) = w_2(x_2 - OR_1).$

Hence $\qquad OR_1 = \dfrac{w_1x_1 + w_2x_2}{w_1 + w_2}.$

Proceeding as before we finally have

$$\bar{x} = \frac{w_1x_1 + w_2x_2 + \ldots + w_nx_n}{w_1 + w_2 + \ldots + w_n}.$$

The theorem of this article may be put somewhat differently as follows :

The distance of the centre of gravity from ***any*** *line in the plane of the particles is equal to a fraction, whose numerator is the sum of the products of each weight into its distance from the given line, and whose denominator is the sum of the weights.*

In other words, the distance of the centre of gravity is equal to the **average** distance of the particles.

112. The formula of the preceding article may be deduced from Article 93. For, since the resultant weight $(w_1 + w_2 + \ldots + w_n)$ acting at G, where G is the centre of gravity of all the weights, is equivalent to the component weights $w_1, w_2 \ldots$ the resultant would, if the line OX be supposed to be a fixed axis, have the same moment about this fixed axis that the component weights have.

But the moment of the resultant is

$$(w_1 + w_2 + \ldots + w_n)\,\bar{y},$$

and the sum of the moments of the weights is

$$w_1y_1 + w_2y_2 + \ldots + w_ny_n.$$

Hence $\qquad \bar{y} = \dfrac{w_1y_1 + w_2y_2 + \ldots + w_ny_n}{w_1 + w_2 + \ldots + w_n}.$

In a similar manner we should have

$$\bar{x} = \frac{w_1x_1 + w_2x_2 + \ldots + w_ny_n}{w_1 + w_2 + \ldots + w_n}.$$

113. Ex. 1. *A square lamina, whose weight is 5 kg, has attached to its angular point particles whose weights, taken in order, are* $1\frac{1}{2}$, 3, $2\frac{1}{2}$, *and* $\frac{1}{2}$ *kg respectively. Find the position of the centre of gravity of the system, if the side of the lamina be 50 cm.*

Let the particles be placed at the angular points *O, A, B,* and *C*. Let the two fixed lines from which the distances are measured be *OA* and *OC*.

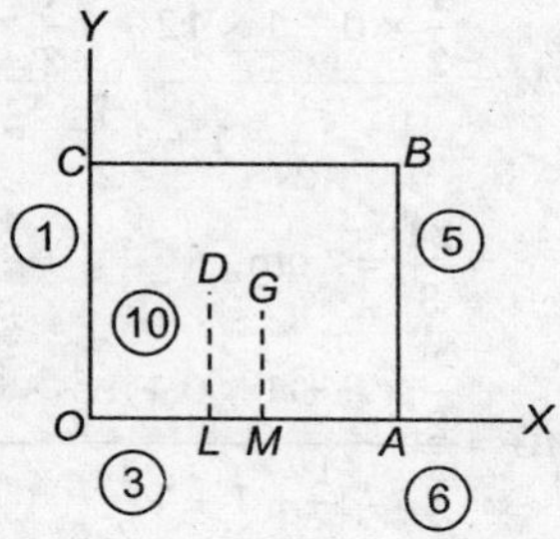

The weight of the lamina acts at its centre *D*. Let *G* be the required centre of gravity and draw *DL* and *GM* perpendicular to *OX*.

The distances of the points *O, A, B, C,* and *D* from *OX* are clearly 0, 0, 50, 50 and 25 cm respectively.

$$\therefore \quad MG = \bar{y} = \frac{1\frac{1}{2} \times 0 + 3 \times 0 + 2\frac{1}{2} \times 50 + \frac{1}{2} \times 50 + \times 5 \times 25}{1\frac{1}{2} + 3 + 2\frac{1}{2} + \frac{1}{2} + 5}$$

$$= \frac{275}{12\frac{1}{2}} = 22 \text{ cm.}$$

So the distances of the particles from *OY* are 0, 25, 25, 0, and $12\frac{1}{2}$ inches respectively.

$$\therefore \quad OM = \bar{x} = \frac{1\frac{1}{2} \times 0 + 3 \times 50 + 2\frac{1}{2} \times 50 + \frac{1}{2} \times 0 + 5 \times 25}{1\frac{1}{2} + 3 + 2\frac{1}{2} + \frac{1}{2} + 5}$$

$$= \frac{400}{12\frac{1}{2}} = 32 \text{ cm.}$$

Hence the required point may be obtained by measuring 32 cm from *O* along *OA* and then erecting a perpendicular of length 22 cm.

Ex. 2. *OAB is an isosceles weightless triangle, whose base OA is 12 cm and whose sides are each 10 cm; at the points O, A, and B are placed particles of weights* $\frac{1}{2}$, 1, *and* $1\frac{1}{2}$ *kg; find their centre of gravity.*

Let the fixed line OX coincides with OA and let OY be a perpendicular to OA through the point O.

If BL be drawn perpendicular to OA, then $OL = 6$ cm, and

$$LB = \sqrt{10^2 - 6^2} = 8 \text{ cm.}$$

Hence, if G is the required centre of gravity and GM is drawn perpendicular to OX, we have

$$OM = \frac{\frac{1}{2} \times 0 + 1 \times 12 + 1\frac{1}{2} \times 6}{\frac{1}{2} + 1 + 1\frac{1}{2}}$$

$$= \frac{21}{3} = 7 \text{ cm,}$$

and
$$MG = \frac{\frac{1}{2} \times 0 + 1 \times 0 + 1\frac{1}{2} \times 8}{\frac{1}{2} + 1 + 1\frac{1}{2}}$$

$$= \frac{12}{3} = 4 \text{ cm.}$$

Hence the required point is obtained by measuring a distance 7 cm from O along OA and then erecting a perpendicular of length 4 cm.

114. *Centre of Parallel Forces.*

The methods and formulae of Arts. 109 and 111 will apply not only to weights, but also to any system of parallel forces and will determine the position of the resultant of any such system. The magnitude of the resultant is the sum of the forces. Each force must, of course, be taken with its proper sign prefixed.

There is one case in which we obtain no satisfactory result; if the algebraic sum of the forces is zero, the resultant force is zero, and the formulae of the Art. 111 give

$$\bar{x} = \infty, \text{and } \bar{y} = \infty.$$

In this case the system of parallel forces is, as in Art. 53, equivalent to a couple.

114 (a) *Determination of the centre of gravity of particles distributed in space*

Let us take axis OZ in the vertical upward direction and axes OX, OY in a horizontal plane. Let A_1, A_2, etc. be the positions of the particles of masses m_1, m_2, etc. respectively and let their respective co-ordinates be $(x_1, y_1, z_1), (x_2, y_2, z_2)$ etc. G is the centre of gravity of the system of particles and its co-ordinates are $(\bar{X}, \bar{Y}, \bar{Z})$.

Taking the algebraic sum of the moments of the forces which are the weights of the particles acting in the vertical downward direction, about the Y axis, we get,

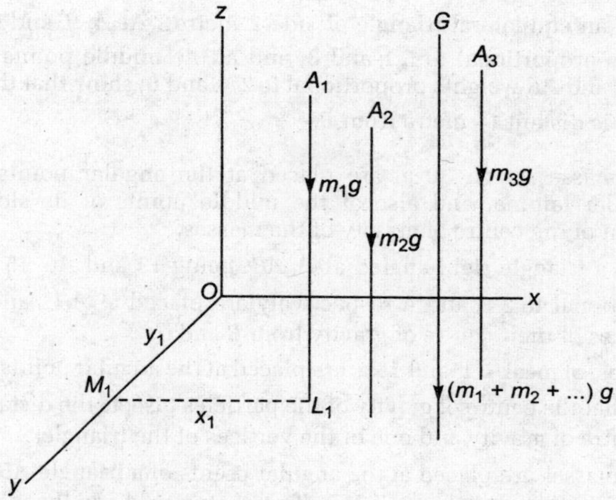

$$\overline{X}(m_1 + m_2 + \ldots)g = m_1g \cdot x_1 + m_2g \cdot x_2 + \ldots$$

or $$\overline{X} = \frac{\Sigma m_1 x_1}{\Sigma m_1}$$

Similarly, $$\overline{Y} = \frac{\Sigma m_1 y_1}{\Sigma m_1}$$

and $$\overline{Z} = \frac{\Sigma m_1 z_1}{\Sigma m_1}$$

N.B. To find $\overline{Z}$, the direction of the forces are altered and are made at right-angles to *YOZ* or *XOZ* plane. This is justified as the centre of a system of like parallel forces does not depend on their directions.

Examples XVIII

1. Particles of 1, 2, 3 and 4 kg weight are placed at the angular points of a square; find the distance of their C.G. from the centre of the square.
2. At two opposite corners *A* and *C* of a square *ABCD* weights of 2 kg each are placed, and at *B* and *D* are placed 1 and 7 kg respectively; find their centre of gravity.
3. Particles of 5, 6, 9, and 7 kg respectively are placed at the corners *A, B, C,* and *D* of a horizontal square, the length of whose side is 27 cm; find where a single force must be applied to preserve equilibrium.
4. Five masses of 30, 60, 90, 120, and 15 g are placed on a square table. The distances from one edge of the table are 4, 8, 12, 16, and 20 cm and from the adjacent edge, 6, 10, 14, 18, and 22 cm respectively. Find the distance of the centre of gravity from the two edges.
5. Weights proportional to 1, 2, and 3 are placed at the corners of an equilateral triangle, whose side is of length *a*; find the distance of their centre of gravity from the first weight.

   Find the distance also if the weights are proportional to 11, 13, and 6.

6. ABC is an equilateral triangle of side 2 metres. At A, B, and C are placed weights proportional to 5, 1, and 3, and at the middle points of the sides BC, CA, and AB weights proportional to 2, 4, and 6; show that their centre of gravity is distant $1\frac{1}{3}$ metre from B.
7. Equal masses, each 30 g, are placed at the angular points of a heavy triangular lamina, and also at the middle points of its sides; find the position of the centre of gravity of the masses.
8. ABC is a triangle right-angled at A, AB being 13 and AC 15 cm; weights proportional to 2, 3, and 4 respectively are placed at A, C, and B; find the distances of their centre of gravity from B and C.
9. Particles, of mass 4, 1, and 1 kg, are placed at the angular points of a triangle; show that the centre of gravity of the particles bisects the distance between the centre of gravity and one of the vertices of the triangle.
10. Three masses are placed at the angular points of a triangle ABC. Find their ratios if their centre of inertia is halfway between A and the middle point of BC.
11. Bodies of mass 2, 3, and 4 kg respectively are placed at the angular points A, B, and C of a triangle; find their centre of gravity G, and show that forces $2GA$, $3GB$, and $4GC$ are in equilibrium.
12. ABC is a uniform triangular plate, of mass 3 kg. Masses of 2, 3, and 5 kg respectively are placed at A, B, and C. Find the position of the centre of gravity of the whole system.
13. To the vertices A, B, and C of a uniform triangular plate, whose mass is 3 kg and whose centre of gravity is G, particles of masses 2 kg, 2 kg, and 11 kg, are attached; show that the centre of gravity of the system is the middle point of GC.
14. Masses of 2, 3, 2, 6, 9, and 6 kg are placed at the angular corners of a regular hexagon, taken in order; find their centre of gravity.
15. Weights proportional to 5, 4, 6, 2, 7, and 3 are placed at the angular points of a regular hexagon, taken in order; show that their centre of gravity is the centre of the hexagon.
16. Weights proportional to 1, 5, 3, 4, 2, and 6 are placed at the angular points of a regular hexagon, taken in order; show that their centre of gravity is the centre of the hexagon.
17. If weights proportional to the numbers 1, 2, 3, 4, 5, and 6 are placed at the angular points of a regular hexagon taken in order, show that the distance of their centre of gravity from the centre of the circumscribing circle of the hexagon is $\frac{2}{7}$ ths of the radius of the circle.
18. At the angular points of a square, taken in order, these act parallel forces in the ratio 1 : 3 : 5 : 7; find the distance from the centre of the square of the point at which their resultant acts.
19. A, B, C, and D are the angles of a parallelogram taken in order; like parallel forces proportional to 6, 10, 14, and 10 respectively act at A, B, C, and D; show that the centre and resultant of these parallel forces remain the same, if,

instead of these forces, parallel forces, proportional to 8, 12, 16, and 4, act at the points of bisection of the sides AB, BC, and CD, and DA respectively.

20. Find the centre of parallel forces equal respectively to P, $2P$, $3P$, $4P$, $5P$, and $6P$, the points of application of the forces being at distances 2, 4, 6, 8, 10, and 12 cm respectively from a given point A measured along a given line AB.

21. Three parallel forces, P, Q, and R, act at the vertices A, B, and C, of a triangle and are proportional respectively to a, b, and c. Find the magnitude and position of their resultant.

115. *Given the centre of gravity of the two portions of a body, to find the centre of gravity of the whole body.*

Let the given centres of gravity be G_1 and G_2, and let the weights of the two portions be W_1 and W_2; the required point G, by Art. 97, divides G_1G_2 so that

$$G_1G : GG_2 :: W_2 : W_1.$$

The point G may also be obtained by the use of Art. 109.

Ex. *On the same base AB, and on opposite sides of it, isosceles triangles CAB and DAB are described whose altitudes are* 12 cm *and* 6 cm *respectively. Find the distance from AB of the centre of gravity of the quadrilateral CADB.*

Let CLD be the perpendicular to AB, meeting it in L, and let G_1, and G_2 be the centres of gravity of the two triangles CAB and DAB respectively.

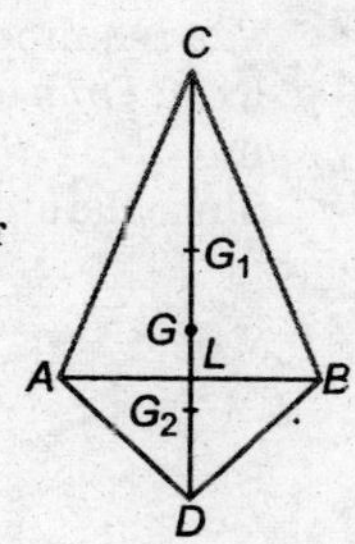

Hence $$CG_1 = \frac{2}{3} \cdot CL = 8.$$

and $$CG_2 = CL + LG_2 = 12 + 2 = 14.$$

The weights of the triangles are proportional to their areas, *i.e.*, to $\frac{1}{2}$ AB. 12 and $\frac{1}{2}$ AB. 6.

If G is the centre of gravity of the whole figure, we have

$$CG = \frac{\Delta CAB \times CG_1 + \Delta DAB \times CG_2}{\Delta CAB + \Delta DAB}$$

$$= \frac{\frac{1}{2} AB.12 \times 8 + \frac{1}{2} AB.6 \times 14}{\frac{1}{2} AB.12 + \frac{1}{2} AB.6}$$

$$= \frac{48 + 42}{6 + 3} = \frac{90}{9} = 10.$$

Hence $$LG = CL - CG = 2 \text{ cm}.$$

This result may be verified experimentally by cutting the figure out of thin cardboard.

116. *Given the centre of gravity of the whole of a body and of a portion of the body, to find the centre of gravity of the remainder.*

Let G be the centre of gravity of a body $ABCD$, and G_1 that of the portion ADC.

Let W be the weight of the whole body and W_1 that of the portion ACD, so that $W_2(= W - W_1)$ is the weight of the portion ABC.

Let G_2 be the centre of gravity of the portion ABC. Since the two portions of the body make up the whole, therefore W_1 at G_1 and W_2 at G_2 must have their centre of gravity at G.

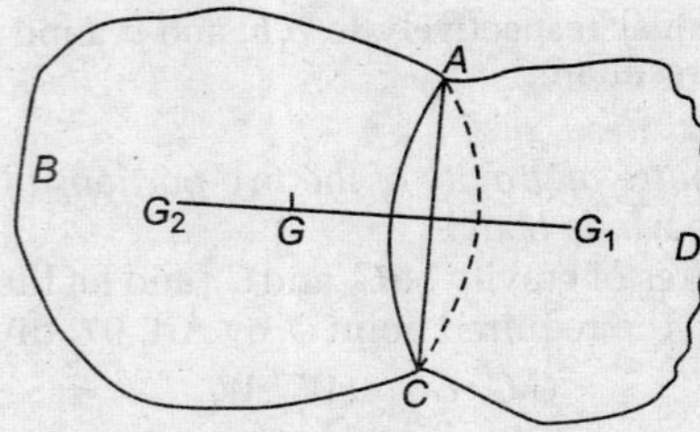

Hence G must lie on G_1G_2 and be such that

$$W_1 \cdot GG_1 = W_2 \cdot GG_2.$$

Hence given G and G_1, we obtain G_2 by producing G_1G to G_2, so that

$$GG_2 = \frac{W_1}{W_2} \cdot GG_1 = \frac{W_1}{W - W_1} \cdot GG_1.$$

The required point may be also obtained by means of Art. 109.

Ex. 1. *From a circular disc, of radius r, is cut out a circle, whose diameter is a radius of the disc; find the centre of gravity of the remainder.*

Since the areas of circles are to one another as the squares of their radii,

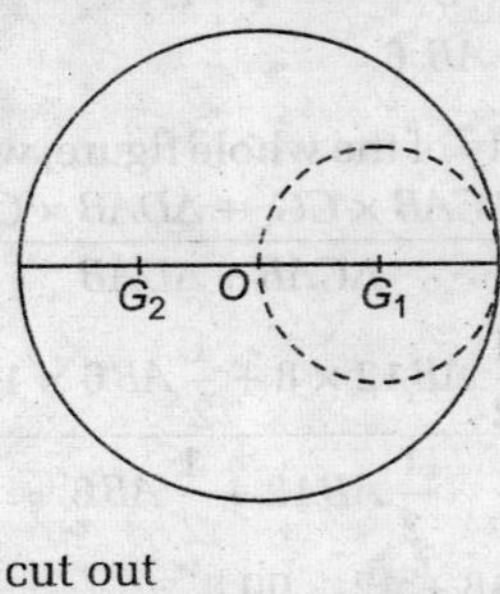

∴ area of the portion cut out

: area of the whole circle

$$:: \left(\frac{r}{2}\right)^2 : r^2$$

$$:: 1 : 4.$$

Hence the portion cut off is one-quarter, and the portion remaining is three-quarters, of the whole, so that $W_1 = \frac{1}{3} W_2$.

Now the portions W_1 and W_2 make up the whole disc, and therefore balance about O.

Hence

$$W_2 \cdot OG_2 = W_1 \cdot OG_1 = \frac{1}{3} W_2 \times \frac{1}{2} r.$$

$$\therefore \quad OG_2 = \frac{1}{6} r.$$

This may be verified experimentally.

Ex. 2. *From a triangular lamina ABC is cut off, by a line parallel to its base BC, one-quarter of its area; find the centre of gravity of the remainder.*

Let AB_1C_1 be the portion cut off, so that

$$\Delta AB_1C_1 : \Delta ABC :: 1 : 4.$$

By geometry, since the triangles AB_1C_1 and ABC are similar, we have

$$\Delta AB_1C_1 : \Delta ABC :: AB_1^2 : AB^2.$$

$$\therefore \quad AB_1^2 : AB^2 :: 1 : 4,$$

and hence $\quad AB_1 = \frac{1}{2} AB.$

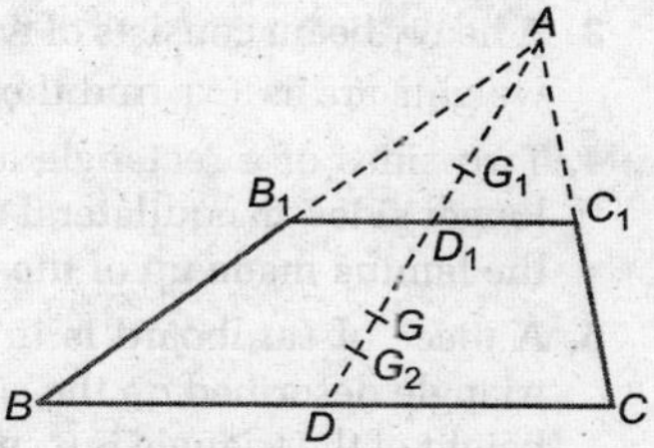

The line B_1C_1 therefore bisects AB, AC, and AD.

Let G and G_1 be the centres of gravity of the triangles ABC and AB_1C_1 respectively; also let W_1 and W_2 be the respective weights of the portion cut off and the portion remaining, so that $W_2 = 3W_1$.

Since W_2 at G_2 and W_1 at G_1 balance about G, we have, by Art. 109,

$$DG = \frac{W_1 \cdot DG_1 + W_2 \cdot DG_2}{W_1 + W_2}$$

$$= \frac{DG_1 + 3DG_2}{4} \quad \text{...(1).}$$

But $\quad DG = \frac{1}{3} DA = \frac{2}{3} DD_1,$

and $\quad DG_1 = DD_1 + \frac{1}{3} D_1A = DD_1 + \frac{1}{3} DD_1 = \frac{4}{3} DD_1.$

Hence (1) is $\quad 4 \times \frac{2}{3} DD_1 = \frac{4}{3} DD_1 + 3DG_2$

$$\therefore \quad DG_2 = \frac{4}{9} DD_1.$$

This result can also be easily verified experimentally.

Examples XIX

[*The student should verify some of the following questions experimentally; suitable ones for this purpose are Nos.* 1, 2, 4, 5, 8, 9, 10, 11, 17, 18, and 19.]

1. A uniform rod, 24 cm in length, is broken into two parts, of lengths 10 and 14 cm, which are placed so as to form the letter T, the longer portion being vertical; find the centre of gravity of the system.

2. Two rectangular pieces of the same cardboard, of lengths 6 and 8 cm and breadths 2 and $2\frac{1}{2}$ cm respectively, are placed touching, but not overlapping, one another on a table so as to form a T-shaped figure, the longer portion being vertical. Find the position of its centre of gravity.

3. A heavy beam consists of two portions, whose lengths are as 3 : 5, and whose weights are as 3 : 1; find the position of its centre of gravity.

4. Two sides of a rectangle are double of the other two, and on one of the longer sides an equilateral triangle is described; find the centre of gravity of the lamina made up of the rectangle and the triangle.

5. A piece of cardboard is in the shape of a square *ABCD* with an isosceles triangle described on the side *BC*; if the side of the square is 12 cm and the height of the triangle is 6 cm, find the distance of the centre of gravity of the cardboard from the line *AD*.

6. An isosceles right-angled triangle has squares described externally on all its sides. Show that the centre of gravity of the figure so formed is on the line, which bisects the hypotenuse and passes through the right angle, and divides it in the ratio 1 : 26.

7. Two uniform spheres, composed of the same materials, and whose diameters are 6 and 12 cm respectively, are firmly united; find the position of their centre of gravity.

8. From a parallelogram is cut one of the four portions into which it is divided by its diagonals; find the centre of gravity of the remainder.

9. A parallelogram is divided into four parts, by joining the middle points of opposite sides, and one part is cut away; find the centre of gravity of the remainder.

10. From a square a triangular portion is cut off, by cutting the square along a line joining the middle points of two adjacent sides; Find the centre of gravity of the remainder.

11. From a triangle is cut off $\frac{1}{5}$th of its area by a straight line parallel to its base. Find the position of the centre of gravity of the remainder.

12. *ABC* is an equilateral triangle, of 6 cm side, of which *O* is the centre of gravity. If the triangle *OBC* is removed, find the centre of gravity of the remainder.

13. If from a triangle *ABC* three equal triangles *ARQ*, *BPR*, and *CQP* are cut off, show that the centres of the inertia of the triangles *ABC* and *PQR* are coincident.

14. *G* is the centre of gravity of a given isosceles triangle, right-angled at *A*, and having *BC* equal to *a*. The portion *GBC* is cut away; find the distance of the centre of gravity of the remainder from *A*.

15. On the same base BC are two triangles, ABC and $A'BC$, the vertex A' falling within the former triangle. Find the position of A' when it is the centre of gravity of the area between the two triangles.

16. Two triangles, each $\frac{1}{m}$th of the whole, are cut off from a given triangle at two of its angular points, B and C, by straight lines parallel to the opposite sides; find the C.G. of remainder.

17. Out of a square plate show how to cut a triangle, having one side of the square for base, so that the remainder may have its centre of gravity at the vertex of this triangle and therefore rest in any position if this point is supported.

18. A uniform plate of metal, 10 cm square has a hole of area 3 square cm cut out of it, the centre of the hole being $2\frac{1}{2}$ cm from the centre of the plate; find the position of the centre of gravity of the remainder of the plate.

19. Where must a circular hole, of 1 metre radius, be punched out of a circular disc, of 3 metres radius, so that the centre of gravity of the remainder may be $\frac{1}{6}$ metre from the centre of the disc?

20. Two spheres, of radii a and b, touch internally; find the centre of gravity of the solid included between them.

21. If a right cone is cut by a plane bisecting its axis at right angles, find the distance of the vertex of the cone from the centre of gravity of the frustum thus cut off.

22. A solid right circular cone of homogeneous iron, of height 128 cm and mass 4096 kg, is cut by a plane perpendicular to its axis so that the mass of the small cone removed is 343 kg. Find the height of the centre of gravity of the truncated portion above the base of the cone.

23. A solid right circular cone has its base scooped out, so that the hollow is a right cone on the same base; how much must be scooped out so that the centre of gravity of the remainder may coincide with the vertex of the hollow?

24. The mass of the moon is 0.013 times that of the earth. Taking the earth's radius as 6400 km and the distance of the moon's centre from the earth's centre as 60 times the earth's radius, find the distance of the C.G. of the earth and moon from the centre of the earth.

117. Centre of gravity of a hemisphere.

If a hemisphere is of radius r, the centre of gravity lies on that radius which is perpendicular to its plane face, and is at a distance $\frac{3r}{8}$ from the centre of the plane face. If the hemisphere is hollow, the distance is $\frac{r}{2}$. The proofs of these statements are difficult by elementary methods; they will be found in the last chapter.

118. *To find the centre of gravity of a quadrilateral lamina having two parallel sides.*

Let *ABCD* be the quadrilateral, having the sides *AB* and *CD* parallel and equal to $2a$ and $2b$ respectively.

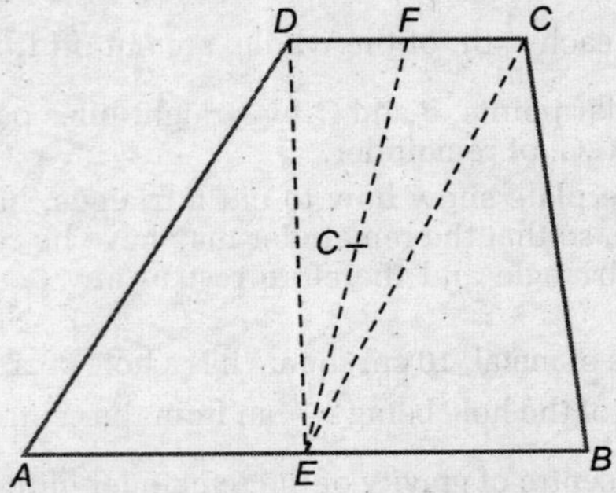

Let *E* and *F* be the middle points of *AB* and *CD* respectively. Join *DE* and *EC*; the areas of the triangles *ADE*, *DEC*, and *BEC* are proportional to their bases *AE*, *DC*, and *EB*, *i.e.*, are proportional to a, $2b$, and a.

Replace them by particles equal to one-third of their weight placed at their angular points (Art. 104).

We thus have weights proportional to

$$\frac{a}{3}+\frac{2b}{3} \text{ at each of } C \text{ and } D,$$

$$\frac{a}{3} \text{ at each of } A \text{ and } B,$$

and

$$\frac{2a}{3}+\frac{2b}{3} \text{ at } E.$$

Again, replace the equal weights at *C* and *D* by a weight proportional to $\frac{2a}{3}+\frac{4b}{3}$ at the middle point *F* of *CD*, and the equal weights at *A* and *B* by a weight proportional to $\frac{2a}{3}$ at *E*.

We thus have weights

$$\frac{2a}{3}+\frac{4b}{3} \text{ at } F,$$

and

$$\frac{4a}{3}+\frac{2b}{3} \text{ at } E.$$

Hence the required centre of gravity *G* is on the straight line *EF*, and is such that

$$\frac{EG}{GF}=\frac{\text{weight at } F}{\text{weight at } E}$$

$$=\frac{a+2b}{2a+b}.$$

Examples XX

1. A triangular table rests on supports at its vertices; weights of 6, 8, and 10 kg are placed at the middle points of the sides. Find by how much the pressures on the legs are increased thereby.
2. A piece of thin uniform wire is bent into the form of a four-sided figure, *ABCD*, of which the sides *AB* and *CD* are parallel, and *BC* and *DA* are equally inclined to *AB*. If *AB* is 36 cm, *CD* 24 cm, and *BC* and *DA* each 10 cm, find the distance from *AB* of the centre of gravity of the wire.
3. *AB*, *BC*, and *CD* are three equal uniform rods firmly joined, so as to form three successive sides of a regular hexagon, and are suspended from the point *A*; show that *CD* is horizontal.
4. *ABC* is a piece of uniform wire; its two parts *AB* and *BC* are straight, and the angle *ABC* is 135°. It is suspended from a fixed point by a string attached to the wire at *B*, and the part *AB* is observed to be horizontal. Show that *BC* is to *AB* as 92 to 1.
5. A rod, of length $5a$, is bent so as to form five sides of a regular hexagon; show that the distance of its centre of gravity from either end of the rod is $\frac{a}{10}\sqrt{133}$.
6. The side *CD* of a uniform trapezoidal lamina *ABCD* is twice as long as *AB*, to which it is opposite and parallel ; compare the distances of the centre of gravity of *ABCD* from *AB* and *CD*.
7. If the centre of gravity of a quadrilateral lamina *ABCD* coincides with one of the angles *A*, show that the distances of *A* and *C* from the line *BD* are as 1 : 2.
8. A uniform quadrilateral *ABCD* has the sides *AB* and *AD*, and the diagonal *AC* all equal, and the angles *BAC* and *CAD* are 30° and 60° respectively. If a weight, equal to two-thirds that of the triangle *ABC*, is attached at the point *B*, and the whole rests suspended from the point *A*, show that the diagonal *AC* will be vertical.
9. Explain what will take place when 3 forces, represented by *AB*, *BC*, and *CA* respectively, act along the sides of a triangular board *ABC* which is supported on a smooth peg passing through its centre of gravity.
10. Three forces act at a point *O* in the plane of a triangle *ABC*, being represented by *OA*, *OB* and *OC*; where must be the point *O* so that the three forces may be in equilibrium?
11. A particle *P* is attracted to three points *A*, *B*, *C* by forces equal to $\mu.PB$, $\mu.PB$ and $\mu.PC$ respectively; show that the resultant is $3\mu.PG$, where *G* is the centre of gravity of the triangle *ABC*.
12. A particle *P* is acted upon by forces towards the points *A*, *B*, *C*, ... which are represented by $\lambda.PA$, $\mu.PB$, $\nu.PC$,...; show that their resultant is represented by $(\lambda + \mu + \nu + ...)PG$, where *G* is the centre of gravity of weights placed at *A*, *B*, *C*,... proportional to λ, μ, ν,... respectively.

   [This is the generalized form of Art. 42, and may be proved by successive applications of that article.]
13. A uniform rod is hung up by two strings attached to its ends, the other ends of the strings being attached to a fixed point; show that the tensions of the strings are proportional to their lengths.

Prove that the same relation holds for a uniform triangular lamina hung up by three strings attached to its angular points.

14. Find the vertical angle of a cone in order that the centre of gravity of its whole surface, including its plane base, may coincide with the centre of gravity of its volume.

15. A cylinder and a cone have their bases joined together,the bases being of the same size; find the ratio of the height of the cone to the height of the cylinder so that the common centre of gravity may be at the centre of the common base.

16. Show how to cut out of a uniform cylinder a cone, whose base coincides with that of the cylinder, so that the centre of gravity of the remaining solid may coincide with the vertex of the cone.

17. If the diameter of the base of a cone is to its altitude as $1:\sqrt{2}$; show that, when the greatest possible sphere has been cut out, the centre of gravity of the remainder coincides with that of the cone.

18. From a uniform right cone, whose vertical angle is $60°$, is cut out the greatest possible sphere; show that the centre of gravity of the remainder divides the axis in the ratio $11:49$.

19. A solid in the form of a right circular cone has its base scooped out, so that the hollow so formed is a right circular cone on the same base and of half the height of the original cone; find the position of the centre of gravity of the cone so formed.

20. A uniform equilateral triangle *ABC* is supported with the angle *A* in contact with a smooth wall by means of a string *BD*, equal in length to a side of the triangle, which is fastened to a point *D* vertically above *A*. Show that the distances of *B* and *C* from the wall are as $1:5$

21. A cone, whose height is equal to four timers the radius of its base, is hung from a point in the circumference of its base; show that it will rest with its base and axis equally inclined to the vertical.

22. Two right cones, consisting of the same material, have equal slant slides and vertical angles of $60°$ and $120°$ respectively, and are so joined that they have a slant side coincident. Show that, if they are suspended from their common vertex, the line of contact will be inclined at $15°$ to the vertical.

23. A triangular piece of paper is folded across the line bisecting two sides, the vertex being thus brought to lie on the base of the triangle. Show that the distance of the centre of inertia of the paper in this position from the base of the triangle is three-quarters that of the centre of inertia of the unfolded paper from the same line.

24. A rectangular sheet of stiff paper, whose length is to its breadth as $\sqrt{2}$ to 1, lies on a horizontal table with its longer sides perpendicular to the edge and projecting over it. The corners on the table are then doubled over symmetrically, so that the creases pass through the middle point of the side joining the corners and make angles of $45°$ with it. The paper is now on the point of falling over; show that it had originally as of its length on the table.

25. At each of $n-1$ of the angular points of a regular polygon of n sides a particle is placed, the particles being equal; show that the distance of their centre of gravity from the centre of the circle circumscribing the polygon is $\frac{r}{n-1}$, where r is the radius of the circle.

26. A square hole is punched out of a circular lamina, the diagonal of the square being a radius of the circle. Show that the centre of gravity of the remainder is at a distance $\frac{a}{8\pi - 4}$ from the centre of the circle, where a is the diameter of the circle.

27. From a uniform, triangular board a portion consisting of the area of the inscribed circle is removed; show that the distance of the centre of gravity of the remainder from any side, a, is

$$\frac{S}{3as}\,\frac{2s^3 - 3\pi aS}{s^2 - \pi S},$$

where S is the area and s the semiperimeter of the board.

28. A circular hole of a given size is punched out of a uniform circular plate; show that the centre of gravity lies within a certain circle.

29. *The distances of the angular points and intersection of the diagonals of a plane quadrilateral lamina from any line in its plane are a, b, c, d, and e; show that the distance of the centre of inertia from the same line is* $\frac{1}{3}(a + b + c + d - e)$.

Let A, B, C, D be the angular points, and E the intersection of the diagonals. Then

$$\frac{\Delta ACD}{\Delta ACB} = \frac{\text{perpendicular from } D \text{ on } AC}{\text{perpendicular from } B \text{ on } AC} = \frac{DE}{EB} = \frac{d-e}{e-b}.$$

By Arts. 104 and 111 the distance of the centre of gravity of the ΔACD from OX is $\frac{a+c+d}{3}$ and that of the ΔACB is $\frac{a+c+b}{3}$.

Hence distance of required C.G. from OX

$$= \frac{\Delta ACD \times \frac{1}{3}(a+c+d) + \Delta ACB \times \frac{1}{3}(a+b+c)}{\Delta ACD + \Delta ACB}$$

$$= \frac{1}{3}\,\frac{(d-e)(a+c+d) + (e-b)(a+b+c)}{(d-e)+(e-b)}$$

$$= \frac{1}{3}(a+b+c+d-e), \text{ on reduction.}$$

30. If A and B are the positions of two masses, m and n, and if G is their centre of gravity, show that, if P is any point, then

$$m\,.\,AP^2 + n\,.\,BP^2 = m\,.\,AG^2 + n\,.\,BG^2 + (m+n)\,PG^2.$$

Similarly, if there are any number of masses, $m, n, p,\ldots$ at points $A, B, C,\ldots$, and G is their centre of gravity, show that

$$m\,.\,AP^2 + n\,.\,BP^2 + p\,.\,CP^2 + \ldots$$
$$= m\,.\,AG^2 + n\,.\,BG^2 + p\,.\,CG^2 + \ldots + (m+n+p\ldots)\,PG^2.$$

10

Centre of Gravity (Continued)

119. *If a rigid body is in equilibrium, one point only of the body being fixed, the centre of gravity of the body will be in the vertical line passing through the fixed point of the body.*

Let O be the fixed point of the body, and G its centre of gravity.

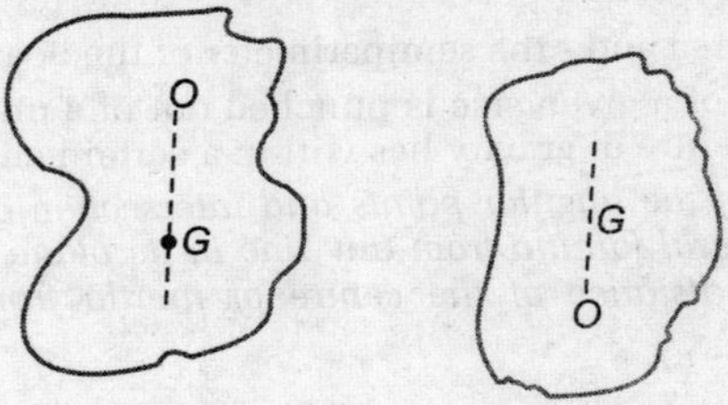

The forces acting on the body are the reaction at the fixed point of support of the body, and the weights of the component parts of the body.

The weights of these component parts are equivalent to a single vertical force through the centre of gravity of the body.

Also, when two forces keep a body in equilibrium, they must be equal and opposite and have the same line of action. But the lines of action cannot be the same unless the vertical line through G passes through the point O.

Two cases arise; the first, in which the centre of gravity G is below the point of suspension O, and the second, in which G is above O.

In the first case, the body, if slightly displaced from its position of equilibrium, will tend to return to this position; in the second case, the body will not tend to return to its position of equilibrium.

120. *To find, by experiment, the centre of gravity of a body of any shape.*

Take a flat piece of cardboard of any shape. Bore several small holes $A, B, C, D, \ldots$ in it of a size just large enough to freely admit of the insertion of a small pin.

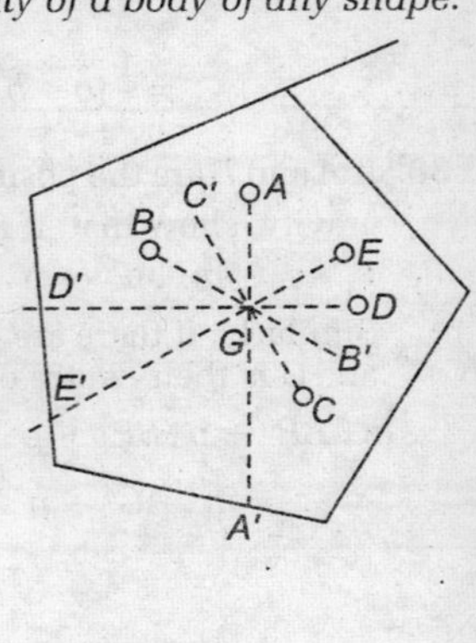

Hang up the cardboard by the hole A and allow it to hang freely and come to rest. Mark on the card-board the line AA' which is now vertical. This may be done by hanging from the pin a fine piece of string with a small plummet of lead at the other end, the string having first been well rubbed with chalk. If the string is now flipped against the cardboard it will leave a chalked line, which is AA'. Now hang up the cardboard with the hole B on the pin, and mark in a similar manner the line BB' which is now vertical.

Perform the experiment again with the points C, D, E as the points through which the small pin passes, and obtain the corresponding vertical lines CC', DD', EE'.

These chalked lines AA', BB', CC', DD', EE' will all be found to pass through the same point G. If the thickness of the cardboard is neglected, this point G is its centre of gravity. If the pin is now passed through G, the cardboard will be found to rest in any position in which it is placed.

121. *If a body is placed with its base in contact with a horizontal plane, it will stand, or fall, according as the vertical line drawn through the centre of gravity of the body meets the plane within, or outside, the base.*

The forces acting on the body are its weights, which act at its centre of gravity G, and the reactions of the plane,

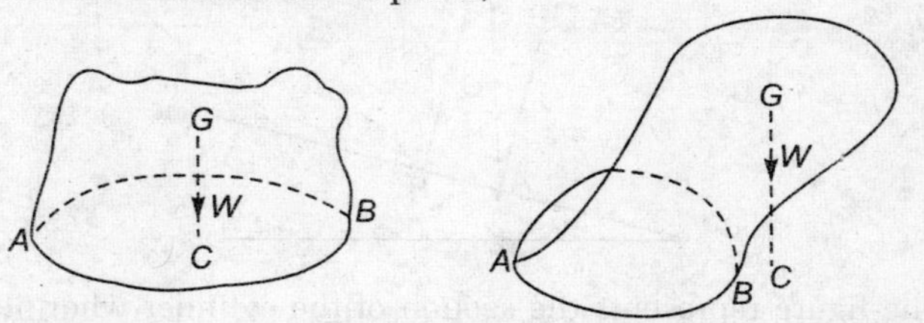

acting at different points of the base of the body. These reactions are all vertical, and hence they may be compounded into a single vertical force acting at some point of the base.

Since the resultant of two *like* parallel forces acts always at a point *between* the forces, it follows that the resultant of all the reactions on the base of the body cannot act through a point *outside* the base.

Hence, if the vertical line through the centre of gravity of the body meets the plane at a point outside the base, it cannot be balanced by the resultant reaction, and the body cannot therefore be in equilibrium, but must fall over.

If the base of the body is a figure having a re-entrant angle, as in the above figure. we must extend the

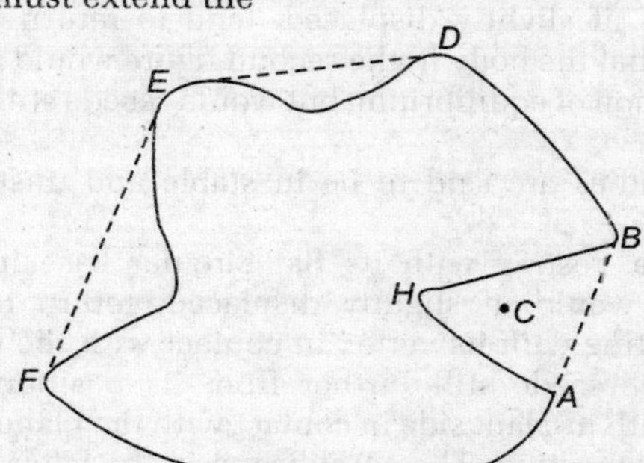

meaning of the word 'base' in the enunciation to mean the area included in the figure obtained by drawing a piece of thread tightly round the geometrical base. In the given figure the 'base' therefore means the area *ABDEFA*.

For example, the point *C*, at which the resultant reaction acts, may lie within the area *AHB*, but it cannot lie outside the dotted line *AB*.

If the point *C* were on the line *AB*, between *A* and *B*, the body would be on the point of falling over.

Ex. *A cylinder, of height h, and the radius of whose base is r, is placed on an inclined plane and prevented from sliding; If the inclination of the plane is gradually increased, find when the cylinder will topple.*

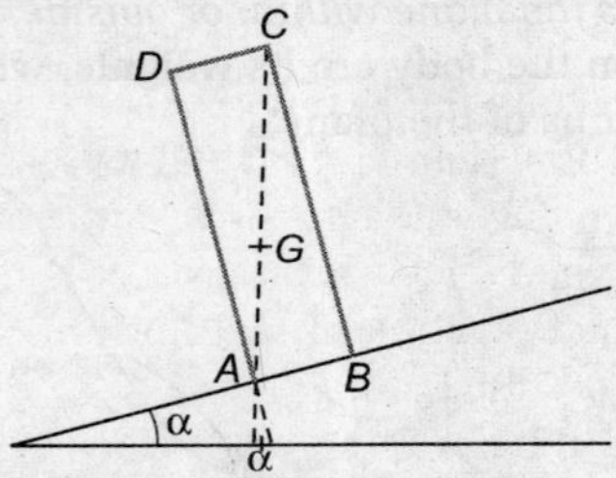

Let the figure represents the section of the cylinder when it is on the point of toppling over; the vertical line through the centre of gravity *G* of the body must therefore just pass through the end *A* of the base. Hence *CAD* must be equal to the angle of inclination, α, of the plane.

Hence $$\frac{h}{2r} = \frac{CB}{AB} = \tan CAB = \cot \alpha;$$

$$\therefore \qquad \tan \alpha = \frac{2r}{h},$$

giving the required inclination of the plane.

Stable, unstable, and neutral equilibrium.

122. We have pointed out in Art. 119 that the body in the first figure of that article would, if slightly displaced, tend to return to its position of equilibrium, and that the body in the second figure would not tend to return to its original position of equilibrium, but would recede still further from that position.

These two bodies are said to be in stable and unstable equilibrium respectively.

Again, a cone, resting with its flat circular base in contact with a horizontal plane, would, if slightly displaced, return to its position of equilibrium; if resting with its vertex in contact with the plane it would, if slightly displaced, recede still further from its position of equilibrium; whilst, if placed with its slant side in contact with the plane, it will remain in equilibrium in any position. The equilibrium in the latter case is said to be neutral.

123. Consider, again, the case of a heavy sphere, resting on a horizontal plane, whose centre of gravity is not at its centre.

Let the first figure represents the position of equilibrium, the centre of gravity being either below the centre O, as G_1,

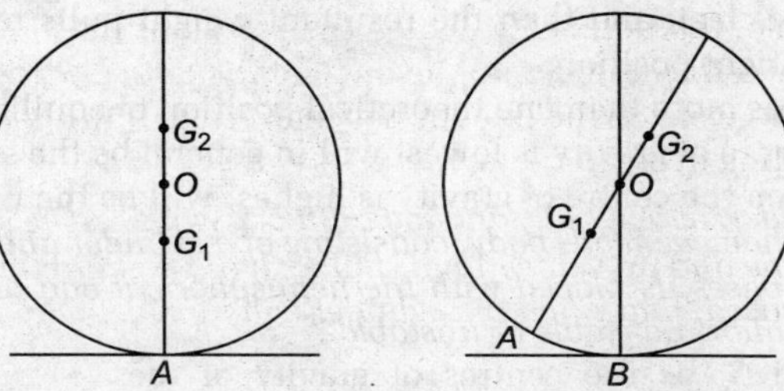

or above, as G_2. Let the second figure represents the sphere turned through a small angle, so that B is now the point of contact with the plane.

The reaction of the plane still acts through the centre of the sphere.

If the weight of the body acts through G_1, it is clear that the body will return towards its original position of equilibrium, and therefore the body was originally in stable equilibrium.

If the weight acts through G_2, the body will move still further from its original position of equilibrium, and therefore it was originally in unstable equilibrium.

If however the centre of gravity of the body had been at O, then, in the case of the second figure, the weight would still be balanced by the reaction of the plane; the body would thus remain in the new position, and the equilibrium would be called neutral.

124. Def. A body is said to be in **stable** equilibrium when, if it is slightly displaced from its position of equilibrium, the forces acting on the body tend to make it return towards its position of equilibrium, it is in **unstable** equilibrium when, if it is slightly displaced, the forces tend to move it still further from its position of equilibrium; it is in **neutral** equilibrium, if the forces acting on it in its displaced position are in equilibrium.

In general bodies which are 'top-heavy,' or which have small bases, are unstable.

Thus in theory a pin might be placed upright with its point on a horizontal table so as to be in equilibrium; in practice the 'base' would be so small that the slightest displacement would bring the vertical through its centre of gravity outside its base and it would fall. So with a billiard cue placed vertically with its end on the table.

A body is, as a general principle, in a stable position of equilibrium when the centre of gravity is in the lowest position it can take up; examples are the case of the last article, and the pendulum of a clock; the latter when displaced always returns towards its position of rest.

Consider again the case of a man walking on a tight rope. He always carries a pole heavily weighted at one end, so that the centre of gravity of himself and the pole is always below his feet. When he feels himself falling in one direction, he shifts his pole so that this centre of gravity shall be on the other side of his feet, and then the resultant weight pulls him back again towards the upright position.

If a body has more than one theoretical position of equilibrium, the one in which its centre of gravity is lowest will in general be the stable position, ant that in which the centre of gravity is highest will be the unstable one.

125. Ex. *A homogeneous body, consisting of a cylinder and a hemisphere joined at their bases, is placed with the hemispherical end on a horizontal table; is the equilibrium stable or unstable ?*

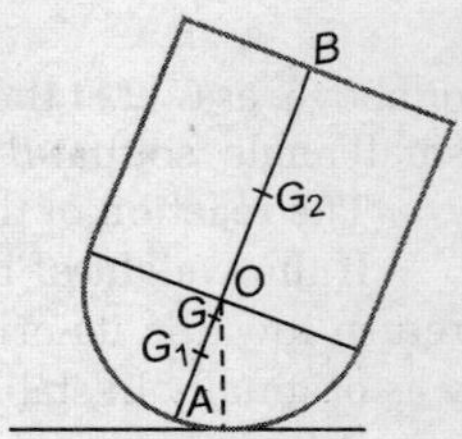

Let G_1 and G_2 be the centres of gravity of the hemisphere and cylinder, and let A be the point of the body which is initially in contact with the table, and let O be the centre of the base of the hemisphere.

If h is the height of the cylinder, and r the radius of the base, we have

$$OG_1 = \frac{2}{3}r, \text{ and } OG_2 = \frac{h}{2} \text{ (Art. 117).}$$

Also the weights of the hemisphere and cylinder are proportional to $\frac{2}{3}\pi r^3$ and $\pi . r^2 h$.

The reaction of the plane, in the displaced position of the body, always passes through the centre O.

The equilibrium is stable or unstable according as G, the centre of gravity of the compound body, is below or above O,

i.e., according as

$$OG_1 \times \text{wt. of hemisphere is } \overset{<}{>} OG_2 \times \text{wt. of cylinder,}$$

i.e., according as $\frac{2}{3}r \times \frac{2}{3}\pi r^3$ is $\frac{>h}{<2} \times \pi r^2 h$,

i.e., according as $\frac{r^2}{2}$ is $\overset{<}{>} h^2$,

i.e., according as r is $\overset{<}{>} \sqrt{2}h$,

i.e., $\overset{<}{>} h \times 1\cdot 42\ldots$

****126.** Within the limits of this book we cannot enter into the general discussion of the equilibrium of one body resting on another; in the following article we shall discuss the case in which the portions of the two bodies in contact are spherical.

A body rests in equilibrium upon another fixed body, the portions of the two bodies in contact being spheres of radii r and R respectively; if the first body is slightly displaced, to find whether the equilibrium is stable or unstable, the bodies being rough enough to prevent sliding.

Let O be the centre of the spherical surface of the lower body, and O_1 that of the upper body; since there is equilibrium, the centre of gravity G_1 of the upper body must be in the line OO_1, which passes through the point of contact A_1 of the bodies.

Let A_1G_1 be h.

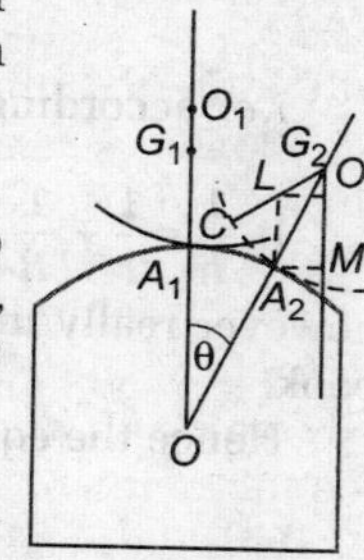

Let the upper body be slightly displaced, by rolling, so that the new position of the centre of the upper body is O_2, the new point of contact is A_2, the new position of the centre of gravity is G_2, and the new position of the point A_1 is C. Hence CG_2 is h.

Through A_2 draw A_2L vertically to meet O_2C in L, and draw O_2M vertically downwards to meet a horizontal line through A_2 in M.

Let the angle A_2OA_1 be θ, and let A_2O_2C be ϕ, so that the angle CO_2M is $(\theta + \phi)$.

Since the upper body has rolled into its new position, the arc A_1A_2 is equal to the arc CA_2.

Hence (*Elements* of *Trigonometry*, Art. 158) we have

$$R \cdot \theta = r \cdot \phi \qquad \text{... (1)}$$

where r and R are respectively the radii of the upper and lower surfaces.

The equilibrium is stable, or unstable, according as G, lies to the left, or right, of the line A_2L,

i.e., according as the distance of G_2 from O_2M is

> or < the distance of L, from O_2M, *i.e.*, A_2M,

i.e., according as

$$O_2G_2 \sin(\theta + \phi) \text{ is } > \text{ or } < O_2A_2 \sin\theta,$$

i.e., according as

$$(r - h)\sin(\theta + \phi) \text{ is } > \text{ or } < r\sin\theta,$$

i.e., according as

$$\frac{r-h}{r} \text{ is } > \text{ or } < \frac{\sin\theta}{\sin(\theta+\phi)}.$$

But

$$\frac{\sin\theta}{\sin(\theta+\phi)} = \frac{\theta}{\theta+\phi},$$

since θ and ϕ are both very small,

$$= \frac{r}{r+R}, \text{ by equation (1).}$$

Hence the equilibrium is stable, or unstable, according as

$$\frac{r-h}{r} \text{ is } > \text{ or } < \frac{r}{r+R},$$

i.e., according as $\quad r - \dfrac{r^2}{r+R}$ is > or < h,

i.e., according as

$$\frac{Rr}{r+R} \text{ is } > \text{ or } < h,$$

i.e., according as $\quad \dfrac{1}{h}$ is > or < $\dfrac{1}{r} + \dfrac{1}{R}$.

If $\dfrac{1}{h} = \dfrac{1}{r} + \dfrac{1}{R}$, the equilibrium is sometimes said to be neutral; it is however really unstable, but the investigation is beyond the limits of this book.

Hence the equilibrium is stable only when

$$\frac{1}{h} \text{ is } > \frac{1}{r} + \frac{1}{R};$$

in all other cases it is unstable.

Cor. 1. If the surface of the lower body, instead of being convex, as in the above figure, is concave, as in the following figure, the above investigation will still apply provided we change the sign of R.

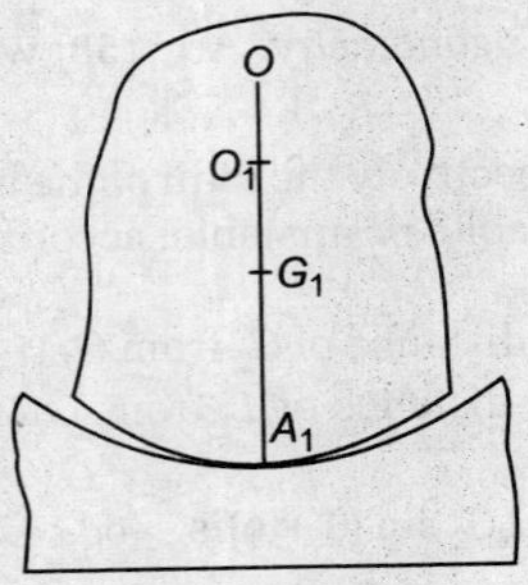

Hence the equilibrium is stable when

$$\frac{1}{h} \text{ is } > \frac{1}{r} - \frac{1}{R};$$

otherwise it is, in general, unstable.

Cor. 2. If the upper body has a plane face in contact with the lower body, as in the following figure, r is now infinite in value, and therefore $\dfrac{1}{r}$ is zero.

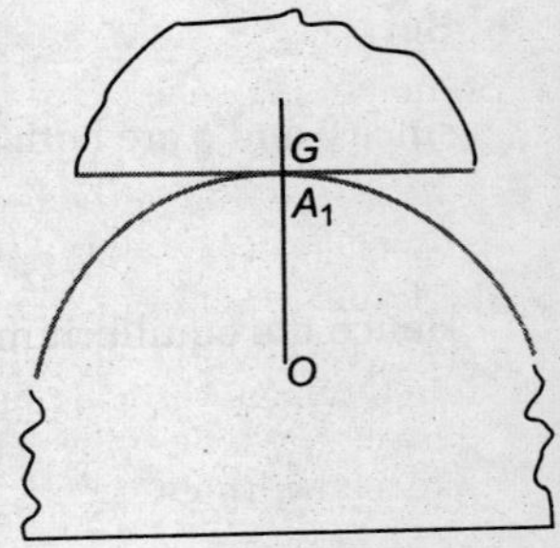

Hence the equilibrium is stable if

$$\frac{1}{h} \text{ is } > \frac{1}{R};$$

i.e., $\quad h$ is < R.

Hence the equilibrium is stable, if the distance of the centre of gravity of the upper body from its plane face is less than the radius of the lower body; otherwise the equilibrium is unstable.

Cor. 3. If the lower body is a plane, so that R is infinity, the equilibrium is stable if

$$\frac{1}{h} \text{ is } > \frac{1}{r}, i.e., \text{if } h \text{ is } < r.$$

Hence if a body of spherical base is placed on a horizontal table, it is in stable equilibrium, if the distance of its centre of gravity from the point of contact is less than the radius of the spherical surface.

Examples XXI

1. A carpenter's rule, 60 cm in length, is bent into two parts at right angles to one another, the length of the shorter portion being 20 cm. If the shorter is placed on a smooth horizontal table, what is the length of the least portion on the table that there may be equilibrium?
2. A piece of metal, 18 cubic cm in volume, is made into a cylinder which rests with its base on an inclined plane, of $30°$ slope, and is prevented from slipping. How tall may the cylinder be made so that it may just not topple over ?
3. If a triangular lamina ABC can just rest in a vertical plane with its edge AB in contact with a smooth table, prove that
$$BC^2 \sim AC^2 = 3AB^2.$$
4. The side CD of a uniform square plate $ABCD$, whose weight is W, is bisected at E and the triangle AED is cut off. The plate $ABCEA$ is placed in a vertical position with the side CE on a horizontal plane. What is the greatest weight that can be placed at A without upsetting the plate ?
5. ABC is a flat board, A being a right angle and AC in contact with a flat table; D is the middle point of AC and the triangle ABD is cut away; show that the triangle is just on the point of falling over.
6. A brick is laid with one-quarter of its length projecting over the edge of a wall; a brick and one-quarter of a brick are then laid on the first with one-quarter of a brick projecting over the edge of the first brick; a brick and a half are laid on this, and so on; show that 4 courses of brick laid in the above manner will be in equilibrium without the aid of mortar, but that, if a fifth course is added, the structure will topple.
7. How many coins, of the same size and having their thicknesses equal to $\frac{1}{50}$th of their diameters, can stand in a cylindrical pile on an inclined plane, whose height is one-sixth of the base, assuming that there is no slipping?
If the edge of each coin overlaps on one side that of the coin below, find by what fraction of the diameter each must overlap so that a pile of unlimited height may stand on the plane.
8. A number of bricks, each 9 cm long, 4 cm wide, and 3 cm thick, are placed one on another so that, whilst their narrowest surfaces, or thicknesses, are in the same vertical plane, each brick overlaps the one underneath it by half a cm; the lowest brick being placed on a table, how many bricks can be so placed without their falling over?

9. ABC is an isosceles triangle, of weights, W, of which the angle A is $120°$, and the side AB rests on a smooth horizontal table, the plane of the triangle being vertical; if a weight $W/3$ is hung on at C, show that the triangle will just be on the point of toppling over.
10. The quadrilateral lamina $ABCD$ is formed of two uniform isosceles triangles ABC and ADC, whose vertices are B and D, on opposite sides of a common base AC, the angle ABC being a right angle. Show that it will rest in a vertical plane with BC on a horizontal plane, provided the area of ADC is not greater than four times that of ABC.
11. A body, consisting of a cone and a hemisphere on the same base, rests on a rough horizontal table, the hemisphere being in contact with the table; find the greatest height of the cone so that the equilibrium may be stable.
12. A solid consists of a cylinder and a hemisphere of equal radius, fixed base to base; find the ratio of the height to the radius of the cylinder, so that the equilibrium may be neutral when the spherical surface rests on a horizontal plane.
13. A hemisphere rests in equilibrium on a sphere of equal radius; show that the equilibrium is unstable when the curved, and stable when the flat, surface of the hemisphere rests on the sphere.
14. A heavy right come rests with its base on a fixed rough sphere of given radius; find the greatest height of the cone if it is in stable equilibrium.
15. A uniform beam, of thickness $2b$, rests symmetrically on a perfectly rough horizontal cylinder of radius a; show that the equilibrium of the beam will be stable or unstable according as b is less or greater than a.
16. A heavy uniform the cube balances on the highest point of a sphere, whose radius is r. If the sphere is rough enough to prevent sliding, and if the side of the cube is $\pi r/2$, show that the cube can rock through a right angle without falling.
17. A lamina in the form of an isosceles triangle, whose vertical angle is α, is placed on a sphere, of radius r, so that its plane is vertical and one of its equal sides is in contact with the sphere; show that, if the triangle is slightly displaced in its own plane, the equilibrium is stable if $\sin\alpha$ is less than $3r/a$, where a is one of the equal sides of the triangle.
18. A weight W is supported on a smooth inclined plane by a given weight P, connected with W by means of a string passing round a fixed pulley whose position is given. Find the position of W on the plane, and determine whether the position is stable or unstable.
19. A rough uniform circular disc, of radius r and weight p, is movable about a point distance c from its centre. A string, rough enough to prevent any slipping, hangs over the circumference and carries unequal weights W and w at its ends. Find the position of equilibrium, and determine whether it is stable or unstable.
20. A solid sphere rests inside a fixed rough hemispherical bowl of twice its radius. Show that, however large a weight is attached to the highest point of the sphere, the equilibrium is stable.
21. A thin hemispherical bowl, of radius b and weight W, rests in equilibrium on the highest point of a fixed sphere, of radius a, which is rough enough to prevent any sliding. Inside the bowl is placed a small smooth sphere of weight w. Show that the equilibrium is not stable unless

$$w < W \cdot \frac{a-b}{2b}.$$

11

Centre of Gravity (Continued)

The formulae of Art. 114 (a) may be used to give the centre of gravity of any arc, area or solid of known shape.

126 (a). *Centre of gravity of any arc*

If P is a point (x, y) on a plane arc, PQ an elementary arc ds, whose density at the point P is ρ and whose weight is therefore proportional to ρds, these formulae give

$$\bar{x} = \frac{\Sigma(\rho ds \cdot x)}{\Sigma(\rho \cdot ds)} = \frac{\int \rho x ds}{\int \rho ds},$$

the limits of the integrals extending from one end to the other.

Similarly, $$\bar{y} = \frac{\int \rho y ds}{\int \rho ds}.$$

Also $\dfrac{ds}{dx} = \sqrt{1 + \dfrac{(dy)^2}{dx}}$, and $\dfrac{dy}{dx}$ is known from the equation of the curve.

If, as is usually the case, the arc is of uniform density, ρ is constant and divides out from both numerator and denominator; if it is of variable density, then ρ must be given as a function of x or y.

126 (b). *Centre of gravity of any plane area.*

In Cartesian co-ordinates the element of area is $\delta x\, \delta y$, and if ρ is its density, the weight w is proportional to $\rho \delta x \delta y$; the fundamental formulae thus become

$$\bar{x} = \frac{\Sigma\, \rho \delta x \delta y \cdot x}{\Sigma\, \rho \delta x \delta y} = \frac{\iint \rho x\, dx\, dy}{\iint \rho\, dx\, dy}, \text{ and } \bar{y} = \frac{\iint \rho y\, dx\, dy}{\rho\, dxdy},$$

the limits being chosen so as to include all the areas considered.

126 (c). *Centre of gravity of a solid and surface of revolution.*

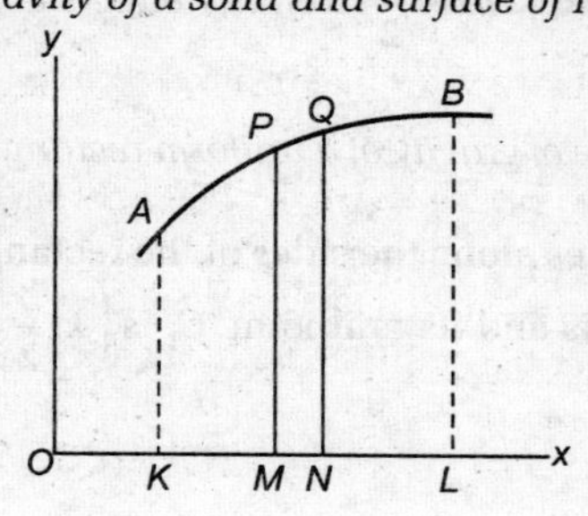

Let the curve AB revolve round the axis of x. The volume generated by the element of $PMNQ$ between two ordinates at distances x and $x + \delta x$ from Oy is $\pi y^2\, \delta x$, and its centre of gravity is at a distance x from O, when δx is indefinitely small.

Hence, if the solid is of uniform density,

$$\bar{x} = \frac{\Sigma \pi y^2\, \delta x\; x}{\Sigma \pi y^2\, \delta x} = \frac{\int y^2 x\, dx}{\int y^2\, dx};$$

where y is known in terms of x from the equation of the curve and the limits of x are OK and OL.

The surface generated by the revolution of the arc PQ $(= \delta s)$ about Ox is $2\pi y \cdot \delta s$. Hence, for the surface,

$$\bar{x} = \frac{\Sigma 2\pi \delta s\; x}{\Sigma 2\pi y\, \delta s} = \frac{\int yx\, dx}{\int y\, ds}$$

Now $\frac{ds}{dx}\left(= \sqrt{1 + \left(\frac{dy}{dx}\right)^2}\right)$ and y are known from the equation to the curve and hence the integration can be performed.

126 (d) *(i). Centre of gravity of a uniform thin rod of length a.*

Let us take the x-axis along AB, the rod, and the y-axis perpendicular to it. Let the co-ordinates of A, and B be $(0, 0)$, and $(a, 0)$ respectively. Taking an element $PQ = \delta x$ we get,

$$\bar{x} = \frac{\int_0^a x\, dx}{\int_0^a dx} = \frac{a}{2}$$

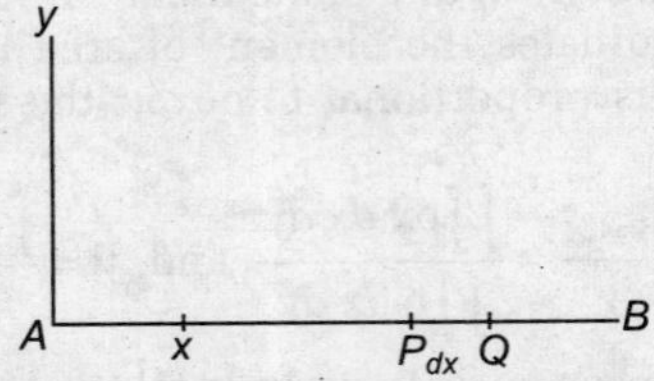

so the C.G. is at a distance $\frac{a}{2}$ from A, *i.e.*, it is at the midpoint of the rod.

Obviously, $\bar{y} = 0$.

126 (d) *(ii). Centre of gravity of a uniform rectangular lamina with sides of lengths a and b.*

Let us take the axes along the sides of the rectangle. The thin strip $PQRS$ is parallel to the y-axis and its midpoint, G_1 is $\left(x, \frac{b}{2}\right)$.

So we get,

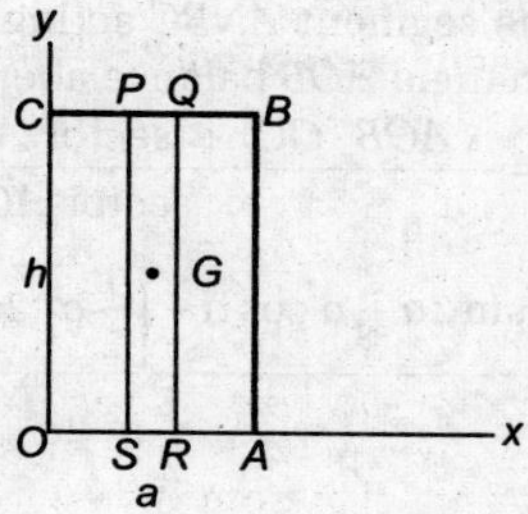

$$\bar{x} = \frac{\int_0^a xbdx}{\int_0^a bdx} = \frac{\frac{a^2b}{2}}{ba} = \frac{a}{2}.$$

and $$\bar{y} = \frac{\int_0^a \frac{b}{2} bdx}{\int_0^a bdx} = \frac{\frac{1}{2}ab^2}{ab} = \frac{b}{2}.$$

126 (d) *(iii). Centre of gravity of the arc, sector and segment of a circle.*

Let the arc ACB subtends an angle 2α at the centre O of the circle, and let C be the midpoint of the arc.

Taking OC as the x-axis, then for the arc

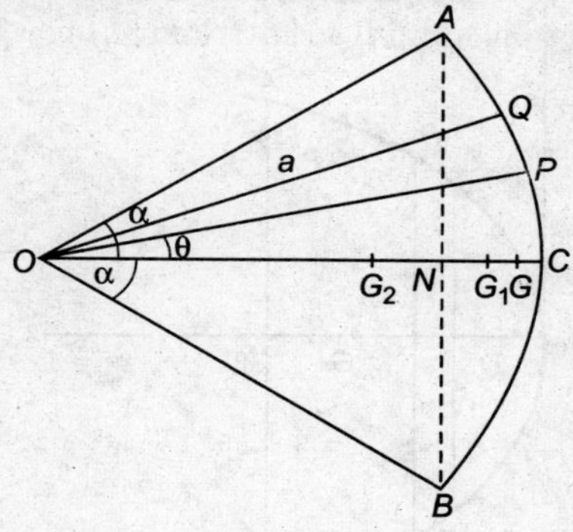

$$\bar{x} = \frac{\int dsx}{\int ds} = \frac{\int_{-a}^{a} ad\theta\, a\cos\theta}{\int_{-a}^{a} a\, d\theta} = a\,\frac{\sin a}{a}$$

For the sector AOB,

$$\bar{x} = \frac{\int_{-a}^{+a} \frac{1}{2} a^2\, d\theta\, \frac{2}{3}\, a\cos\theta}{\int_{-a}^{+a} -a^{+a}\, \frac{1}{2}\, a^2 d\theta} = \frac{2}{3}\, a\, \frac{\sin a}{a} = OG_1.$$

Let G_2 be the centre of gravity of the triangle AOB, so that

$$OG_2 = \frac{2}{3}\, ON = \frac{2}{3}\, a\cos a$$

Then the weight of the segment *ANBC* acting at its centre of gravity *G* together with that of the triangle *AOB* balance about G_1.

$$\frac{2}{3}a\frac{\sin a}{a} = OG_1 = \frac{\Delta\, AOB \cdot OG_2 + [\text{sector } AOB - \Delta\, AOB]\, OG}{\text{sector } AOB}$$

$$= \frac{\frac{1}{2}a^2 \sin 2a \frac{2}{3} a \cos a + \left[\frac{1}{2}a^2\, 2a - \frac{1}{2}a^2 \sin 2a\right] OG}{\frac{1}{2}a^2\, 2a}$$

This gives $OG = \dfrac{2a}{3} \cdot \dfrac{\sin^3 a}{a - \sin\cos a}$

N.B. In each of the above cases, by symmetry, the G.'s lie on *OC*.

Cor. By putting $a = \frac{\pi}{2}$, we see that the centre of gravity of the arc of a semicircle is distance $\frac{2a}{\pi}$ from the centre, and that the centre of gravity of a semi-circular arc is $\frac{4a}{3\pi}$ from the centre.

126 (d) *(iv). Centre of the gravity of a parabolic lamina bounded by a double ordinate.*

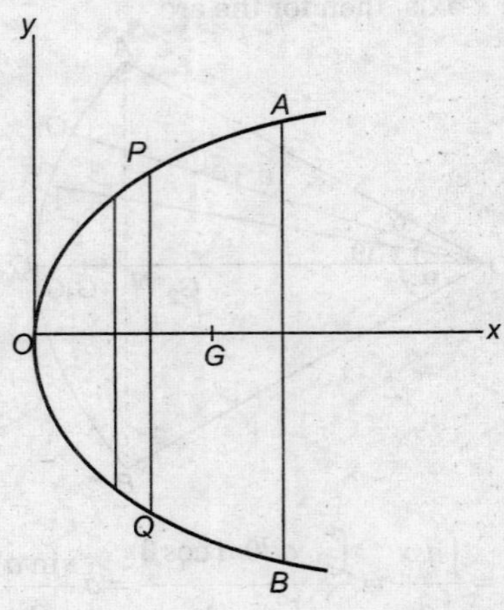

The parabolic lamina in the figure, *OAB*, is bounded by the parabola $y^2 = 4ax$ and the straight line $x = h$. Let us take a thin strip *PQ* (area *ds*) parallel to the *y*-axis. Obviously, the C.G. will lie on the *x*-axis.

Here

$$\bar{x} = \frac{\int x\,ds}{\int ds} = \frac{\int_0^h x\, 2y\,dx}{\int_0^h 2y\,dx} = \frac{2\int_0^h x\sqrt{4ax}\,dx}{2\int_0^h \sqrt{4ax}\,dx}$$

$$= \frac{\frac{8}{5}\sqrt{a}\, h^{5/2}}{\frac{8}{3}\sqrt{a}\, h^{3/2}} = \frac{3}{5}h.$$

126 (d) *(v). Centre of gravity of a uniform hemispherical shell.*

Let the hemisphere be of radius, with its centre O taken as the origin and axis of symmetry as the x-axis. We take a zonal strip $P'PQQ'$. Here, $P'P = Q'Q = r d\theta$. So the area of this strip $= 2\pi r \sin\theta . r d\theta = 2\pi r^2 \sin\theta\, d\theta$ and the distance of its C.G. from the origin is $X = r\cos\theta$. We then have,

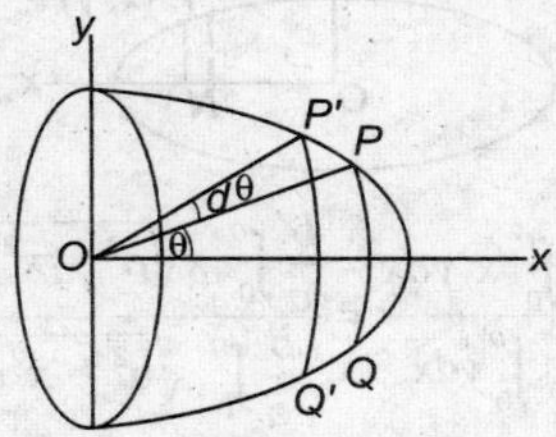

$$\bar{x} = \frac{\int_0^{\pi/2} (2\pi r^2 \sin\theta)(r\cos\theta) d\theta}{\int_0^{\pi/2} 2\pi r^2 \sin\theta\, d\theta} = \frac{\pi r^3}{2\pi r^2} = \frac{r}{2}.$$

126 (d) *(vi). Centre of gravity of a uniform solid hemisphere.*

Let the hemisphere be of radius r and let us choose its centre as origin and axis of symmetry as x-axis. Obviously, by symmetry, the C.G. lies on the x-axis and so $\bar{y} = 0$.

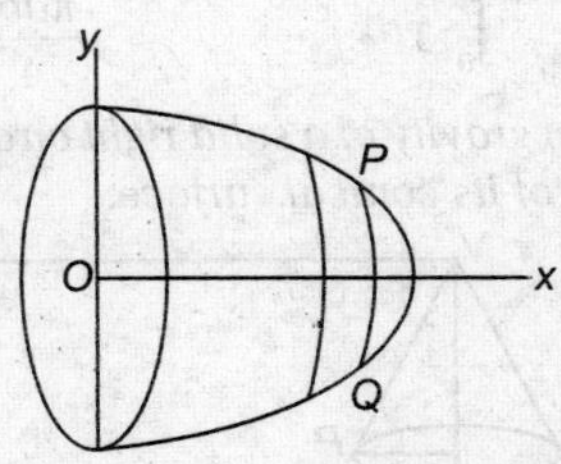

We take an element PQ, a thin circular plate of radius y and width dx.

So, $$\bar{x} = \frac{\int_0^r x\pi y^2\, dx}{\int_0^r \pi y^2\, dx} = \frac{\int_0^r x(r^2 - x^2)\, dx}{\int_0^r (r^2 - x^2)\, dx} = \frac{r^2 \cdot \frac{r^2}{2} - \frac{r^4}{4}}{r^3 - \frac{r^2}{3}}$$

$$= \frac{\frac{r^4}{4}}{\frac{2r^3}{3}} = \frac{3}{8} r$$

126 (d) *(vii) Centre of gravity of a quadrant of the ellipse*

$$\frac{x^2}{a^2} + \frac{y^2}{b^2} = 1.$$

We take a thin strip *PN* parallel to the *y*-axis. Its C.G. is at the mid-point of *PN*, with co-ordinates $\left(x, \frac{y}{2}\right)$. So we have,

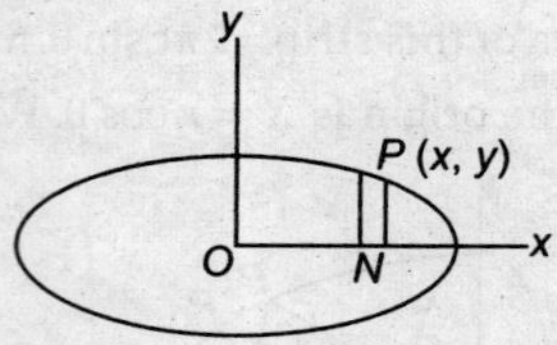

$$\bar{x} = \frac{\int_0^a x\,ydx}{\int_0^a ydx} = \frac{\frac{b}{a}\int_0^a x\sqrt{a^2 - x^2}\,dx}{\frac{b}{a}\int_0^a \sqrt{a^2 - x^2}dx}$$

Putting $x = a\sin\theta$,

$$\bar{x} = \frac{\int_0^{\pi/2} a^3\cos^2\theta\sin\theta d\theta}{\int_0^{\pi/2} a^2\cos^2\theta d\theta} = \frac{a^2b/3}{ab\pi/4} = \frac{4\,a}{3\,\pi},$$

Similarly,

$$\bar{y} = \frac{\int_0^a \frac{1}{2}y\,ydx}{\int_0^a ydx} = \frac{\frac{1}{2}\frac{b^2}{a^2}\int_0^a (a^2 - x^2)\,dx}{\frac{\pi ab}{4}} = \frac{\frac{1}{3}ab^2}{\frac{ab\pi}{4}} = \frac{4b}{3\pi}.$$

126 (d) *(viii). Centre of gravity of a solid right circular cone of height h and semi-vertical angle a, and of its conical surface.*

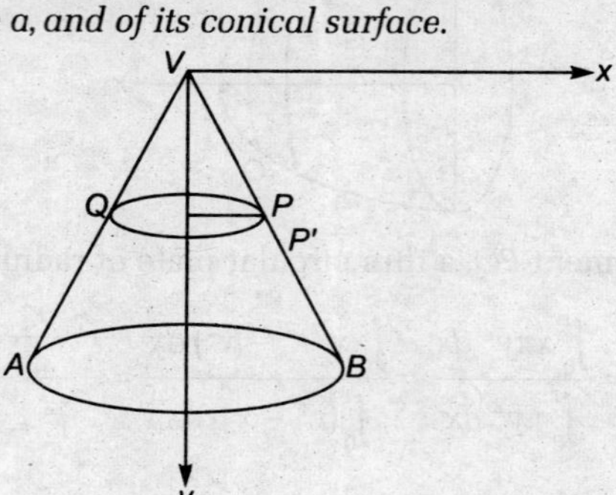

We choose the vertex *V* as the origin and the axis of the cone as *y*-axis.

Let *P*(*x*, *y*) be a point on the conical surface. The area of the elementary disc $PQ = \pi x^2 dy$. By symmetry, the C.G. will lie on the *y*-axis.

So,

$$\bar{y} = \frac{\int_0^k y\pi x^2\, dy}{\int_0^k \pi x^2\, dy} = \frac{\int_0^k \pi y^3 \tan^2 a\, dy}{\int_0^k \pi y^2 \tan^2 a\, dy}$$

$$= \frac{h^4/4}{h^3/3} = \frac{3}{4} h.$$

To find the C.G. of the conical surface, we consider a strip generated by revolving PP', an elementary length ds, about the y-axis. The area of the strip $= 2\pi x\, dx = 2\pi x \operatorname{cosec} a dy$. By symmetry, the C.G. lies on the y-axis. So we get,

$$\bar{y} = \frac{\int y\, 2\pi x\, ds}{\int 2\pi x\, ds} = \frac{2\pi \int_0^k y^2 \tan a \operatorname{cosec} a\, dy}{2\pi \int_0^k y \tan a \operatorname{cosec} a\, dy}$$

$$= \frac{2\pi \sec a \dfrac{h^3}{3}}{\pi \sec a\, h^2} = \frac{2}{3} h.$$

12

Work

127. Work Def. A force is said to do work when its point of application moves in the direction of the force.

The force exerted by a horse, in dragging a waggon, does work.

The force exerted by a man, in raising a weight, does work.

The pressure of the steam, in moving the piston of an engine, does work.

When a man winds up a watch or a clock he does work.

The measure of the work done by a force is the product of the force and the distance through which it moves its point of application in the direction of the force.

Suppose that a force acting at a point A of a body

moves the point A to D, then the work done by P is measured by the product of P and AD.

If the point D is on the side of A toward which the force acts, this work is positive; if D lie on the opposite side, the work is negative.

Next, suppose that the point of application of the force is moved to a point C, which does not lie on the line AB. Draw CD perpendicular to AB, or AB produced. Then AD is the distance through which the point of application is moved in the direction of the force. Hence in the first figure the work done is $P \times AD$; in the second figure the work done is $-P \times AD$. When

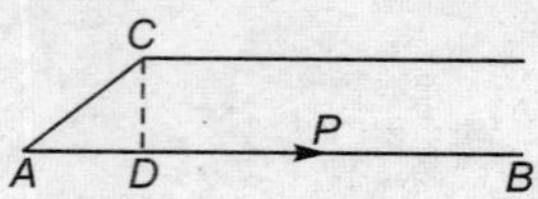

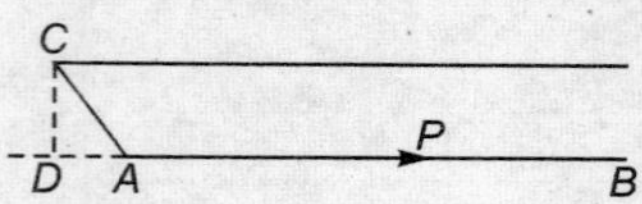

the work done by the force is negative, this is sometimes expressed by saying that the force has work done against it.

In the case when AC is at right angles to AB, the points A and D coincide, and the work done by the force P vanishes.

As an example, if a body is moved about on a horizontal table the work done by its weight is zero. So, again, if a body be moved on an inclined plane. no work is done by the normal reaction of the plane.

128. The gravitational units of work are called a foot-pound in F.P.S. system and a gramme-centimetre in C.G.S. system. A foot-pound is defined as the work done by a force, equal to the weight of a pound, when it moves its point of application through one foot in its own direction. A gramme-centimetre is defined as the work done by a force, equal to the weight of a gramme, when it moves its point of application through one centimetre in its own direction. The unit of work may also be measured in the absolute system. the absolute unit of work in F.P.S. system is a foot-poundal and is the work done by a force of one poundal, when it moves its point of application through one foot in its own direction. The absolute unit of work in C.G.S. system is an erg and is defined as the work done by a force of one dyne, when it moves its point of application through one centimetre in its own direction.

Since the gravitational units of force is g times the absolute unit of force,

$$1 \text{ foot-pound} = 32.2 \text{ foot-poundals}$$

$$1 \text{ gramme-centimetre} = 981 \text{ ergs.}$$

$$\text{Also } 1 \text{ joule (s)} = 10^7 \text{ ergs.}$$

Conversion of one system of unit to the other.

$$1 \text{ foot-poundal} = 4.2139 \times 10^5 \text{ ergs}$$

$$1 \text{ foot-pound} = 1.356 \times 10^7 \text{ ergs.}$$

129. It will be noticed that the definition of work, given in Art. 127, necessarily implies motion. A man may use great exertion in *attempting* to move a body, and yet does not work on the body.

For example, suppose a man pulls at the shafts of a heavily-loaded van, which he cannot move. He may pull to the utmost of his power, but, since the force which he exerts does not move its point of application, he does not work (in the technical sense of the word).

130. Theorem. *To show that the work done is raising a number of particles from one position to another is Wh, where W is the total weight of the particles, and h is the distance through which the centre of gravity of the particles has been raised.*

Let $w_1, w_2, w_3, \ldots w_n$ be the weights of the particles; in the initial position let $x_1, x_2, x_3, \ldots x_n$ be their heights above a horizontal plane, and $\bar{x}$ that of their centre of gravity, so that, as in Art. 111 or Art. 114(a), we have

$$\bar{x} = \frac{w_1 x_1 + w_2 x_2 + \ldots w_n x_n}{w_1 + w_2 + .. + w_n} \qquad \ldots(1)$$

In the final position let $x'_1, x'_2, \ldots x'_n$ be the heights of the different particles, and $\bar{x}'$ the height of the new centre of gravity, so that

$$\bar{x}' = \frac{w_1 x'_1 + w_2 x'_2 + \ldots w_n x'_n}{w_1 + w_2 + \ldots w_n} \qquad \ldots(2)$$

But, since $w_1 + w_2 + \ldots = W$, equations (1) and (2) give

$$w_1 x_1 + \ldots w_2 x_2 + \ldots = W \cdot \bar{x},$$

and

$$w_1 x'_1 + w_2 x'_2 + \ldots = W \cdot \bar{x}'.$$

By subtraction we have

$$w_1(x'_1 - x_1) + w_2(x'_2 - x_2) + \ldots = W(\bar{x}' - \bar{x}).$$

But the left-hand member of this equation gives the total work done in raising the different particles of the system from their initial position to their final position; also the right-hand side

$$= W \times \text{height through which the centre of gravity has been raised}$$
$$= W \cdot h$$

Hence the proposition is proved.

130 (a). When a number of forces acts upon a particle which undergoes a small displacement,the algebraical sum of the work done by the separate forces is equal to the work done by their resultant.

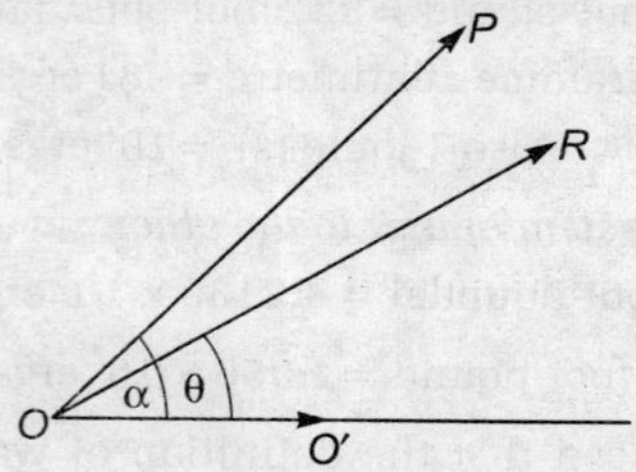

Let the particles at O be displaced to O'. We denote one of the forces acting at O by P and the resultant by R. Let the direction of P and R make angles θ and ϕ respectively with the displacement OO' of the particle.

Then the algebraical sum of the work done by the forces

$$= \Sigma P \cdot OO' \cos\theta$$
$$= OO' \, \Sigma P \cos\theta$$
$$= OO' \cdot R \cos\phi$$
$$= R \cdot OO' \cos\phi$$
$$= \text{work done by the resultant force.}$$

Cor. If $X, Y,$ and Z are the rectangular components of a force R acting on a particle which receives s small displacement dr along R, we have

$$X\,dx = Y\,dy + Z\,dz = R\,dr,$$

where dx, dy and dz are the components of dr along the co-ordinate axis.

131. Power. Def. *The power of an agent is the amount of work that would be done by the agent if working uniformly for the unit of time.*

The unit of power used by engineers is called is **horse-power.** An agent is said to be working with one horse-power when it performs 33,000 foot-pounds in a minute, *i.e.*, when it would raise 33,000 lb through a foot in a minute, or when it would raise 330 lb through 100 feet in a minute, or 33 lb through 1000 feet in a minute. The word horse-power is usually abbreviated into H.P.

The MKS unit of power is the watt (w) 1 watt = 1 joule/sec = 10^7 ergs/sec. A kilowatt (kw) is 1000 watts. 1 H.P. = $\frac{3}{4}$ kw.

132. It will be noted that the result of Art. 130 does not in any way depend on the initial of final arrangement of the particles amongst themselves, except in so far as the initial and final positions of the centre of gravity depend on these arrangements.

For example, a hole may be dug in the ground, the soil lifted out, and spread on the surface of the earth at the top of the hole. We only want the positions of the C.G. of the soil initially and finally, and then the work done is known. This work is quite independent of the path by which the soil went from its initial to its final position.

Ex. *A well, of which the section is a square whose side is 4 feet, and whose depth is 300 feet, is full of water; find the work done, in foot-pounds, in pumping the water to the level of the top of the well.*

Find also the H.P. of the engine which would just accomplish this work in one hour.

[**N.B.** A cubic foot of water weighs 1000 ounces.]

Initially the height of the centre of gravity of the water above the bottom of the well was 150 feet and finally it is 300 feet, so that the height through which the centre of gravity has been raised is 150 feet.

The volume of the water = $4 \times 4 \times 300$ cubic feet.

Therefore its weight $= 4 \times 4 \times 300 \times \frac{1000}{16}$ lb = 300,000 lb.

Hence the work done = $300{,}000 \times 150$ ft-lb = 45,000,000 ft-lb

Let x be the required H.P. Then the work done by the engine in one hour

$$= x \times 60 \times 33{,}000.$$

Hence we have $\quad x \times 60 \times 33{,}000 = 45{,}000{,}000;$

$$\therefore \qquad x = 22\frac{8}{11}.$$

133. *Graphical representation of the work done by a force.*

It is sometimes difficult to calculate directly the work done by a varying force, but it may be quite possible to obtain the result to a near degree of approximation.

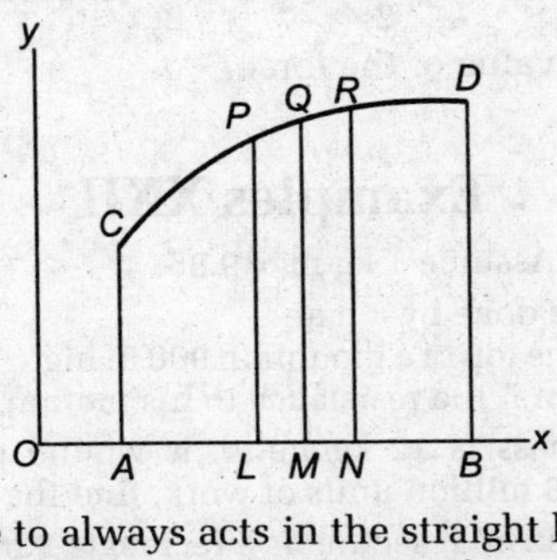

Suppose the force to always acts in the straight line OX, and let us find the work done as its point of application moves from A to B. At A and B erect ordinates AC and DB to represent the value of the force for these two points of application. For any and every intermediate point of application L erect the ordinate LP to represent the corresponding value of the acting force; then the tops of these ordinates will clearly lie on some such curve as CPD.

Take M a very near point to L, so near that the force may be considered to have remained constant as its point of application moved through the small distance LM.

Then the work done by the force

= its magnitude × distance through which its point of application has moved

$$= LP \times LM = \text{area } PM \text{ very nearly.}$$

Similarly whilst the point of application moves from M to N the work done

= are QN very nearly, and so on.

Hence it follows that the work done as the point of application moves from A to B is, when the lengths LM, MN,... are taken indefinitely small, equal more and more nearly to the area $ACDB$.

[Where the shape of the curve CPD is irregular a rough approximation to its area may be found as follows; divide AB into a number, say 10, of equal strips; take the middle ordinates of these strips and obtain the average of these middle ordinates; and multiply this average ordinate to the distance AB. This clearly gives an approximation by the area of $ACDB$.]

134. As an example of the above construction let us find the work done by a force which was initially zero and which varied as the distance through which its point of application was moved.

In this case $\angle C$ is zero, and $NP = \lambda . AN$, where λ is some constant.

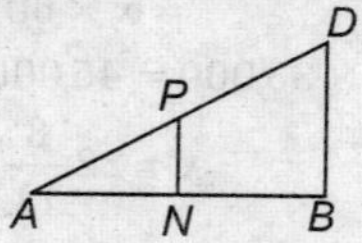

$\therefore \tan PAN = \dfrac{PN}{AN} = \lambda$, so that P lies on a straight line passing through A.

The work done = area $ABD = \dfrac{1}{2} AB \cdot BD = \dfrac{1}{2}$. displacement of the point of application × the final value of the force.

Examples XXII

Assume 1 kg-m = 9.85.

1. How much work is done by a man
(1) in climbing to the top of a mountain 900 m high, if his weight is 70 kg ?
(2) in cycling 16 km if the resistance to his motion is equal to 3 kgf.?

2. A chain, whose mass is 12 kg/metre, is wound up from a shaft by the expenditure of 2.16 million units of work; find the length of the chain.

3. A shaft, whose horizontal section is a rectangle 3 m by 2.5 m, is to be sunk 24 m into the earth. If the average weight of the soil is 2000 kg per cu.m., find the work done in bringing the soil to the surface.

4. How many cu. m. of water will an engine of 75 kw raise in one hour from a depth of 45 m ?

5. In how many hours would an engine of 14 kw empty a vertical shaft full of water if the diameter of the shaft is 2.7 m, and the depth 126 m ?
6. Find the H.P. of an engine that would empty a cylindrical shaft full of water in 32 hours, if the diameter of the shaft is 2.4 m and its depth 180 m.
7. Find how long engine of 20 H.P. would take to pump 5000 cu.m. of water to a height of 100 m, one-third of the work being wasted by friction, etc.
8. A man whose weight is 70 kg climbs a rope at the rate of 45 cm per second. Prove that he is working at just over $\frac{3}{10}$ kw.
9. A tower is to be built of brickwork, the base being a rectangle whose external measurements are 6.6 m by 2.7 m, the height of the 19.8 m, and the walls 0.6 thick; find the number of hours in which an engine of 25 kw would raise the bricks from the ground, the weight of a cubic metre of brickwork being 1500 kg.
10. At the bottom of a coal mine, 275 feet deep, there is an iron cage containing coal weighing 14 cwt, the cage itself weighing 4 cwt 109 Ib, and the wire rope that raises it 6 lb per yard. Find the work done when the load has been lifted to the surface, and the H.P. of the engine that can do this work in 40 seconds.
11. A steamer is going at the rate of 24 km per hour; if the effective H.P. of her engines is 10,000, what is the resistance to her motion ?
12. A man is cycling at the rate of 9 km per hour up a hill whose slope is 1 in 20; if the weight of the man and the machine is 100 kg, prove that he must at the least be working at the rate of nearly 12 kw.
13. A man rowing 40 strokes per minute propels a boat at the rate of 16 km an hour, and the resistance to his motion is equal to 3 kgf; find the work he does in each stroke and the H.P. at which he is working.
14. A Venetian blind consists of 30 movable bars, the thickness of each bar being negligible, and, when it is hanging down,the distance between each pair of consecutive bars is 5 cm; if the weight of each bar is 125 g, find the work done in drawing up the blind.
If there were n such bars, what would be the corresponding work ?
15. A Venetian blind consists of n thin bars, besides the top fixed bar, and the weight of the movable part is W. When let down the length of the blind is a, and when pulled up it is b; show that the work done against gravity in drawing up the blind is
$$W \cdot \frac{n+1}{2n}(a-b).$$
16. A solid hemisphere of weight 6 kg and radius 30 cm rests with its flat face on a table. How many joules of work are required to turn it over so that it may rest with its curved surface in contact with the table ? [Use the result of Art. 130.]
17. A uniform log weighing 450 kg is in the form of a triangular prism, the sides of whose cross section are 45 cm,60 cm, and 75 cm respectively, and the log is resting on the ground on its narrowest face. Prove that the work which must be done to raise it on its edge so that it may fall over on to its broadest face is approximately 72.9 kg-m.
18. A force acts on a particle, its initial value being 10 kgf and its values being 12.5, 14.5, 16, 15.0, 13.5, and 12 kgf in the direction of the particle's motion when the latter has moved through 30, 60, 90, 120, 150, and 180 cm respectively; find, by means of a graph, the work done by the force, assuming that it varies uniformly during each foot of the motion.

13

Machines

135. In the present chapter we shall explain and discuss the equilibrium of some of the simpler machines, *viz.*, (1) the lever, (2) the pulley and systems of pulleys, (3) the inclined plane, (4) the wheel and axle, (5) the common balance, (6) the steelyards, and (7) the screw.

The lever, the wheel and axle, the balance, and the steelyards are similar machines. In each we have either a point, or an axis, fixed about which the machine can revolve.

In the pulleys an essential part is a flexible string or strings.

We shall suppose the different portions of these machines to be smooth and rigid, that all cords or strings used are perfectly flexible,and that the forces acting on the machines always balance, so that they are at rest.

In actual practice these conditions are not even approximately satisfied in the cases of many machines.

136. When two external forces applied to a machine balance, one is called the load and the other the effort.

A machine is always used in practice to overcome some resistance; the force we exert on the machine is the effort; the resistance to be overcome, in whatever form it may appear, is called the load.

The words resistance and weight are also used for load.

137. Mechanical Advantage. If in any machine an effort P balances a resistance W, the ratio $W : P$ is called the mechanical advantage of the machine, so that

$$\frac{\text{Resistance}}{\text{Effort}} = \text{Mechanical Advantage},$$

and $$\text{Resistance} = \text{Effort} \times \text{Mechanical Advantage}.$$

Almost all machines are constructed so that the mechanical advantage is a ratio greater than unity.

If in any machine the mechanical advantage is less than unity, it may, with more accuracy, be called mechanical disadvantage.

The term Force-Ratio is sometimes used instead of Mechanical Advantage.

Velocity Ratio. The velocity ratio of any machine is the ratio of the distance through which the point of application of the effort moves to the distance through which the point of application of the resistance, or weight, moves in the same time; so that

$$\text{Velocity Ratio} = \frac{\text{Distance through which } P \text{ moves}}{\text{Distance through which } W \text{ moves}}.$$

If the machine is such that no work has to be done in lifting its component parts, and if it is perfectly smooth throughout, it will be found that the Mechanical Advantage and the Velocity Ratio are equal, so that in this case

$$\frac{W}{P} = \frac{\text{Distance through which } P \text{ moves}}{\text{Distance through which } W \text{ mvoes}},$$

and then

$$P \times \text{distance through which } P \text{ moves}$$
$$= W \times \text{distance through which } W \text{ moves},$$

or, in other words,

work done by P will = work done against W.

138. The following we shall thus find to be a universal principle, known as the **Principle of Work,** *viz., Whatever is the machine we use, provided that there is no friction and that the weight of the machine is neglected, the work done by the effort is always equivalent to the work done against the weight, or resistance.*

Assuming that the machine we are using gives mechanical advantage, so that the effort is less than the weight, the distance moved through by the effort is therefore greater than the distance moved through by the weight in the same proportion. This is sometimes expressed in popular language in the form; *What is gained in power is lost in speed.*

More accurate is the statement that mechanical advantage is always gained at a proportionate diminution of speed. No work is ever gained by the use of a machine though mechanical advantage is generally obtained.

139. It will be found in the next chapter that, as a matter of fact, some work, in practice, is always lost by the use of any machine.

The uses of a machine are

(1) to enable a man to lift weights or overcome resistances much greater than he could deal with unaided, *e.g.*, by the use of a system of pulleys,or a wheel and axle, or a screw-jack, etc.

(2) to cause a motion imparted one point to be changed into a more rapid motion at some other point, *e.g.*, in the case of bicycle.

(3) to enable a force to be applied at a more convenient point or in a more convenient manner, *e.g.*, in the use of a poker to stir the fire, or in the lifiting of a bucket of mortar by means of a long rope passing over a pulley at the top of a building, the other end being pulled by a man standing on the ground.

I. The Lever

140. The lever consists essentially of a rigid bar, straight or bent, which has one point fixed about which the rest of the lever can turn. This fixed point is called the fulcrum, and the perpendicular distances between the fulcrum and the lines of action of the effort and the weight are called the arms of the lever.

When the lever is straight, and the effort and weight act perpendicular to the lever, it is usual to distinguish three classes or orders.

Class I. Here the effort P and the weight W act on opposite sides of the fulcrum C.

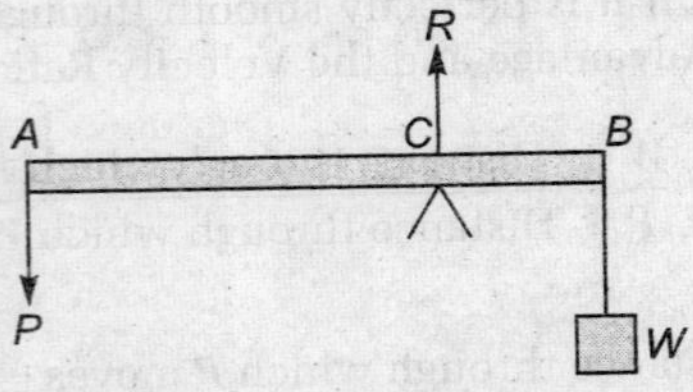

Class II. Here the effort P and the weight W act on the same side of the fulcrum C, but the former acts at a greater distance than the latter from the fulcrum.

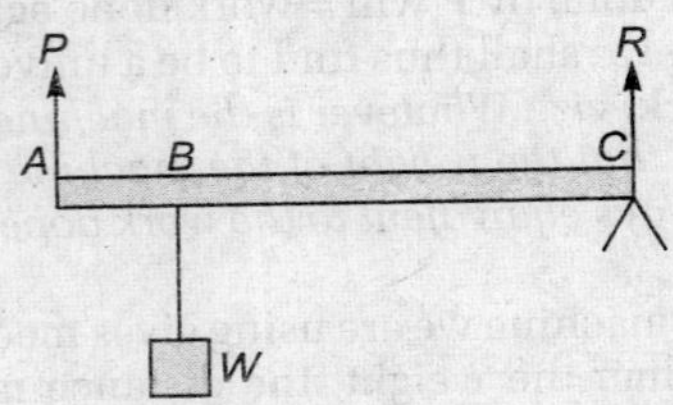

Class III. Here the effort P and the weight W act on the same side of the fulcrum C, but the former is closer to the fulcrum.

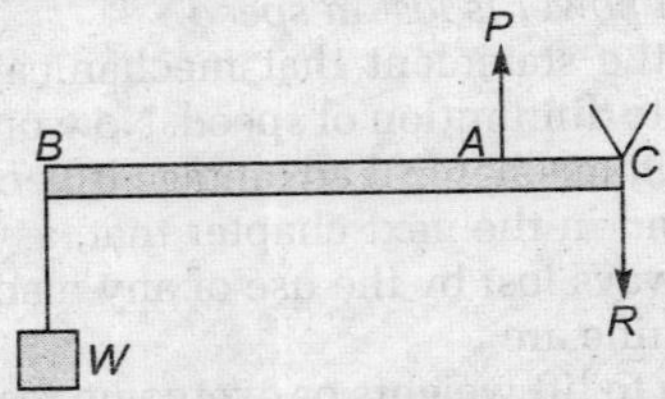

141. *Conditions of equilibrium of a straight lever.*

In each case we have three parallel forces acting on the body, so that the reaction, R, at the fulcrum must be equal and opposite to the resultant of P and W.

In the first class P and W are like parallel forces, so that their resultant is $P + W$. Hence

$$R = P + W.$$

In the second class P and W are unlike parallel forces, so that

$$R = W - P.$$

So in the third class $\qquad R = P - W.$

In the first and third classes we see that R and P act in opposite directions; in the second class they act in the same direction.

In all three classes, since the resultant of P and W passes through C, we have, as in Art. 52,

$$P \cdot AC = W \cdot BC,$$

i.e., $P \times$ the arm of $P = W \times$ the arm of W.

Since $\frac{W}{P} = \frac{\text{arm of } P}{\text{arm of } W}$, we observe that generally in Class I, and always in Class II, there is mechanical advantage, but that in Class III there is mechanical disadvantage.

The practical use of levers of the latter class is to apply a force at some point at which it is not convenient to apply the force directly.

In this article we have neglected the weight of the lever itself.

If this weight is taken into consideration we must, as in Art. 91, obtain the conditions of equilibrium by equating to zero the algebraic sum of the moments of the forces about the fulcrum C.

The principle of the lever was known to Archimedes who lived in the third century B.C.; until the discovery of the parallelogram of forces in the sixteenth century it was the fundamental principle of statics.

142. Examples of the different classes of levers are;

Class I. A poker *(when used to stir the fire, the bar of the grate being the fulcrum)*; a claw-hammer *(when used to extract nails)*; a crowbar *(when used with a point in it resting on a fixed support)*; a pair of scales; the brake of a pump.

Double levers of this class are; a pair of scissors, a pair of pincers.

Class II. A wheelbarrow; a cork squeezer; a crowbar *(with one end in contact with the ground)*; an oar *(assuming the end of the oar in contact with the water to be at rest)*.

A pair of nutcrackers is a doble lever of this class.

Class III. The treadle of a lathe; the human forearm *(when the latter is used to support a weight placed on the palm of the hand. The fulcrum is the elbow, and the tension exerted by the muscles is the effort.)*

A pair of sugar-tongs is a double lever of this class.

143. *Bent Levers.*

Let AOB be a bent lever, of which O is the fulcrum, and let OL and OM be the perpendiculars from O upon the lines action AC and BC of the effort P and resistance W.

The condition of equilibrium of Art. 91 again applies, and we have, by taking moments about O,

$$P \cdot OL = W \cdot OM \qquad \ldots(1)$$

$$\therefore \quad \frac{P}{W} = \frac{OM}{OL}$$

$$= \frac{\text{perpendicular from fulcrum on direction of resistance.}}{\text{perpendicular from fulcrum on direction of effort}}$$

To obtain the reaction at O let the directions of P and W meet in C. Since there are only three forces acting on the body, the direction of the reaction R at O must pass through C, and then, by Lami's Theorem, we have

$$\frac{R}{\sin ACB} = \frac{P}{\sin BCO} = \frac{W}{\sin ACO}.$$

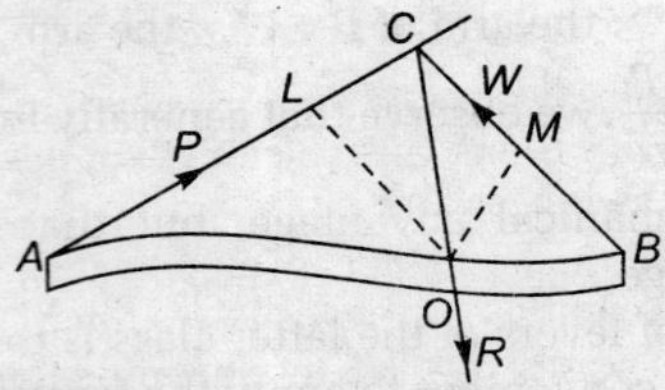

The reaction may also be obtained, as in Art. 46, by resolving the forces R, P, and W in two directions at right angles.

If the effort and resistance are parallel forces, the reaction R is parallel to either of them and equal to $(P + W)$, and, as before, we have

$$P \cdot OL = W \cdot OM,$$

where OL and OM are the perpendiculars from O upon the lines of action of the forces.

If the weight W' of the lever is not neglected, we have an additional term to introduce into our equation of moments.

144. *If two weights balance, about a fixed fulcrum, at the extremities of a straight lever, in any position inclined to the vertical, they will balance in any other position.*

Let AB be the lever, of weight W, and let its centre of gravity be G. Let the lever balance about a fulcrum O in any position inclined at an angle θ to the horizontal, the weights at A and B being P and W respectively.

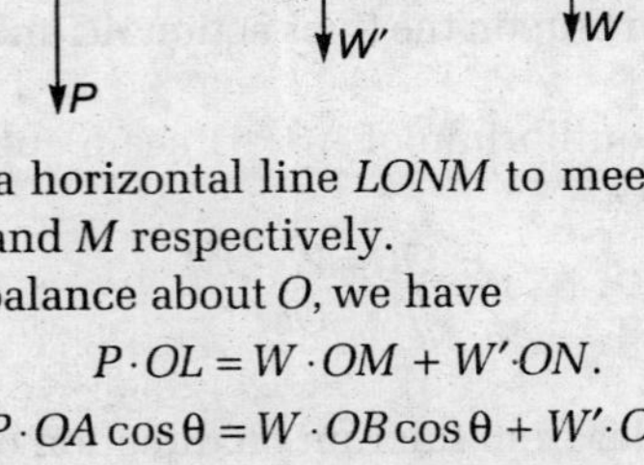

Through O draw a horizontal line $LONM$ to meet the lines of action of P, W', and W in L, N, and M respectively.

Since the forces balance about O, we have

$$P \cdot OL = W \cdot OM + W' \cdot ON.$$

$$\therefore \quad P \cdot OA \cos\theta = W \cdot OB \cos\theta + W' \cdot OG \cos\theta.$$

$$\therefore \quad P \cdot OA = W \cdot OB + W' \cdot OG.$$

This condition of equilibrium is independent of the inclination θ of the lever to the horizontal; hence in any other position of the lever the condition would be the same.

Hence, if the lever is in equilibrium in one position, it will be in equilibrium in all positions.

Examples XXIII

1. In a weightless lever, if one of the forces is equal to 10 kgf and the thrust on the fulcrum is equal to 16 kgf, and the length of the shorter arm is 3 metres, find the length of the longer arm.
2. Where must the fulcrum be so that a weight of 6 kg may balance a weight of 8 kg on a straight weightless lever, 7 metres long ?

   If each weight is increased by 1 kg, in what direction will the lever turn ?
3. If two forces, applied to a weightless lever, balance, and if the thrust on the fulcrum is ten times the difference of the forces, find the ratio of the arms.
4. A lever, 90 cm long, has weights of 3 and 10 kg fastened to its ends, and balances about a point distant 25 cm from one end; find its weight.
5. A straight lever, AB, 3.6 m long, balances about a point, 30 cm from A, when a weight of 6.5 kg is suspended from A. It will balance about a point, which is 30 cm from B, when a weight of 5.5 kg is suspended from B. Show that the centre of gravity of the lever is 12.5 cm from the middle point of the lever.
6. A straight uniform lever is kept in equilibrium by weights of 12 and 5 kg respectively attached to the ends of its arms, and the length of one arm is double that of the other. What is the weight of the lever ?
7. A straight uniform lever, of the length 5 decimetres and weight 10 kg, has fulcrum at one end and weights of 3 and 6 kg are fastened to it at distances of 1 and 3 decimetres respectively from the fulcrum; it is kept horizontal by a force at its other end; find the thrust on the fulcrum.
8. A uniform lever is 45 cm long and is of weight 54 g, find the position of the fulcrum when a weight of 756 g at one end of the lever balances one of 252 g at the other.

   If the lesser weight is doubled, by how much must the position of the fulcrum be shifted so as to preserve equilibrium ?
9. Two weights, of 224 and 112 g, are in equilibrium when attached to the opposite ends of a rod of negligible weight; if 56 g is added to the greater, the fulcrum must be moved through $\frac{10}{7}$th of a cm to preserve equilibrium; find the length of the lever.
10. The short arm of one lever is hinged to the long arm of a second lever, and the short arm of the latter is attached to a press; the long arms being each 90 cm in length, and the short arms 15 cm. Find what thrust will be produced on the press by a force, equal to 70 kg weight, applied to the long end of the first lever.
11. A straight heavy uniform lever, 42 cm long, has a fulcrum at its end. A force, equal to the weight of 6 kg, acting at a distance of 14 cm from the fulcrum, supports a weight of 1.5 kg hanging at the other end of the lever. If the weight is increased by $\frac{1}{2}$ kg, what force at a distance of 10 cm from the fulcrum will support the lever ?
12. On a lever, forces of 13 and 14 kg weights balance, and their directions meet at an angle whose cosine is $-\frac{5}{13}$; find the thrust on the fulcrum.
13. A straight lever is acted on, at its extremities, by forces in the ratio $\sqrt{3}+1:\sqrt{3}-1$, and which are inclined at angles of 30° and 60° to its length.

Find the magnitude of the thrust on the fulcrum, and the direction in which it acts.

14. The arms of a bent lever are at right angles to one another, and the arms are in the ratio of 5 to 1. The longer arm is inclined to the horizon at an angle of 45°, and carries at its end a weight of 5 kg; the end of the shorter arm presses against a horizontal plane; find the thrust on the plane.

15. The arms of a uniform heavy bent rod are inclined to one another at an angle of 120°, and their lengths are in the ratio of 2 : 1; if the rod is suspended from its angular point, find the position in which it will rest.

16. A uniform bar, of length 2.25 m and weight 8.5 kg, rests on a horizontal table with one end projecting 75 cm over the edge; find the greatest weight that can be attached to its end, without making the bar topple over.

17. A straight weightless lever has for its fulcrum a hinge at one end A, and from a point B is hung a body of weight W. If the strain at the hinge must not exceed $\frac{1}{2}W$ in either direction, upwards or downwards, show that the effort must act somewhere within a space equal to $\frac{4}{3}AB$.

18. Show that the propelling force on an eight-oared boat is 112 kg weight, supposing each man to pull his oar with a force of 28 kg weight, and that the length of the oar from the middle of the blade to the handle is three times that from the handle to the row-lock.

19. In a pair of nutcrackers, 5 cm long, if the nut is placed at a distance of $\frac{7}{3}$ cm from the hinge, a force equal to $3\frac{1}{2}$ kg wt applied to the ends of the arms will crack the nut. What weight placed on the top of the nut will crack it ?

20. A man raises a 90 cm cube of stone, weighing 1800 kg, by means of a crowbar, 1.2 m long, after having thrust one end of the bar under the stone to a distance of 15 cm; what force must be applied at the other end of the bar to raise the stone ?

21. A cubical block, of edge a, is being turned over by a crowbar applied at the middle point of the edge in a plane through its centre of gravity; if the crowbar is held at rest when it is inclined at an angle of 60° to the horizon, the lower face of the block being then inclined at 30° to the horizon, and if the weight of the block be n times the force applied, find the length of the crowbar, the force being applied at right angles to the crowbar.

II. Pulleys

145. A Pulley is composed of a wheel of wood,or metal, grooved along its circumference to receive a string or rope; it can turn freely about an axle passing through its centre perpendicular to its plane, the ends of this axle being supported by a frame of wood called the block.

A pulley is said to be movable or fixed according as its block is movable or fixed.

The weight of the pulley is often so small, compared with the weights which it supports, that it may be neglected; such a pulley is called a weightless pulley.

We shall always neglect the weight of the string or rope which passes round the pulley.

We shall also in this chapter consider the pulley to be perfectly smooth, so that the tension of a string which passes round a pulley is constant throughout its length.

146. Single Pulley. The use of a single pulley is to apply an effort in a different direction from that in which it is convenient to us to apply the effort.

Thus, in the first figure, a man standing on the ground and pulling vertically at one end of the rope might support a weight W hanging at the other end; in the second figure the same man pulling sideways might support the weight.

In each case the tension of the string passing round the pulley is unaltered; the effort P is therefore equal to the weight W.

In the first figure the action on the fixed support to which the block is attached must balance the other forces on the pulley-block, and must therefore be equal to

$$W + P + w$$

i.e., $2W + w$, where w is the weight of the pulley-block.

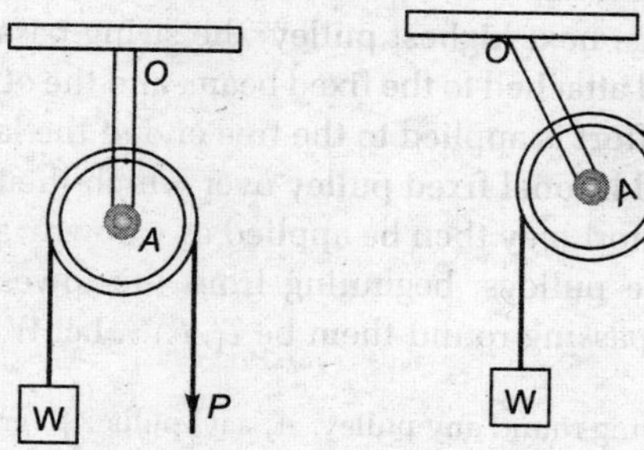

In the second figure, if the weight of the pulley is neglected, the effort P, and the weight W, being equal, must be equally inclined to the line OA.

Hence, if T is the tension of the supporting OB and 2θ the angle between the direction of P and W, we have

$$T = P\cos\theta + W\cos\theta = 2W\cos\theta$$

If w is the weight of the pulley, we should have,

$$T^2 = (W + w)^2 + P^2 + 2(W + w)\cdot P\cdot\cos 2\theta$$

$$= 2W^2 + 2Ww + w^2 + 2(W + w)\cdot W(2\cos^2\theta - 1), \text{ since } P \text{ and } W \text{ are equal,}$$

$$= w^2 + 4W(W + w)\cos^2\theta$$

147. We shall discuss three systems of pulleys and shall follow the usual order; there is no particular reason for this order, but it is convenient to retain it for purposes of reference.

First system of Pulleys. *Each string attached to the supporting beam. To find the relation between the effort and the weight.*

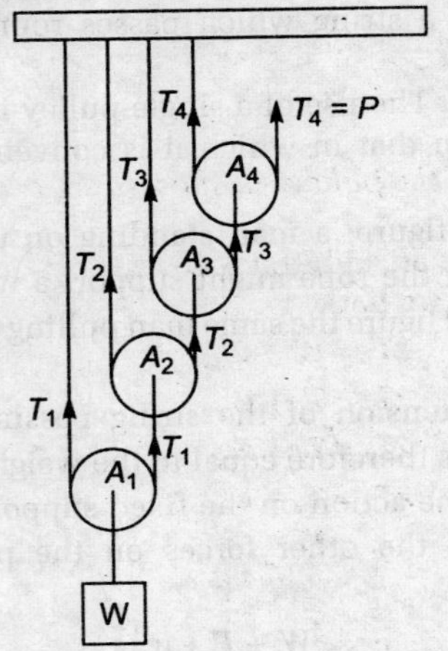

In this system of pulleys the weight is attached to the lowest pulley, and the string passing round it has one end attached to the fixed beam, and the other end attached to the next highest pulley; the string passing round the latter pulley has one end attached to the fixed beam, and the other to the next pulley, and so on; the effort is applied to the free end of the last string.

Often there is an additional fixed pulley over which the free end of the last string passes; the effort may then be applied as a downward force.

Let $A_1, A_2, \ldots$ be the pulleys, beginning from the lowest, and let the tensions of the strings passing round them be $T_1, T_2, \ldots$ Let W be the weigh and P the power.

[**N.B.** The string passing round any pulley, A_2 say, pulls A_1 vertically *upwards* and pulls a_3 *downwards*]

I. *Let the weights of the pulleys be neglected.*

From the equilibrium of the pulleys $A_1, A_2, \ldots$, taken in order, we have

$$2T_1 = W; \quad \therefore \quad T_1 = \frac{1}{2}W.$$

$$2T_2 = T_1; \quad \therefore \quad T_2 = \frac{1}{2}T_1 = \frac{1}{2^2}W.$$

$$2T_3 = T_2; \quad \therefore \quad T_3 = \frac{1}{2}T_2 = \frac{1}{2^3}W.$$

$$2T_4 = T_3; \quad \therefore \quad T_4 = \frac{1}{2}T_3 = \frac{1}{2^4}W.$$

But, with our figure, $T_4 = P$.

$$\therefore \quad P = \frac{1}{2^4}W.$$

Similarly, if there were *n* pulleys, we should have

$$P = \frac{1}{2^n} W.$$

Hence, in this system of pulleys, the mechanical advantage

$$= \frac{W}{P} = 2^n.$$

II. *Let the weights of the pulleys in succession, beginning from the lowest, be* $w_1, w_2, \ldots$

In this case we have an additional downward force on each pulley. Resolving as before, we have

$$2T_1 = W + w_1,$$
$$2T_2 = T_1 + w_2,$$
$$2T_3 = T_2 + w_3,$$
$$2T_4 = T_3 + w_4.$$

$$\therefore \quad T_1 = \frac{W}{2} + \frac{w_1}{2},$$

$$T_2 = \frac{1}{2}T_1 + \frac{w_2}{2} = \frac{W}{2^2} + \frac{w_1}{2^2} + \frac{w_2}{2},$$

$$T_3 = \frac{1}{2}T_2 + \frac{w_3}{2} = \frac{W}{2^3} + \frac{w_1}{2^3} + \frac{w_2}{2^2} + \frac{w_3}{2},$$

and
$$P = T_4 = \frac{1}{2}T_3 + \frac{w_4}{2} = \frac{W}{2^4} + \frac{w_1}{2^4} + \frac{w_2}{2^3} + \frac{w_3}{2^2} + \frac{w_4}{2}.$$

Similarly, if there were *n* pulleys, we should have

$$P = \frac{W}{2^n} + \frac{w_1}{2^n} + \frac{w_2}{2^{n-1}} + \ldots + \frac{w^n}{2}.$$

$$\therefore \quad 2^n P = W + w_1 + 2 \cdot w_2 + 2^2 w_3 + \ldots + 2^{n-1} w_n.$$

If the pulleys are all equal, we have

$$w_1 = w_2 = \ldots = w_n = w.$$

$$\therefore \quad 2^n P = W + w(1 + 2 + 2^2 + \ldots + 2^{n-1})$$
$$= W + w\,(2^n - 1),$$

by summing the geometrical progression.

If follows that the mechanical advantage, $\frac{W}{P}$, depends on the weight of he pulleys.

If this system of pulleys we observe that the greater the weight of the ulleys, the greater must *P* be to support a given weight *W*; the weights of the ulleys oppose the effort, and the pulleys should therefore be made as light s is consistent with the required strength.

Stress on the beam from which the pulleys are hung.

Let *R* be the stress on the beam. Since *R*, together with the force *P*, upports the system of pulleys, together with the weight *W*, we have

$$R + P = W + w_1 + w_2 + \ldots + w_n.$$

$$\therefore \quad R = W + w_1 + w_2 + \ldots + w_n - \frac{W + w_1 + 2w_2 + 2^2 w_3 + \ldots + 2^{n-1} w_n}{2^n}$$

$$= W\left(1 - \frac{1}{2^n}\right) + w_1\left(1 - \frac{1}{2^n}\right) + w_2\left(1 - \frac{1}{2^{n-1}}\right)$$

$$+ w_3\left(1 - \frac{1}{2^{n-2}}\right) + \ldots + w_n\left(1 - \frac{1}{2}\right).$$

Ex. *If there are* 4 *movable pulleys, whose weights, commencing with the lowest, are* 4, 5, 6, *and* 7 *kg, what effort will support a body of weight* 112 *kg?*

Using the notation of the previous article, we have

$$2T_1 = 112 + 4; \qquad \therefore \; T_1 = 58.$$

$$2T_2 = T_1 + 5 = 63; \qquad \therefore \; T_2 = 31\frac{1}{2}.$$

$$2T_3 = T_2 + 6 = 37\frac{1}{2}; \qquad \therefore \; T_3 = 18\frac{3}{4}.$$

$$2P = T_3 + 7 = 25\frac{3}{4}; \qquad \therefore \; P = 12\frac{7}{8} \text{ kgf}.$$

148. Verification of the Principle of Work. Neglecting the weights of the pulleys we have, if there are four pulleys,

$$P = \frac{1}{2^4} W.$$

If the weight W is raised through a distance x, the pulley A_2 would, if the distance A_1A_2 remained unchanged, rise a distance x; but, at the same time, the length of the string joining A_1 to the beam is shortened by x, and a portion x of the string therefore slips round A_1; hence, altogether, the pulley A_2 rises through a distance $2x$.

Similarly, the pulley A_3 rises a distance $4x$, and the pulley A_4 a distance $8x$.

Since A_4 rises a distance $8x$, the strings joining it to the beam and to the point at which P is applied both shorten by $8x$.

Hence, since the slack string runs round the pulley A_4, the point of application of P rises through $16x$, *i.e.*, through sixteen times as far as the point of application of W.

Hence the velocity-ratio (Art. 137) $= 16$, so that it is equal to the mechanical advantage in this case.

Also
$$\frac{\text{work done by the effort}}{\text{work done a against the weight}} = \frac{P \cdot 16x}{W \cdot x}$$

$$= \frac{\frac{1}{2^4} W \cdot 16x}{W \cdot x} = \frac{W \cdot x}{W \cdot x} = 1.$$

Hence the principle is verified.

Taking the weights of the pulleys into account, and taking the case of four pulleys, we have

$$P = \frac{W}{2^4} + \frac{w_1}{2^4} + \frac{w_2}{2^3} + \frac{w_3}{2^2} + \frac{w_4}{2}.$$

As before, if A_1 ascends a distance x, the other pulleys ascend distances $2x$, $4x$, and $8x$, respectively. Hence the work done on the weight and the weights of the pulleys

$$= W \cdot x + w_1 \cdot x + w_2 \cdot 2x + w_3 \cdot 4x + w_4 \cdot 8x$$

$$= 16x\left[\frac{W}{2^4} + \frac{w_1}{2^4} + \frac{w_2}{2^3} + \frac{w_3}{2^2} + \frac{w_4}{2}\right]$$

$$= 16x \times P = \text{work done by the effort.}$$

A similar method of proof would apply, whatever the number of pulleys.

Examples XXIV

1. In the following cases, the movable pulleys are weightless, their number is n, the weight is W, and the effort is P;
   (1) If $n = 4$ and $P = 10$ kgf, find W;
   (2) If $n = 4$ and $W = 64$ kg, find$P$;
   (3) If $W = 28$ kgf and $P = 3.5$ kgf, find n.
2. In the following cases, the movable pulleys are of equal weight w, and are n in number, P is the effort, and W is the weight :
   (1) If $n = 4$, $w = 0.5$ kgf, and $W = 48.5$ kgf, find P;
   (2) If $n = 3$, $W = \frac{3}{4}$ kgf, and $P = 3.5$ kgf, find W;
   (3) If $n = 5$, $W = 387.5$ kgf, and $P = 15.5$ kgf, find w;
   (4) If $W = 53.5$ kgf, $P = 1$ kgf, and $w = \frac{1}{6}$ kgf, find n.
3. In the first system of pulleys, if there are 4 pulleys, each of weight 2 kg, what weight can be raised by an effort equal to the weight of 20 kg ?
4. If there are 3 movable pulleys, whose weights, commencing with the lowest, are 9, 2, and 1 kg respectively, what force will support a weight of 69 kg ?
5. If there are 4 movable pulleys, whose weights commencing with the lowest, are 4, 3, 2, and 1 kg respectively, what force will support a weight of 54 kg ?
6. If there are 4 movable pulleys, each of weight w, and the effort by P, show that the stress on the beam is $15P - 11w$.
7. If there are 3 movable pulleys and their weights beginning from the lowest are 4, 2, and 1 kg respectively, what force will be required to support a weight of 28 kg ?
8. Show that, on the supposition that the pulleys are weightless, the mechanical advantage is greater than it actually is.
9. In the system of pulleys in which each hangs by a separate string, if there are 3 pulleys, it is found that a certain weight can be supported by an effort equal to 7 kg weight; but, if there are 4 pulleys, the same weight can be supported by an effort equal to 4 kg weight; find the weight supported and the weight of the pulleys, which are equal.
10. A system consists of 4 pulleys, arranged so that each hangs by a separate string, one end being fastened to the upper block, and all the free ends being

vertical. If the weights of the pulleys, beginning at the lowest, are w, $2w$, $3w$, and $4w$, find the power necessary to support a weight of $15w$, and the magnitude of the single force necessary to support the beam to which the other ends of the string are attached.

11. In the system of 4 heavy pulleys, if P is the effort and W the weight, show that the stress on the beam is intermediate between $\frac{15}{16}W$ and $15P$.

12. A man, of 84 kg weight, is suspended from the lowest of a system of 4 weightless pulleys, in which each hangs by a separate string, and supports himself by pulling at the end of the string which passes over a fixed pulley. Find the amount of his pull on this string.

13. A man, whose weight is 156 kg, is suspended from the lowest of a system of 4 pulleys, each being of weight 10 kg, and supports himself by pulling at the end of the string which passes over the fixed pulley. Find the force which he exerts on the string; supposing all the strings to be vertical.

---

149. Second system of pulleys. *The same string passing round all the pulleys. To find the relation between the effort and the weight.*

In this system there are two blocks, each containing pulleys, the upper block being fixed and the lower block movable . The same string passes round all the pulleys as in the figures.

If the number of pulleys in the upper block be the same as in the lower block (Fig. 1), one end of the string must be fastened to the upper block; if the number in the upper block be

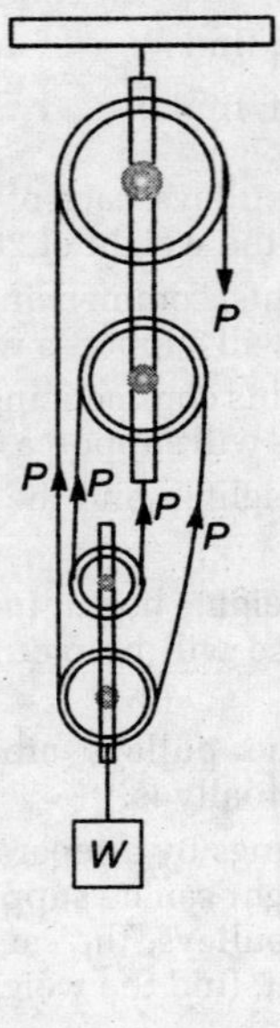

Fig. 1

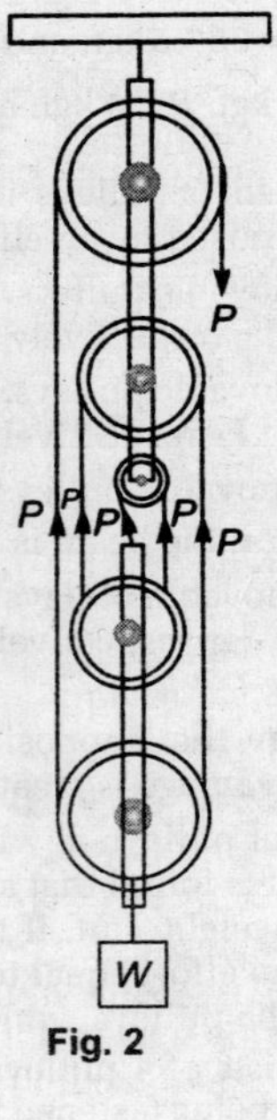

Fig. 2

greater by one than the number in the lower block (Fig. 2), the end of the string must be attached to the lower block.

In the first case, the number of portions of string connecting the blocks is even; in the second case, the number is odd.

In either case, let n be the number of portions of string at the lower block. Since we have only one string passing over smooth pulleys, the tension of each of these portions is P, so that the total upward force at the lower block is $n \cdot P$.

Let W be the weight supported, and w the weight of the lower block.

Hence $W + w = nP$, giving the relation required.

In practice the pulleys of each block are often placed parallel to one another, so that the strings are not mathematically parallel; they are however, very approximately parallel, so that above relation is very approximately true.

Examples XXV

1. If a weight of 5 kg supports a weight of 24 kg, find the weight of the lower block, when there are 3 pulleys in each block.
2. If weights of 5 and 6 kg respectively at the free ends of the string support weights of 18 and 22 kg at the lower block, find the number of the strings and the weights of the lower block.
3. If weight of 2 kg and 2.5 kg support weights of 2.5 kg and 9 kg respectively, what is the weight of the lower block, and how many pulleys are there in it?
4. A weight of 6 kg just supports a weight of 28 kg, and a weight of 8 kg just supports a weight of 42 kg; find the number of strings and the weight of the lower block.
5. In the second system of pulleys, if a basket be suspended from the lower block and a man in the basket supports himself and the basket, by pulling at the free end of the rope, find the tension he exerts, neglecting the inclination of the rope to the vertical, and assuming the weight of the man and basket to be W.

   If the free end of the rope passes round a pulley attached to the ground and then be held by the man, find the force he exerts.
6. A man, whose weight is 84 kg, raises 168 kg by means of a system of pulleys in which the same rope passes round all the pulleys, there being 4 in each block, and the rope being attached to the upper block; neglecting the weights of the pulleys, find what will be his thrust on the ground if he pulls vertically downwards.
7. We are told that the cable by which 'Great Paul', whose weight is 18 tonnes, was lifted into its place in the cathedral tower, passed four times through the two blocks of pulleys. From this statement give a description of the pulleys, and estimate the strength of the cable.
8. Prove the Principle of Work in this system of pulleys, and find the Velocity Ratio.
9. An ordinary block and tackle have two pulleys in the lower block and two in the upper. What force must be exerted to lift a load of 150 kg ? If on account of friction a given force will only lift 0.45 times as much as if the system were frictionless, find the force required.

10. In a block and tackle the velocity ratio is 8 : 1. The friction is such that only 55% of the force applied can be usefully employed. Find what force will raise 250 kg by its use.

---

150. Third system of pulleys. *All the strings attached to the weight. To find the relation between the effort and the weight.*

In this system the string passing round any pulley is attached at one end to a bar, from which the weight is suspended, and at the other end to the next lower pulley; the string round the lowest pulley is attached at one end to the bar, whilst at the other end of this string the power is applied. In this system the upper pulley is fixed.

Let A_1, A_2, A_3,... be the movable pulleys, beginning from the lowest, and let the tensions of the strings passing round these pulleys respectively be T_1, T_2, T_3....

If the power is P, we have clearly $T_1 = P$.

I. *Let the weights of the pulleys be neglected.*

For the equilibrium of the pulleys, taken in order and commencing from the lowest, we have

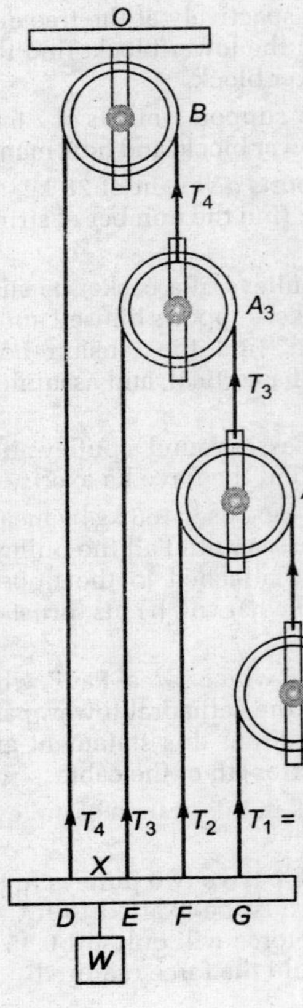

$$T_2 = 2T_1 = 2P,$$
$$T_3 = 2T_2 = 2^2 P,$$
and
$$T_4 = 2T_3 = 2^3 P.$$

But, since the bar, from which W is suspended, is in equilibrium, we have

$$W = T_1 + T_2 + T_3 + T_4 = P + 2P + 2^2 P + 2^3 P$$
$$= P\frac{2^4 - 1}{2 - 1} = P(2^4 - 1) \qquad \ldots(1)$$

If there were n pulleys, of which $(n-1)$ would be movable, we should have, similarly,

$$W = T_1 + T_2 + T_3 + \ldots + T_n$$
$$= P + 2P + 2^2 P + \ldots + 2^{n-1} P$$
$$= P\left[\frac{2^n - 1}{2 - 1}\right],$$

by summing the geometrical progression,

$$= P(2^n - 1) \qquad \ldots(2)$$

II. *Let the weights of the movable pulleys, taken in order and commencing with the lowest, be* $w_1, w_2, \ldots$

Considering the equilibrium of the pulleys in order, we have

$$T_2 = 2T_1 + w_1 = 2P + w_1,$$
$$T_3 = 2T_2 + w_2 = 2^2 P + 2w_1 + w_2,$$
$$T_4 = 2T_3 + w_3 = 2^3 P + 2^2 w_1 + 2w_2 + w_3.$$

But, from the equilibrium of the bar,

$$W = T_4 + T_3 + T_2 + T_1$$
$$= (2^3 + 2^2 + 2 + 1)P + (2^2 + 2 + 1)w_1 + (2 + 1)w_2 + w_3$$
$$= \frac{2^4 - 1}{2 - 1} P + \frac{2^3 - 1}{2 - 1} w_1 + \frac{2^2 - 1}{2 - 1} w_2 + w_3$$
$$= (2^4 - 1)P + (2^3 - 1)w_1 + (2^2 - 1)w_2 + w_3 \qquad \ldots(3)$$

If there were n pulleys, of which $(n-1)$ would be movable, we should have, similarly,

$$W = T_n + T_{n-1} + \ldots + T_2 + T_1$$
$$= (2^{n-1} + 2^{n-2} + \ldots + 1)P + (2^{n-2} + 2^{n-3} + \ldots + 1)w_1$$
$$+ (2^{n-3} + 2^{n-4} + \ldots + 1)w_2 + \ldots + (2 + 1)w_{n-2} + w_{n-1}$$
$$= \frac{2^n - 1}{2 - 1} P + \frac{2^{n-1} - 1}{2 - 1} w_1 + \frac{2^{n-2} - 1}{2 - 1} w_2$$
$$+ \ldots + \frac{2^2 - 1}{2 - 1} w_{n-2} + w_{n-1}$$

$$= (2^n - 1)P + (2^{n-1} - 1)w_1 + (2^{n-2} - 1)w_2 + \dots$$
$$+ (2^2 - 1)w_{n-2} + (2 - 1)w_{n-1} \quad \dots(4)$$

If the pulleys be all equal, so that

$$w_1 = w_2 = \dots = w_{n-1} = w,$$

the relation (4) becomes

$$W = (2^n - 1)P + w[2^{n-1} + 2^{n-2} + \dots + 2 - (n-1)]$$
$$= (2^n - 1)P + w[2^n - n - 1],$$

by summing the geometrical progression.

Stress on the supporting beam. This stress balances the effort, the weight, and the weight of the pulleys, and therefore equals

$$P + W + w_1 + w_2 + \dots + w_n,$$

and hence is easily found.

Ex. *If there are* 4 *pulleys, whose weights, commencing with the lowest, are* 4, 5, 6, *and* 7 *kg, what effort will support a body of weight* 112 *kg* ?

Using the notation of the previous article, we have

$$T_2 = 2P + 4,$$
$$T_3 = 2T_2 + 5 = 4P + 13,$$
$$T_4 = 2T_3 + 6 = 8P + 32.$$

Also $\quad 112 = T_4 + T_3 + T_2 + P = 15P + 49.$

$\therefore \quad P = \dfrac{63}{15} = 4\dfrac{1}{5}$ kgf.

151. In this system we observe that, the greater the weight of each pulley, the less is P required to be in order that it may support a given weight W. Hence the weights of the pulleys assist the effort. If the weights of the pulleys be properly chosen, the system will remain in equilibrium without the application of any effort whatever.

For example, suppose we have 3-movable pulleys, each of weight w, the relation (3) of the last article will become

$$W = 15P + 11w.$$

Hence, if $11w = W$, we have P zero, so that no power need be applied at the free end of the string to preserve equilibrium.

152. In the third system of pulleys, the bar supporting the weight W will not remain horizontal, unless the point at which the weight is attached be properly chosen. In any particular case the proper point of attachment can be easily found.

Taking the figure of Art. 146 let there be three movable pulleys, whose weights are negligible. Let the distances between the points D, E, F, and G at which the strings are attached, be successively a, and let the point at which the weight is attached be X.

The resultant of T_1, T_2, T_3, and T_4 must pass through X.
Hence by Art. 109,

$$DX = \frac{T_4 \times 0 + T_3 \times a + T_2 \times 2a + T_1 \times 3a}{T_4 + T_3 + T_2 + T_1}$$

$$= \frac{4P \cdot a + 2P \cdot 2a + P \cdot 3a}{8P + 4P + 2P + P} = \frac{11a}{15}.$$

$$\therefore \quad DX = \frac{11}{15} DE, \text{ giving the position of } X.$$

153. This system of pulleys was not however designed in order to lift weights. If it is used for that purpose it is soon found to be unworkable. Its use is to give a short strong pull. For example it is used on board a yacht to set up the back stay.

In the figure of Art 150, *DEFG* is the deck of the yacht to which the strings are attached and there is no W. The strings to the pulleys A_1, A_2, A_3, A_4 are inclined to the vertical and the point O is at the top of the mast which is to be kept erect. The resistance in this case is the force at O necessary to keep the mast up, and the effort is applied as in the figure.

154. Verification of the Principle of Work.

Suppose the weight W to ascend through a space x. The string joining B to the bar shortens by x, and hence the pulley A_3 descends a distance x. Since the pulley A_3 descends x and the bar rises x, the string joining A_3 to the bar shortens by $2x$, and this portion slides over A_3; hence the pulley A_2 descends a distance equal to $2x$ together with the distance through which A_3 descends, *i.e.*, A_2 descends a distance $2x + x$, or $3x$. Hence the string A_2F shortens by $4x$, which slips over the pulley A_2, so that the pulley A_1 descends a distance $4x$ together with the distance through which A_2 descends, *i.e.*, $4x + 3x$, or $7x$. Hence the string A_1G shortens by $8x$, and A_1 itself descends $7x$, so that the point of application of P descends $15x$.

Neglecting the weight of the pulleys, the work done by P therefore

$$= 15x \cdot P = x(2^4 - 1)P = x \cdot W \text{ by equation (1), Art. 150,}$$

$$= \text{work done on the weight } W.$$

Taking the weights of the pulleys into account, the work done by the effort and the weights of the pulleys [which in this case assist the power]

$$= P \cdot 15x + w_1 \cdot 7x + w_2 \cdot 3x + w_3 \cdot x$$

$$= x[P(2^4 - 1) + w_1(2^3 - 1) + w_2(2^2 - 12) + w_3]$$

$$= x \cdot W \text{ by equation (3), Art. 150,}$$

$$= \text{work done on the weight } W.$$

If there were n pulleys we should in a similar manner find the point of application of P moved through $(2^n - 1)$ times the distance moved through by W, so that the velocity ratio is $2^n - 1$.

Examples XXVI

1. In the following cases, the pulleys are weightless and n in number, P is the effort and W the weight ;
   (1) If $n = 4$ and $P = 2$ kgf, find W;
   (2) If $n = 5$ and $W = 124$ kgf, find P;
   (3) If $W = 105$ kg and $P = 7$ kgf, find n.
2. In the following cases, the pulleys are equal and each of weight w, P is the effort and W is the weight ;
   (1) If $n = 4$, $w = 1$ kgf, and $P = 10$ kgf, find W;
   (2) If $n = 3$, $w = \frac{1}{2}$ kgf, and $W = 114$ kgf, find P;
   (3) If $n = 5$, $P = 3$ kgf, and $W = 106$ kgf, find w;
   (4) If $P = 4$ kgf, $W = 137$ kgf, and $w = \frac{1}{2}$ kgf, find n.
3. If there are 5 pulleys, each of weight $\frac{1}{2}$ kg, what effort is required to support 168 kg ?
   If the pulleys are of equal size, find to what point of the bar the weight must be attached, so that the beam may be always horizontal.
4. If the strings passing round a system of 4 weightless pulleys are fastened to a rod without weight at distances successively a cm apart, find to what point of the rod the weight must be attached, so that the rod may be horizontal.
5. Find the mechanical advantage, when the pulleys are 4 in number, and each is of weight $\frac{1}{54}$th that of the weight.
6. In a system of 3 weightless pulleys, in which each string is attached to a bar which carries the weight, if the diameter of each pulley is 2 cm, find to what point of the bar the weight should be attached so that the bar may be horizontal.
7. If the pulleys are equal, and the effort be equal to the weight of one of them, and the number of pulleys be 5, show that the weight is 57 times the power.
8. In the third system of 3 pulleys, if the weights of the pulleys are all equal, find the relation of the effort to the weight when equilibrium is established. If each pulley weighs 50 g, what weight would be supported by the pulleys only ?
   If the weights supported are 12.5 kgf, and the effort be $1\frac{1}{2}$ kgf, find what must be the weight of each pulley.
9. In the third system of weightless pulleys, the weight is supported by an effort of 70 kg. The hook by which one of the strings is attached to the weight breaks, and the string is then attached to the pulley which it passed over, and an effort of 150 kg is now required. Find the number of pulleys and the weight supported.
10. In the third system of weightless pulleys, if the string round the last pulley is tied to the weight, show that the tension of the string is diminished in a ratio depending on the number of pulleys.
    If the tension is decreased in the ratio 16 : 15, find the number of pulleys.

11. In the system of pulleys in which each string is attached to the weight, if each pulley has a weight w, and the sum of the weights of the pulleys is W', and P and W are the effort and weight in this case, show that the effort $P + w$ would support the weight $W + W'$ in the same system if the pulleys had no weight.
12. If there are n weightless pulleys and if a string, whose ends are attached to the weights P and W, carry a pulley from which a weight W' is suspended, find the relation between P, W, and W'.
13. If there are n pulleys, each of diameter $2a$ and of negligible weight, show that the distance of the point of application of the weight from the line of action of the effort should be $\frac{2^n}{2^n - 1} na$.

III. The Inclined Plane

155. The inclined plane, considered as a mechanical power,is a rigid plane inclined at an angle to the horizon.

It is used to help raise of heavy bodies.

In the present chapter we shall only consider the case of a body resting on the plane, and acted upon by forces in a plane perpendicular to the intersection of the inclined plane and the horizontal, *i.e.*, in a vertical plane through the line of greatest slope.

The reader can picture to himself the line of greatest slope on an inclined plane in the following manner : take a rectangular sheet of cardboard $ABCD$, and place it at an angle to the horizontal, so that the line AB is in contact with a horizontal table : take any point P on the cardboard and draw PM perpendicular to the line AB; PM is the line of greatest slope passing through the point P.

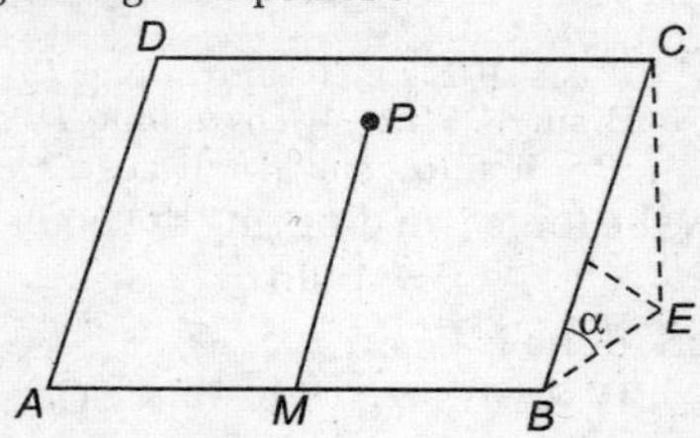

From C draw CE perpendicular to the horizontal plane through AB, and join BE. The lines BC, BE, and CEf are called respectively the length, base, and height of the inclined plane; also the angle CBE is the inclination of the plane to the horizon.

In this chapter the inclined plane is supposed to be smooth, so that the only reaction between it and any body resting on it is perpendicular to the inclined plane.

Since the plane is rigid, it is capable of exerting any reaction, however great, that may be necessary to give equilibrium.

156. *A body, of given weight, rests on an inclined plane ; to determine the relations between the effort, the weight, and the reaction of the plane.*

Let W be the weight of the body, P the effort, and R the reaction of the plane; also let α be the inclination of the plane to the horizon.

Case I. *Let the effort act up the plane along the line of greatest slope.*

Let AC be the inclined plane, AB the horizontal line through A, DE a vertical line, and let the perpendicular to the plane through D meet AB in F.

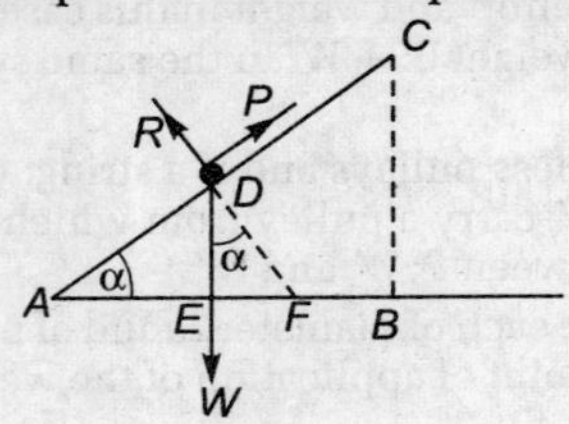

Then clearly

$$\angle FDE = 90° - \angle ADE = \angle DAE = \alpha.$$

By Lami's Theorem (Art. 40), since only three forces act on the body, each is proportional to the sine of the angle between the other two.

$$\therefore \qquad \frac{P}{\sin(R, W)} = \frac{R}{\sin(W, P)} = \frac{W}{\sin(P, R)},$$

$$i.e., \qquad \frac{P}{\sin(180° - \alpha)} = \frac{R}{\sin(90° + \alpha)} = \frac{W}{\sin 90°},$$

$$i.e., \qquad \frac{P}{\sin \alpha} = \frac{R}{\cos \alpha} = W \qquad \text{...(1)}$$

$$\therefore \qquad P = W \sin \alpha, \text{ and } R = W \cos \alpha.$$

The relation (1) may be written in the form

$$P : R : W$$

:: height of plane : base of plane : length of plane.

Otherwise thus : Resolve W along and perpendicular to the plane : its components are

$W \cos ADE$, *i.e.*, $W \sin \alpha$, along DA,

and $W \sin ADE$, *i.e.*, $W \cos \alpha$, long DF.

Hence $P = W \sin \alpha$, and $R = W \cos \alpha$.

The work done by the force P in dragging the body from A to C is $P \times AC$.

But $P = W \sin \alpha$.

Therefore the work done is $W \sin \alpha \times AC$,

i.e., $W \times AC \sin \alpha$, *i.e.*, $W \times BC$.

Hence the work done is the same as that which would be done in lifting the weight of the body through the same height without the intervention of the inclined plane. Hence the Principle of Work is true in this case.

Case II. *Let the effort acts horizontally.*

[In this case we must imagine a small hole in the plane at D through which a string is passed and attached to the body, or else that the body is *pushed* toward the plane by a horizontal force.]

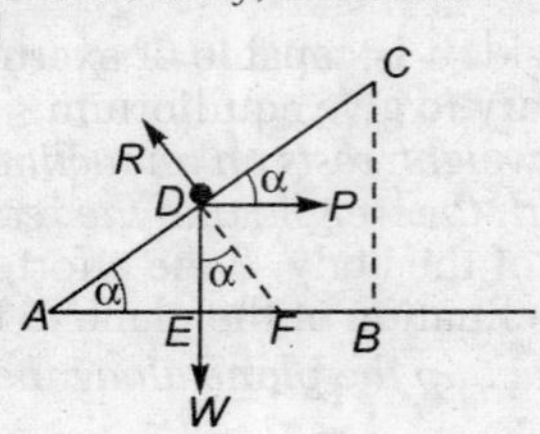

As in Case I, we have

$$\frac{P}{\sin(R, W)} = \frac{R}{\sin(W, P)} = \frac{W}{\sin(P, R)},$$

i.e., $$\frac{P}{\sin(180° - \alpha)} = \frac{R}{\sin 90°} = \frac{W}{\sin(90° + \alpha)}$$

i.e., $$\frac{P}{\sin\alpha} = \frac{R}{1} = \frac{W}{\cos\alpha} \qquad \ldots(1)$$

$\therefore$ $$P = W\tan\alpha, \text{ and } R = W\sec\alpha.$$

The relation (1) may be written in the form

$$P : R : W$$

:: height of plane : length of plane : base of plane.

Otherwise thus : The components of W along and perpendicular to the plane are $W\sin\alpha$ and $W\cos\alpha$; the components of P, similarly, are $P\cos\alpha$ and $P\sin\alpha$.

$\therefore$ $P\cos\alpha = W\sin\alpha$, and

$$R = P\sin\alpha + W\cos\alpha$$

$$= W\left[\frac{\sin^2\alpha}{\cos\alpha} + \cos\alpha\right] = W\frac{\sin^2\alpha + \cos^2\alpha}{\cos\alpha}1 = W\sec\alpha.$$

$\therefore$ $$P = W\tan\alpha, \text{ and } R = W\sec\alpha.$$

Case III. *Let the effort acts at an angle θ with the inclined plane.*

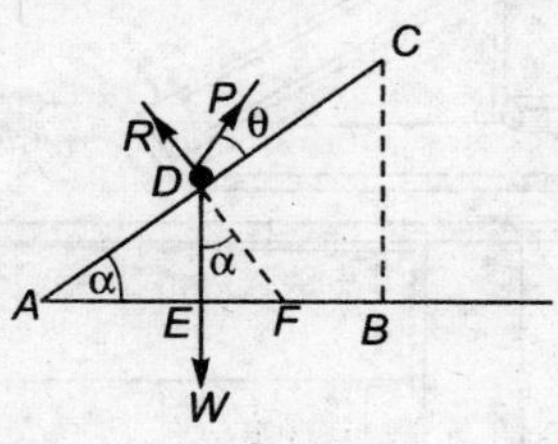

By Lami's Theorem we have

$$\frac{P}{\sin(R, W)} = \frac{R}{\sin(W, P)} = \frac{W}{\sin(P, R)},$$

i.e., $$\frac{P}{\sin(180° - \alpha)} = \frac{R}{\sin(90° + \theta + \alpha)} = \frac{W}{\sin(90° - \theta)},$$

i.e., $$\frac{P}{\sin\alpha} = \frac{R}{\cos(\theta + \alpha)} = \frac{W}{\cos\theta}.$$

$\therefore$ $$P = W\frac{\sin\alpha}{\cos\theta}, \quad \text{and} \quad R = W\frac{\cos(\theta + \alpha)}{\cos\theta}.$$

Otherwise thus : Resolving along and perpendicular to the plane, we have

$$P\cos\theta = W\sin\alpha, \quad \text{and } R + P\sin\theta = W\cos\alpha.$$

$\therefore$ $$P = W\frac{\sin\alpha}{\cos\theta},$$

and $$R = W\cos\alpha - P\sin\theta = W\left[\cos\alpha - \frac{\sin\alpha\sin\theta}{\cos\theta}\right]$$

$$= W\frac{\cos\alpha\cos\theta - \sin\alpha\sin\theta}{\cos\theta} = W\frac{\cos(\alpha+\theta)}{\cos\theta}.$$

If through E we draw EK parallel to P to meet DF in K, then DEK is a triangle of force, and

$$\therefore \quad P : R : W :: EK : KD : DE,$$

and thus we have a graphic construction for P and R.

It will be noted that Case III includes both Cases I and II; if we make θ zero, we obtain Case I; if we put θ equal to $(-\alpha)$, we have Case II.

Verification of the Principle of Work. In Case III let the body move a distance x along the plane; the distance through which the point of application of P moves, measured along its direction of application, is clearly $x\cos\theta$; also the vertical distance through which the weight moves is $x\sin\alpha$.

Hence the work done by the power is $P\cdot x\cos\theta$, and that done against the weight is $W\cdot x\sin\alpha$. These are equal by the relation proved above.

157. Experiment. *To find experimentally the relation the effort and the weight in the case of an inclined plane.*

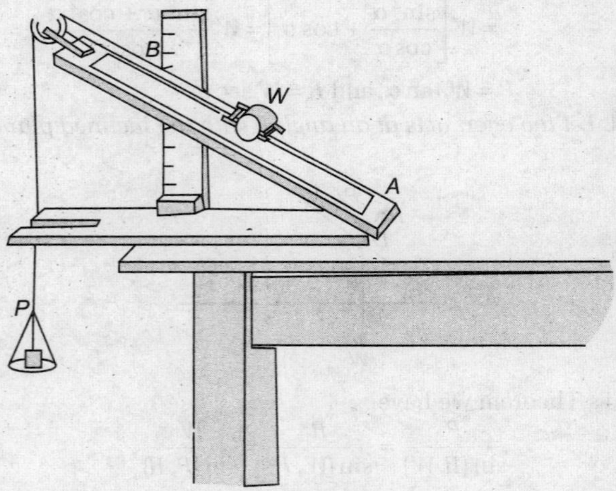

Take a wooden board AB, hinged at A to a second board, which can be clamped to a table; to the board AB let a sheet of glass be fixed in order to minimise the friction. At B is fixed a vertical graduated scale, so that the height of B above A can be easily read off.

The weight consists of a heavy brass roller to which is attached a string which after passing over a pulley supports a scale-pan in which weights can be placed. These weights, together with the weight of the scale-pan, form the 'effort' P.

The pulley is so arranged that the string between it and W is parallel to the plane.

Set the arm AB at any convenient angle; load the scale-pan so that W is just supported. [In actual practice it is better to take for P the mean of the values of the weights which will let W just run down and just drag it up respectively.]

Observe h the height of B above A, and l the length AB.

Then it will be found $\dfrac{P}{W} = \dfrac{h}{l}$.

Now set the board at a different angle and determine F, h, l for this second experiment. The same relation will be found to be true.

If there is a slit along the length of the board through which the string can pass, then a pulley can be arranged in such a position that the string can be horizontal. In this case the effort, as in Case II of Art. 156, will be horizontal and we shall find that

$$\frac{P}{W} = \frac{\text{Height of the plane}}{\text{Base of the plane}}.$$

158. If the power does not act in a vertical plane through the line of greatest slope there could not be equilibrium on a smooth inclined plane; in this case we could, however, have equilibrium if the inclined plane were rough. We shall return to this case in the next chapter.

Examples XXVII

1. What force, acting horizontally, could keep a mass of 16 kg at rest on a smooth inclined plane, whose height is 3 metres and length of base 4 metres, and what is the reaction of the plane ?

2. A body rests on an inclined plane, being supported by a force acting up the plane equal to half its weight. Find the inclination of the plane to the horizon and the reaction of the plane.

3. A rope, whose inclination to the vertical is 30°, is just strong enough to support a weight of 90 kg on a smooth plane, whose inclination to the horizon is 30°. Find approximately the greatest tension that the rope could exert.

4. A body rests on a plane, inclined at an angle of 60° to the horizon, and is supported by a force inclined at an angle of 30° to the horizon ; show that the force and the reaction of the plane are each equal to the weight of the body.

5. A body, of weight $2P$, is kept in equilibrium on an inclined plane by a horizontal force P, together with a force P acting parallel to the plane; find the ratio of the base of the plane to the height and also the reaction of the plane.

6. A body rests on a plane, inclined to the horizon at an angle of 30° being supported by a force inclined at 30° to the plane; find the ratio of the weight of the body to the force.

7. A weight is supported on an inclined plane by a force inclined to the plane; if the weight, the force and the reaction be as the numbers 4, 3 and 2, find the inclination of the plane and the direction of the force.

8. A body, of 5 kgf is placed on a smooth plane inclined at 30°, to the horizon, and is acted on by two forces, one equal to the weight of 2 kg and acting parallel to the plane and upwards, and the other equal to P and acting at an angle of 30° with the plane. Find P and the reaction of the plane.

9. Find the force which acting up an inclined plane will keep a body, of 10 kg weight, in equilibrium, it being given that the force, the reaction of the plane and the weight of the body are in arithmetical progression.

10. If a force P, acting parallel to an inclined plane and supporting a mass of weight W, produces on the plane a thrust R, show that the same power, acting horizontally and supporting a mass of weight R, will produce on the plane a thrust W.

11. Two boards, of lengths 3.3 and 2.4 m, are fixed with their lower ends on a horizontal plane and their upper ends in contact; on these planes rest bodies of weights W and 6 kg respectively, which are connected by a string passing over the common vertex of the boards; find the value of W. (assume the boards meet at right angles)
12. A number of loaded trucks, each containing 1 tonne, on one part of a tramway inclined at an angle α to the horizon supports an equal number of empty trucks on another part whose inclination is β. Find the weight of a truck.
13. A body rests on a plane inclined to the horizon at an angle α; if the reaction of the plane is equal to the effort applied, show that the inclination of the effort to the inclined plane is $90° - 2\alpha$.
14. A heavy string is placed with a portion of it resting on a given inclined plane, the remaining part hanging vertically over small pulley at the top of the plane. Find what point of the string should be placed over the pulley for equilibrium.
15. On two inclined planes, of equal heights, two weights are respectively supported, by means of a string passing over the common vertex and parallel to the planes; the length of one plane is double its height, and the length of the other plane is double its base; show that the reaction of one plane is three times the reaction of the other.
16. A body,of weight 25 kg, is in equilibrium on a smooth plane inclined at an angle of 20°20′ to the horizon, being supported by a force acting up the plane; find graphically or by use of trigonometrical tables, the force and the reaction of the plane.
17. A body, of weight 10 kg, rests on a smooth plane inclined at an angle of 25° to the horizon, being supported by a force P acting at an angle of 35° with the plane; find graphically or by use of trigonometrical tables, P and the reaction of the plane.
18. A body, of weight 15 kg, rests on a smooth plane inclined at an angle of 28°15′ to the horizon, being supported by a horizontal force P; find, graphically or by use of trigonometrical tables, P and the reaction of the plane.

IV. The Wheel and Axle

159. This machine consists of a strong circular cylinder, or axle, terminating in two pivots, A and B, which can turn freely on fixed supports.

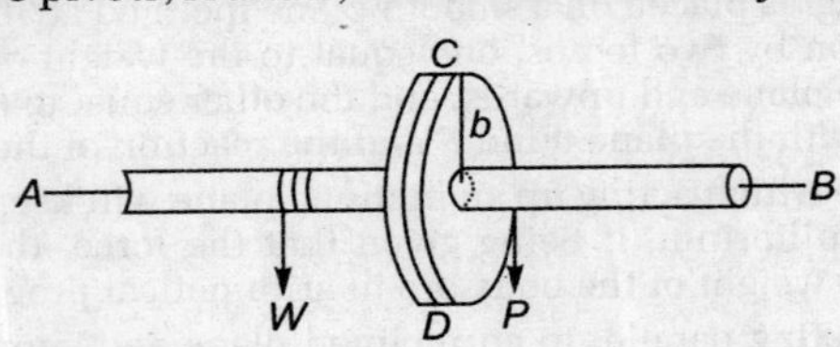

To the cylinder is rigidly attached a wheel, CD, the plane of the wheel being perpendicular to the axle.

Round the axle is coiled a rope, one end of which is firmly attached to the axle, and the other end of which is attached to the weight.

Round the circumference of the wheel, in a direction opposite to that of the first rope, is coiled a second rope, having one end firmly attached to the wheel, and having the effort, applied at its other end. The circumference of the wheel is grooved to prevent the rope from slipping off.

160. *To find the relation between the effort and the weight.*

In Art. 93, we have shown that a body, which can turn freely about a fixed axis, is in equilibrium if the algebraic sum of the moments of the forces about the axis vanishes. In this case, the only forces acting on the machine are the effort P and the weight W, which tend to turn the machine in opposite directions. Hence, if a is the radius of the axle, and b is the radius of the wheel, the condition of equilibrium is

$$P \cdot b = W \cdot a \qquad \ldots(1)$$

Hence the mechanical advantage $= \dfrac{W}{P}$

$$= \frac{b}{a} = \frac{\text{radius of the wheel}}{\text{radius of the axle}}$$

Verification of the Principle of Work. Let the machine turn through four right angles. A portion of string whose length is $2\pi b$ becomes unwound from the wheel, and hence P descends through this distance. At the same time a portion equal to $2\pi a$ becomes wound upon the axle, so that W rises through this distance. The work done by P is therefore $P \times 2\pi b$ and that done against W is $W \times 2\pi a$. These are equal by the relation (1).

Also the velocity-ratio (Art. 137)

$$= \frac{2\pi b}{2\pi a} = \frac{b}{a} = \text{the mechanical advantage.}$$

161. Theoretically, by making the quantity $\dfrac{b}{a}$ very large, we can make the mechanical advantage as great as we please; practically however there are limits. Since the pressure of the fixed supports on the axle must balance P and W, it follows that the thickness of the axle, *i.e.*, $2a$, must not be reduced unduly, for then the axle would break. Neither can the radius of the wheel in practice become very large, for then the machine would be unwieldy. Hence the possible values of the mechanical advantage are bounded, in one direction by the strength of our materials, and in the other direction by the necessity of keeping the size of the machine within reasonable limits.

162. In Art. 160 we have neglected the thicknesses of the ropes. If, however, they are too great to be neglected, compared with the radii of the wheel and axle, we may take them into consideration by supposing the tensions of the ropes to act along their middle threads.

Suppose the radii of the ropes which pass round the axle and wheel to be x and y respectively ; the distances from the line joining the pivots at which the tensions now act are $(a + x)$ and $(b + y)$ respectively. Hence the condition of equilibrium is

$$P(b + y) = W(a + x),$$

so that $$\frac{P}{W} = \frac{\text{sum of the radii of the axle and its rope}}{\text{sum of the radii of the wheel and its rope}}.$$

163. Other forms of the wheel and axle are the windlass, used for drawing water from a well, and capstan, used on board ship. In these machines the effort instead of being applied, as in Art. 159, by means of a rope passing round a cylinder, is applied at the ends of a spoke, or spokes, which are inserted in a plane perpendicular to the axle.

In the windlass the axle is horizontal, and in the capstan it is vertical.

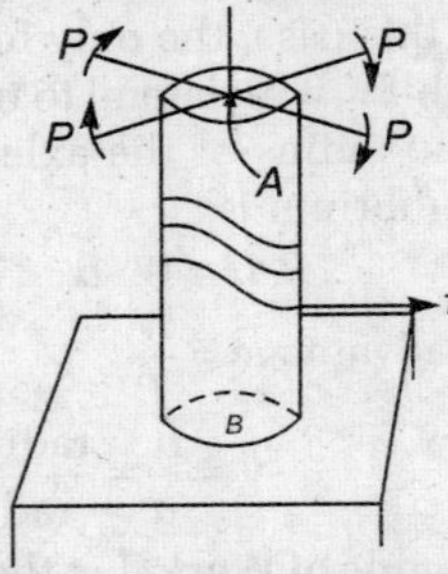

In the latter case the resistance consists of the tension T of the rope round the axle, and the effort consists of the forces applied at the ends of bars inserted into sockets at the point A of the axle. The advantage of pairs of arms is that the strain on the bearings of the capstan is thereby much diminished or destroyed. The condition of equilibrium may be obtained as in Art. 160.

164. Differential Wheel and Axle. A slightly modified form of the ordinary wheel and axle is the differential wheel and axle. In this machine the axle consists of two cylinders, having a common axis, joined at their ends, the radii of the two cylinders being different. One end of the rope is wound round one of these cylinders, and its other end is wound in a contrary direction round the other cylinder. Upon the slack portion of the rope is slung a pulley to which the weight is attached. The part of the rope which passes round the smaller cylinder tends to turn the machine in the same direction as the effort.

As before, let b be the radius of the wheel and let a and c be the radii of the portion AC and CB of the axle, a being the smaller.

Since the pulley is smooth, the tension T of the string round it is the same throughout its length, and hence, for the equilibrium of the weight, we have $t = \frac{1}{2}W$.

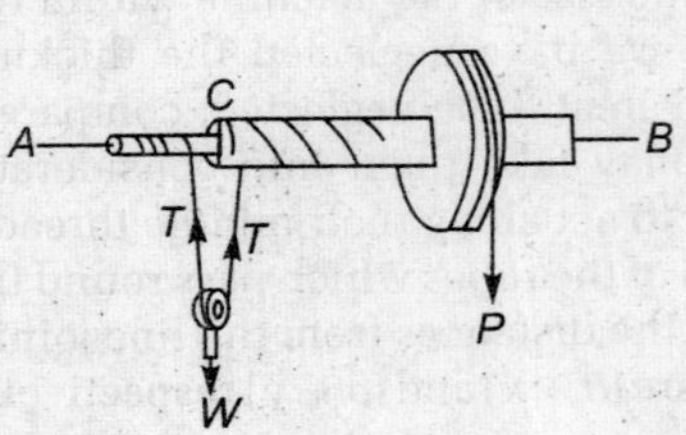

Taking moments about the line AB for the equilibrium of the machine, we have

$$P \cdot b + T \cdot a = T \cdot c.$$

$$\therefore \qquad P = T\frac{c-a}{b} = \frac{W}{2}\frac{c-a}{b}.$$

Hence the mechanical advantage $= \dfrac{W}{P} = \dfrac{2b}{c-a}$.

By making the radii c and a of the two portions of the axle very nearly equal, we can make the mechanical advantage very great, without unduly weakening the machine.

165. Weston's Differential Pulley. In this machine there are two blocks, the upper contains two pulleys of nearly the same size which turn together as one pulley; the lower consists of one pulley to which the weight W is attached.

The figure represents a section of the machine.

An endless chain passes round the larger of the upper pulleys, then round the lower pulley and the smaller of the upper pulleys; the remainder of the chain hangs slack and is joined on to the first portion of the chain. The effort P is applied as in the figure. The chain is prevented from slipping by small projections on the surfaces of the upper pulleys, or by depressions in the pulleys into which the links of the chain fit.

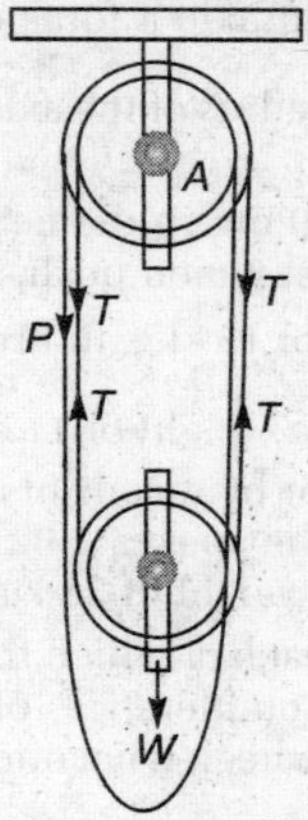

If T is the tension of the portions of the chain which support the weight W, we have, since these portions are approximately nearly vertical, on neglecting the weight of the chain and the lower pulley,

$$2T = W \qquad \ldots(1)$$

If R and r are the radii of the larger and smaller pulleys of the upper block we have, by taking moments about the centre A of the upper block,

$$P \cdot R + T \cdot r = T \cdot R.$$

$$\text{Hence} \qquad P = T\frac{R-r}{R} = \frac{W}{2}\frac{R-r}{R}.$$

The mechanical advantage of this system therefore

$$= \frac{W}{P} = \frac{2R}{R-1}.$$

Since R and r are nearly equal this mechanical advantage is therefore very great.

The differential pulley-block avoids one great disadvantage of the differential wheel and axle. In the latter machine a very great amount of rope is required in order to raise the weight through an appreciable distance.

Examples XXVIII

1. If the radii of the wheel and axle are respectively 60 cm and $7\frac{1}{2}$ cm, find what force must be applied to raise a weight of 28 kg.
2. If the radii of the wheel and axle are respectively 75 cm and $12\frac{1}{2}$ cm, find what weight would be supported by a force equal to the weight of 10 kg, and find also the pressures on the supports on which the axle rests.

   If the thickness of the rope is $2\frac{1}{2}$ cm , find what weight would now be supported.
3. If by means of a wheel and axle a force equal to $1\frac{1}{2}$ kg weight balances a weight of 15 kg, and if the radius of the axle is 5 cm, what is the radius of the wheel ?
4. The axle of a capstan is 40 cm in diameter and there are 8 bars. At what distance from the axis must 8 men push, 1 at each bar and each exerting a force equal to the weight of $13\frac{1}{3}$ kg, in order that they may just produce a strain sufficient to raise the weight of 1120 kg ?
5. Four sailors raise an anchor by means of a capstan, the radius of which is 10 cm and the length of the spekes 1.8 m from the capstan; if each man exerts a force equal to the weight of 56 kg, find the weight of the anchor.
6. Four wheels and axles, in each of which the radii are in the ratio of 5 : 1, are arranged so that the circumference of each axle is applied to the circumference of the next wheel; what effort is required to support a weight of $937\frac{1}{2}$ kg ?
7. The radii of a wheel and axle are 60 cm and 5 cm respectively and the strings which hang from them are tied to the two ends of a uniform rod, 65 cm length and 5 kg in weight; what weight must be also hung from one of the strings that the rod may hang in a horizontal position ?
8. A pulley is suspended by a vertical loop of string from a wheel-and-axle and supports a weight of 56 kg, one end of the string being wound round the axle and the other in a contrary direction round the wheel. Find the force which acting at one end of an arm, 60 cm in length, so as to turn the axle, will support the weight, assuming the radii of the wheel and axle to be 30 cm and 5 cm.

9. In the differential wheel and axle, if the radius of the wheel is 30 cm and the radii of the two portions of the axle $12\frac{1}{2}$ and 10 cm respectively, what force will support a weight of 28 kg ?

10. In the differential wheel and axle, if the radius of the wheel is 45 cm and the radii of the two portions of the axle 15 and 10 cm respectively, what weight will be supported by and effort equal to 10 kg weight ?

11. In a wheel and axle the radius of the wheel is 30 cm and that of the axle is $2\frac{1}{2}$ cm; if 2 weights, each 5 kg, are fastened to 2 points on the rim of the wheel, so that the line joining them subtends an angle of 120° at the centre of the wheel, find the greatest weight which can be supported by a string hanging from the axle in the usual way.

12. In a wheel and axle, if the radius of the wheel be six times that of the axle, and if by means of an effort equal to 2.5 kgf a body is lifted through 15 m, find the amount of work expended.

13. A capstan, of diameter 50 cm, is worked by means of a lever, which measures 1.5 m from the axis of the capstan. Find the work done in drawing up by a rope a body of weight 1120 kg, over 10.5 m of the surface of a smooth plane inclined to the horizon at an angle $\cos^{-1}\frac{4}{5}$. Find also the force applied to the end of the lever, and the distance through which the point of application moves.

14. Verify the principle of work in the cases of the differential wheel-and-axle and Weston's differential pulley, finding the velocity ratio in each case.

V. The Common Balance

166. The common balance consists of a rigid beam *AB* (Art. 167), carrying a scale-pan suspended from each end, which can turn freely about a fulcrum *O* outside the beam. The fulcrum and the beam are rigidly connected and, if the balance is well constructed, at the point *O* is a hard steel wedge, whose edge is turned downward and which rests on a small plate of agate.

The body to be weighed is placed in one scale-pan and in the other are placed weights, whose magnitudes are known; these weights are adjusted until the beam of the balance rests in a horizontal position. If *OH* is perpendicular to the beam, and the arms *HA* and *HB* are of equal lengths, and if the centre of gravity of the beam lies in the line *OH,* and the scale-pans are of equal weights, then the weight of the body is the same as the sum of the weights placed in the other scale-pan.

If the weight of the body is not equal to the sum of the weights placed in the other scale-pan, the balance will not rest with its beam horizontal, but will rest with the beam inclined to the horizon.

In the best balances the beam is usually provided with a long pointer attached to the beam at *H*. The end of this pointer travels along a graduated scale and, when the beam is horizontal, the pointer is vertical and points to the zero graduation on the scale.

167. *To Find the position of equilibrium of a balance when the weights placed in the scale-pans are not equal.*

Let the weights placed in the scale-pans be P and W, the former being the greater; let S be the weight of each scale-pan, and let the weight of the beam (and the parts rigidly connected with it) be W', acting at a point K on OH.

[*The figure is drawn out of proportion so that the points may be distinctly marked; K is actually very near the beam.*]

When in equilibrium let the beam be inclined at an angle θ to the horizontal, so that OH is inclined at the same angle θ to the vertical.

Let OH and OK be h and k respectively, and let the length of AH or HB be a.

Let horizontal lines through O and H meet the vertical lines through the ends A and B of the beam in the points L, M, L', and M' respectively.

Also let the vertical lines through H and K meet LM in F and G respectively.

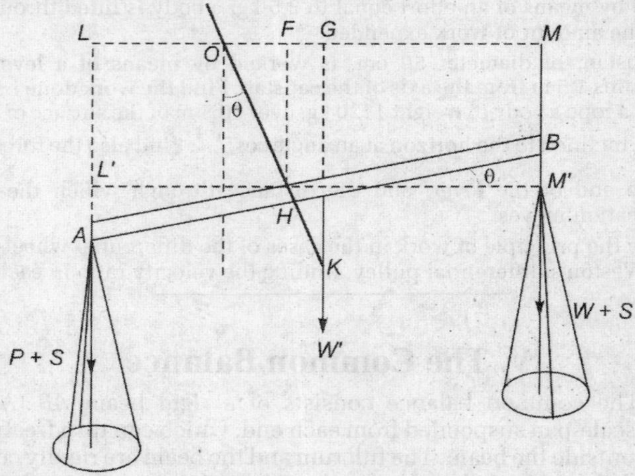

When the system is in equilibrium, the moments of the forces about O must balance.

$$\therefore \quad (P+S)\cdot OL = (W+S)OM + W'\cdot OG'$$

i.e.,
$$(P+S)(FL-FO) = (W+S)(FM+OF) + W'\cdot OG,$$

$$\therefore \quad (P+S)(a\cos\theta - h\sin\theta) = (W+S)(a\cos\theta + h\sin\theta) + W'\cdot k\sin\theta$$

[For $\quad OF = OH\cos FOH = h\sin\theta;\ OG = OK\sin\theta;$

and $\quad FL = HL' = a\cos\theta$]

$$\therefore \quad a\cos\theta\,(P-W) = \sin\theta\,[W'k + (P+W+2S)h].$$

$$\therefore \quad \tan\theta = \frac{(P-W)a}{W'k + (P+W+2S)h}.$$

168. *Requisites of a good balance.*

(1) The balance must be **true.**

This will be the case if the arms of the balance are equal, if the weights of the scale-pans are equal, and if the centre of gravity of the beam is on the line through the fulcrum perpendicular to the beam; for the beam will now be horizontal when equal weights are placed in the scale-pans.

To test whether the balance is true, first see if the beam is horizontal when the scale-pans are empty; then make the beam horizontal by putting sufficient weights in one scale-pan to balance the weight of a body placed in the other; now interchange the body and the weights; if they still balance one another, the balance must be true; if in the second case the beam assumes any position inclined to the vertical, the balance is not true.

(2) The balance must be **sensitive**, *i.e.*, the beam must for any difference, however small, between the weights in the scale-pans, be inclined at an appreciable angle to the horizon.

For a *given* difference between P and W, the greater the inclination of the beam to the horizon the more sensitive is the balance; also the less the difference between the weights required to produce a given inclination θ, the greater is the sensitiveness of the balance.

Hence, when $P - W$ is given, the sensitiveness increases as θ increases, and therefore as $\tan\theta$ increases; also, when θ given, it varies as

$$\frac{1}{P - W}.$$

The sensitiveness is therefore appropriately measured by

$$\frac{\tan\theta}{P - W},$$

i.e., by
$$\frac{a}{W'k + (P + W + 2S)h}. \qquad \text{(Art. 167.)}$$

Hence, the sensitiveness of a balance will be greater if the arm a is fairly long in comparison with the distances h and k and the weight W of the beam is as small as is consistent with the length and rigidity of the machine.

If L is not zero, it follows that the sensitiveness depends on the values of P and W, *i.e.*, depends on the loads on the scale-pans. In a balance for use in a chemical laboratory this is undesirable. Such balances are therefore made with h zero, *i.e.*, with the point O in the figure coinciding with H. The sensibility then varies inversely with k, the distance of the centre of gravity of the beam below O or H.

But we must not make both h and k zero; for then the points O and K would both coincide with H. In this case the balance would either when the weights in the scale-pans were equal, be, as in Art. 144, in equilibrium in *any* position or else, if the weights in the scale-pans were not equal, it would take up a position as nearly vertical as the mechanism of the machine would allow.

(3) The balance must be **stable** and must quickly take up its position of equilibrium.

The determination of the time taken by the machine to take up its position of equilibrium is essentially a dynamical question. We may however *assume* that this condition is best satisfied when the moment of the forces about the fulcrum O is greatest. When the weights in the scale-pans are each P, the moment of the forces tending to restore equilibrium

$$= (P + S)(a\cos\theta + h\sin\theta) - (P + S)(a\cos\theta - h\sin\theta) + W' \cdot k\sin\theta$$
$$= [2(P + S)h + W' \cdot k]\sin\theta.$$

This expression is greatest when h and k are greatest.

Since the balance is most sensitive when h and k are small, and most stable when these quantities are large, we see that in any balance great sensitiveness and quick weighing are to a certain extent incompatible. In practice this is not very important; for in balances where great sensitiveness is required (such as balances used in a laboratory) we can afford to sacrifice quickness of weighing; the opposite is the case when the balance is used for ordinary commercial purposes.

To insure as much as possible both the qualities of sensitiveness and quick weighing, the balance should be made with fairly light long arms, and at the same time the distance of the fulcrum from the beam should be considerable.

169. Double weighing. By this method the weight of a body may be accurately determined even if the balance is not accurate.

Place the body to be weighed in one scale-pan and in the other pan put sand, or other suitable material, sufficient to balance the body. Next remove the body, and in its place put known weights sufficient to again balance the sand. The weight of the body is now clearly equal to the sum of the weights.

This method is used even in the case of extremely good machines when very great accuracy is desired. It is known as Borda's Method.

170. Ex. 1. *The arms of a balance are equal in length but the beam is unjustly loaded; if a body is placed in each scale-pan in succession and weighed, show that its weight is the arithmetic mean between its apparent weights.*

For let the length of the arms be a, and let the horizontal distance of the centre of gravity of the beam from the fulcrum be x.

Let a body, whose true weight is W, appears to weigh W_1 and W_2 successively.

If W' be the weight of the beam, we have

$$W \cdot a = W' \cdot x + W_1 \cdot a,$$

and

$$W_2 \cdot a = W' \cdot x + W \cdot a.$$

Hence, by subtraction

$$(W - W_2)a = (W_1 - W)\,a$$

$$\therefore \quad W = \frac{1}{2}(W_1 + W_2)$$

= arithmetic mean between the apparent weights.

Ex. 2. *The arms of a balance are of unequal lengths, but the beam remains in a horizontal position when the scale-pans are not loaded ; show that, if a body is placed successively in each scale-pan, its true weight is the geometrical mean between its apparent weight.* [Method of Gauss]

Show also that if a tradesman appears to weigh out equal quantities of the same substance, using alternately each of the scale-pans, he will defraud himself.

Since the beam remains horizontal when there are no weights in the scale-pans, it follows that the centre of gravity of the beam and scale-pans must be vertically under the fulcrum.

Let a and b be the lengths of the arms of the beam and let a body, whose true weight is W, appears to weigh W_1 and W_2 successively.

Hence $$W \cdot a = W_1 \cdot b \qquad ...(1)$$

and $$W_2 \cdot a = W \cdot b \qquad ...(2)$$

Hence, by multiplication, we have

$$W^2 \cdot ab = W_1 W_2 \cdot ab.$$

$$\therefore \qquad W = \sqrt{W_1 \cdot W_2},$$

i.e., the true weight is the geometrical mean between the apparent weights.

Again, if the tradesman appears to weigh out in succession quantities equal to W, he really gives his customers $W_1 + W_2$.

Now, $$W_1 + W_2 - 2W = W\frac{a}{b} + W\frac{b}{a} - 2W$$

$$= W\frac{a^2 + b^2 - 2ab}{ab} = W\frac{(a-b)^2}{ab}.$$

Now, whatever be the values of a and b, the right-hand member of this equation is always positive, so that $W_1 + W_2$ is always $> 2W$. Hence, the tradesman defrauds himself.

Numerical example. If the lengths of the arms are 22 and 24 cm respectively, and if the nominal quantity weighed be 33 kg in each case, the real quantities are $\frac{22}{24} \times 33$ and $\frac{24}{22} \times 33$, *i.e.*, $30\frac{1}{4}$ and 36, *i.e.*, $66\frac{1}{4}$ kg, so that the tradesman loses $\frac{1}{4}$ kg.

Ex. 3. *If a balance is unjustly weighted, and has unequal arms, and if a tradesman weigh out to a customer a quantity 2W of some substance by weighing equal portions in the two scale-pans, show that he will defraud himself if the centre of gravity of the beam is in the longer arm.*

Let a and b be the lengths of the arms; and let the weight W' of the machine acts at a point in the arm b at a distance x from the fulcrum. Let a body of weight W, placed in the two pans in succession, be balanced by W_1 and W_2 respectively. Then we have

$$W \cdot a = W_1 \cdot b + W' \cdot x,$$

and $$W_2 \cdot a = W \cdot b + W' \cdot x.$$

$$\therefore \qquad W_1 + W_2 - 2W = \frac{W \cdot a - W' \cdot x}{b} + \frac{W \cdot b + W' \cdot x}{a} - 2W$$

$$= \frac{W(b-a)^2}{ab} + W'\frac{b-a}{ab}x.$$

If b is $> a$, the right-hand member of this equation is positive, and then $W_1 + W_2$ is $> 2W$.

Hence, if the centre of gravity of the beam is in the longer arm, the tradesman will defraud himself.

Examples XXIX

1. The only fault in a balance being the unequalness in weight of the scale-pans, what is the real weight of a body which balances 10 kg when placed in one scale-pan, and 12 kg when placed in the other ?
2. The arms of a balance are $43\frac{3}{4}$ and 45 cm respectively, the goods be weighed being suspended from the longer arm; find the real weight to of goods whose apparent weight is 13.5 kg.
3. One scale of a common balance is loaded so that the apparent weight of a body, whose true weight is 450 g, is 500 g; find the weight with which the scale is loaded.
4. A substance, weighed from the two arms successively of a balance, has apparent weights 9 and 4 kg. Find the ratio of the lengths of the arms and the true weight of the body.
5. A body, when placed in one scale-pan, appears to weigh 12 kg and, when placed in the other, 12.5 kg. Find its true weight to three places of decimals, assuming the arms of the scale-pans to be of unequal length.
6. A piece of lead in one pan A of a balance is counterpoised by 25 grammes in the pan B; when the same piece of lead is put into the pan B it requires 26 grammes in A to balance it; what is the ratio of the lengths of the arms of the balance ?
7. A body, placed in a scale-pan, is balanced by 5 kg placed in the other pan; when the position of the body and the weights are interchanged, 5.5 kg are required to balance the body. If the length of the shorter arm is 30 cm, find the length of the longer arm and the weight of the body.
8. The arms of a false balance, whose weight is neglected, are in the ratio of 10 : 9, If goods be alternately weighed from each arm, show that the seller loses $\frac{5}{9}$ th per cent.
9. If the arms of a false balance are 20 and $22\frac{1}{2}$ cm long respectively, find the prices really paid by a person for tea at four rupees per kg, if the tea is weighed out from the end of (1) the longer, (2) the shorter arm.
10. A dealer has correct weights, but one arm of his balance is $\frac{1}{20}$th part shorter than the other. If he sells two quantities of a certain drug, each apparently weighing $4\frac{3}{4}$ kg, at Rs. 18/kg, weighing one in one scale and the other in the other, what will he gain or lose ?
11. When a given balance is loaded with equal weights, it is found that the beam is not horizontal, but it is not known whether the arms are of unequal lengths, or the scale-pans of unequal weights; 102.150 g in one scale balances 102.724 in the other, and 51.184 g balances 51.758 g; show that the arms are equal, but that the scale-pans differ in weight by 0.574 g.
12. P and Q balance on a common balance; on interchanging them it is found that we must add to Q one-hundredth part of itself; what is the ratio of the arms and the ratio of P to Q ?
13. A true balance has one scale unjustly loaded; if a body is successively weighed in the two scales and appears to weigh P and Q pounds respectively, find the amount of the unjust load and also the true weight of the body.

14. The arms of a false balance are unequal and the scale loaded; a body, whose true weight is P kg, appears to weigh w kg when placed in one scale and w' kg when placed in the other; find the ratio of the arms and the weight with which the scale is loaded.

15. In a loaded balance with unequal arms, P appears to weigh Q, and Q appears to weigh R; find what R appears to weigh.

16. A piece of wood in the form of a long wedge, of uniform width, one end being 1 cm and the other $\frac{1}{2}$ cm thick, is suspended by its centre of gravity and used as the beam of a balance, the goods to be weighed being suspended from the longer arm; find the true weight of goods whose apparent weight is 10 kg.

17. The arms of a false balance are a and b and a weight W balances P at the end of the shorter arm b, and Q at the end of the arm a; show that

$$\frac{a}{b} = \frac{P - W}{W - Q}.$$

18. If a man, sitting in one scale of a weighing-machine, presses with a stick against any point of the beam between the point from which the scale is suspended and the fulcrum, show that he will appear to weigh more than before.

VI. The Steelyards

171. The common, or roman, steelyard is machine for weighing bodies and consists of a rod AB, movable about a fixed fulcrum at a point C.

At the point A is attached a hook or scale-pan to carry the body to be weighed, and on the arm CB slides a movable weight P. The point at which P must be placed, in order that the beam may rest in a horizontal position, determines the weight of the body in the scale-pan. The arm CB has numbers engraved on it at different points of its length, so that the graduation at which the weight P rests gives the weight of the body.

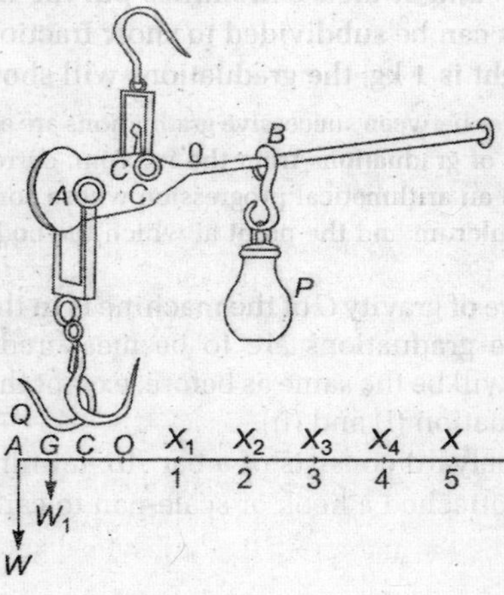

172. *To graduate the Steelyard.* Let W' be the weight of the steelyard and the scale-pan, and let G be the point of the beam through which W' acts. The beam is usually constructed so that G lies in the shorter arm AC.

When there is no weight in the scale-pan, let O be the point in CB at which the movable weight P must be placed to balance W'.

Taking moments about C, we have

$$W' \cdot GC = P \cdot CO \qquad \text{...(i)}$$

This condition determines the position of the point O which is the zero of graduation.

When the weight in the scale-pan is W, let X be the point at which P must be placed. Taking moments, we have

$$W \cdot CA + W' \cdot GC = P \cdot CX \qquad \text{...(ii)}$$

By subtracting equation (i) from equation (ii), we have

$$W \cdot CA = P \cdot OX$$

$$\therefore \qquad OX = \frac{W}{P} \cdot CA \qquad \text{...(iii)}$$

First, let $W = P$; then, by (iii), we have

$$OX = CA.$$

Hence, if from O we measure off a distance $OX_1 (= CA)$, and if we mark the point X_1 with the figure 1, then, when the movable weight rests here, the body in the scale-pan is P kg.

Secondly, let $W = 2P$; then, from (iii), $OX = 2CA$.

Hence from O mark off a distance $2CA$, and at the extremity put the figure 2. Thirdly, let $W = 3P$; then, from (iii), $OX = 3CA$, and we therefore mark off a distance from O equal to $3CA$, and mark the extremity with the figure 3.

Hence, to graduate the steelyard, we must mark off from O successive distances CA, $2CA$, $3CA$... and at their extremities put the figures 1, 2, 3, 4, ... The intermediate spaces can be subdivided to show fractions of P kg.

If the movable weight is 1 kg, the graduations will show kilogrammes.

Cor. Since, the distances between successive graduations are equal, if follows that the distances of the points of graduations from the fulcrum, corresponding to equal increments of weight, form an arithmetical progression whose common difference is the distance between the fulcrum and the point at which the body to be weighed is attached.

173. When the centre of gravity G of the machine is in the longer arm, the point O from which the graduations are to be measured must lie in the shorter arm. The theory will be the same as before, except that in this case we shall have to add the equation (i) and (ii).

174. The Danish steelyard consists of a bar AB, terminating in a heavy knob, or ball, B. At A is attached a hook or scale-pan to carry the body to be weighed.

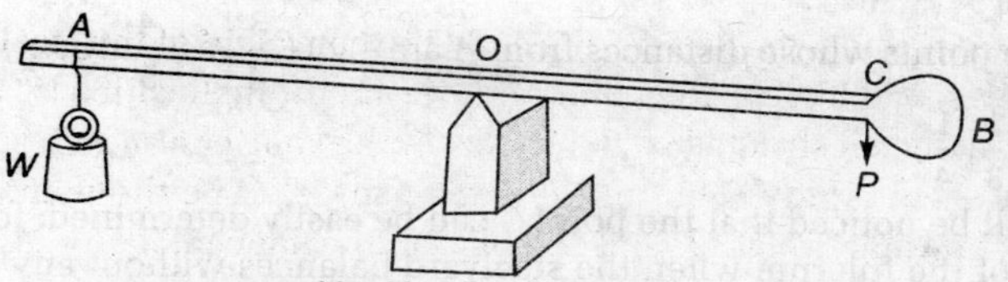

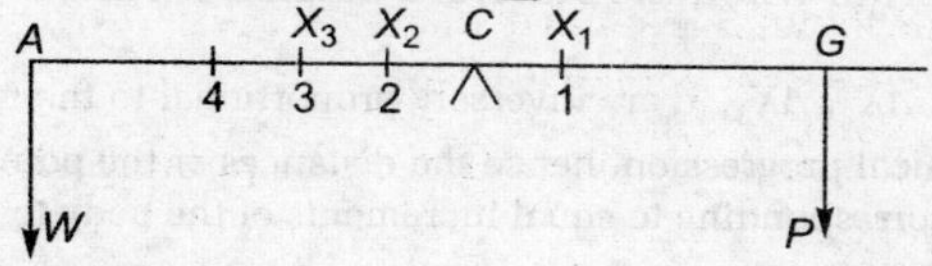

The weight of the body is determined by observing about what point of the bar the machine balances.

[This is often done by having a loop of string, which can slide along the bar, and finding where the loop must be to give equilibrium].

175. *To graduate the Danish steelyard.* Let P be the weight of the bar and scale-pan, and let G be their common centre of gravity. When a body of weight W is placed in the scale-pan, let C be the position of the fulcrum.

By taking moments about C, we have

$$AC \cdot W = CG \cdot P = (AG - AC) \cdot P.$$

$$\therefore \quad AC\,(P + W) = P \cdot AG.$$

$$\therefore \quad AC = \frac{P}{P+W} \cdot AG \qquad \text{...(i)}$$

First, let $\quad W = P$, then $AC = \frac{1}{2}\,AG.$

Hence, bisect AG and at the middle point, X_1, engrave the figure 1; when the steelyard balances about this point the weight of the body in the scale-pan is P.

Secondly, let $\quad W = 2P$; then $AC = \frac{1}{3}\,AG.$

Take a point at a distance from A equal to $\frac{1}{3}\,AG$ and mark it 2.

Next, let W in succession be equal to $3P, 4P, \ldots$; from (i), the corresponding values of AC are $\frac{1}{4}\,AG, \frac{1}{5}\,AG, \ldots$ Take points of the bar at these distances from A and mark them 3, 4, ...

Finally, let $\quad W = \frac{1}{2}\,P$ then from (i), $AC = \frac{2}{3}\,AG;$

and let $\quad W = \frac{1}{2}\,P$ then, from (i) $AC = \frac{3}{4}\,AG.$

Take points whose distances from A are $\frac{2}{3}AG, \frac{3}{4}AG, \frac{4}{5}AG, \ldots$, and mark them $\frac{1}{2}, \frac{1}{3}, \frac{1}{4}, \ldots$

It will be noticed that the point G can be easily determined; for it is the position of the fulcrum when the steelyard balances without any weight in the scale-pan.

Cor. Since AX_1, AX_2, AX_3, ... are inversely proportional to the numbers 2, 3, 4,... they form an harmonical progression, hence the distances of the points of graduation from the scale-pan (corresponding to equal increments of the body to be weighed) are in harmonical progression.

Ex. *A Danish steelyard weighs* 3 kg *, and the distance of its centre of gravity from the scale-pan is* 30 cm*; find the distances of the successive points of graduation from the fulcrum.*

Taking the notation of the preceding article, we have $P = 3$, and $AG = 30$ cm.

$$\therefore \quad AC = \frac{3}{3+W} \times 30 = \frac{90}{W+3} \text{ cm.}$$

$$\therefore \text{ when} \quad W = 1,\ AX_1 = \frac{90}{4} = 22\frac{1}{2} \text{ cm,}$$

$$\text{when} \quad W = 2,\ AX_2 = \frac{90}{5} = 18 \text{ cm,}$$

$$\text{when} \quad W = 3,\ AX_3 = \frac{90}{6} = 15 \text{ cm.}$$

....

$$\text{when} \quad W = \frac{1}{2},\ AX_{\frac{1}{2}} = \frac{90}{\frac{1}{2}+3} = 25\frac{5}{7} \text{ cm}$$

and so on.

These give the required graduations.

Examples XXX

1. A common steelyard weighs 5 kg; the weight is suspended from a point 8 cm from the fulcrum, and the centre of gravity of the steelyard is 6 cm on the other side of the fulcrum; the movable weight is 6 kg; where should the graduation corresponding to 56 kg be situated ?
2. A heavy tapering rod, 29 cm long and of weight 1.5 kg, has its centre of gravity $3\frac{1}{3}$ cm from the thick end and is used as a steelyard with a imovable weight of 1 kg; where must the fulcrum be placed, so that it may weigh up 6 kg, and what are the intervals between the graduations that denote pounds ?
3. In a steelyard, in which the distance of the fulcrum from the point of suspension of the weight is 2 cm and the movable weight is 150 g, to weigh 6.0 kg the weight must be placed 16 cm from the fulcrum ; where must it be placed to weigh 9.6 kg ?
4. The fulcrum is distant $2\frac{2}{3}$ cm from the point at which are suspended the goods to be weighed, and is distant 4 cm from the centre of gravity of the

bar; the bar itself weighs 1.5 kg and a 1 kg weight slides on it. At what distance apart are the graduations marking successive kg weight, and what is the least weight that can be weighed ?

5. A steelyard, AB, 1.2 m long, has its centre of gravity $27\frac{1}{2}$ cm and its fulcrum 20 cm, from A. If the weight of the machine is 2 kg and the movable weight is 1.5 kg, find how many cm from B is the graduation marking 7.5 kg.

6. A uniform bar, AB, 60 cm long and weighing 1.5 kg, is used as a steelyard, being supported at a point 10 cm from A. Find the greatest weight that can be weighed with a movable weight of 1 kg, and find also the point from which the graduations are measured.

7. A uniform rod being divided into 20 equal parts, the fulcrum is placed at the first graduation. The greatest and least weights which the instrument can weigh are 10 and 1 kg; find its weight and the magnitude of the movable weight.

8. A uniform rod, 60 cm long and of weight 1.5 kg, is used as a steelyard, whose fulcrum is 5 cm from one end, the sliding weight being $\frac{1}{2}$ kg. Find the greatest and the least weights that can be measured.
Where should the sliding weight be to show 10 kg ?

9. The beam of a steelyard is 66 cm in length; the fulcrum is distant 8 cm and the centre of gravity of the beam 11 cm from the point of attachment of the weight; if the weight of the beam is 3 kg and the heaviest weight that can be weighted be 12 kg, find the magnitude of the movable weight.

10. A steelyard is formed of a uniform bar, 90 cm long and weighing $1\frac{1}{4}$ kg, and the fulcrum is distant 10 cm from one end; if the movable weight is $\frac{1}{2}$ kg, find the greatest and least weights that can be weighed by the machine and the distance between the graduations when it is graduated to show kg.

11. A common steelyard, supposed uniform, is 80 cm long, the weight of the beam is equal to the movable weight, and the greatest weight that can be weighed by it is four times the movable weight; find the position of the fulcrum.

12. In a Danish steelyard the distance between the zero graduations and the end of the instrument is divided into 20 equal parts and the greatest weight that can be weighed is 1.425 kg; find the weight of the instrument.

13. Find the length of the graduated arm of a Danish steelyard, whose weight is $\frac{1}{2}$ kg, and in which the distance between the graduations denoting 2 and 2.5 kg is 2 cm.

14. In a Danish steelyard the fulcrum rests halfway between the first and second graduation; show that the weight in the scale-pan is $\frac{7}{5}$th of the weight of the bar.

15. If the weight of a steelyard be worn away to one-half, its length and centre of gravity remaining unaltered, what correction must be applied to make the weighing true, if the distance of the zero point of graduation from the fulcrum were originally one-third of the distance between successive graduations, and if the movable weight be one kg ?

16. A steelyard by use loses $\frac{1}{10}$th of its weight, its centre of gravity remaining unaltered; show how to correct its graduations.

17. A shopman, using a common steelyard, alters the movable weight for which it has been graduated; does he cheat himself or his customers

18. In a weighing machine constructed on the principle of a common steelyard, the kg are read off by graduations reading from 0 to 7 kg and the stones by a weight hung at the end of the arm; if the weight corresponding to 7 kg is $218\frac{3}{4}$g, the movable weight $\frac{1}{4}$ kg, and the length of the arm measured from the fulcrum 30 cm, show that the distance between successive graduations is $1\frac{7}{8}$ cm.

19. A weighing machine is constructed so that for each complete kg placed in the weighing pan an additional mass of m grammes has to be placed at the end of the arm, which is 30 cm in length mesured from the fulcrum, whilst the odd grammes in the weighing pan are measured by a mass of n grammes sliding along the weighing arm. Show that the distances between the graduations for successive kg must be $\frac{6m}{7n}$ cm, and that the distance from the fulcrum of the point of suspension of the weight is $\frac{3m}{5n}$ cm.

VII. The Screw

176. A screw consists of a cylinder of metal round the outside of which runs a protuberant thread of metal.

Let $ABCD$ be a solid cylinder, and let $EFGH$ be a rectangle, whose base

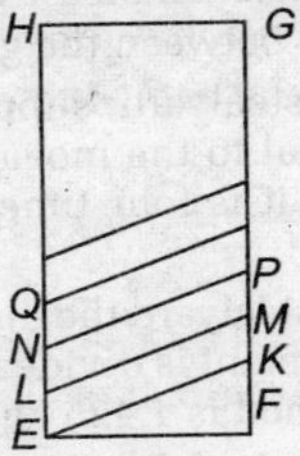

EF is equal to the circumference of the solid cylinder. On EH and FG take points

$$L, N, Q \ldots \quad \text{and} \quad K, M, P \ldots$$

such that $\quad EL, LN, \ldots \; FK, KM, MP \ldots$

are all equal, and join EK, LM, NP, ...

Wrap the rectangle round the cylinder, so that the point E coincides with A and EH with the line AD. On being wrapped round the cylinder the point F will coincide with E at A.

The lines EK, LM, NP, ... will now become a continuous spiral line on the surface of the cylinder and, if we imagine the metal along this spiral line to become protuberant, we shall have the thread of a screw.

It is evident, by the method of construction, that the thread is an inclined plane running round the cylinder and that its inclination of the horizon is the same everywhere and equal to the angle *KEF*. This angle is often called the angle of the screw, and the distance between two consecutive threads, measured parallel to the axis, is called the pitch of the screw.

It is clear that *FK* is equal to the distance between consecutive threads on the screw, and that *EF* is equal to the circumference of the cylinder on which the thread is traced.

$$\therefore \tan(\text{angle of screw}) = \frac{FK}{EF}$$

$$= \frac{\text{pitch of screw}}{\text{circumference of a circle whose radius is the distance from the axis of any point of the screw.}}$$

The section of the thread of the screw has, in practice, various shapes. The only kind that we shall consider has the section rectangular.

177. The screw usually works in a fixed support, along the inside of which is cut out a hollow of the same shape as the thread of the screw, and along which the thread slides. The only movement admissible to the screw is to revolve about its axis, and at the same time to move in a direction parallel to its length.

If the screw were placed in an upright position, and a weight placed on its top, the screw would revolve and descend since there is supposed to be no friction between it and its support. Hence, if the screw is to remain in equilibrium, some force must act on it; this force is usually applied at one end of a horizontal arm, the other end of which is rigidly attached to the screw.

178. *In a smooth screw, to find the relation between the effort and the weight.*

Let a be the distance of any point on the thread of the screw from its axis and b the distance, *AB*, from the axis of the screw, of the point at which the effort is applied.

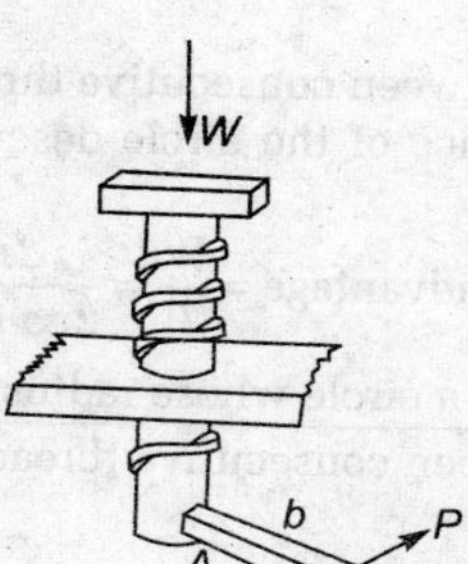

The screw is in equilibrium under the action of the effort P, the weight W, and the reactions at the points in which the fixed block touches the thread of the screw. Let $R, S, T, \ldots$ Denote the reactions of the block at different points of the thread of the screw. These will be all perpendicular to the thread of the screw, since it is smooth.

Let α be the inclination of the thread of the screw to the horizontal.

The horizontal and vertical components of the reaction R are $R \sin \alpha$ and $R \cos \alpha$ respectively.

Similarly, we may resolve $S, T, \ldots$

Hence the reactions of the block are equivalent to a set of forces $R \cos \alpha$, $S \cos \alpha$, $T \cos \alpha, \ldots$ vertically, and a set $R \sin \alpha$, $S \sin \alpha$, $T \sin \alpha, \ldots$ horizontally.

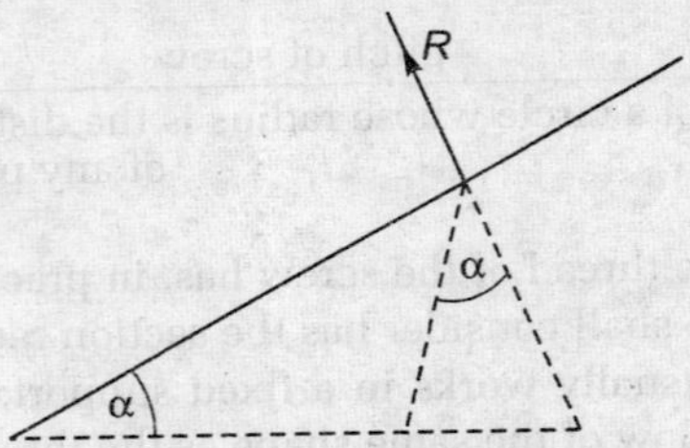

These latter forces, though they act at different points of the screw, all act at the same distance from the axis of the screw; they also tend to turn the screw in the opposite direction to that of P.

Equating the vertical forces, we have

$$W = R \cos \alpha + S \cos \alpha + \ldots = (R + S + T + \ldots) \cos \alpha \qquad \ldots (1)$$

Also, taking moments about the axis of the screw, we have, by Art. 93,

$$P \cdot b = R \sin \alpha \cdot a + S \sin \alpha \cdot a + T \sin \alpha \cdot a + \ldots$$

$$= a \sin \alpha \, (R + S + T + ..) \qquad \ldots (2).$$

From equations (1) and (2) we have, by division,

$$\frac{P \cdot b}{W} = \frac{a \sin \alpha}{\cos \alpha},$$

$$\therefore \quad \frac{P}{W} = \frac{a}{b} \tan \alpha = \frac{2\pi a \tan a}{2\pi b}.$$

But, by Art. 176,

$2\pi a \tan \alpha$ = distance between consecutive threads = pitch of the screw.

Also $2\pi b$ = circumference of the circle described by the end B of the effort-arm.

Hence the mechanical advantage $= \dfrac{W}{P} = \dfrac{2\pi b}{2\pi a \tan \alpha}$

$$= \frac{\text{circumference of a circle whose radius is the effort-arm}}{\text{distance between consecutive threads of the screw}}$$

Verification of the Principle of Work.

For each revolution made by the effort-arm the screw rises through a distance equal to the distance between two consecutive threads.

Hence, during each revolution, the work done by the effort is

$P \times$ circumference of the circle described by the end of the effort-arm and that done against the weight is

$W \times$ distance between two consecutive threads.

These are equal by the relation just proved.

***179.** Theoretically, the mechanical advantage in the case of the screw can be made as large as we please, by decreasing sufficiently the distance between the threads of the screw. In practice, however, this is impossible; for, if we diminish the distance between the threads to too small a quantity, the threads themselves would not be sufficiently strong to bear the strain put upon them.

By means of **Hunter's Differential Screw** this difficulty may be overcome.

In this machine we have a screw AD working in a fixed block. The inside of the screw AD is hollow and is grooved to admit a smaller screw DE. The screw DE is fastened at E to a block, so that it cannot rotate, but can only move in the direction of its length.

When the effort-arm AB has made one revolution, the screw AD has advanced a distance equal to the distance between two consecutive threads, and at the same time the smaller screw goes into DA a distance equal to the

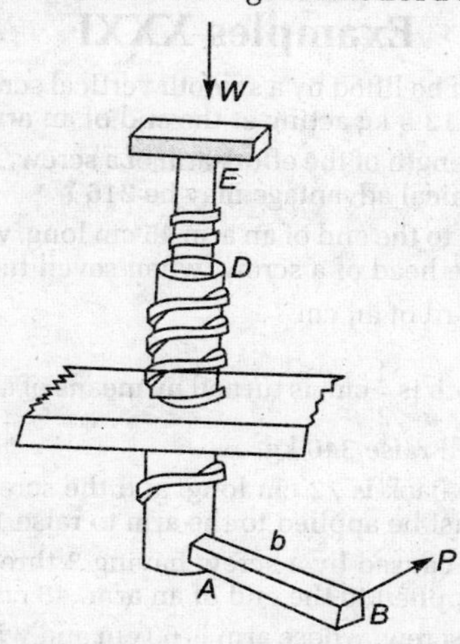

distance between two consecutive threads of the smaller screw. Hence the smaller screw and therefore also the weight, advances a distance equal to the *difference* of these two distances.

When in equilibrium let $R, S, T, \ldots$ be the reactions between the larger screw and its block, and $R', S', T', \ldots$ the reactions between the inner and outer screws; let a and a' be the radii, and α and α' the angles of the screws.

As in the last article, since the outer screw is in equilibrium, we have

$$P \cdot b = (R + S + T + \ldots) \sin \alpha \cdot a - (R' + S' + \ldots) \sin \alpha' \cdot a' \qquad \ldots(1)$$

and

$$(R + S + T + \ldots) \cos \alpha = (R' + S' + \ldots) \cos \alpha' \cdot a' \qquad \ldots(2)$$

Also, since the inner screw is in equilibrium, we have

$$W = (R' + S' + T' \ldots) \cos \alpha' \qquad \ldots(3)$$

From (2) and (3), we have

$$R' S' + \ldots = \frac{W}{\cos \alpha'}, \quad \text{and} \quad R + S + \ldots \frac{W}{\cos \alpha}.$$

Hence, from (1),

$$P \cdot b = W \cdot a \tan \alpha - W \cdot a \tan \alpha'.$$

$$\therefore \frac{W}{P} = \frac{2\pi b}{2\pi a \tan \alpha - 2\pi a' \tan \alpha}$$

$$= \frac{\text{circum. of the circle described by the end of the effort-arm}}{\text{difference of the pitches of the two screws}}$$

By making the pitches of the two screws nearly equal, we can make the mechanical advantage very great without weakening the machine.

The principle of work is seen to be true in this case also; for the weight rises in this case a distance equal to the difference between the pitches of the screws.

Examples XXXI

1. Find what mass can be lifted by a smooth vertical screw of 5 cm pitch, if the power is a force of 12.5 kg acting at the end of an arm, 84 cm long.
2. What must be the length of the effort-arm of a screw, having 3 threads to the cm, so that mechanical advantage may be 216 ?
3. What force applied to the end of an arm 45 cm long, will produce a pressure of 550 kgf upon the head of a screw, when seven turns cause the screw to advance through $\frac{5}{3}$ rd of an cm ?
4. A screw, whose pitch is $\frac{1}{2}$ cm, is turned by means of a lever, 96 cm long; find the force which will raise 340 kg.
5. The arm of a screw-jack is 72 cm long, and the screw has 1 threads to the cm. What force must be applied to the arm to raise 1120 kg ?
6. What is the thrust caused by a screw having 2 threads to the cm, when a force of 25 kgf is applied to the end of an arm, 48 cm long ?
7. What thrust will a screw, whose arm is 60 cm and with one thread per 3 cm of its length, produce, if the effort is a force of 56 kg weight ?
8. If the effort is applied at the end of an arm of 30 cm in length, and if the screw makes seven complete turns in 30 cm of its length, find the effort that will support a weight of 1120 kg.
9. If the lever by which a screw is worked is 1.8 m in length, determine the distance between two successive threads of the screw, in order that a thrust

of 5 kg applied to each end of the lever may produce a thrust of 500 kg at the end of the screw.

10. Find the mechanical advantage in a differential screw, having 5 threads to 2 cm and 3 threads to the cm, the effort being applied at the circumference of a wheel of diameter 96 cm.

11. Find the mechanical advantage in a differential screw, the larger screw having 4 threads to the cm and the smaller 9 threads to 2 cm the length of the effort-arm being 24 cm.

12. If the axis of a screw is vertical and the distance between the threads 5 cm, and a door, of weight 50 kg, is attached to the screw as to a hinge, find the work done in turning the door through a right angle.

13. Prove that the tension of a stay is equal to 10080 kg if it be set up by a force of $24\frac{1}{2}$ kg at a leverage of 48 cm acting on a double screw having a right-handed screw of 5 threads to 2 cm and a left-handed one of 3 threads to the cm.

[For one complete turn of the screw its ends are brought nearer by a distance of $\left(\frac{2}{5}+\frac{1}{3}\right)$ cm. Hence the principle of work gives

$$T \times \left(\frac{2}{5}+\frac{1}{3}\right) = 24\frac{1}{2} \times 2\pi \cdot 48,$$

where T is the tension of the stay in kg.]

14

Friction

180. In Art. 20 we defined smooth bodies to be bodies such that, if they are in contact, the only action between them is perpendicular to both surfaces at the point of contact. With smooth bodies, therefore, there is no force tending to prevent one body sliding over the other. If a perfectly smooth body is placed on a perfectly smooth inclined plane, there is no action between the plane and the body to prevent the latter from sliding down the plane, and hence the body will not remain at rest on the plane unless some external force is applied to it.

Practically, however, there are no bodies which are perfectly smooth ; there is always *some* force between two bodies in contact to prevent one sliding upon the other. Such a force is called the force of friction.

Friction. Def. *If two bodies are in contact with one another, the property of the two bodies, by virtue of which a force is exerted between them at their point of contact to prevent one body sliding on the other, is called friction ; also the force exerted is called the force of friction.*

181. Friction is a self-adjusting force; no more friction is called into play than is sufficient to prevent motion.

Let a heavy slab of iron with a plane base be placed on a horizontal table. If we attach a piece of string to some point of the body, and pull in a horizontal direction passing through the centre of gravity of the slab, a resistance is felt which prevents our moving the body; this resistance is exactly equal to the force which we exert on the body.

If we now stop pulling, the force of friction also ceases to act ; for, if the force of friction did not cease to act, the body would move.

The amount of friction which can be exerted between two bodies is not, however, unlimited. If we continually increase the force which we exert on the slab, we find that finally the friction is not sufficient to overcome this force, and the body moves.

182. Friction plays an important part in the mechanical problems of ordinary life. If there were no friction between our boots and the ground, we should not be able to walk; if there were no friction between a ladder and the ground, the ladder would not rest, unless held, in any position inclined to the vertical; without friction nails and screws would not remain in wood, nor would a locomotive engine be able to draw a train.

183. The laws of static friction are as follows :

Law I. *When two bodies are in contact, the direction of the friction on one of them at its point of contact is opposite to the direction in which this point of contact would commence to move.*

Law II. *The magnitude of the friction is, when there is equilibrium, just sufficient to prevent the body from moving.*

184. Suppose, in Art. 156, Case I, the plane to be rough, and that the body, instead of being supported by a force, rested freely on the plane. In this case the force P is replaced by the friction, which is therefore equal to $W \sin \alpha$.

Ex. 1. In what direction does the force of friction act in the case of (1) the wheel of a carriage, (2) the feet of a man who is walking ?

Ex. 2. A body, of weight 30 kg, rests on a rough horizontal plane and is acted upon by a force, equal to 10 kg wt, making an angle of 30° with the horizontal ; show that the force of friction is equal to about 8.66 kg wt.

Ex. 3. A body, resting on a rough horizontal plane, is acted on by two horizontal forces, equal respectively to 7 and 8 kg wt, and acting at an angle of 60° ; show that the force of friction is equal to 13 kg wt in a direction making an angle $\sin^{-1} \dfrac{4\sqrt{3}}{13}$ with the first force.

Ex. 4. A body, of weight 40 kg, rests on a rough plane inclined at 30° to the horizon, and is supported by (1) a force of 14 kg wt acting up the plane, (2) a force of 25 kg acting up the plane, (3) a horizontal force equal to 20 kg wt, (4) a force equal to 30 kg wt making an angle of 30° with the plane.

Find the force of friction in each case.

Ans. (1) 6 kg wt up the plane; (2) 5 kg wt down the plane ; (3) 2.68 kg wt up the plane ; (4) 5.98 kg wt down the plane.

185. The above laws hold good, in general ; but the amount of friction that can be exerted is limited, and equilibrium is sometimes on the point of being destroyed, and motion often ensues.

Limiting Friction. Def. *When one body is just on the point of sliding upon another body, the equilibrium is said to be limiting, and the friction then exerted is called limiting friction.*

186. The direction of the limiting friction is given by Law I. (Art. 183).

The magnitude of the limiting friction is given by the three following laws.

Law III. *The magnitude of the limiting friction always bears a constant ratio to the normal reaction, and this ratio depends only on the substances of which the bodies are composed.*

Law IV. *The limiting friction is independent of the extent and shape of the surfaces in contact, so long as the normal reaction is unaltered.*

Law V. *When motion ensues, by one body sliding over the other, the direction of friction is opposite to the direction of motion ; the magnitude of the friction is independent of the velocity, but the ratio of the friction of the normal reaction is slightly less than when the body is at rest and just on the point of motion.*

The above laws are experimental, and cannot be accepted as rigorously accurate, though they represent, however, to a fair degree of accuracy the facts under ordinary conditions.

For example, if one body is pressed so closely on another that the surfaces in contact are on the point of being crushed, Law III is no longer true; the friction then increases at a greater rate than the normal reaction.

187. Coefficient of Friction. The constant ratio of the limiting friction to the normal pressure is called the coefficient of friction, and is generally denoted by μ ; hence, if F is the friction, and R the normal pressure, between two bodies when equilibrium is on the point of being destroyed, we have $\frac{F}{R} = \mu$, and hence $F = \mu R$.

The values of μ are widely different for different pairs of substances in contact ; no pairs of substances are, however, known for which the coefficient of friction is as great as unity.

188. *To verify the laws of friction by experiment.*

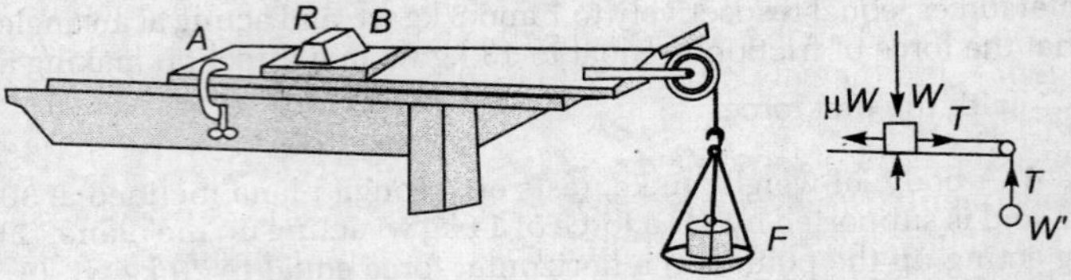

Experiment 1. Take a large smooth piece of wood (A) and clamp it firmly so as to be horizontal. Take a second piece of wood (B) to act as a sliding piece and make it as smooth as possible ; attach a light string to it and pass the string over a light pulley fixed at the end of the piece A, and at the other end of the string attach a scale-pan.

The pulley should be so placed that the part of the string, which is not vertical, should be horizontal.

Upon the sliding piece put a known weight R, and into the scale pan put known weights, F, until the slider is just on the point oOf motion. The required weight F can be very approximately ascertained by gently tapping the fixed piece A.

Consider now the right-hand diagram.

Let W is the total weight of R and the sliding piece, and W' the total weight of F and the scale-pan. Since the slider is just on the point of motion the friction on it is μW ; also the tension T of the string is equal to W', since it just balances the scale-pan and F.

From the equilibrium of the slider we have

$$\mu W = T = W'.$$

$$\mu = \frac{W'}{W}.$$

Next, put a different weight on the slider, and adjust the corresponding weight F until the slider is again on the point of motion and calculate the new values, W_1 and W_1' of W and W'. Then, as before,

$$\mu = \frac{W_1'}{W_1}.$$

Perform the experiment again with different weights on the slider and obtain the values of

$$\frac{W_2'}{W_2}, \frac{W_3'}{W_3}, \ldots$$

The, approximately, it will be found that

$$\frac{W'}{W}, \frac{W_1'}{W_1}, \frac{W_2'}{W_2}, \ldots$$

Will be the same.

Hence, the truth of the first part of Law III, *viz. that the value of* μ *is independent of the normal reaction.*

Experiment 2. Take another piece of wood (B) whose shape is quite different from the piece used in Experiment 1. [This should be obtained by cutting it from the same piece of well-planed wood from which the first piece B was taken.]

The area of this piece B in contact with the board A should differ considerably from that in Experiment 1, whether greater or less is immaterial.

Perform the Experiment 1 over again and deduce the corresponding value of μ. It will be found to be, within the limits of experiment, the same as in Experiment 1. but the only difference in the two experiments is the extent of the rough surfaces in contact.

Hence the truth of Law IV.

Experiment 3. Take another piece of a different kind of wood (C) and plane it well. Cut out from it pieces, of different area, but with surfaces otherwise as nearly alike as possible.

Perform Experiments 1 and 2 over again and obtain the value of μ. This value of μ will be found to differ from the value of μ found when the slider was made of wood B. Hence the truth of the second part of Law III, *viz.* that *the ratio depends on the substances of which the bodies are composed.*

Experiment 4. Perform the above three experiments over again but in this case choose F not so that the slider shall just be on the point of motion, but so that *the slider shall move with a constant velocity.* The truth of Law V will then approximately appear.

However carefully the surfaces of the wood used in the previous experiments are prepared, the student must expect to find some considerable discrepancies in the actual numerical results obtained. There must also be applied a correction for the force necessary to make the pulley turn. However light and well-made it may be, there will always be a certain amount of friction on its axis. Hence the tensions of the string on each side of it will not quite be equal, as we have assumed ; in other words some part of F will be used in turning the pulley.

189. Angle of Friction. When the equilibrium is limiting, if the friction and the normal reaction are compounded into one single force, the angle which this force makes with the normal is called the angle of friction, and the single force is called the resultant reaction.

Let A be the point of contact of the two bodies, and let AB and AC be the directions of the normal force R and the friction μR.

Let AD be the direction of the resultant reaction S, so that the angle of friction is BAD. Let this angle be λ.

Since R and μR are the components of S. we have

$$S \cos \lambda = R,$$

and

$$S \sin \lambda = \mu R.$$

Hence by squaring and adding, we have

$$S = R\sqrt{1 + \mu^2},$$

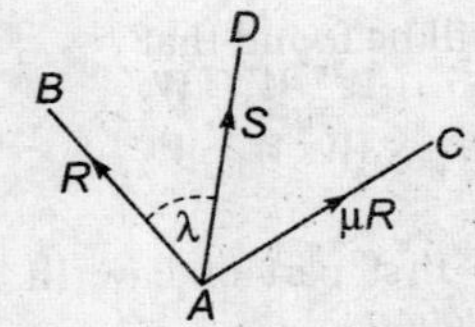

and, by division

$$\tan \lambda = \mu.$$

Hence, we see that *the coefficient of friction is equal to the tangent of the angle of friction.*

190. Since the greatest value of the friction is μR, it follows that the greatest angle which the direction of resultant reaction can make with the normal is λ, *i.e.*, $\tan^{-1} \mu$.

Hence, if two bodies are in contact and if, with the common normal as axis, and the point of contact as vertex, we describe a cone whose semi-vertical angle is $\tan^{-1} \mu$, it is possible for the resultant reaction to have any direction lying within, or upon, this cone, but it cannot have any direction lying without the cone.

This cone is called the **Cone of friction.**

191. The following table, taken from Prof. Rankine's *Machinery and Millwork*, gives the coefficients and angles of friction for a few substances.

Substances		μ	λ
Wood on wood	—Dry	0.25 to 0.5	$14°$ to $26\frac{1°}{2}$
Wood on wood	—Soaped	0.04 to 0.2	$2°$ to $11\frac{1°}{2}$
Metals on metals	—Dry	0.15 to 0.2	$8\frac{1°}{2}$ to $11\frac{1°}{2}$
Metals on metals	—Wet	0.3	$16\frac{1°}{2}$
Leather on metals	—Dry	0.56	$29\frac{1°}{2}$
Leather on metals	—Wet	0.36	$20°$
Leather on metals	—Oily	0.15	$8\frac{1°}{2}$

192. *If a body is placed upon a rough inclined plane, and is on the point of sliding down the plane under the action of its weight and the reactions of the plane* only, *the angle of inclination of the plane to the horizon is equal to the angle of friction.*

Let θ be the inclination of the plane to the horizon, W the weight of the body, and R the normal reaction.

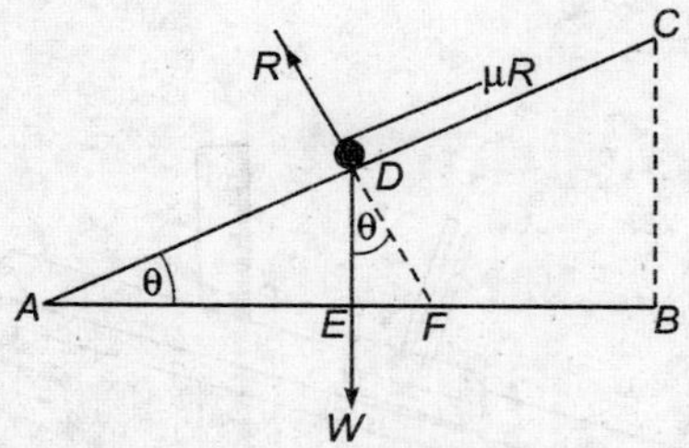

Since the body is on the point of motion *down* the plane, the friction acts *up* the plane and is equal to μR.

Resolving perpendicular and parallel to the plane, we have

$$W \cos\theta = R,$$

and $$W \sin\theta = \mu R.$$

Hence, by division,

$$\tan\theta = \mu = \tan \text{(angle of friction)},$$

$$\therefore \quad \theta = \text{the angle of friction.}$$

This may be shown otherwise thus :

Since the body is an equilibrium under the action of its weight and the resultant reaction, the latter must be vertical ; but, since the equilibrium is limiting, the resultant reaction makes with the normal the angle cf friction.

Hence the angle between the normal and the vertical is the angle of friction, *i.e.*, the indination of the plane to the horizon is the angle of friction.

On account of the property just proved the angle of friction is sometimes called the angle of repose.

The student must carefully notice that, when the body rests on the inclined plane *supported by an external force*, it must not be assumed that the coefficient of friction is equal to the tangent of inclination of the plane to the horizon.

193. *To determine the coefficient of friction experimentally, and to verify the laws of friction.* [Second Method.]

By means of the theorem of the previous article the coefficient of friction between two bodies may be experimentally obtained.

For let an inclined plane be made of one of the substances and let its face be made as smooth as is possible; on this face let there be placed a slab, having a plane face, composed of the other substance.

If the angle of inclination of the plane be gradually increased, until the slab *just* slides, the tangent of the angle of inclination is the coefficient of friction.

To obtain the result as accurately as possible, the experiment should be performed a large number of times with the same substances, and the mean of all the results taken.

In the apparatus here drawn we have a board hinged at one end to another board which can be clamped to the table. The hinged board can be raised or lowered by a string attached to it whose other end passes over the top of a fixed support.

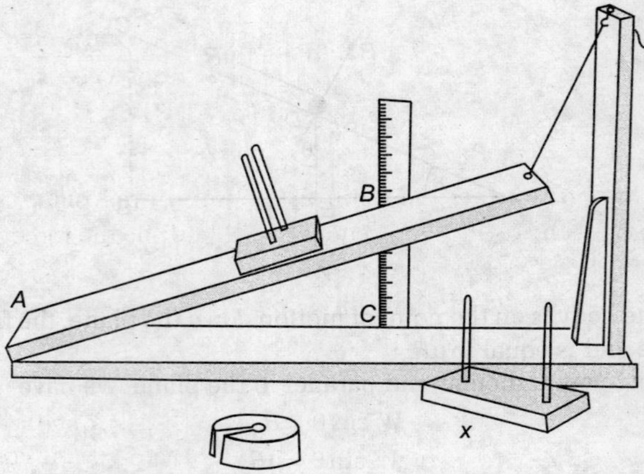

On the hinged board can be placed sliders of different sizes and materials upon which various weights can be placed. Each slider x has two thin brass rods screwed to it on which weights can be piled so that they shall not slip during the experiment. A graduated vertical scale is attached to the lower board, so that the height of the hinged boards at B is easily seen. The value of $\frac{BC}{AC}$, *i.e.*, $\tan\theta$ of Art. 185, in then easily obtained.

By this apparatus the laws of friction can be verified ; for within the limits of experiment, it will be found that the value of $\frac{BC}{AC}$, *i.e.*, μ,

(1) is always the same so long as the slide x is made of the same material in the same state of preparedness of surface,

(2) is independent of the weights put upon the slide, or of its shape,

(3) is different for different substances.

This method is the one used by Coulomb in the year 1785.

194. Equilibrium on a rough inclined plane. *A body is placed on a rough plane inclined to the horizon at an angle greater than the angle of friction, and is supported by a force, acting parallel to the plane, and along a line of greatest slope ; to find the limits between which the force must lie.*

Let α be the inclination of the plane to the horizontal, W the weight of the body, and R the normal reaction (Fig. I, Art. 156).

(i) Let the body be on the point of motion *down* the plane, so that the friction acts *up* the plane and is equal to μR ; let P be the force required to keep the body at rest.

Resolving parallel and perpendicular to the plane, we have

$$P + \mu R = W \sin\alpha \quad \text{...(1),}$$

and $$R = W \cos\alpha \quad \text{...(2).}$$

$\therefore$ $$P = W(\sin\alpha - \mu\cos\alpha).$$

If $\mu = \tan\lambda$, we have

$$P = W[\sin\alpha - \tan\lambda\cos\alpha]$$

$$= W\left[\frac{\sin\alpha\cos\lambda - \sin\lambda\cos\alpha}{\cos\lambda}\right]$$

$$= W\,\frac{\sin(\alpha - 1)}{\cos\lambda} \quad \text{...(3).}$$

(ii) Let the body be on the point of motion *up* the plane, so that the friction acts *down* the plane and is equal to μR ; let P_1 be the force required to keep the body at rest. In this case, we have

$$P_1 - \mu R = W\sin\alpha,$$

and $$R = W\cos\alpha.$$

Hence $$P_1 = W(\sin\alpha + \mu\cos\alpha)$$

$$= W[\sin\alpha + \tan\lambda\cos\alpha] = W\,\frac{\sin(\alpha+\lambda)}{\cos\lambda} \quad \text{...(4).}$$

These values, P and P_1, are the limiting values of the force, if the body is to remain in equilibrium ; if the force lies between P and P_1, the body remains in equilibrium, but is not on the point of motion in either direction.

Hence, for equilibrium, the force must lie between the values

$$W\,\frac{\sin(\alpha \pm \lambda)}{\cos\lambda}.$$

It will be noted that the value of P_1 may be obtained from that of P by changing the sign of μ.

195. If the power P acts at an angle θ with the inclined plane (as in Art. 156, Case III), when the body is on the point of motion *down* the plane and the friction acts therefore *up* the plane, the equations of equilibrium are

$$P\cos\theta + \mu R = W\sin\alpha \quad \text{...(1),}$$

$$P\sin\theta + R = W\cos\alpha \quad \text{...(2).}$$

Hence, multiplying (2) by μ, and subtracting, we have

$$P = W\,\frac{\sin\alpha - \mu\cos\alpha}{\cos\theta - \mu\sin\theta} = W\,\frac{\sin(\alpha-\lambda)}{\cos(\theta+\lambda)}$$

By substituting this value of P in (2), the value of R may be found.

When the body is on the point of motion *up* the plane we have, by changing the sign of μ,

$$P_1 = W\,\frac{\sin(\alpha+\lambda)}{\cos(\theta-\lambda)}$$

Cor. The force that will just be on the point of moving the body up the plane is least when

$$W\,\frac{\sin(\alpha+\lambda)}{\cos(\theta+\lambda)} \text{ is least,}$$

i.e., when $$\cos(\theta - \lambda) \text{ is unity,}$$

i.e., when $$\theta = \lambda.$$

Hence the force required to move the body up the plane will be least when it is applied in a direction making with the inclined plane an angle equal to the angle of friction.

196. The results of the previous article may be found by geometric construction.

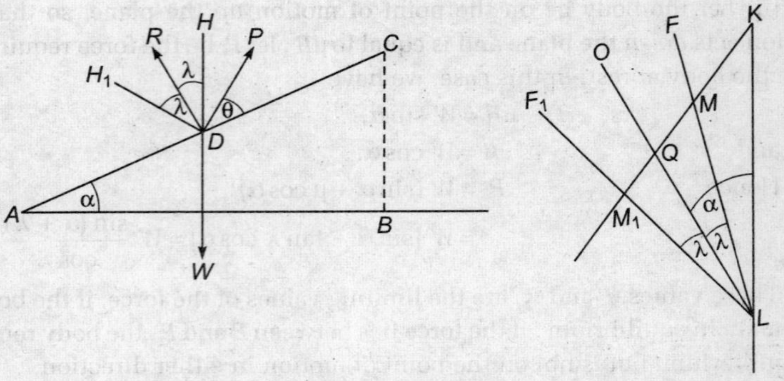

Draw a vertical line KL to represent W on any scale that is convenient (*e.g.* one inch per lb or one inch per 10 lb).

Draw LO parallel to the direction of the normal reaction R. Make OLF, OLF_1 each equal to the angle of friction λ, as in the figure.

Then LF, LF_1 are parallel to the directions DH, DH_1 of the resulting reaction at D according as the body is on the point of motion down or up the plane.

Draw KMM_1 parallel to the supporting force P to meet LF, LF_1 in M and M_1.

Then clearly KLM and KLM_1 are respectively the triangles of forces for the two extreme positions of equilibrium.

Hence, on the same scale that KL represents W, KM and KM_1 represent the P and P_1 of the previous article.

Clearly $\quad OLK = \angle$between R and the vertical $= \alpha$, so that

$$\angle MLK = \alpha - \lambda \text{ and } \angle M_1LK = \alpha + \lambda.$$

Similarly

$$\angle KQO = \angle \text{between the directions of } R \text{ and } P = 90° - \theta,$$

so, that $\quad \angle KQL = 90° + \theta, \angle KM_1L = 90° + \theta - \lambda,$

and $\quad \angle KML = 90° + \theta + \lambda.$

Hence,

$$\frac{P}{W} = \frac{KM}{KL} = \frac{\sin KLM}{\sin KML} = \frac{\sin(\alpha - \lambda)}{\sin(90° + \theta + \lambda)} = \frac{\sin(\alpha - \lambda)}{\cos(\theta + \lambda)},$$

and $$\frac{P_1}{W} = \frac{KM_1}{KL} = \frac{\sin KLM_1}{\sin KM_1L} = \frac{\sin(\alpha + \lambda)}{\sin(90° + \theta - \lambda)} = \frac{\sin(\alpha + \lambda)}{\cos(\theta - \lambda)}.$$

Cor. It is clear that KM_1 is least when it is drawn perpendicular to LF_1, *i.e.*, when P_1 is inclined at a right angle to the direction of resultant reaction DH_1, and therefore at an angle λ to the inclined plane.

Examples XXXII

1. A body, of weight 40 kg, rests on a rough horizontal plane whose coefficient of friction is .25 ; find the least force which acting horizontally would move the body.

   Find also the least force which, acting at an angle $\cos^{-1}\frac{3}{5}$ with the horizontal, would move the body.

   Determine the direction and magnitude of the resultant reaction of the plane in each case.

2. A heavy block with a plane base is resting on a rough horizontal plane. It is acted on by a force at an inclination of 45° to the plane, and the force is gradually increased till the block is just going to slide. If the coefficient of friction is .5, compare the force with the weight of the block.

3. A mass of 30 kg is resting on a rough horizontal plane and can be just moved by a force of 10 kgf acting horizontally ; find the coefficient of friction and the direction and magnitude of the resultant reaction of the plane.

4. Show that the least force which will move a weight W along a rough horizontal plane is $W \sin\phi$, where ϕ is the angle of friction.

5. The inclination of a rough plane to the horizon is $\cos^{-1}\frac{12}{13}$; show that, if the coefficient of friction is $\frac{1}{3}$, the least force, acting parallel to the plane, that will support 56 kg placed on the plane is $4\frac{4}{13}$ kgf; show also that the force that would be on the point of moving the body up the plane is $38\frac{10}{13}$ kgf.

6. The base of an inclined plane is 4 metres in length and the height is 3 metres; a force of 8 kg, acting parallel to the plane, will just prevent a weight of 20 kg from sliding down; find the coefficient of friction.

7. A body, of weight 2 kg, rests in limiting equilibrium on a rough plane whose slope is 30°; the plane being raised to a slope of 60°, find the force along the plane required to support the body.

8. A weight of 15 kg just rests on a rough inclined plane, the height of the plane being $\frac{3}{5}$ th of its length. Show that it will require a force of 18 kg acting parallel to the plane just to be on the point of moving the weight up the plane.

9. A weight of 60 kg is on the point of motion down a rough inclined plane when supported by a force of 24 kgf acting parallel to the plane, and is on the point of motion up the plane when under the influence of a force of 36 kgf parallel to the plane; find the coefficient of friction.

10. Two inclined planes have a common vertex, and a string, passing over a small smooth pulley at the vertex, supports two equal weights. If one of the planes is rough and the other smooth, find the relation between the two angles of inclination of the two planes when the weight on the smooth plane is on the point of moving down.

11. Two unequal weights on a rough inclined plane are connected by a string which passes round a fixed pulley in the plane; find the greatest inclination of the plane consistent with the equilibrium of the weights.

12. Two equal weights are attached to the ends of a string which is laid over the top of two equally rough planes, having the same altitude and placed back to back, the angles of inclination of the planes to the horizon being 30° and 60° respectively; show that the weights will be on the point of motion if the coefficient of friction is $2 - \sqrt{3}$.

13. A particle is placed on the outside surface of a rough sphere whose coefficient of friction is μ. Show that it will be on the point of motion when the radius from it to the centre makes an angle $\tan^{-1}\mu$ with the vertical.

14. How high can a particle rest inside a hollow sphere, of radius a, if the coefficient of friction is $\frac{1}{\sqrt{3}}$?

15. At what angle of inclination should the traces be attached to a sledge that it may be drawn up a given hill with the least exertion ?

16. A cubical block of stone, of weight 280 kg, is to be drawn along a rough horizontal plane by a force P inclined at 40° to the horizontal. If the angle of friction is 25°, find, by a graphic construction, the least value of P.

17. A body, of weight 56 kg, rests on a plane inclined at 25° to the horizontal, being just prevented from sliding down by a force of 7.5 kg acting up the plane; find, by a graphic construction, the force that will just drag it up and the value of the coefficient of friction.

---

197. *To find the work done in dragging a body up a rough inclined plane.*

From Art. 194, Case II, we know that the force P_1 which would just move the body up the plane is

$$W(\sin\alpha + \mu\cos\alpha).$$

Hence, the work done in dragging it from A to C

$$= P_1 \times AC \text{(Fig. Art. 156)}$$
$$= W(\sin\alpha + \mu\cos\alpha)\cdot AC$$
$$= W\cdot AC\sin\alpha + \mu W\cdot AC\cos\alpha$$
$$= W\cdot BC + \mu W\cdot AB$$

= work done in dragging the body through the same vertical height without the intervention of the plane

+ the work done in dragging it along a horizontal distance equal to the base of the inclined plane and of the same roughness as the plane.

198. From the preceding article we see that, if our inclined plane is rough, the work done by the effort is more than the work done against the weight. This is true for any machine; the principle may be expressed thus,

In any machine, the work done by the effort is equal to the work done against the weight, together with the work done against the frictional resistances of the machine, and the work done against the weights of the component parts of the machine.

The ratio of the work done on the weight to the work done by the effort is, for any machine, called the efficiency of the machine, so that

$$\text{Efficiency} = \frac{\text{Useful work done by the machine}}{\text{Work supplied to the machine}}.$$

Let P_0 be the effort required if there were no friction, and P the actual effort. Then, by Art. 138,

Work done against the weight

$= P_0 \times$ distance through which its point of application moves, and work supplied to the machine

$= P \times$ distance through which its point of application moves.

Hence, by division,

$$\text{Efficiency} = \frac{P_0}{P}$$

$$= \frac{\text{Effort when there is no friction}}{\text{Actual effort}}$$

We can never get rid entirely of frictional resistances, or make our machine without weight, so that some work must always be lost through these two causes. Hence the efficiency of the machine can never be so great as unity. The more nearly the efficiency approaches to unity, the better is the machine.

There is no machine by whose use we can create work, and in practice, however smooth and perfect the machine may be, we always lose work. The only use of any machine is to multiply the force we apply, whilst at the same time the distance through which the force works is more than proportionately lessened.

199. Equilibrium of a rough screw. *To find the relation between the effort and the resistance in the case of a screw, when friction is taken into account.*

Using the same notation as in Art. 178, let the screw be on the point of motion *downwards*, so that the friction acts *upwards* along the thread. [As in Art. 176, its section is rectangular.]

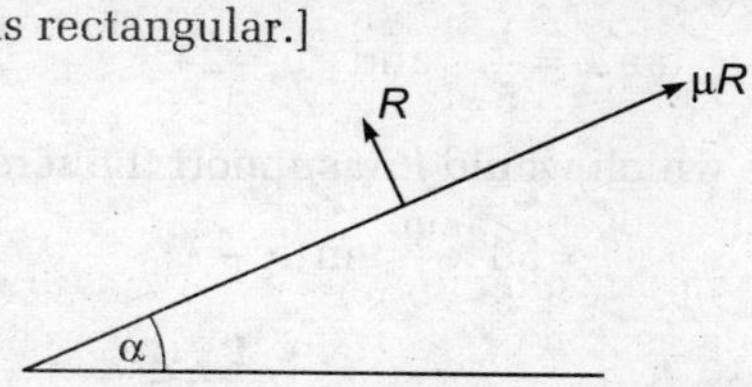

In this case the vertical pressures of the block are $R(\cos\alpha + \mu \sin\alpha), S(\cos\alpha + \mu\sin\alpha), \ldots$

and the horizontal components of these pressure are

$$R(\sin\alpha - \mu\cos\alpha), S(\sin\alpha - \mu\cos\alpha), \ldots$$

Hence the equations (1) and (2) of Art. 178 become

$$W = (R + S + T + \ldots)(\cos\alpha + \mu\sin\alpha) \qquad \ldots(1),$$

and

$$P \cdot b = a(R + S + T + \ldots)(\sin\alpha - \mu\cos\alpha) \qquad \ldots(2).$$

Hence, by division,

$$\frac{P \cdot b}{W} = a\frac{\sin\alpha - \mu\cos\alpha}{\cos\alpha + \mu\sin\alpha} = a\frac{\sin\alpha\cos\lambda - \cos\alpha\sin\lambda}{\cos\alpha\cos\lambda + \sin\alpha\sin\lambda}$$

$$= a\frac{\sin(\alpha - \lambda)}{\cos(\alpha - \lambda)}.$$

$$\therefore \qquad \frac{P}{W} = \frac{a}{b}\tan(\alpha - \lambda).$$

Similarly, if the screw is on the point of motion upwards, we have, by changing the sign of μ,

$$\frac{P_1}{W} = \frac{a\sin\alpha + \mu\cos\alpha}{b\cos\alpha - \mu\sin\alpha} = \frac{a}{b}\tan(\alpha + \lambda).$$

If the effort has any value between P and P_1, the screw will be in equilibrium, but the friction will not be limiting friction.

It will be noted that if the angle α of the screw is equal to the angle of friction, λ, then the value of the effort P is zero. In this case the screw will just remain in equilibrium supported only by the friction along the thread of the screw.

If $\alpha < \lambda$, P will be negative, *i.e* the screw will not descend unless it is forced down.

Ex. 1. *If the circumference of a screw is four cm, the distance between its threads one cm, and the coefficient of friction* $\frac{1}{5}$, *find the limits between which the effort must lie, so that the screw may be in equilibrium when it is supporting a body of weight* 56 *kg, the length of the effort-arm being* 24 *cm.*

Here $\qquad 2\pi a = 4$ and $2\pi a\tan\alpha = 1$.

$$\therefore \qquad a = \frac{2}{\pi} \quad \text{and} \quad \tan\alpha = \frac{1}{4}.$$

Also $\qquad \tan\lambda = \frac{1}{5}$, and $b = 24$

Hence, the force which would *just* support the screw

$$= 56 \times \frac{a}{b}\tan(\alpha - \lambda)$$

$$= 56 \times \frac{1}{12\pi} \times \frac{\frac{1}{4} - \frac{1}{5}}{1 + \frac{1}{4}\cdot\frac{1}{5}}$$

$$= \frac{56}{12\pi} \times \frac{1}{21} = \frac{7}{99}\text{ kgf}$$

$$= 70.7\text{ gf, nearly.}$$

Again, the force which would just be on the point of moving the screw upwards

$$= 56 \times \frac{a}{b} \tan(\alpha + \lambda) = \frac{56}{12\pi} \times \frac{\frac{1}{4} + \frac{1}{5}}{1 - \frac{1}{4} \cdot \frac{1}{5}} = \frac{56}{12\pi} \times \frac{9}{19}$$

$$= \frac{147}{209} \text{ kgf} = 0.7033 \text{ kgf nearly.}$$

Hence the screw will be in equilibrium if the effort lies between 70.7 and 703.3 gf nearly.

If the screw were smooth, the force required would

$$= 56 \frac{a}{b} \tan\alpha = \frac{56}{12\pi} \times \frac{1}{4} = \frac{49}{132} = 0.371 \text{ kgf}$$

The efficiency therefore, by Art. 198,

$$= \frac{0.371}{0.7033} = 0.527.$$

Ex. 2. The coefficient of friction of wrought iron on wood being .15, show that the least angle of inclination of the thread of a screw, so that it may slide into a prepared hole in the wood under the influence of its own weight, is $\tan^{-1}\frac{3}{20}$.

Ex. 3. If the circumference of a screw is 3 cm, the coefficient of friction 0.15 the length of the power-arm 24 cm, and if there are 3 threads to 2 cm, find the forces which will respectively just support and just move, the screw when it supports a weight W. Find also the value of the effort, when the same screw is smooth, and deduce its efficiency.

Ans. $\frac{W}{16\pi}(0.07)$; $\frac{W}{16\pi}(0.385)$; $\frac{W}{16\pi}(0.2)$; 0.577.

Ex. 4. *Show that the efficiency of a screw is greatest when its angle is* $45° - \frac{\lambda}{2}$.

The force required to lift the weight W, when there is friction,

$$= W \frac{a}{b} \tan \overline{\alpha + \lambda},$$

and where there is no friction it

$$= W \frac{a}{b} \tan\alpha \quad .$$

As in Art. 198 the efficiency, $E =$ the ratio of these

$$= \frac{\tan\alpha}{\tan(\alpha + \lambda)} = \frac{\sin\alpha \cos(\alpha + \lambda)}{\cos\alpha \sin \overline{\alpha + \lambda}}.$$

$$\therefore \quad 1 - E = 1 - \frac{\sin\alpha\cos(\alpha + \lambda)}{\cos\alpha\sin(\alpha + \lambda)} = \frac{\sin\lambda}{\cos\alpha\sin(\alpha + \lambda)}$$

$$= \frac{2\sin\lambda}{\sin(2\alpha + \lambda) + \sin\lambda}$$

$\therefore$ E is greatest when $1 - E$ is least,

i.e., when $\sin(2\alpha + \lambda)$ is greatest,

i.e., when $2\alpha + \lambda = 90°$,

and then $\alpha = 45° - \frac{\lambda}{2}$.

200. *Wheel and axle with the pivot resting on rough bearings.*

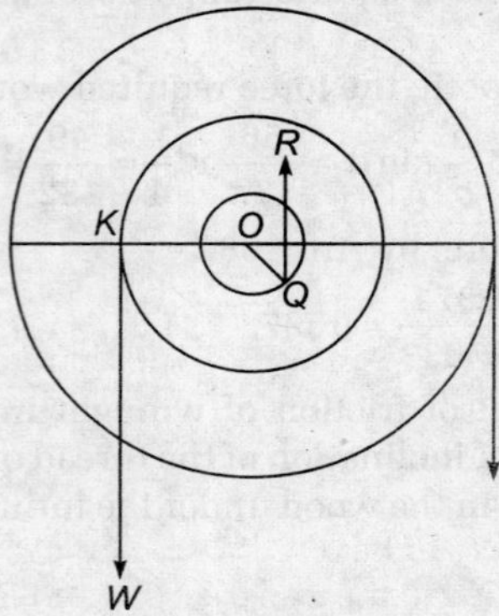

Let the central circle represent the pivots A or B of Fig. Art. 159 (much magnified) when looked at endways.

The resultant action between these pivots and the bearings on which they rest must be vertical, since it balances P and W.

Also it must make an angle λ, the angle of friction, with the normal at the point of contact Q, if we assume that P is just on the point of overcoming W.

Hence Q cannot be at the lowest point of the pivot, but must be as denoted in the figure, where OQ makes an angle λ with the vertical. The resultant reaction at Q is thus vertical.

Since R balances P and W,

$$\therefore \quad R = P + W \quad \text{...(1).}$$

Also, by taking moments about O, we have

$$P \cdot b - R \cdot c \sin\lambda = W \cdot a \quad \text{...(2),}$$

Where c is the radius of the pivot and b, a the radii of the wheel and the axle (as in Art. 159).

Solving (1) and (2), we have

$$P = W\frac{a + c\sin\lambda}{b - c\sin\lambda}.$$

If P is only just sufficient to support W, *i.e.* if the machine is on the point of motion in the direction, then by changing the sign of λ, we have

$$P_1 = W\frac{a - c\sin\lambda}{b + c\sin\lambda}.$$

In this case the point of contact Q is on the left of the vertical through O.

201. The Wedge is a piece of iron, or metal, which has two plane faces meeting in a sharp edge. It is used to split wood or other tough substances, its edge being forced in by repeated blows applied by a hammer to its upper surface.

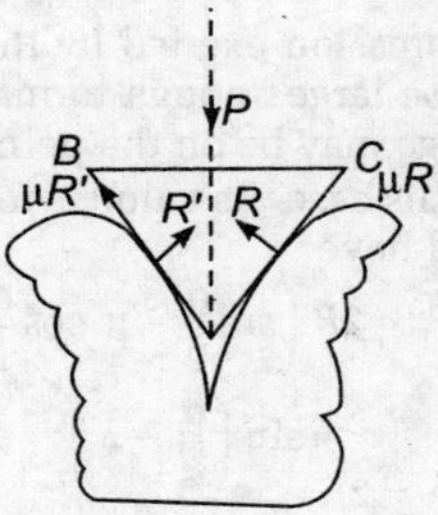

The problem of the action of a wedge is essentially a dynamical one.

We shall only consider the statical problem when the wedge is just kept in equilibrium by a steady force applied to its upper surface.

Let ABC be a section of the wedge and let its faces be equally inclined to the base BC. Let the angle CAB be α.

Let P be the force applied to the upper face, R and R' the normal reactions of the wood at the points where the wedge touches the wood, and μR and $\mu R'$ the frictions, it being assumed that the wedge is on the point of being pushed in.

We shall suppose the force P applied at the middle point of BC and that its direction is perpendicular to BC and hence bisects the angle BAC.

Resolving along and perpendicular to BC, we have

$$\mu R \sin\frac{\alpha}{2} - R\cos\frac{\alpha}{2} = \mu R' \sin\frac{\alpha}{2} - R'\cos\frac{\alpha}{2} \qquad \text{...(1),}$$

and
$$P = \mu(R + R')\cos\frac{\alpha}{2} + (R + R')\sin\frac{\alpha}{2} \qquad \text{...(2).}$$

From equation (1) we have $R = R'$, and then (2) gives

$$P = 2R\left(\mu\cos\frac{\alpha}{2} + \sin\frac{\alpha}{2}\right),$$

Hence
$$\frac{2R}{P} = \frac{1}{\mu\cos\frac{\alpha}{2} + \sin\frac{\alpha}{2}} = \frac{\cos\lambda}{\sin\frac{\alpha}{2}\cos\lambda + \cos\frac{\alpha}{2}\sin\lambda}$$

$$= \frac{\cos\lambda}{\sin\left(\frac{\alpha}{2} + \lambda\right)},$$

if λ be the coefficient of friction.

The splitting power of the wedge is measured by R. For a given force P this splitting power is therefore greatest when α is least.

Theoretically this will be when α is zero, *i.e.*, when the wedge is of infinitesimal strength. Practically the wedge has the greatest splitting power when it is made with as small an angle as is consistent with its strength.

202. If there is no friction between the wedge and wood (though this is practically an impossible supposition), we should have $\lambda = 0$, and therefore,

$$\frac{2R}{P} = \frac{1}{\sin\frac{\alpha}{2}} = \operatorname{cosec}\frac{\alpha}{2}.$$

203. If the force of compression exerted by the wood on the wedge is great enough the force P may not be large enough to make the wedge on the point of motion down; in fact the wedge may be on the point of being forced out.

If P_1 is the value of P in this case, its value is found by changing the sign of μ in Art. 201, so that we should have

$$P_1 = 2R\left(\sin\frac{\alpha}{2} - \mu\cos\frac{\alpha}{2}\right)$$

$$= 2R\,\frac{\sin\left(\frac{\alpha}{2} - \lambda\right)}{\cos\lambda}.$$

If $\frac{\alpha}{2}$ is $> \lambda$, the value of P_1 is positive.

If $\frac{\alpha}{2}$ is $< \lambda$, P_1 is negative and the wedge could therefore only be on the point of slipping out if a pull were applied to its upper surface.

If $\frac{\alpha}{2} = \lambda$, the will just stick fast without the application of any force.

Ex. Prove that the multiplication of force produced by a screw-press, in which the distance between successive threads is c and the power is applied at the extremities of a cross-bar of length $2b$, is the same as the produced by a thin isosceles wedge of angle α such that

$$\sin\frac{\alpha}{2} = c \div 4\pi b.$$

204. Friction exerts such an important influence on the practical working of machines that the theoretical investigations are not of much actual use and recourse must for any particular machine be made to experiment. The method is the same for all kinds of machines.

The velocity-ratio can be obtained by experiment; for in all machines it equals the distance through which the effort moves divided by the corresponding distance through which the weight, or resistance, moves. Call it n.

Let the weight raised be W. Then the theoretical effort P_0, corresponding to no friction, is $\frac{W}{n}$. Find by experiment the actual value of the effort P which just raises W. The actual mechanical advantage of the machine is $\frac{W}{P}$, and the efficiency of it is, by Art. 198, $\frac{P_0}{P}$. The product of the efficiency and the velocity ratio $= \frac{P_0}{P}\cdot\frac{W}{P_0} = \frac{W}{P} =$ the mechanical advantage.

205. As an examples take the case of a class-room model of a differential wheel and axle on which some experiments were performed. The machine was not at all in good condition and was not cleaned before use and no lubricants were used for the bearings of either it or its pulley.

With the notation of Art. 164 the values of a, b, and c were found to be 3, 6, and $13\frac{1}{2}$ cm, so that the value of the velocity ratio n

$$= \frac{2b}{c-b} = \frac{2 \times 6\frac{3}{4}}{3 - 1\frac{1}{2}} = 9.$$

This valu[illegible] [illegible]lso verified by experiment; for it was found that for every inch that W wen[illegible] P went down nine inches.

P was measu[illegible]ed by means of weights put into a scale-pan whose weight is included in that of P; similarly for W.

The weight of the pulley to which W is attached was also included in the weight of W.

The corresponding values of P and W, in gramme weight are given in the following table; the value of P was that which just overcame the weight W. The third column gives the corresponding values of P_0 *i.e.*, the effort which would have been required has there been no frictional resistances.

W	P	$P_0 = \frac{W}{n}$	$E = \frac{P_0}{P}$	$M = \frac{W}{P}$
50	28	5.55	.2	1.79
100	36	11.11	.31	2.78
150	45	16.67	.37	3.3
250	60	27.78	.46	4.17
450	90	50	.56	5
650	119	72.22	.61	5.46
850	147	94.44	.64	5.78
1050	175	116.67	.67	6
1250	203	138.88	.68	6.16
1450	232	161.11	.694	6.25

The fourth column gives the values of E, the corresponding efficiency, and the last column gives the values of M, the mechanical advantages.

On plotting out on squared paper the above results, which the student should do for himself, the points giving P are found to roughly be on a straight line going through the third and last of the above. Hence, according to the theory of graphs, the relation between P and W is of the form $P = aW + b$, where a and b are constants.

Also, $P = 45$ when $W = 150$, and $P = 232$ when $W = 1450$.

$\therefore$ $45 = 150a + b$ and $232 = 1450a + b$.

Solving, we have $a = .144$ and $b = 23.4$ approximately, so that

$$P = .144\,W + 23.4$$

This is called the Law of the Machine.

Also $$P_0 = \frac{1}{5}W = .111W.$$

Hence $$E = \frac{P_0}{P} = \frac{.111\,W}{.144W + 23.4}.$$

and $$M = \frac{W}{P} = \frac{W}{.144W + 23.4}.$$

These give E and M for any weight W.

The values of E and M get bigger as W increases. Assuming the above value of E to be true for all values of W, then its greatest value is when W is infinitely great, and

$$= \frac{.111}{.144} = \text{about } .77,$$

so that in this machine at least 23% of the work put into it is lost.

The corresponding greatest value of the mechanical advantage

$$= \frac{1}{.144} = \text{about } 7.$$

If the machine had been well cleaned and lubricated before the experiment, much better results would have been obtained.

206. Just as in the example of the last article, so, with any other machine, the actual efficiency is found to fall considerably short of unity.

There is one practical advantage which, in general, belongs to machines having a comparatively small efficiency.

It can be shown that, in any machine in which the magnitude of the effort applied has no effect on the friction, the load does not run down of its own accord when no effort is applied provided that the efficiency is less than $\frac{1}{2}$.

Examples of such machines are a screw whose pitch is small and whose effort is applied horizontally as in Art. 178, and an inclined plane where the effort acts up the plane as in Art. 194.

In machines where the friction does depend on the effort applied no such general rule can be theoretically proved, and each case must be considered separately. But it may be taken as a rough general rule that where the effort has a comparatively small effect on the amount of friction then the load will not run down if the efficiency be less than $\frac{1}{2}$. Such a machine is said not to 'reverse' or 'ouverhaul'.

Thus in the case of the differential pulley (Art. 165), as usually constructed the efficiency is less than $\frac{1}{2}$, and the load W does not run down when no force P is applied, that is, when the machine is left alone and the chain let go.

This property of not overhauling compensates, in great measure, for the comparatively small efficiency.

In a wheel and axle the mechanical advantage is usually great and the efficiency usually considerably more than $\frac{1}{2}$; but the fact that it reverses does not always make it a more useful machine than the differential pulley.

The student, who desires further information as to the practical working of machines, should consult Sir Robert Ball's *Experimental Mechincs* or works on Applied Mechanics.

Examples XXXIII

1. How much work is done in drawing a load of 336 kg up a rough inclined plane, whose height is 90 cm and base 6 metres, the coefficient of friction being $\frac{2}{15}$?
2. A weight of 104 kg is dragged in half an hour through a length of 99 m up an inclined plane, of inclination 30°, the coefficient of friction being $\frac{1}{\sqrt{3}}$; find the work expended and the H.P. of the engine which could do the work.
3. A tank, 7.2 m long, 3.6 m broad, and 4.8 m deep, is filled by water from a well the surface of which is always 24 m below the top of the tank; find the work done in filling the tank, and the H.P. of an engine, whose efficiency is 0.5, that will fill the tank in 4 hours.
4. The diameter of the circular piston of a steam engine is 150 cm and it makes 11 strokes per minute, the length of each stroke being 2.4 m the mean pressure per square cm on the piston being 1.2 kg, and the efficiency of the engine .65. Find the number of cubic m of water that it will raise per hour from a wel whose depth is 90 m, on the supposition that no work is wasted.
5. The diameter of the piston of an engine is 2.0 metres, the mean pressure of steam .46 kg per square cm, the length of the stroke 3 m and the number of double strokes per minute is 11. The engine is found to raise 1.1475 cu.m of water per minute from a depth of 900 metres. Show that its efficiency is .6 nearly.
6. The radii of a wheel and axle are 1.2 m and 15 cm. If a force of 28 kgf is required to overcome a resistance of 100 kgf; what is the efficiency of the machine ?
7. In some experiments with a block and tackle (second system of pulleys), in which the velocity-ratio was 4, the weights lifted were 5, 40, and 80 kg and the corresponding values of the effort were 11.5, 29, and $42\frac{1}{2}$ kg. Find the efficiency in each case.
8. With a certain machine it is found that, with efforts equal to 6 and 3.75 kgf respectively, resistances equal to 350 and 150 kgf are overcome; assuming that $P = a + bW$, find the values of a and b.

9. In some experiments with a screw-jack the values of the load W were 75, 90, 105, 120 and 135 kgf and the corresponding values of the effort P were found to be 10.45, 11.35, 12.875, 14.2 and 15.7 kgf; plot the results on squarred paper and assuming that $P = a + bW$, find the approximate values of a and b.

10. In some experiments with a model block and tackle (the second system of pulleys), the values of W (including the weight of the lower block) and P expressed in gramme weight were found to be as follows :

$W = 75$, 175, 275, 475, 675, 875, 1075;

$P = 25$, 48, 71, 119, 166, 214, 264.

Also there were five strings at the lower block. Find an approximate relation between P and W and the corresponding values for the efficiency and mechanical advantage.

Draws the graphs of P, P_0, E, and M.

11. The following table gives the load in tonnes upon a crane, and the corresponding effort in kgf :

Load	1,	3,	5,	7,	8,	10,	11.
Effort	9,	20,	28,	37,	42,	51,	56.

Find the law of the machine, and calculate the efficiency at the loads 5 and 10 tonnes given that the velocity-ratio is 500.

12. A weight is lifted by a screw-jack, of pitch $\frac{1}{2}$ cm, the force being applied at right angles to a lever of length 30 cm. The values of the weight in tonnes, and the corresponding force in kg, are given in the following table :

Weight	1,	2.5,	5,	7,	8,	10.
Force	24,	32,	46,	57,	63,	73.

Find the law of the machine, and calculate its efficiency for the weights 4 and 9 tonnes.

15

Friction (Continued)

207. In this chapter we give some further examples of the solution of problems where friction is involved.

Ex. 1. *A uniform ladder is in equilibrium, with one end resting on the ground, and the other end against a vertical wall; if the ground and wall are both rough, the coefficients of friction being μ and μ' respectively, and if the ladder is on the point of slipping at both ends, find the inclination of the ladder to the horizon.*

Let AB be the ladder, and G is centre of gravity; let R and S be the normal reactions at A and B respectively; the end A of the ladder is on the point of slipping *from* the wall, and hence the friction μR is *towards* the wall; the end B is on the point of motion vertically *downwards*, and therefore the friction $\mu' S$ acts *upwards*.

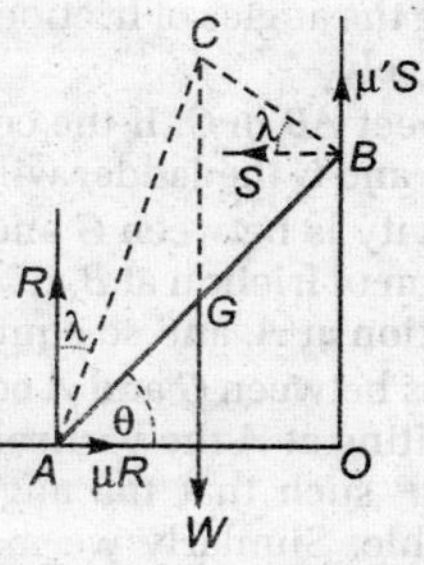

Let θ be the inclination of the ladder to the ground, and $2a$ its length.

Resolving horizontally and vertically, we have

$$\mu R = S \quad \text{...(1),}$$

and

$$R + \mu' S = W \quad \text{...(2).}$$

Also, taking moments about A, we have

$$W \cdot a\cos\theta = \mu' S \cdot 2a\cos\theta + S \cdot 2a\sin\theta$$

$\therefore$

$$W\cos\theta = 2S\,(\mu'\cos\theta + \sin\theta) \quad \text{...(3).}$$

From (1) and (2), we have

$$\mu\,(W - \mu' S) = S,$$

and $\therefore$

$$\mu W = S\,(1 + \mu\mu') \quad \text{...(4).}$$

By (3) and (4), we have, by division,

$$\frac{\cos\theta}{\mu} = \frac{2\,(\mu'\cos\theta + \sin\theta)}{1 + \mu\mu'},$$

$\therefore$

$$\cos\theta\,(1 - \mu\mu') = 2\mu\sin\theta.$$

Hence, $$\tan\theta = \frac{1-\mu\mu'}{2\mu}.$$

Otherwise thus ;

Let λ and λ' be the angles of friction at A and B; draw AC making an angle λ with the normal at A, and BC making an angle λ' with the normal at B, as in the figure.

By Art. 189, AC and BC are the directions of the resultant reactions at A and B.

The ladder as kept in equilibrium by these resultant reactions and its weight; hence their directions must meet in a point and therefore the vertical line through G must pass through C.

Formula (1) of Art. 79 gives

$$(a+a)\cot CGB = a\cot ACG - a\cot BCG,$$

i.e. $$2\tan\theta = \cot\lambda - \tan\lambda' = \frac{1}{\mu} - \mu'.$$

$\therefore$ $$\tan\theta = \frac{1-\mu\mu'}{2\mu}.$$

Ex. 2. *A ladder is placed in a given position with one end resting on the ground and the other against a vertical wall. If the ground and wall are both rough, the angles of friction being λ and λ' respectively, find by a graphic construction how high a man can ascend the ladder without its slipping.*

Let AB (Fig. Ex. 1) be the ladder.

Draw AC and BC making the angles of friction with the normals at A and B to the wall and ground respectively.

Draw CG vertically to meet AB in G. If the centre of gravity of the man and ladder together is between A and G the ladder will rest; if not, it will slide.

For if this centre of gravity is between G and B the vertical through it will meet BC, the limiting direction of friction at B, in a point P such that the $\angle PAR$ is greater than the angle of friction at A, and so equilibrium will be impossible.

If this centre of gravity is between G and A equilibrium will be possible; for even if the friction were limiting at A the vertical through this centre of gravity would meet AC in a point P such that the angle PBS would be $< \lambda'$, so that equilibrium would be possible. Similarly we may show that if the friction is limiting at B, there is still equilibrium.

If then G_1 is the centre of gravity of the ladder, G_2 the highest possible position of the man, and W_1 and W_2 be their respective weights, then G_2 is determined by the relation

$$W_1 \cdot GG_1 = W_2 \cdot GG_2.$$

Examples XXXIV

1. A uniform ladder, 3.9 m long, rests with one end against a smooth vertical wall and the other on a rough horizontal plane at a point 1.5 m from the wall; find the friction between the ladder and the ground, if the weight of the ladder is 28 kg.
2. A uniform ladder rests with one end on a horizontal floor and the other against a vertical wall, the coefficients of friction being respectively $\frac{3}{7}$ and $\frac{1}{3}$; find the inclination of the ladder when it is about to slip.

3. If in the last example the coefficient of friction in each case is $\frac{1}{3}$, show that the ladder will slip when its inclination to the vertical is $\tan^{-1}\frac{3}{4}$.

4. A uniform ladder rests in limiting equilibrium with one end on a rough floor, whose coefficient of friction is μ, and with the other against a smooth vertical wall; show that its inclination to the vertical is $\tan^{-1}(2\mu)$.

5. A uniform ladder is placed against a wall; if the ground and wall are equally rough, the coefficient of friction being $\tan\theta$, show that the limiting inclination of the ladder to the vertical is 2θ.

When the ladder is in this position can it be ascended without its slipping ?

6. A uniform ladder rests in limiting equilibrium with one end on a rough horizontal plane, and the other against a smooth vertical wall; a man then ascends the ladder; show that he cannot go more than half-way up.

7. A uniform ladder rests with one end against a smooth vertical wall and the other on the ground, the coefficient of friction being $\frac{3}{4}$; if the inclination of the ladder to the ground is 45°, show that a man, whose weight is equal to that of the ladder, can just ascend to the top of the ladder without its slipping.

8. A uniform ladder, of length 21 m, rest against a vertical wall with which it makes an angle of 45°, the coefficients of friction between the ladder and the wall and ground respectively being $\frac{1}{3}$ and $\frac{1}{2}$. If a man, whose weight is one-half that of the ladder, ascends the ladder show high will be when the ladder slips ?

Now stands on the bottom rung of the ladder what must be his least weight so that the man may go to the top of the ladder ?

9. Two equal ladders, of weight w, are placed so as to lean against each other with their ends resting on a rough horizontal floor; given the coefficient of friction, μ; and the angle 2α, that they make with each other, find what weight on the top would cause them to slip.

Explain the meaning of the result when $\tan\alpha > 2\mu$ or $< \mu$.

10. A uniform ladder rests, at an angle of 45° with the horizontal, with its upper extremity against a rough vertical wall and its lower extremity on the ground. If μ and μ' are the coefficients of limiting friction between the ladder and the ground and wall respectively, show that the least horizontal force which will move the lower extremity towards the wall is $\frac{1}{2}W \cdot \frac{1+2\mu-\mu\mu'}{1-\mu}$.

11. In Ex. 9 if the weight is placed at the middle point of one leg and be heavy enough to cause slipping, show that the other leg will be the one that will slide first.

208. Ex. 1. *A uniform cylinder is placed with its plane base on a rough inclined plane and the inclination of the plane to the horizontal is gradually increased; show that the cylinder will topple over before it slides if the ratio of the diameter of the base of the cylinder to its height is less than the coefficient of friction.*

Let ϕ be the inclination of the plane to the horizontal when the cylinder is on the point of tumbling over. The vertical line through the centre of gravity G of the cylinder must just fall within the base.

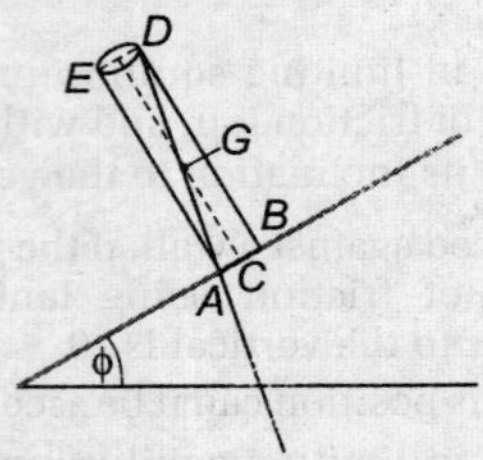

Hence, if AB is the base, the line GA must be vertical.

Let C be the middle point of the base; r its radius, and let h be the height of the cylinder,

$$\therefore \qquad \tan\phi = \cot CAG = \frac{AC}{CG} = \frac{r}{\frac{1}{2}h} = \frac{2r}{h} \qquad \text{...(1).}$$

Also the inclination θ of the plane to the horizon, when the cylinder is about to slide. is given by

$$\tan\theta = \mu \qquad \text{...(2).}$$

Hence, the cylinder will topple before it slides if ϕ is less than θ,

i.e., if $\qquad \dfrac{2r}{h}$ be $< \mu$.

Ex. 2. *A rectangle ABCD rests on a vertical plane, with its base AB on a rough table; a gradually increasing force acts along DC; will equilibrium be broken by sliding or toppling ?*

Let F be the force, and W the weight of the rectangle

Let $\qquad AB = 2a \quad$ and $\quad BC = h$.

If the rectangle topples it will clearly turn about B, and this will be when the moments of F and W about B just balance,

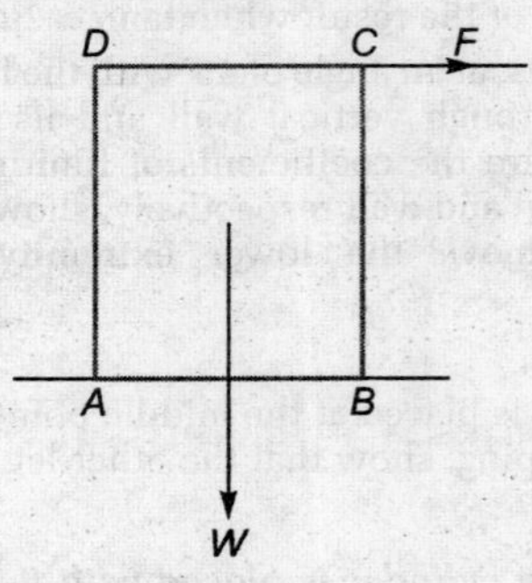

i.e., when $\qquad F \cdot h = W \cdot a \qquad$ ...(1).

Also the rectangle will slide when F is equal to the limiting friction,

i.e., when $\qquad F = \mu W \qquad$ ...(2).

The rectangle will topple or slide according as the value of F given by (1) is less or greater than the value of F given by (2),

i.e., according as $\frac{a}{h} \lessgtr \mu$.

i.e., according as μ is $\lessgtr$ the ratio of the base of twice the height of the rectangle.

Examples XXXV

1. A cylinder rests with its circular base on a rough inclined plane, the coefficient of friction being $\frac{1}{2}$. Find the inclination of the plane and the relation between the height and diameter of the base of the cylinder, so that it may be on the point of sliding and also of toppling over.
2. A solid cylinder rests on a rough horizontal plane with one of its flat ends on the plane, and is acted on by a horizontal force through the centre of its upper end; if this force is just sufficient to move the solid, show that it will slide, and not topple over, if the coefficient of friction be less than the ratio of the radius of the base of the cylinder to its height.
3. An equilateral triangle rests in a vertical plane with its base resting on a rough horizontal plane; a gradually increasing horizontal force acts on its vertex in the plane of the triangle; prove that the triangle will slide before it turns about the end of its base, if the coefficient of friction is less than $\frac{1}{3}\sqrt{3}$.
4. A conical sugarloaf, whose height is equal to twice the diameter of its base, stands on a table rough enough to prevent sliding; one end is gently raised till the sugarloaf is on the point of falling over; find the inclination of the plane to the horizontal in this position.
5. A cone, of given vertical angle 2α, rests on a rough plane which is inclined to the horizontal. As the inclination of the plane is increased, show that the cone will slide, before it topples over, if the coefficient of friction be less than $4 \tan\alpha$.
6. A right cone is placed with its base on a rough inclined plane; if $\frac{1}{\sqrt{3}}$ is the coefficient of friction, find the angle of the cone when it is on the point of both slipping and turning over.
7. A cone rests on a rough table, and a cord fastened to the vertex of the cone passes over a smooth pulley at the same height as the top of the cone, and supports a weight. Show that, if the weight is continually increased, the cone will turn over, or slide, according as the coefficient of friction is $>$ or $<$ $\tan\alpha$, where α is the semi-vertical angle of the cone.
8. A cubical block rests on a rough inclined plane with its edges parallel to the edges of the plank. If, as the plank is gradually raised, the block turns on it before slipping, what is the least value that the coefficient of friction can have ?
9. The triangular lamina ABC, right angled at B, stands with BC upon a rough horizontal plane. If the plane is gradually tilted round an axis in its own plane perpendicular to BC, so that the angle B is lower than the angle C, show that the lamina will begin to slide, or topple over, according as the coefficient of friction is less, or greater, than $\tan A$.

10. A square uniform metallic plate *ABCD* rests with its side *BC* on a perfectly rough plane inclined to the horizon at an angle α. A string *AP* attached to *A*, the highest point of the plate, and passing over a smooth pulley at *P*, the vertex of the plane, supports a weight *w*, and *AP* is horizontal. If *W* is the weight of the plane, show that, as *w* increases, it will begin to turn when

$$w > W\frac{1+\tan\alpha}{2}.$$

11. A block, of weight 1 tonne, is in the form of a rectangular parallelopiped, 2.4 m high, standing on a square base whose side is 1.8 m. It is placed on a rough weightless board with the sides of its base parallel to the length and breadth of the board, and the centre of the base is distant 1.8 m from one extremity of the board. The board is now tilted round this extremity until the block topples without sliding; find the work done.

209. Ex. *A uniform rod rests in limiting equilibrium within a rough hollow sphere; if the rod subtends an angle 2α at a the centre of the sphere, and if λ is the angle of friction, show that the angle of inclination of the rod to the horizontal is*

$$\tan^{-1}\left[\frac{\tan(\alpha+\lambda)-\tan(\alpha-\lambda)}{2}\right]$$

Let *AB* be the rod, *G* its centre of gravity, and *O* the centre of the sphere, so that

$$\angle GOA = \angle GOB = \alpha.$$

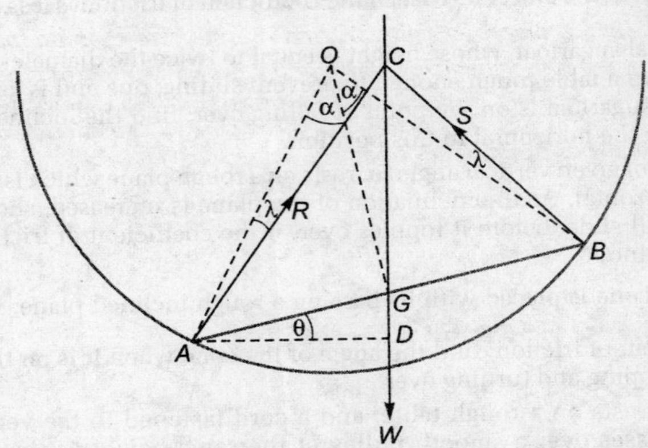

Through *A* and *B* draw lines *AC* and *BC* making an angle λ with the line joining *A* and *B* to the centre. By Art. 189, these are the directions of the resultan reactions, *R* and *S*, at *A* and *B* respectively.

Since these reactions and the weight keep the rod in equilibrium, th vertical line through *G* must pass through *C*.

Let *AD* be the horizontal line drawn through *A* to meet *CG* in *D* so that th angle *GAD* is θ.

The angle $CAG = \angle OAG - \lambda = 90° - \alpha - \lambda$,

and the angle $CBG = \angle OBG + \lambda = 90° - \alpha + \lambda$.

Hence theorem (2) of Art. 79 gives

$$(a + a)\cot CGB = a\cot CAB - a\cot CBA$$

i.e. $$2\tan\theta = \cot(90° - \alpha - \lambda) - \cot(90° - \alpha + \lambda)$$

$$= \tan(\alpha + \lambda) - \tan(\alpha - \lambda) \qquad ...(1),$$

Otherwise thus; The solution may be also obtained by using the condition of Art. 83.

Resolving the forces along the rod, we have

$$R\cos(90° - \alpha - \lambda) - S\cos(90° - \alpha + \lambda) = W\sin\theta,$$

i.e., $$R\sin(\alpha + \lambda) - S\sin(\alpha - \lambda) = W\sin\theta \qquad ...(2).$$

Resolving perpendicular to the rod, we have

$$R\cos(\alpha + \lambda) + S\cos(\alpha - \lambda) = W\cos\theta \qquad ...(3).$$

By taking moments about A, we have

$$S \cdot AB\sin(90° - \alpha + \lambda) = W \cdot AG\cos\theta,$$

i.e., $$2S\cos(\alpha - \lambda) = W\cos\theta \qquad ...(4).$$

From equations (3) and (4), we have

$$R\cos(\alpha + \lambda) = S\cos(\alpha - \lambda) = \frac{1}{2}W\cos\theta$$

Substituting these values of R and S in (2), we have

$$\tan(\alpha + \lambda) - \tan(\alpha - \lambda) = 2\tan\theta.$$

Numerical Example. If the rod subtends a right angle at the centre of the sphere, show that its inclination to the horizontal is twice the angle of friction.

210. Ex. *Two bodies, of weights W_1 and W_2, are placed on an inclined plane and are connected by a light string which coincides with a line of greatest slope of the plane; if the coefficient of friction between the bodies and the plane are respectively μ_1 and μ_2, find the inclination of the plane to the horizontal when both bodies are on the point of motion, it being assumed that the smoother body is below the other.*

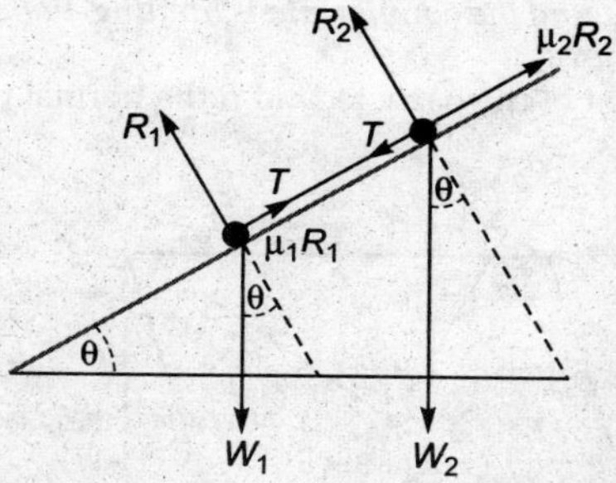

The lower body would slip when the inclination is $\tan^{-1}\mu_1$, but the upper would not do so till the inclination had the value $\tan^{-1}\mu_2$. When the two are tied together the inclination for slipping would be between these two values. Let it be and let R_1 and R_2 be the normal reactions of the bodies; also let T be the tension of the string.

The frictions $\mu_1 R_1$ and $\mu_2 R_2$ both act up the plane.

For the equilibrium of W_1, we have

$$W_1 \sin\theta = T + \mu_1 R_1,$$

and $$W_1 \cos\theta = R_1.$$

$\therefore$ $$T = W_1(\sin\theta - \mu_1 \cos\theta) \qquad ...(1).$$

For the equilibrium of W_2, we have

$$W_2 \sin\theta + T = \mu_2 R_2,$$

and $$W_2 \cos\theta = R_2.$$

$\therefore$ $$T = \mu_2 R_2 - W_2 \sin\theta = W_2(\mu_2 \cos\theta - \sin\theta) \qquad ...(2).$$

Hence, from (1) and (2),

$$W_1(\sin\theta - \mu_1 \cos\theta) = W_2(\mu_2 \cos\theta - \sin\theta).$$

$\therefore$ $$(W_1 + W_2)\sin\theta = (W_1\mu_1 + W_2\mu_2)\cos\theta.$$

$\therefore$ $$\tan\theta = \frac{W_1\mu_1 + W_2\mu_2}{W_1 + W_2}.$$

Ex. 1. Two equal bodies are placed on a rough inclined plane, being connected by a light string; if the coefficients of friction are respectively $\frac{1}{2}$ and $\frac{1}{3}$, show that they will both be on the point of motion when the inclination of the plane is $\tan^{-1}\frac{5}{12}$.

Ex. 2. Show that the greatest angle at which a plane may be inclined to the horizon so that three equal bodies, whose coefficients o friction arc $\frac{1}{2}, \frac{5}{8}$ and $\frac{3}{8}$ respectively, when rigidly connected together may rest on it without slipping, is $\tan^{-1}\frac{1}{2}$.

211. Ex. *A particle is placed on a rough plane, whose inclination to the horizontal is α, and is acted upon by a force P acting parallel to the plane and in a direction making an angle β with the line of greatest slope in the plane, if the coefficient of friction is μ and the equilibrium is limiting, find the direction in which the body will begin to move.*

Let W be the weight of the particle, and R the normal reaction.

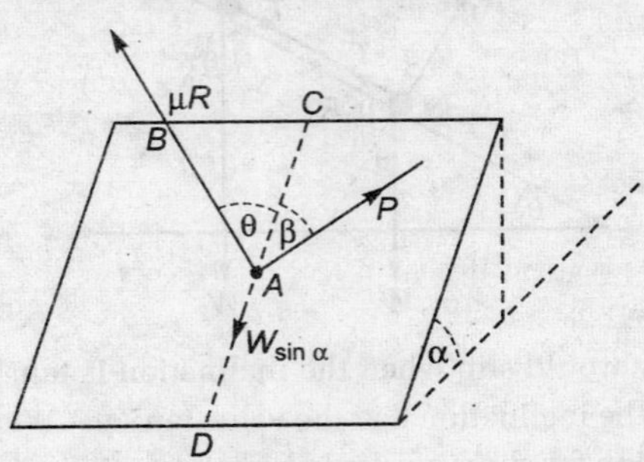

The forces perpendicular to the inclined plane must vanish.

$\therefore$ $$R = W\cos\alpha \qquad ...(1).$$

The other component of the weight will be $W \sin\alpha$, acting down the line of greatest slope.

Let the friction, μR, act in the direction AB, making an angle θ with the line of greatest slope, so that the particle would begin to move in the direction BA produced.

Since the forces acting along the surface of the plane are in equilibrium, we have, by Lami's Theorem,

$$\frac{\mu R}{\sin\beta} = \frac{W \sin\alpha}{\sin(\theta+\beta)} = \frac{P}{\sin\theta} \qquad \text{...(2).}$$

From (1) and (2), eliminating E and W, we have

$$\cos\alpha = \frac{R}{W} = \frac{\sin\alpha \sin\beta}{\mu \sin(\theta+\beta)}.$$

Hence $$\sin(\theta+\beta) = \frac{\tan\alpha \sin\beta}{\mu} \qquad \text{...(3),}$$

giving the angle θ.

Numerical Example. Suppose the inclination of the plane to be 30° the coefficient of friction to be $\frac{1}{3}$ and the angle between the force P and the line of greatest slope to be 30°.

In this case we have

$$\sin(\theta + 30°) = \frac{\tan 30° \cdot \sin 30°}{\frac{1}{3}} = \frac{\sqrt{3}}{2} = \sin 60° \qquad \text{...(4).}$$

Hence θ is 30°, and the body begins to slide down the plane in a direction making an angle of 30° with the line of greatest slope.

The force P could be easily shown to be $\frac{W}{6}\sqrt{3}$.

If the force is on the point of overcoming the weight, it can be easily shown [or it follows from (4), since another solution is $\theta = 90°$], that the friction μR acts horizontally, so that the particle would start in a horizontal direction, and that the corresponding value of P is $\frac{W}{3}\sqrt{3}$.

Examples XXXVI

1. A ladder, whose centre of gravity divides it into two portions of length a and b, rests with one end on a rough horizontal floor, and the other end against a rough vertical wall. If the coefficients of friction at the floor and wall are respectively μ and μ', show that the inclination of the ladder to the floor, when the equilibrium is limiting, is $\tan^{-1}\frac{a - b\,\mu\mu'}{\mu(a+b)}$.
2. A weightless rod is supported horizontally between two rough inclined planes at right angles to each other, the angle of friction λ being less than the inclination of either plane. Show that the length of that portion of the rod on which a weight may be placed without producing motion is $\sin 2\alpha \cdot \sin 2\lambda$ of the whole length of the rod, where α is the inclination of either plane to the horizontal.

3. A heavy uniform rod is placed over one and under the other on two horizontal pegs, so that the rod lies in a vertical plane; show that the length of the shortest rod which will rest in such a position is

$$a(1 + \tan\alpha \cot\lambda),$$

where a is the distance between the pegs, α is the angle of inclination to the horizon of the line joining them, and λ is the angle of friction.

4. A uniform heavy rod, 30 cm long, one end of which is rough and the other smooth, rests within a circular hoop in a vertical plane, the radius of the hoop being 25 cm. If the rod is in limiting equilibrium when its rough end is at the lowest point of the hoop, show that the coefficient of friction is $\frac{24}{48}$.

5. A heavy uniform rod rests with its extremities on a rough circular hoop fixed in a vertical plane; the rod subtends an angle of 120° at the centre of the hoop, and in the limiting position of equilibrium is inclined to the horizon at an angle θ. If $\sqrt{3}\,\mu = \tan\alpha$, μ being the coefficient of friction, show that

$$\tan\theta : \tan 2\alpha : 2 : \sqrt{3}.$$

6. A and B are two small equal heavy rings which slide on a rough horizontal rod, the coefficient of friction being $3^{-\frac{3}{2}}$. Another equal heavy ring C slides on a weightless smooth string connecting A and B; show that, in the position of limiting equilibrium, ABC is an equilateral triangle.

7. One end of a heavy uniform rod AB can slide along a rough horizontal rod AC, to which it is attached by a ring; B and C are joined by a string. If ABC is a right angle when the rod is on the point of sliding, μ the coefficient of friction, and α the angle between AB and the vertical, show that

$$\mu = \frac{\tan\alpha}{\tan^2\alpha + 2}.$$

8. A uniform rod slides with its ends on two fixed equally rough rods, one being vertical and the other inclined at an angle α to the horizon. Show that the inclination θ to the horizon of the movable rod, when it is on the point of sliding, is given by

$$\tan\theta = \frac{1 \mp 2\mu \tan\alpha - \lambda^3}{2(\tan\alpha \pm \mu)}.$$

9. A uniform ladder, whose length is a and whose weight is W, makes an angle θ with the horizontal, and rests with one end against a vertical wall and the other upon a horizontal floor, the wall and floor being equally rough, and the coefficient of friction being $\tan\lambda$. Show that a man, whose weight is P, can never get nearer to the top of the ladder than

$$\frac{W\cot 2\lambda + P\cot\lambda - (W + P)\tan\theta}{2P}\, a \sin 2\lambda.$$

10. The poles supporting a lawn-tennis net are kept in a vertical position by guy ropes, one to each pole, which pass round pegs 60 cm distant from the poles. If the coefficient of limiting friction between the ropes and pegs is $\frac{4}{3}$, show that the inclination of the latter to the vertical must not be less than $\tan^{-1}\frac{8}{11}$, the height of the poles being 120 cm.

11. A chest in the form of a rectangular parallelopiped, whose weight without the lid is 100 kg, and width from back to front 30 cm, has a lid weighing 25 kg and stands with its back 15 cm from a smooth wall, and parallel to it. If the lid is open and leans against the wall find the least coefficient of friction between the chest and the ground that three may be no motion.

12. A heavy circular disc, whose plane is vertical, is kept at rest on a rough inclined plane by a string parallel to the plane and touching the circle. Show that the disc will slip on the plane if the coefficient of friction is less than $\frac{1}{2}\tan i$, where i is the slope of the plane.

13. A particle resting on a rough table, whose coefficient of friction is μ, is fastened by a string, of length a, to a fixed point A on the table. Another string is fastened to the particle and, after passing over the smooth edge of the table, supports an equal particle hanging freely. Show that the particle on the table will rest at any point P of the circle, whose centre is A and whose radius is a, which is such that the string AP is kept taut and the distance of the second string from A is not greater than μa.

14. A heavy rod, of length $2a$, lies over a rough peg with one extremity leaning against a rough vertical wall; if c is the distance of the peg from the wall and λ be the angle of friction both at the peg and the wall, show that, when the point of contact of the rod with the wall is above the peg, then the rod is on the point of sliding downwards when

$$\sin^2\theta = \frac{c}{a}\cos^2\lambda,$$

where θ is the inclination of the rod to the wall. If the point of contact of the rod and wall is below the peg, prove that the rod is or the point of slipping downwards when

$$\sin^2\theta\sin(\theta + 2\lambda) = \frac{c}{a}\cos^2\lambda,$$

and on the point of slipping upwards when

$$\sin^2\theta\sin(\theta - 2\lambda) = \frac{c}{a}\cos^2\lambda.$$

15. A circular disc, of radius a and weight W, is placed withing a smooth sphere, of radius b and a particle, of weight w, is placed on the disc, If the coefficient of friction between the particle and the disc is μ, find the greatest distance from the centre of the disc at which the particle can rest.

16. A smooth sphere, of given weight W, rests between a vertical wall and a prism, one of whose faces rests on a horizontal plane; if the coefficient of friction between the horizontal plane and the prism is μ, show that the least weight of the prism consistent with equilibrium is $W\left(\frac{\tan\alpha}{\mu} - 1\right)$, where α is the inclination to the horizon of the face in contact with the sphere.

17. Two equal rods, of length $2a$, are fastened together so as to form two sides of a square, and one of them rests on a rough peg. Show that the limiting distances of the points of contact from the middle point of the rod are $\frac{a}{2}(1 \pm \mu)$, where μ is the coefficient of friction.

18. Two uniform rods, AC and BC, are rigidly joined at C so that they form one uniform bent rod, whose two portions are at right angles. This bent rod is supported on the edge of a rough table which touches AC at its middle point. If BC is three times AC, show that the tangent of the inclination of AC to the horizontal is $\frac{1}{3}$.

Find also the least value of the coefficient of friction that the rod may rest with the point A on the edge of the table.

19. A heavy string rests on two given inclined planes, of the same material, passing over a small pulley at their common vertex. If the string is on the point of motion, show that the line joining its two ends is inclined to the horizontal at the angle of friction.

20. On a rough inclined plane $\left(\mu = \frac{1}{2}\right)$ a weight W is just supported by a force $\frac{W}{2}$ acting up the plane and parallel to it. Find the magnitude and direction of the least additional force, acting along the plane, which will prevent motion when the force $\frac{W}{2}$ acts along the plane, but at 60° with the line of greatest slope.

21. A weight W is laid upon a rough place $\left(\mu = \frac{1}{\sqrt{3}}\right)$, inclined at 45° to the horizontal, and is connected by a string passing through a smooth ring, A, at the top of the plane, with a weight P hanging vertically. If $W = 3P$, show that, if θ is the greatest possible inclination of the string AW to the line of greatest slope in the plane, then

$$\cos\theta = \frac{2\sqrt{2}}{3}.$$

Find also the direction in which W would commence to move.

22. A weight W rests on a rough inclined plane inclined at an angle α to the horizontal, and the coefficient of friction is 2 $\tan\alpha$. Show that the least horizontal force along the plane which will move the body is $\sqrt{3}W \sin\alpha$, and that the body will begin to move in a direction inclined at 60° to the line of greatest slope on the plane.

23. If two equal weights, unequally rough, are connected by a light rigid rod and placed on an inclined plane whose inclination, α, to the horizontal is the angle whose tangent is the geometric mean between the coefficients of friction, show that the greatest possible inclination to the line of greatest slope which the rod can make when at rest is $\cos^{-1}\left(\frac{\mu_1 + \mu_2}{2\sqrt{2\mu_1\mu_2}}\right)$, where μ_1 and μ_2 are the coefficients of friction.

24. A heavy particle is placed on a rough plane inclined at an angle α to the horizon, and is connected by a stretched weightless string AP to a fixed point A in the plane. If AB is the line of greatest slope and θ the angle PAB when the particle is on the point of slipping, show that $\sin\theta = \mu \cot\alpha$. Interpret the result when $\mu \cot\alpha$ is greater than unity.

25. A hemispherical shell rests on a rough plane, whose angle of friction is λ; show that the inclination of the plane base of the rim to the horizontal cannot be greater than $\sin^{-1}(2 \sin\lambda)$.

26. A solid homogeneous hemisphere rests on a rough horizontal plane and against a smooth vertical wall. Show that, if the coefficient of friction is greater than $\frac{3}{6}$, the hemisphere can rest in any position and, if it is less, the least angle that the base of the hemisphere can make with the vertical is $\cos^{-1}\frac{8\mu}{3}$.

If the wall is rough (coefficient of friction μ') show that this angle is $\cos^{-1}\left(\frac{8\mu}{3} \cdot \frac{1+\mu'}{1+\mu\mu'}\right)$.

27. A heavy homogeneous hemisphere rests with its convex surface in contact with a rough inclined plane; show that the greatest possible inclination of the plane to the horizontal is $\sin^{-1}\frac{3}{8}$.

Show that a homogeneous sphere cannot rest in equilibrium on any inclined plane, whatever its roughness.

28. If a hemisphere rests in equilibrium with its curved surface in contact with a rough plane inclined to the horizontal at an angle $\sin^{-1}\frac{3}{16}$, find the inclination of the plane base of the hemisphere to the vertical.

29. A uniform hemisphere, of radius a and weight W, rests with its spherical surface on a horizontal plane, and a rough particle, of weight W', rests on the plane surface; show that the distance of the particle from the centre of the plane face is not greater than $\frac{3W\mu a}{8W'}$, where μ is the coefficient of friction.

30. A sphere, whose radius is a and whose centre of gravity is at a distance c from the centre, rests in limiting equilibrium on a rough plane inclined at an angle α to the horizon; show that it may be turned through an angle $2\cos^{-1}\left(\frac{a\sin\alpha}{c}\right)$, and still be in limiting equilibrium.

16

Miscellaneous

212. Bodies connected by smooth hinges. When two bodies are hinged together, it usually happens that, either a rounded end of one body fits loosely into a prepared hollow in the other body, as in the case of a ball and socket joint; or that a round pin, or other separate fastening, passes through a hole in each body, as in the case of the hinge of a door.

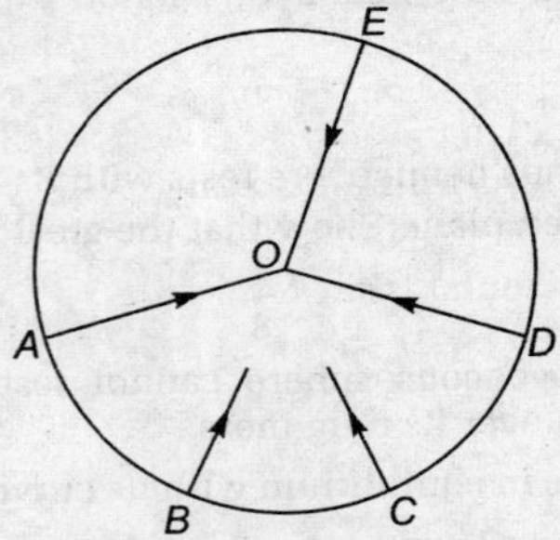

In either case, if the bodies are smooth, the action on each body at the hinge consists of a single force. Let the figure represent a section of the joint connecting two bodies. If it is smooth the actions at all the points of the joint pass through the centre of the pin and thus have as resultant a single force passing through O. Also the action of the hinge on the one body is equal and opposite to the action of the hinge on the other body; for forces, equal and opposite to these actions, keep the pin, or fastening, in equilibrium, since its weight is negligible.

If the joint is not smooth, then at the points of contact A, B, C, D,.. there will also be frictional resistances acting in directions perpendicular to OA, OB, OC ,..... . The forces acting on such a joint will not, in general, reduce to a single force but to a force and a couple (Art. 87).

In solving question concerning smooth hinges, the direction and magnitude of the action at the hinge are usually both unknown. Hence it is generally most convenient to assume the action of a smooth hinge on one body to consist of two unknown components at right angles to one another; the action of the hinge on the other body will then consist of components equal and opposite to these.

The forces acting on each body, together with the actions of the hinge on it, are in equilibrium, and the general conditions of equilibrium of Art. 83 will now apply.

In order to avoid mistakes as to the components of the reaction acting on each body, it is convenient, as in the second figure of the following example, not to produce the beams to meet but to leave a space between them.

213. Ex. *Three equal uniform rods, each of weight W , are smoothly jointed so as to form an equilateral triangle. If the system is supported at the middle point of one of the rods, show that the action at the lowest angle is* $\frac{\sqrt{3}}{6}$ *W and that at each of the others is* $W\sqrt{\frac{13}{12}}$.

Let ABC be the triangle formed by the rods, and D the middle point of the side AB at which the system is supported.

Let the action of the hinge at A on the rod AB consist of two components, respectively equal to Y and X, acting in vertical and horizontal directions; hence the action of the hinge on AC consists of components equal and opposite to these.

Since, the whole system is symmetrical about the vertical line through D, the action at B will consist of components, also equal to Y and X, as in the figure.

Let the action of the hinge C on CB consist of Y_1 vertically upwards, and X_1 horizontally to the right, so that the action of the same hinge on CA consists of two components opposite to these, as in the figure.

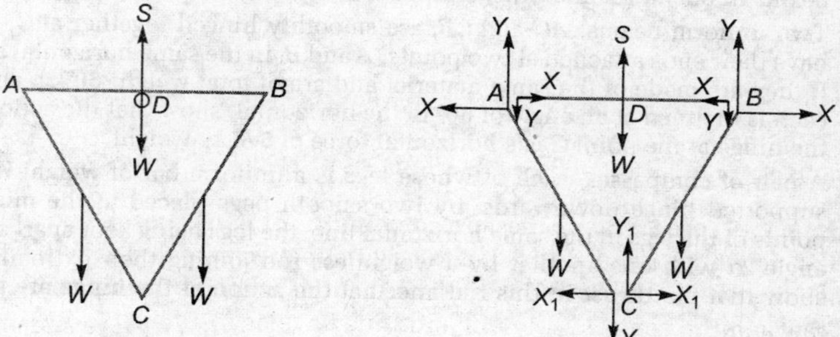

For AB, resolving vertically, we have

$$S = W + 2Y \qquad \text{...(1)},$$

where S is the vertical reaction of the peg at D.

For CB, resolving horizontally and vertically, and taking moments about C, we have

$$X + X_1 = 0 \qquad \text{...(2)},$$

$$W = Y + Y_1 \qquad \text{...(3)},$$

and $$W \cdot a\cos 60° + X \cdot 2a\sin 60° = Y \cdot 2a\cos 60° \qquad \text{...(4)}.$$

For CA, by resolving vertically, we have

$$W = Y - Y_1 \qquad \text{...(5)}.$$

From equations (3) and (5) we have,

$$Y_1 = 0, \text{ and } Y = W.$$

Hence equation (4) is

$$X = \frac{1}{2} W\cot 60° = \frac{W}{2\sqrt{3}} = \frac{\sqrt{3}}{6} W.$$

Therefore, from (2), $X_1 = -\frac{\sqrt{3}}{6}W$.

Also (1) gives $S = 3W$.

Hence the action of the hinge at B consists of a force $\sqrt{X^2 + Y^2}$ $\left(i.e., W\sqrt{\frac{13}{12}}\right)$ acting at an angle $\tan^{-1}\frac{Y}{X}$ (*i.e.* $\tan^{-1} 2\sqrt{3}$), to the horizon; also the action of the hinge at C consists of a horizontal force equal to $\frac{\sqrt{3}}{6}W$.

A priori reasoning would have shown us that the action of the hinge at C must be horizontal; for the whole system is symmetrical about the line CD, and, unless the component Y_1 vanished; the reaction at C would not satisfy the condition of symmetry.

Examples XXXVII

1. Two equal uniform beams, AB and BC, are freely jointed at B and A is fixed to a hinge at a point in a wall about which AB can turn freely in a vertical plane. At what point in BC must a vertical force be applied to keep the two beams in one horizontal line, and what is the magnitude of the force ?
2. Two uniform beams, AC and CB, are smoothly hinged together at C, and have their ends attached at two points, A and B, in the same horizontal line. If they are made of the same material and are of total weight 60 kg, and if each is inclined at an angle of 60° to the horizontal, show that the action of the hinge at the point C is a horizontal force of $5\sqrt{3}$ kg weight.
3. A pair of compasses, each of whose legs is a uniform bar of weight W, is supported hinge downwards, by two smooth pegs placed at the middle points of the legs in the same horizontal line, the legs being kept apart at an angle 2α with one another by a weightless rod joining their extremities; show that the thrust in this rod and that the action at the hinge are each $\frac{1}{2}W\cot\alpha$.
4. Two equal uniform rods, AB and AC, each of weight W, are smoothly joined at A and placed in a vertical plane with the ends B and C resting on a smooth table. Equilibrium is preserved by a string which attaches C to the middle point of AB. Show that the tension of the string and the reaction of the rods at A are both equal to
$$\frac{W}{4}\operatorname{cosec}\alpha\sqrt{1 + 8\cos^2\alpha},$$
and that each is inclined at an angle $\tan^{-1}\left(\frac{1}{3}\tan\alpha\right)$ to the horizontal, where α is the inclination of either rod to the horizon.
5. Two equal beams, AC and BC, freely jointed together at C, stand with their ends, A and B, in contact with a rough horizontal plane, and with the plane ABC vertical. If the coefficient of friction is $\frac{1}{2}$, show that the angle ACB cannot be greater than a right angle, and find the thrust at C in any position of equilibrium.

6. Three uniform heavy rods, AB, BC, and CA, of lengths 1.5, 1.2, and .9 m respectively, are hinged together at their extremities to form a triangle. Show that the whole will balance, with AB horizontal about a fulcrum which is distant 3 cm from the middle point towards A.
Prove also that the vertical components of the actions at the hinges A and B, when the rod is balanced, are $\frac{187}{600}W$ and $\frac{163}{600}W$ respectively, where W is the total weight of the rods.

7. Two equal rods, AB and BC, are jointed at B, and have their middle points connected by an inelastic string of such a length that, when it is straightened, the angle ABC is a right angle; if the system is freely suspended from the point A, show that the inclination of AB to the vertical will be $\tan^{-1}\frac{1}{3}$, and find the tension of the string and the action at the hinge.

8. Two equal bars, AB and BC, each 1 metre long and each of weight W, are jointed together at B and suspended by strings OA, OB, and OC, each 1 metre long, from a fixed peg O; find the tensions of the three strings and the magnitude of the action at the hinge, the strings and bars being all in one plane.

9. Three uniform beams AB, BC, and CD, of the same thickness, and of lengths l, $2l$, and l respectively, are connected by smooth hinges at B and C, and rest on a perfectly smooth sphere, whose radius is $2l$, so that the middle point of BC and the extremities, A and D, are in contact with the sphere; show that the pressure at the middle point of BC is $\frac{91}{100}$ of the weight of the beams.

10. Three uniform rods AB, BC, and CD, whose weights are proportional to their lengths a, b, and c are jointed at B and C and are in a horizontal position resting on two pegs P and Q; find the actions at the joints B and C, and show that the distance between the pegs must be

$$\frac{a^2}{2a+b}+\frac{c^2}{2c+b}+b.$$

11. AB and AC are similar uniform rods, of length a, smoothly jointed at A. BD is a weightless bar, of length b, smoothly jointed at B, and fastened at D to a smooth ring sliding on AC. The system is hung on a small smooth pin at A. Show that the rod AC makes with the vertical an angle

$$\tan^{-1}\frac{b}{a+\sqrt{a^2-b^2}}.$$

12. A square figure $ABCD$ is formed by four equal uniform rods jointed together, and the system is suspended from the joint A, and kept in the form of a square by a string connecting A and C; show that the tension of the string is half the weight of the four rods, and find the direction and magnitude of the action at either of the joints B or D.

13. Four equal rods are jointed together to form a rhombus, and the opposite joints are joined by strings forming the diagonals, and the whole system is placed on a smooth horizontal table. Show that their tensions are in the same ratio as their lengths.

214. Funicular, *i. e.* Rope, Polygon. If a light cord has its ends attached to two fixed points, and if at different points of the cord are weights attached, the figure formed by the cord is called a funicular polygon.

Let O and O_1 be the two fixed points at which the ends of the cord are tied, and let $A_1, A_2, \dots A_n$ be the points of the cord at which are attached bodies, whose weights are $w_1, w_2, \dots w_n$ respectively.

Let the lengths of the portions.

$OA_1, A_1A_2, A_2A_3, \dots A_nO_1$, be $\alpha_1, \alpha_2, \alpha_3, \dots \alpha_{n+1}$, respectively, and let their inclinations to the horizontal be

$$\alpha_1, \alpha_2, \dots \alpha_{n+1}.$$

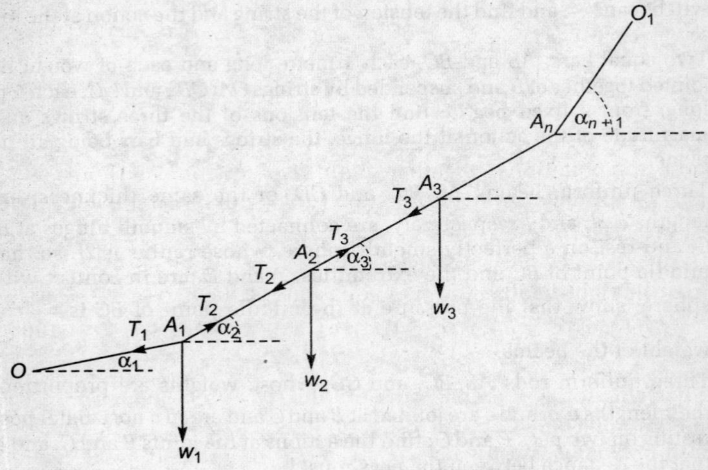

Let h and k be respectively the horizontal and vertical distances between the points O and O_1, so that

$$a_1 \cos\alpha_1 + a_2 \cos\alpha_2 + \alpha_{n+1} \cos\alpha_{n+1} = h \qquad \text{...(1),}$$

and $$a_1 \sin\alpha_1 + a_2 \cos\alpha_2 + \dots + \alpha_{n+1} \sin\alpha_{n+1} = k \qquad \text{...(2),}$$

Let $T_1, T_2, \dots T_{n+1}$ be respectively the tensions of the portions of the cord.

Resolving vertically and horizontally for the equilibrium of the different weights in succession, we have

$$T_2 \sin\alpha_2 - T_1 \sin\alpha_1 = w_1, \text{ and } T_2 \cos\alpha_2 - T_1 \cos\alpha_1 = 0;$$

$$T_3 \sin\alpha_3 - T_2 \sin\alpha_2 = w_2, \text{ and } T_3 \cos\alpha_3 - T_2 \cos\alpha_2 = 0;$$

$$T_4 \sin\alpha_4 - T_3 \sin\alpha_3 = w_3, \text{ and } T_4 \cos\alpha_4 - T_3 \cos\alpha_3 = 0;$$

....

$$T_{n+1} \sin\alpha_{n+1} - T_n \sin\alpha_n = w_n, \text{ and } T_{n+1} \cos\alpha_{n+1} - T_n \cos\alpha_n = 0.$$

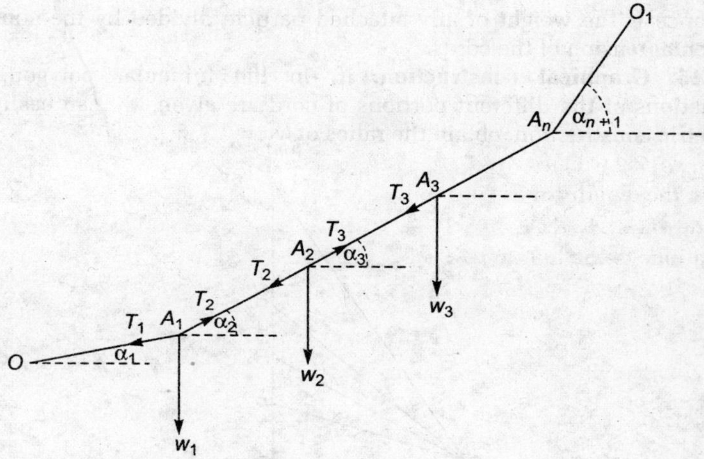

These $2n$ equations, together with the equations (1) and (2), are theoretically sufficient to determine the $(n+1)$ unknown tensions, and the $(n+1)$ unknown inclinations

$$\alpha_1, \alpha_2, \ldots \alpha_{n+1}.$$

From the right-hand column of equations we have

$$T_1 \cos\alpha_1 = T_2 \cos\alpha_2 = T_3 \cos\alpha_3 = \ldots = T_{n+1} \cos\alpha_{n+1}$$
$$= K \text{ (say)} \qquad \ldots(3),$$

so that the horizontal component of the tension of the cord is constant throughout and is denoted by K.

From (3), substituting for $T_1, T_2, \ldots T_{n+1}$ in the left-hand column of equations, we have

$$\tan\alpha_2 - \tan\alpha_1 = \frac{w_1}{K},$$

$$\tan\alpha_3 - \tan\alpha_2 = \frac{w_2}{K},$$

$$\tan\alpha_4 - \tan\alpha_3 = \frac{w_3}{K}.$$

....

$$\tan\alpha_{n+1} - \tan\alpha_n = \frac{w_n}{K}$$

If the weights are all equal, the right-hand members of this latter column of equations are all equal and it follows that $\tan\alpha_1, \tan\alpha_2, \ldots \tan\alpha_{n+1}$, are in arithmetical progression.

Hence when a set of equal weights is attached to different points of a cord, as above, the tangents of inclination to the horizon of successive portions of the cord form an arithmetical progression whose constant difference is the weight of any attached particle divided by the constant horizontal tension of the cords.

215. Graphical construction. If, in the funicular polygon, the inclinations of the different portions of cord are given, we can easily, by geometric construction, obtain the ratios of $w_1, w_2, \ldots w_n$.

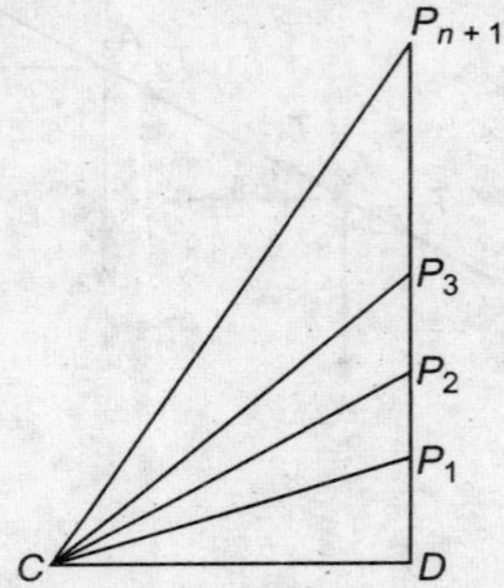

For let C be any point and CD the horizontal line through C. Draw $CP_1, CP_2, \ldots CP_{n+1}$ parallel to the cords $OA_1, A_1A_2, \ldots A_nO_1$, so that the angles $P_1CD, P_2CD, \ldots$ are respectively $\alpha_1, \alpha_2, \ldots$

Draw any vertical line cutting these lines in $D, P_1, P_2, \ldots$

Then, by the previous article,

$$\frac{w_1}{K} = \tan\alpha_2 - \tan\alpha_1 = \frac{DP_2}{CD} - \frac{DP_1}{CD} = \frac{P_1P_2}{CD},$$

$$\frac{w_2}{K} = \tan\alpha_3 - \tan\alpha_2 = \frac{DP_3}{CD} - \frac{DP_2}{CD} = \frac{P_2P_3}{CD},$$

and so on.

Hence the quantities $K, w_1, w_2, \ldots w_n$ are respectively proportional to the lines $CD, P_1P_2, P_2P_3, \ldots P_nP_{n+1}$, and hence their ratios are determined.

This result also follows the fact that CP_2P_1 is a triangle of forces for the weight at A_1, CP_3P_2 similarly for he weight at A_2, and so on.

Similarly, if the weights hung on at the joints be given and the directions of any two of the cords be also known, we can determine the directions of the others. We draw a vertical line and on it mark off $P_1P_2, P_2P_3, \ldots$ proportional to the weights $W_1, W_2, \ldots$. If the directions of the cords OA_1, A_1A_2 are given, we draw P_1O, P_2O parallel to them and thus determine the point O. Join O to $P_3, P_4, \ldots$ etc., and we have the directions of the rest of the cords.

216. Tensions of Elastic Strings. All through this book we have assumed our strings and cords to be inextensible, *i.e.*, that they would bear any tension without altering their length.

In practice, all strings are extensible, although the extensibility is in many cases extremely small, and practically negligible. When the extensibility of the string cannot be neglected, there is a simple experimental law connecting the tension of the string with the amount of extension of the string. It may be expressed in the form.

The tension of an elastic string varies as the extension of the string beyond its natural length.

Suppose a string to be naturally of length 24 cm; its tension, when the length is 26 cm, will be to its tension, when of length 30 cm, as

$$26 - 24 : 30 - 24, i.e., \text{as } 1 : 3.$$

This law may be verified experimentally thus; take a spiral spring, or an India-rubber band. Attach one end A to a fixed point and at the other end B attach weights, and observe the amount of the extensions produced by the weights. These extensions will be found to be approximately proportional to the weights. The amount of the weights used must depend on the strength of the spring or of the rubber band; the heaviest must not be large enough to injure or permanently deform the spring or band.

217. The student will observe carefully that the tension of the string is not proportional to its stretched length, but to its extension.

The above law was discovered by Hooke (A.D. 1635-1703), and enunciated by him in the form *Ut tension, sic vis.* From it we easily obtain a formula giving us the tension in any case.

Let a be the unstretched length of a string, and T its tension when it is stretched to be of length x. The extension is now $x - a$, and the law states that

$$T \propto x - a.$$

This is generally expressed in the form

$$T = \lambda \cdot \frac{x - a}{a},$$

the constant of variation being $\frac{\lambda}{a}$.

The quantity λ depends only on the thickness of the string and on the material of which it is made, and is called the *Modulus of Elasticity of the String.*

It is equal to the force which would stretch the string, if placed on a smooth horizontal table, to twice its natural length; for, when $x = 2a$, we have the tension

$$= \lambda \frac{2a - a}{a} = \lambda.$$

No elastic string will however bear an unlimited stretching; when the string, through being stretched, is on the point of breaking, its tension then is called the *breaking tension.*

Hooke's Law holds also for steel and other bars, but the extensions for which it is true in these cases are extremely small. We cannot stretch a bar to twice its natural length; but λ will be 100 times the force which will extend the bar by $\frac{1}{100}$ th of its natural length. For if $x - a = \frac{a}{100}$, then

$$T = \frac{\lambda}{100}.$$

The value of T will depend also on the thickness of the bar, and the bar is usually taken as one square inch section. Thus the modulus of elasticity of a steel bar is about 13500 tons per square inch.

By the method of Art. 134 it is easily seen that the work done in stretching an elastic string is equal to the extension multiplied by the mean of the initial and final tensions.

Ex. *ABC is an elastic string, hanging vertically from a fixed point A; at B and C are attached particles, of weights 2W and W respectively. If the modulus of elasticity of the string is 3W, find the ratio of the stretched lengths of the portions of the string to their unstretched lengths.*

Let c and c_1 be the unstretched lengths of AB and BC, and x and y their stretched lengths.

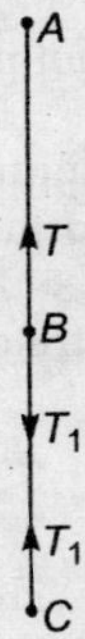

Let T and T_1 be their tensions, so that

$$T = \lambda \frac{x - c}{c} = 3W \frac{x - c}{c},$$

and $$T_S = \lambda \frac{y - c_1}{c_1} = 3W \frac{y - c_1}{c_1}.$$

From the equilibrium of B and C, we have

$$T - T_1 = 2W, \text{ and } T_1 = W.$$

Hence $$T = 3W.$$

$\therefore$ $$3W \frac{x - c}{c} = 3W, \text{ and } 3W \frac{y - c_1}{c_1} = W.$$

$\therefore$ $$x = 2c, \text{and } y = \frac{4}{2} c_1,$$

so that the stretched lengths are respectively twice and four-thirds of the natural lengths.

Examples XXXVIII

1. ABC is an elastic string, whose modulus of elasticity is $4W$, which is tied to a fixed point at A. At B and C are attached weights each equal to W, the unstretched lengths of AB and BC being each equal to c. Show that, if the string and bodies take up a vertical position of equilibrium, the stretched lengths of AB and BC are $\frac{2}{8}c$ and $\frac{8}{4}c$ respectively.
2. An elastic string has its ends attached to two points in the same horizontal plane, and initially it is just tight and unstretched; a particle, of weight W, is tied to the middle point of the string; if the modulus of elasticity is $\frac{W}{\sqrt{3}}$, show that, in the position of equilibrium, the two portions of the string will be inclined at an angle of 60° to one another.
3. In the previous question if, $12a$ is the distance between the two points, $2c$ the unstretched length of the string, and λ the modulus of elasticity, show that the inclination, θ, of the strings to the vertical is given by

$$\frac{W}{2\lambda} \tan\theta + \sin\theta = \frac{a}{c}.$$

4. A body rests on a rough inclined plane whose inclination α to the horizontal is greater than λ, the angle of friction; it is held at rest by an elastic string attached to it and to a point on the plane. If the modulus of elasticity is equal to the weight of the body, prove that in the position of equilibrium the ratio of the length of the string to its original length is

$$1 + \sin(\alpha - \lambda) \cdot \sec \lambda$$

5. Four equal jointed rods, each of length a, are hung from an angular point, which is connected by an elastic string with the opposite point. If the rods hang in the form of a square, and if the modulus of elasticity of the string is equal to the weight of a rod, show that the unstretched length of the string is $\frac{a\sqrt{2}}{3}$.

6. An elastic cord, whose natural length is 20 cm, can be kept stretched to a length of 30 cm by a force of 2.5 kgf; find the amount of work done in stretching it from a length of 24 cm to a length of 30 cm.

7. A spiral spring requires a force of $\frac{1}{2}$ kilogram weight to stretch it two cm. How much work is done in stretching it six cm more ?

Graphic Constructions

218. *To find the resultant of any number of coplanar forces.*

Let the forces be $P, Q, R,$ and S whose lines of action are as in the left-hand figure.

Draw the figure $ABCDE$ having its sides $AB, BC, CD,$ and DE respectively parallel and proportional to $P, Q, R,$ and S. Join AE, so that by the polygon of foces AE represents the required resultant in magnitude and direction.

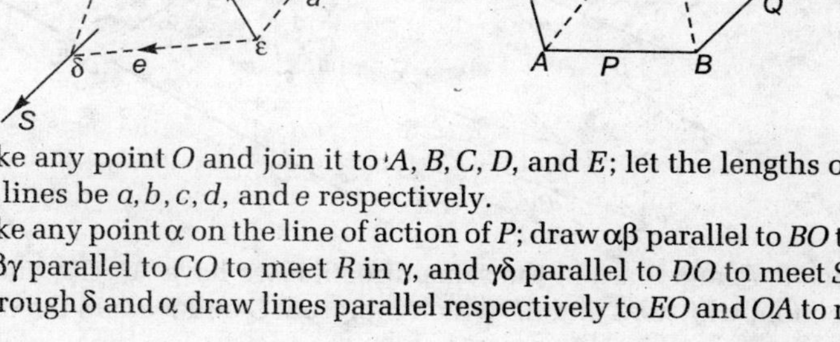

Take any point O and join it to $A, B, C, D,$ and E; let the lengths of these joining lines be $a, b, c, d,$ and e respectively.

Take any point α on the line of action of P; draw $\alpha\beta$ parallel to BO to meet Q in β, $\beta\gamma$ parallel to CO to meet R in γ, and $\gamma\delta$ parallel to DO to meet S in δ.

Through δ and α draw lines parallel respectively to EO and OA to meet in ϵ.

Through ϵ draw ϵL parallel and equal to AE. Then ϵL shall represent the required resultant in magnitude and line of action, on the same scale that AB represents P.

For P, being represented by AB, is equivalent to forces represented by AO and OB and therefore may be replaced by forces equal to a and b in the directions $\in \alpha$ and $\beta\alpha$. So Q may be replaced by b and c in directions $\alpha\beta$ and $\gamma\beta$, R by c and d in directions $\beta\gamma$ and $\delta\gamma$, and S by forces d and e in directions $\gamma\delta$ and $\in \delta$.

The forces P, Q, R, and S have therefore been replaced by forces acting along the sides of the figure $\alpha\beta\gamma\delta \in$, of which the forces along $\alpha\beta$, $\beta\gamma$ and $\gamma\delta$ balance.

Hence we have left forces at $\in$ which are parallel and equal to AO and OE, whose resultant is AE.

Since $\in L$ is drawn parallel and equal to AE, it therefore represents the required resultant in magnitude and line of action.

Such a figure as $ABCDE$ is called a Force Polygon and onr such as $\alpha\beta\gamma\delta \in$ is called a Link of Funicular Polygon, because it represents a set of links or cords in equilibrium.

219. If the point E of the Force Polygon coincides with the point A it is said to close, and then the resultant force vanishes.

If the Force Polygon closed, but the Funicular Polygon did not close, *i.e.*, if $\delta \in \alpha$ was not a straight line, we should have left forces acting at δ and α parallel to OE and AO, *i.e.* we should in this case have two equal, opposite, and parallel forces forming a couple.

If however the Funicular Polygon also closed, then $\delta \in \alpha$ would be a straight line and these two equal, opposite, and parallel forces would now be in the same straight line and would balance.

Hence, if the forces P, Q, R, S are in equilibrium, both their Force and Funicular Polygons must close.

220. If the forces are parallel the construction is the same as in the previous article. The annexed figure is drawn for the case in which the forces are parallel and two of the five forces are in the opposite direction to that of the other three.

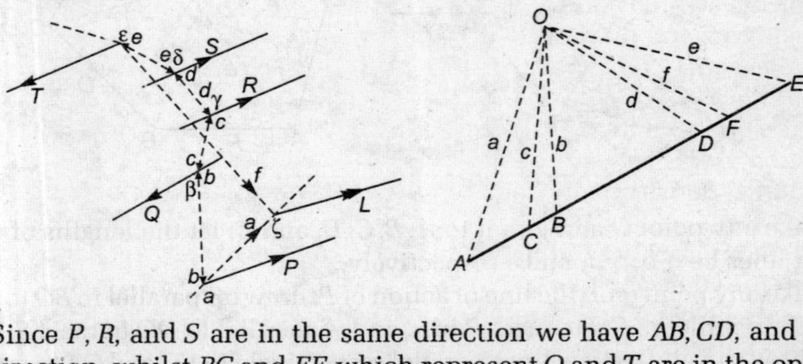

Since P, R, and S are in the same direction we have AB, CD, and DE in one direction, whilst BC and EF which represent Q and T are in the opposite direction.

The proof of the construction is the same as in the last article. The line ζL, equal and parallel to AF, represents the required resultant both in magnitude and line of action.

This construction clearly applies to finding the resultant weight of a number of weights.

221. *A closed polygon of light rods freely jointed at their extremities is acted upon by a given system of forces acting at the joints which are in equilibrium; find the actions along the rods.*

Let $A_1A_2, A_2A_3, \ldots, A_5A_1$ be a system of five rods freely jointed at their ends and at the joints let given forces P_1, P_2, P_3, P_4, and P_5 act as in the figure.

Let the consequent actions along the rods be t_1, t_2, t_3, t_4, and t_5, as marked.

Draw the pentagon $a_5a_1a_2a_3a_4$ having its sides parallel and proportional to the forces $P_1, P_2, \ldots P_5$. Since the forces are in equilibrium this polygon is a closed figure.

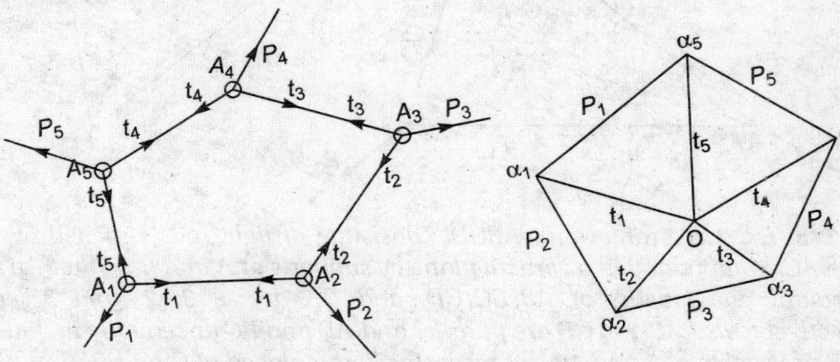

Through a_1 draw a_1O parallel to A_1A_2 and through a_5 draw a_5O parallel to A_5A_1.

Now the triangle a_5Oa_1 has its sides parallel to the forces P_1, t_1, and t_5 which act on the joint A_1. Its sides are therefore proportional to these forces; hence, on the same scale that a_5a_1 represents P_1, the sides Oa_5 and a_1O represents t_5 and t_1.

Join Oa_2, Oa_3, and Oa_4.

The sides a_1a_2 and Oa_1 represent two of the forces, P_2 and t_1, which act on A_2. Hence a_2O, which completes the triangle a_1Oa_2, represents the third force t_2 in magnitude and direction.

Similarly Oa_3 and Oa_4 represent t_3 and t_4 respectively.

The lines Oa_1, Oa_2, Oa_3, Oa_4, and Oa_5 therefore represent, both in magnitude and direction, the forces along the sides of the framework. The figure $a_1a_2a_3a_4a_5$ is called the force polygon.

A similar construction would apply whatever be the number of sides in the framework.

222. It is clear that the figure and construction of the preceding article are really the same as those of Art. 218.

If the right-hand figure represents a frame-work of rods $a_1a_2, a_2a_3, a_3a_4 \ldots$ acted on at the joints by forces along $a_1O, a_2O, \ldots$ then the polygon $A_1A_2A_3A_4A_5$ of the left-hand figure is clearly its force polygon, since $A_1A_2, A_2A_3, \ldots$ are respectively parallel to $a_1O, a_2O, \ldots$

Hence either of these two polygons may be taken as the Framework, or Funicular Polygon, and then the other is the Force Polygon. For this reason such figures are called Reciprocal.

As another example we give a triangular framework acted on at its joints by three forces P_1, P_2, P_3 in equilibrium whose force polygon is $a_2a_3a_1$; conversely, $A_2A_3A_1$ is the force polygon for the triangle $a_1a_2a_3$ acted on by forces T_1, T_2, and T_3.

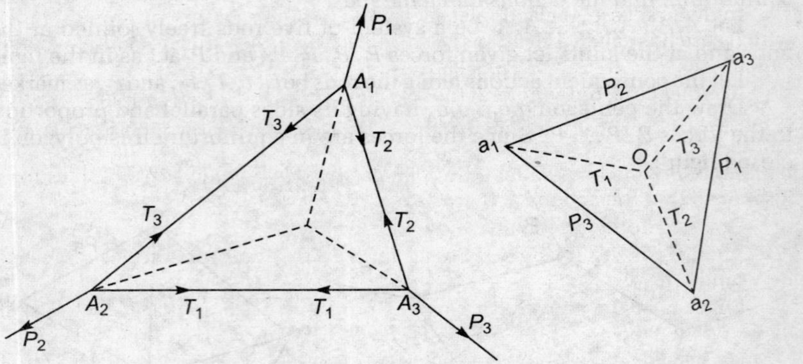

223. Ex. 1. *A framework, ABCD, consisting of light rods stiffened by a brace AC, is supported in a vertical plane by supports at A and B, so that AB is horizontal; the lengths of AB, BC, CD, and DA are 4, 3, 2, and 3 feet respectively; also AB and CD are parallel and AD and BC are equally inclined to AB. If weights of 5 and 10 cwt respectively are placed at C and D, find the reactions of the supports at A and B, and the forces exerted by the different portions of the framework.*

Let the forces in the sides be as marked in the figure and let P and Q be the reactions at A and B.

Draw a vertical line $\alpha\beta$, 5 inches in lengths to represent the weight 10 cwt at D; also draw $\alpha\delta$ parallel to AD and $\beta\delta$ parallel to CD. Then $\alpha\beta\delta$ is the Triangle of Forces for the joint D, and the forces at D must be in the directions marked.

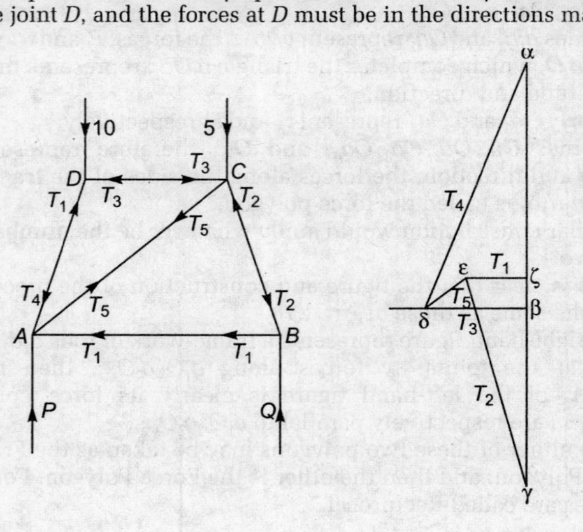

Note that the force at C in the bar DC must be along DC or CD, and that at D in the same bar along CD or DC.

[This is an important general principle; for any bar, which undergoes stress, is either resisting a tendency to compress it, or a tendency to stretch it.

In the first case, the action at each end is from its centre towards its ends, in which case it is called a strut; in the second case it is towards its centre, when it is called a tie.

In *either* case, the actions at the two ends of the rod are equal and opposite].

Draw $\beta\gamma$ vertical and equal to $2\frac{1}{2}$ in to represent the weight at C. Draw $\gamma\epsilon$ parallel to BC and $\delta\epsilon$ parallel to AC. Then $\delta\beta\gamma\epsilon\delta$ is the Polygon of Forces for the joint C, so that the actions at C are as marked.

Draw $\epsilon\zeta$ horizontal to meet $\alpha\gamma$ in ζ.

Then $\epsilon\gamma\zeta$ is the Triangle of Forces for B, so that the reaction Q is represented by $\gamma\zeta$ and T_1 by $\zeta\epsilon$.

Finally, for the joint A, we have the polygon $\delta\epsilon\zeta\alpha\delta$, so that P is represented by $\zeta\alpha$.

On measuring, we have, in inches,

$$\epsilon\zeta = 1.10,\ \gamma\epsilon = 3.31,\ \delta\beta = 1.77,\ \delta\alpha = 5.30,\ \delta\epsilon = 0.91$$
$$\gamma\zeta = 3.125,\ \text{and}\ \zeta\alpha = 4.375$$

Hence since one inch represents 2 cwt, we have, in cwt,

$$T_1 = 2.20,\ T_2 = 6.62,\ T_3 = 3.54,\ T_4 = 10.6,\ T_5 = 1.82$$
$$Q = 6.25,\ \text{and}\ P = 8.75.$$

It will be noted that the bars AB and AC are in a state of tension, *i.e.* they are ties, whilst the other bars of the framework are in a state of compression, *i.e.* they are struts.

The values of P and Q may be also found, as R and S are found in the next example, by the construction of Art. 220.

Ex. 2. *A portion of a Warren Girder consists of a light frame composed of three equilateral triangles ABC, CBD, CDE and rests with ACE horizontal being supported at A and E,. Loads of 2 and 1 tons are hung on at B and D; find the stresses in the various members.*

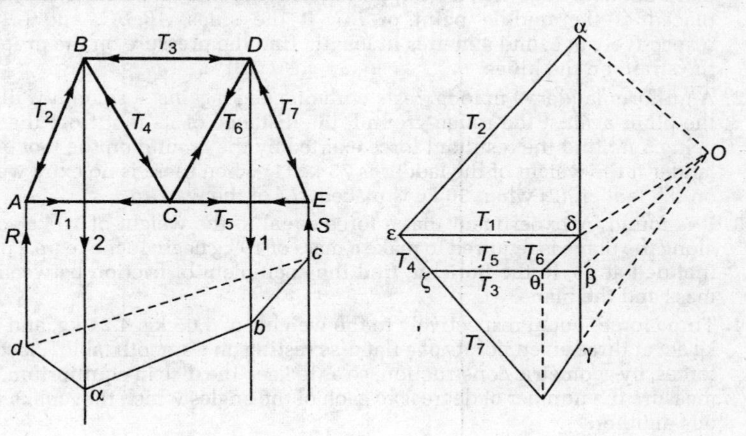

Draw $\alpha\beta$, $\beta\gamma$ vertical, and equal to 2 inches and 1 inch respectively, to represent 2 tons and 1 ton. Take any pole O and join $O\alpha$, $O\beta$, $O\gamma$.

Take any point a on the line of action of the 2 ton wt; draw ad parallel to αO to meet the reaction R in d, and ab parallel to βO to meet the vertical through D in b, and then bc parallel to γO to meet S in c. Join cd. Then $abcd$ is the funicular polygon of which (if we draw $O\delta$ parallel to cd) $\alpha\beta\gamma\delta$ is the force polygon (in this case a straight line). Hence $\delta\alpha$ represents R and $\gamma\delta$ represents S.

Let the forces exerted by the rods, whether thrusts or tensions, be $T_1, T_2, \ldots$ as marked.

Draw $\delta\in$ parallel to CA and $\alpha\in$ Parallel to AB; then $\alpha\in\delta$ is a triangle of forces for the joint A, so that $\alpha\in$ and $\in\delta$ represent T_2 and T_1.

Draw $\in\zeta$ and $\beta\zeta$ parallel to BC and BD respectively. Then $\in\alpha\beta\zeta$ is the polygon of forces for the joint B so that T_4 and T_3 are given by $\in\zeta$ and $\zeta\beta$ respectively.

Draw $\delta\theta$ parallel to DC; then $\delta\in\zeta\theta$ is the polygon of forces for the joint C and hence $\zeta\theta$ and $\theta\delta$ represent T_5 and T_6.

Draw γi parallel to DC to meet $\in\zeta$ produced in then $\zeta\beta\gamma i$ is the polygon of forces for the joint D so that γi and $i\zeta$ represent T_6 and T_7 respectively; [it follows that γi must be equal and parallel to $\delta\theta$, and hence $i\theta$ must be equal and parallel to $\gamma\delta$ and therefore represent S.]

Finally $i\theta\zeta$ is the triangle of forces for the joint E.

Hence if we measure off the lengths $\alpha\delta$, $\delta\gamma$, $\in\delta$, $\in\alpha$, $\zeta\beta$, $\in\zeta$, $\zeta\theta$, $\theta\delta$, $i\zeta$ in inches, we shall have the values of $R, S, T_1, T_2, T_3, T_4, T_5, T_6, T_7$ respectively expressed in tons wt.

They are found to be 1.75, 1.25, 1.01, 2.02, .87, .29, .72, .29, and 1.44 tons wt respectively.

From the figure it is clear that AC, CE, and CD are ties and that the others are struts.

Examples XXXIX

[*The following are to be solved by graphic methods*].

1. A uniform triangular lamina A its of 30 kg weight, can turn in a vertical plane about a hinge at B; it is supported with the side AB horizontal by a peg placed at the middle point of BC. If the sides AB, BC, and CA are respectively 6, 5, and 4 metres in length, find the pressure on the prop and the strain on the hinge.
2. A uniform ladder, 9 m long, rests with one end against a smooth wall and the other against the rough ground, the distance of its foot from the wall being 3 m; find the resultant force exerted by the ground on the foot of the ladder if the weight of the ladder is 75 kg (1) when there is no extra weight on the ladder, (2) when 56 kg is placed 3 / 4 of the way up.
3. It is found by experiment that a force equal to the weight of 10 kg acting along the plane is required to make a mass of 10 kg begin to move up a plane inclined at 45° to the horizon; find the coefficient of friction between the mass and the plane.
4. Three forces equal respectively to the weights of 5.05 kg, 4.24 kg, and 3.85 kg act at three given points of a flat disc resting on a smooth table. Place the forces, by geometric construction, so as to keep the disc in equilibrium, and measure the number of degrees in each of the angles which they make with one another.

5. A uniform rectangular block, of which *ABCD* is the symmetrical section through its centre of gravity, rests with *CD* in contact with a rough horizontal plane $\left(\mu = \frac{1}{2}\right)$; the weight of the block is 20 kg and a force equal to 5 kgf acts at *D* in the direction *CD*; if the lengths of *BC* and *CD* are respectively 90 and 150 cm, find the value of the least force which, applied at the middle point of *CB* parallel to the diagonal *DB*, would move the block.

6. A body, of weight 100 kg, rests on a rough plane whose slope is 1 in 3, the coefficient of friction being $\frac{1}{2}$; find the magnitude of the force which, acting at an angle of 40° with the plane, is on the point of dragging the body up the plane. Find also the force which, acting at an angle of 40° with the plane, is on the point of dragging the body down the plane.

7. *ABC* is a triangle whose sides *AB*, *BC*, *CA* are respectively 24, 20, and 30 cm long and *BD* is the perpendicular from *B* on *CA*. Find by means of a force and funicular polygon the magnitude and the line of action of the resultant of the following forces; 8 from *A* to *C*, 8 from *C* to *B*, 3 from *B* to *A*, and 2 from *B* to *D*.

8. *AB* is a straight line, 90 cm long; at *A* and *B* act parallel forces equal to 392 and 280 kg respectively which are (1) like, (2) unlike; construct for each case the position of the point *D* at which their resultant meets *AB* and measure its distance from *A*.

9. Loads of 112, 224, 168 kg are placed on a beam 3 m long at distances of 30 cm, 80 cm, 2.1 m from one end. Find by an accurate drawing the line of action of the resultant.

10. A horizontal beam 6 m long is supported at its ends and carries loads of 168, 112, 280 and 224 kg at distances of 90, 210, 360, and 450 cm respectively from one end. Find by means of a funicular polygon the thrusts on the two ends.

11. A triangular frame of jointed rod *ABC*, right-angled at *A*, can turn about *A* in a vertical plane. The side *AB* is horizontal and the corner *C* rests against a smooth vertical stop below *A*. If $AB = 90$ cm, $AC = 30$ cm and a weight of 25 kg be hung on at *B*, find graphically the stresses in the various bars.

12. Forces equal to 1, 2, 4, and 4 kg weight respectively act along the sides *AB*, *BC*, *CD*, and *DA* of a square. Prove that their resultant is 3.6 kg weight in a direction inclined at $\tan^{-1}\frac{3}{2}$ to *CB* and intersecting *BC* produced at *G*, where *CG* is equal to $\frac{5}{3}$ *BC*.

13. *AC* and *CB* are two equal beams inclined to one another at an angle of 40°, the ends *A* and *B* resting on the ground, which is rough enough to prevent any slipping, and the plane *ACB* being inclined at an angle of 70° to the ground. At *C* is attached a body of weight 560 kg, and the system is

supported by a rope, attached to C, which is in the vertical plane passing through C and the middle point of AB. If the rope is attached to the ground and is inclined at an angle of 50° to the ground, find the tension of the rope and the action along the beams.[This arrangement is called a Sheer-legs].

14. A beam, AB, of weight 140 kg, rests with one end A on a rough horizontal plane, the other end B, being supported by a cord, passing over a smooth pulley at C, whose horizontal and vertical distances from A are respectively 15 and 20 metres. If the length of the beam is 15 metres, and it is on the point of slipping when the end B is at a height of 9 metres above the horizontal plane, find the magnitudes of the coefficient of friction, the tension of the chord, and the resultant reaction at A.

15. A triangular framework ABC, formed of three bars jointed at its angular points, is in equilibrium under the action of three forces P, Q, and R acting outwards at its angular points, the line of action of each being the line joining its point of application to the middle of the opposite bar. If the sides BC, CA, and AB are 2.7 m, 2.4 m and 2.1 m in length respectively, and if the force P is equal to 25 kgf, find the values of Q and R, and the forces acting along the bars of the framework.

16. A and B are two fixed pegs, B being the higher, and a heavy rod rests on B and passes under A; show that, the angle of friction between the rod and the pegs being the same for both, the rod will rest in any position in which its centre of gravity is beyond B, provided that the inclination of AB to the horizontal is less than the angle of friction; also for any greater inclination, determine graphically the limiting distance of the centre of gravity beyond B consistent with equilibrium.

17. A uniform beam AB, weighing 100 kg, is supported by strings AC and BD, the latter being vertical, and the angles CAB and ABD are each 105°. The rod is maintained in this position by a horizontal force P applied at B. Show that the value of P is about 25 kg weight.

18. AB and AC are two equal rods of no appreciable weight smoothly jointed together at A, which rest in a vertical plane with their ends upon a smooth horizontal plane BC. D is a point in AB such that $AD = \frac{1}{3} AB$ and E and F are the points of trisection of AC, E being the nearer to A. A fine string connects D and F and is of such a length that the angle A is 60°. Show that, if a weight W is attached to E, the tension of the string is $W/2$.

19. $ABCDEF$ is a regular hexagon. Show that the forces which must act along AC, AF, and DE to produce equilibrium with a force of 20 kg weight acting along EC are respectively 5, 8.66, and 17.32 kg weight.

20. Fig. 1 consists of a symmetrical system of light rods freely jointed and supported vertically at the extremities; vertical loads of 560 and 280 kg are placed at the points indicated; find the thrusts or tensions of the rods, if the side rods are inclined at 50° to the horizontal.

21. Fig. 2 consists of a symmetrical system of light rods freely jointed and supported by vertical reactions at *A* and *B*; if a weight of 560 kg is placed at *D* find the thrusts or tensions in the rods, given that $\angle DAB = 55°$ and $\angle CAB = 35°$.

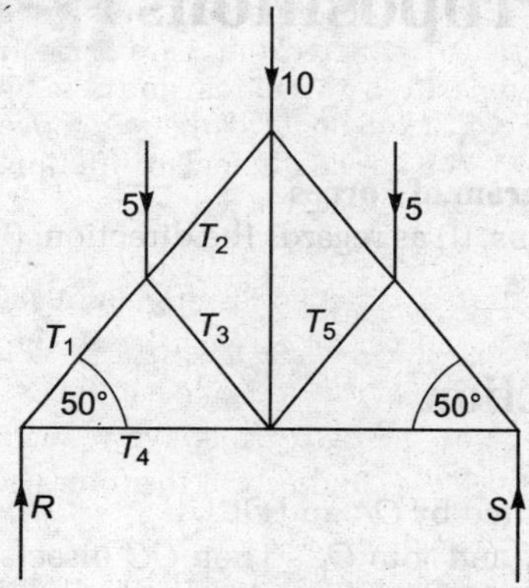

Fig. 1

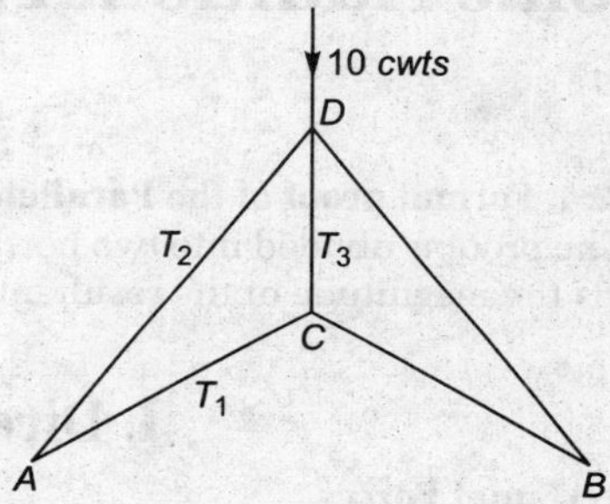

Fig. 2

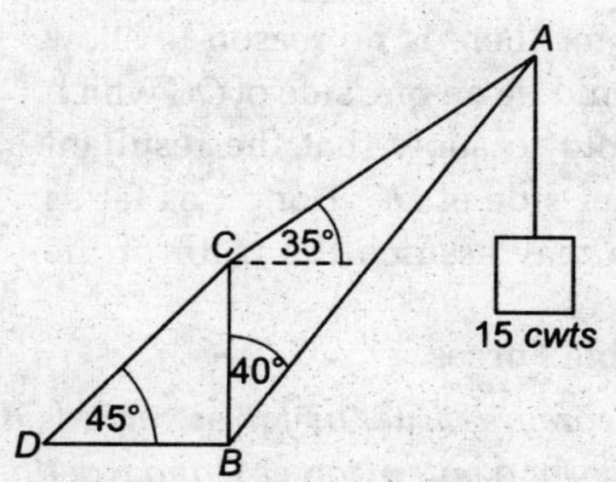

Fig. 3

22. A crane is constructed as in Fig. 3, and 840 kg is hung on at *A*; find the forces along the parts *AC* and *AB*.

If the post *BC* is free to move, and *BD* is rigidly fixed, find the pull in the tie *CD*.

23. A portion of a Warren girder consists of three equilateral triangles *ABC*, *ADC*, *BCE*, the lines *AB*, *DCE* being horizontal and the latter the uppermost. It rests on vertical supports at *A* and *B* and carries 5 tonnes at *D* and 3 tonnes at *E*. Find the reactions at the supports and the stresses in the four inclined members.

24. *ABCD* consists of a quadrilateral consisting of four light rods loosely jointed, which is stiffened by a rod *BD*; at *A* and *C* act forces equal to 20 kg weight. Given that $AB = 60$ cm, $BC = 90$ cm, $CD = 120$ cm, $DA = 135$ cm and $DB = 150$ cm, find the tensions or thrusts of the rods.

17

Some Additional Propositions

224. Formal proof of the Parallelogram of Forces.

The proof is divided into two portions, (I) as regards the direction, (II) as regards the magnitude of the resultant.

I. Direction

(α) Equal Forces.

Let the forces be equal and represented by *OA* and *OB*.

Complete the parallelogram *OACB*, and join *OC*. Then *OC* bisects the angle *AOB*.

Since the forces are equal, it is clear that the resultant must bisect the angle between them; for there is no reason to show why the resultant should lie on one side of *OC* which would not equally hold to show that the resultant should lie on the other side of *OC*. Hence, as far as regards direction, we may assume the truth of the theorem for equal forces.

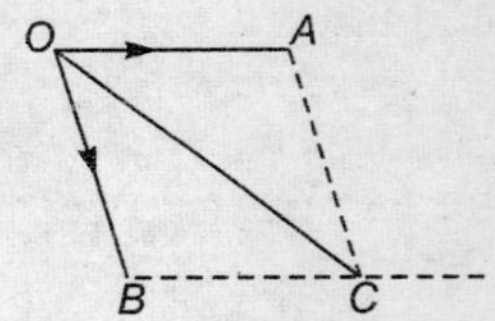

(β) Commensurable Forces.

Lemma. *If the theorem is true, as far as regards direction, for a pair of forces P and Q, and also for a pair of forces P and R acting at the same angle, to show that it is true for the pair of forces P and* (*Q* + *R*).

Let the forces act at a point *A* of a rigid body, and let *AB* be the direction of *P*, and *ACD* that of *Q* and *R*.

Let *AB* and *AC* represent the forces *P* and *Q* in magnitude.

Since, by the principle of The Transmissibility of Force, the force *R* may be supposed to act at any points in its one of action, let it act at *C* and be represented by *CD*.

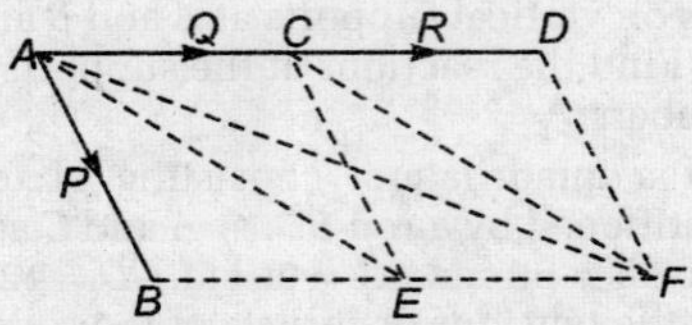

Complete the parallelograms *ABEC* and *ABFD*.

The resultant of P and Q is, by supposition, equal to some force T acting in the direction AE; let them be replaced by this resultant and let its point of application be removed to E.

This force T, acting at E, may now be replaced by forces, equal to P and Q, acting in the directions CE and EF respectively.

Let their points of application be removed to C and F.

Again, by the supposition, the resultant of P and R, acting at C, is equivalent to some force acting in the direction CF; let them be replaced by their resultant and let its point of application be removed to F.

All the forces have now been applied at F without altering their combined effect; hence F must be a point on the line of action of their resultant; therefore AF is the direction of the required resultant.

Hence the Lemma is proved.

Application of the lemma.

By (α) we know that the theorem is true for forces which are each equal to S.

Hence, by the lamma, putting P, Q, and R each equal to S, we see that the theorem is true for forces S and $2S$. Again, by the lemma, since the theorem is true for forces (S, S) and $(S, 2S)$ we see that it is true for forces $(S, 3S)$. Similarly for forces $(S, 4S)$ and so on,

Continuing in this way, we see that it is true for forces S and mS, where m is any positive integer.

Again, from the lemma, putting P equal to mS, and Q and R both equal to S, the theorem is true for forces mS and $2S$.

Again, putting P equal to mS, Q to $2S$, and R to S, the theorem is true for forces mS and $3S$.

Proceeding in this way we see that the theorem is true for forces mS and nS, where m and n are positive integers.

Also any two commensurable forces can be represented by mS and nS.

(γ) Incommensurable Forces.

Let P and Q be incommensurable forces, and let AB and AC represent them.

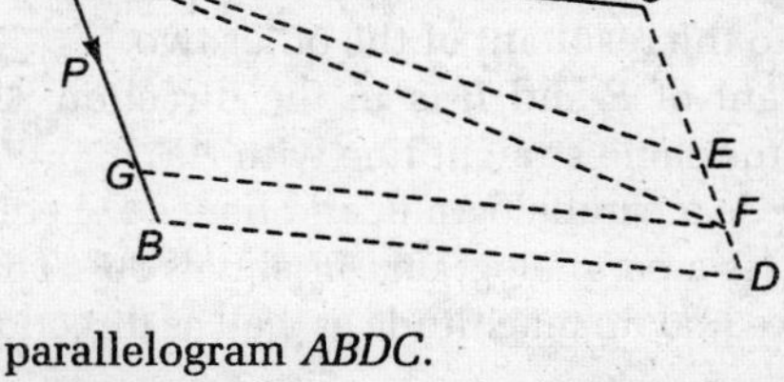

Complete the parallelogram $ABDC$.

If the resultant of P and Q be not in the line AD let it act in the line AE meeting CD in E.

Divide *AC* into any number of equal parts *x*, *each less than ED*, and from *CD* cut off successively portions, each equal to *x*. The last point of subdivision *F* must fall between *E* and *D*, *since x is less than ED*.

Draw *FG* parallel to *CA* to meet *AB* in *G*, and join *AF*.

The lines *AC* and *AG* represent commensurable forces, and therefore their resultant is, by (β), in the direction *AF*.

Hence the resultant of forces *AC* and *AB* must lie within the angle *BAF*. But this resultant acts in the direction *AE*, which is without the angle *BAF*.

But this is absurd.

Hence *AE* cannot be the direction of the resultant.

In a similar manner it can be shown that no other line, except *AD*, can be the direction of the resultant.

Hence *AD* is the direction of the resultant.

II. Magnitude

As before let *AB* and *AC* represent the forces *P* and *Q*. Complete the parallelogram *ABDC*.

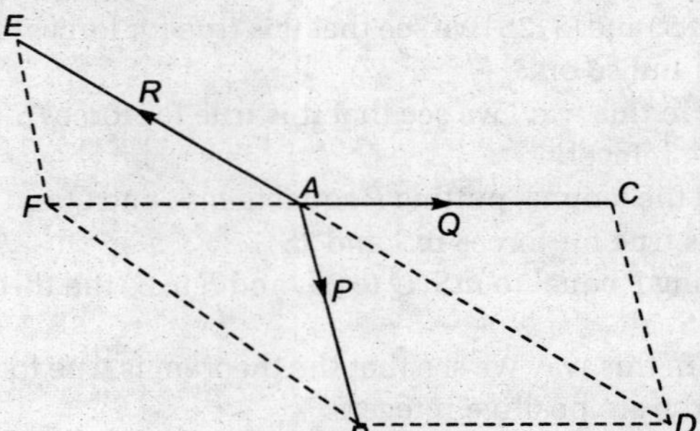

Take a force *R*, represented both in magnitude and direction by *AE*, to balance the resultant of *P* and *Q*.

Then, by the first part of the proof, *AE is in the same straight line with AD*. *AE* shall also be equal to *AD*.

Complete the parallelogram *AEFB*.

Since the three forces *P*, *Q*, and *R* are in equilibrium, each of them is equal and opposite to the resultant of the other two.

Now the resultant of *P* and *R* is in the direction *AF*; hence *AC*, the direction of *Q*, is in the same straight line with *AF*.

Therefore *ADBF* is a parallelogram, and hence *DA* equals *BF*.

But, since *AEFB* is a parallelogram, *BF* equals *AF*. Therefore *AD* equals *AE*, and hence *AD* is equal, in magnitude as well as direction, to the resultant of *P* and *Q*.

The above proof is known as **Duchayla's Proof**.

225. Centre of gravity of a uniform circular arc.

Let AB be a circular arc, subtending an angle 2α at its centre O, and let OC bisect the angle AOB.

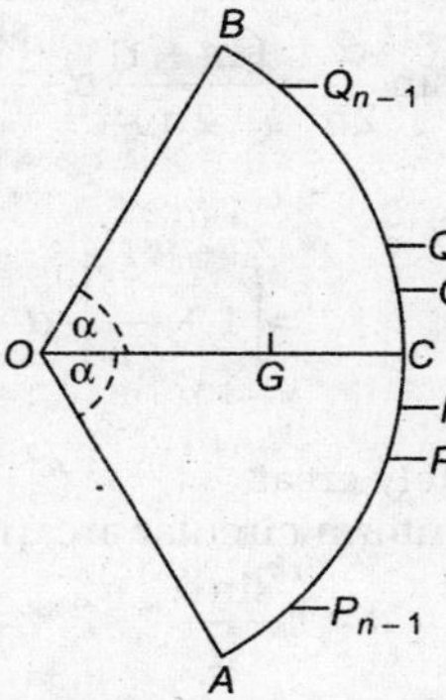

Let the arc AB be divided into $2n$ equal portions, the points of division, starting from C, being $P_1, P_2, \ldots P_{n-1}$ towards A, and $Q_1, Q_2, \ldots Q_{n-1}$ towards B.

At each of these points of division, and at the extremities A and B, and also at the point C, let there be placed equal particles, each of mass m.

Let the arc joining two successive particles subtend an angle β at the centre O, so that $2n\beta = 2\alpha$.

Since the system of particles is symmetrical with respect to the line OC, the centre of gravity, G, must lie on the line OC. Let $\bar{x}$ be the distance OG.

Then, by Art. 111,

$$\bar{x} = \frac{mr + 2m \cdot r\cos\beta + 2m \cdot r\cos 2\beta + \ldots + 2\,mr\cos n\beta}{m + 2m + 2m + \ldots + 2m}$$

$$= \frac{r}{2n+1}[1 + 2\cos\beta + 2\cos 2\beta + \ldots + 2\cos n\beta]$$

$$= \frac{r}{2n+1}\left[1 + 2\,\frac{\cos\frac{n+1}{2}\beta\,\sin\frac{n\beta}{2}}{\sin\frac{\beta}{2}}\right], \text{ [}\textit{Trig.}\text{ Art. 242]}$$

by summing the trigonometrical series,

$$= \frac{r}{2n+1}\left[1 + \frac{\sin\left(n+\frac{1}{2}\right)\beta - \sin\frac{\beta}{2}}{\sin\frac{\beta}{2}}\right]$$

$$= r\,\frac{\sin\left(n+\frac{1}{2}\right)\beta}{(2n+1)\sin\frac{\beta}{2}} = r\,\frac{\sin\left(\alpha+\frac{\alpha}{2n}\right)}{(2n+1)\sin\frac{\alpha}{2n}} \quad \ldots(1).$$

Now let the number of particles be increased without limit, α remaining constant, and consequently β decreasing without limit. We thus obtain the case of a uniform circular arc.

Now $$(2n+1)\sin\frac{\alpha}{2n} = \frac{(2n+1)}{2n}\alpha\cdot\frac{\sin\frac{\alpha}{2n}}{\frac{\alpha}{2n}}$$

$$= \left[1+\frac{1}{2n}\right]\cdot\alpha\cdot\frac{\sin\frac{\alpha}{2n}}{\frac{\alpha}{2n}} = \alpha,$$

when n is made indefinitely great.

Hence in the case of a uniform circular arc, (i) becomes

$$\bar{x} = r\frac{\sin\alpha}{\alpha}\ *.$$

Cor. In the case of a semicircular arc, in which $\alpha = \frac{\pi}{2}$, the distance of the centre of gravity from the centre

$$= r\frac{\sin\frac{\pi}{2}}{\frac{\pi}{2}} = \frac{2r}{\pi}.$$

226. Centre of gravity of a sector of a circle.

With the same notation as in the last article, let P and Q be two consecutive points on the circular boundary of the sector, so that PQ is very approximately a straight line, and OPQ is a triangle with a very small vertical angle at O.

Take P' on OP such that $OP' = \frac{2}{3}OP$; when PQ is very small, P' is the centre of gravity of the triangle OPQ.

*The student who is acquainted with the Integral Calculus can obtain this result very much easier thus;

Let P be a point on the arc such that $\angle POC = \theta$, and P' a very close point such that $\angle P'OP = \delta\theta$.

If M be the mass of the whole arc the mass of the element PP' is $\frac{\delta\theta}{2\alpha}\cdot M$, and the abscissa of the point P is $r\cos\theta$. Hence, by Art. 111,

$$x = \frac{\int_{-\alpha}^{+\alpha}\frac{\delta\theta}{2\alpha}M\cdot r\cos\theta}{\int_{-\alpha}^{+\alpha}\frac{\theta\delta}{2\alpha}M} = r\frac{\int_{-\alpha}^{+\alpha}\cos\theta\,d\theta}{\int_{-\alpha}^{+\alpha}d\theta}$$

$$= r\frac{[\sin\theta]_{-\alpha}^{+\alpha}}{[\theta]_{-\alpha}^{+\alpha}} = r\frac{\sin\alpha}{\alpha}.$$

Also, by symmetry, it is clear that the centre of gravity must lie on OC.

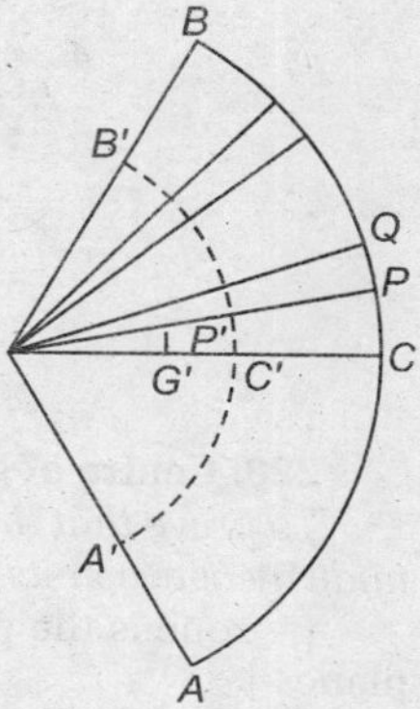

By joining O to an indefinitely large number of consecutive points on the arc AB, the sector can be divided into an indefinitely large number of triangles, each of whose centres of gravity lies on the dotted circular arc, whose radius is $\frac{2}{3}r$.

Hence the centre of gravity of the sector is the same as that of the circular arc $A'C'B'$, so that, by the last article,

$$OG' = OC'\frac{\sin\alpha}{\alpha} = \frac{2}{3}r\frac{\sin\alpha}{\alpha}.$$

Cor. If the sector be a semi-circle, $\alpha = \frac{\pi}{2}$, and the distance $OG' = \frac{4r}{3\pi}$.

227. Centre of gravity of the segment of a circle.

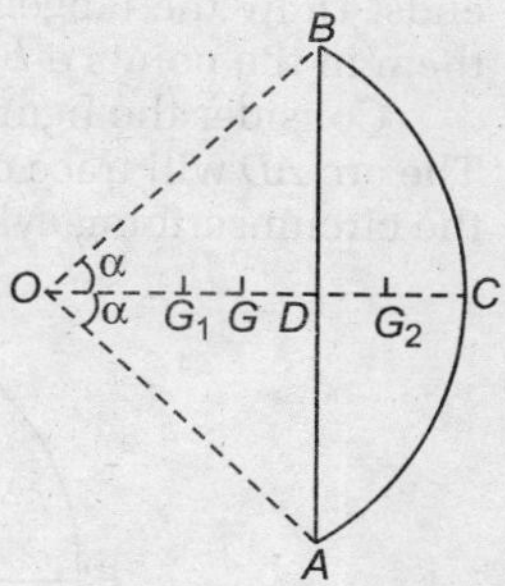

The segment of a circle ACB is the difference between the sector $OACB$ and the triangle OAB.

Using the same notation as in the two previous articles, let G_1 and G_2 be respectively the centres of gravity of the triangle AOB and the segment ACB. Also let G be the centre of gravity of the sector and let AB meet OC in D.

We have, by Art. 109,

$$OG = \frac{\Delta\, AOB \times OG_1 + \text{segment } ACB \times OG_2}{\Delta\, AOB + \text{segment } ACB} \quad ...(1).$$

But $$OG_1 = \frac{2}{3}OD = \frac{2}{3}r\cos\alpha,$$

and $$OG = \frac{2}{3}r\frac{\sin\alpha}{\alpha},$$

Also $$\Delta\, AOB = \frac{1}{2}r^2\sin 2\alpha,$$

and segment ABC = sector $AOB - \Delta\, AOB$

$$= \frac{1}{2}r^2\cdot 2\alpha - \frac{1}{2}r^2\sin 2\alpha.$$

Hence equation (1) becomes

$$\frac{2}{3}r\frac{\sin\alpha}{\alpha} = \frac{\frac{1}{2}r^2\sin 2\alpha \times \frac{2}{3}r\cos\alpha + \frac{1}{2}r^2(2\alpha - \sin 2\alpha)\times OG_2}{\frac{1}{2}r^2\cdot 2\alpha}$$

$$= \frac{\frac{2}{3}r\cos\alpha\sin 2\alpha + OG_2(2\alpha - \sin 2\alpha)}{2\alpha};$$

$$\therefore \quad \frac{4}{3} r \sin\alpha - \frac{2}{3} r \cos\alpha \sin 2\alpha = OG_2(2\alpha - \sin 2\alpha);$$

$$\therefore \quad OG_2 = \frac{4}{3} r \frac{\sin\alpha - \cos^2\alpha \sin\alpha}{2\alpha - \sin 2\alpha}$$

$$= \frac{4}{3} r \frac{\sin^3\alpha}{2\alpha - \sin 2\alpha}.$$

228. Centre of gravity of a Zone of a Sphere.

To prove that the centre of gravity of the surface of any zone of a sphere is midway between its plane ends.

[A zone is the portion of a sphere intercepted between any two parallel planes.]

Let $ABCD$ be the section of the zone which is made by a plane through the centre of the sphere perpendicular to its plane ends.

In the plane of the paper let ROR' be the diameter parallel to the plane ends. Draw the tangents RU and $R'U'$ at its ends, and let AB and CD meet them in the points $a, b, c,$ and d.

Consider the figure obtained by revolving the above figure about EOE'. The arc AD will trace out the zone and the line ad will trace out a portion of the circumscribing cylinder.

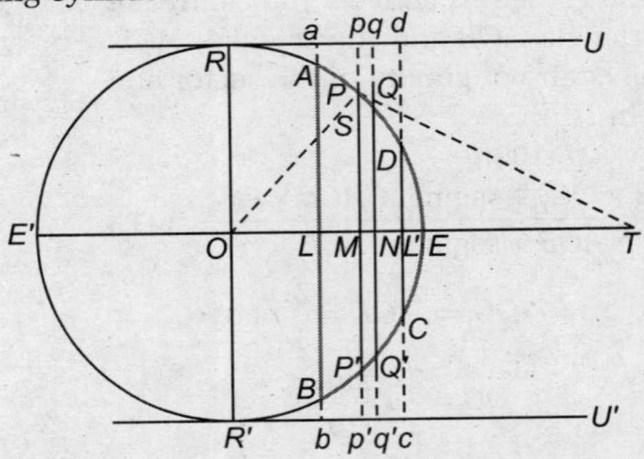

We shall show that the areas of the portions of the zone and cylinder intercepted between the planes ab and cd are the same.

Take any point P on the arc between A and D and another point Q *indefinitely close to P*. Draw the lines $pPMP'p'$ and $qQNQ'q'$ perpendicular to OE as in the figure.

Let PQ meet $E'E$ in T and draw QS perpendicular to PM.

Since Q is the very next point to P on the arc, the line PQ is, by the definition of a tangent, the tangent at P and hence OPT is a right angle. Also in the limit, when P and Q are very close to one another, the area traced out by PQ, which really lies between $2\pi MP \cdot PQ$ and $2\pi NQ \cdot PQ$, is equal to either of them.

We then have

$$\frac{\text{element of the zone}}{\text{element of the cylinder}} = \frac{\text{area traced out by } PQ}{\text{aera traced out by } pq}$$

$$= \frac{2\pi \cdot MP \cdot PQ}{2\pi \cdot Mp \cdot pq} = \frac{MP}{Mp} \cdot \frac{PQ}{SQ} = \frac{MP}{Mp} \cdot \frac{1}{\cos SQP}$$

$$= \frac{MP}{Mp} \cdot \frac{1}{\cos OTP} = \frac{MP}{Mp} \cdot \frac{1}{\sin MOP} = \frac{MP}{Mp} \cdot \frac{OP}{MP}$$

$$= \frac{OP}{Mp} = 1.$$

The portions of the zone and cylinder cut off by these two indefinitely close planes are therefore the same and hence their centres of gravity are the same.

If we now take an indefinitely large number of thin sections of the zone and cylinder starting with *AB* and

---

By Integral Calculus. Let $\angle AOE = \alpha$, $\angle DOE = \beta$, and $\angle POE = \theta$. The element of area at $P = \alpha\delta\theta \times 2\pi\alpha \sin\theta$, and the abscissa of P is $\alpha\cos\theta$. Hence, by Art. 111,

$$x = \frac{\int_\beta^\alpha 2\pi a^2 \sin\theta\delta\theta \cdot \alpha\cos\theta}{\int_\beta^\alpha 2\pi a^2 \sin\theta\, d\theta} = a\frac{\int_\beta^\alpha \sin\theta\cos\theta\, d\theta}{\int_\beta^\alpha \sin\theta\, d\theta}$$

$$= a\frac{\left[\frac{1}{2}\sin^2\theta\right]_\alpha^\beta}{[-\cos\theta]_\beta^\alpha} = \frac{a}{2}\frac{\sin^2\alpha - \sin^2\beta}{\cos\beta - \cos\alpha}$$

$$= \frac{a}{2}\frac{\cos^2\beta - \cos^2\alpha}{\cos\beta - \cos\alpha} = \frac{a}{2}(\cos\beta + \cos\alpha) = \frac{1}{2}[OL + OL'].$$

Ending with *CD* the corresponding sections have the same mass and the same centre of gravity.

The centre of gravity of the zone and cylinder are therefore the same, and the centre of gravity of the latter is clearly the middle point of *LL'*.

Hence the centre of gravity of any zone of a sphere is midway between its plane ends.

229. *Centre of gravity of a* **hollow hemisphere.**

Let *AB* pass through the centre of the sphere and therefore coincide with *RR'*. Also let *D* and *C* move up to coincide with *E*, so that the bounding plane *DC* becomes a point at *E*.

The zone thus becomes the hemisphere *RDECR'* and its centre of gravity is therefore at the middle point of *OE*, *i.e.*, it bisects the radius of the sphere perpendicular to the plane base of the hemisphere.

230. *To find the position of the centre of gravity of a* **solid hemisphere**.

*Let *LAM* be the section of **hemisphere made by the**

***By Integral Calculus.** Let P be any point on the arc AL; draw PN perpendicular to OA and let $ON = x$, $NP = y$; then clearly

$$x^2 + y^2 = a^2,$$

where a is the radius of the hemisphere.

The element of volume included between PN and the plane at distance $x + \delta x$ is $\pi y^2 \delta x$. Also the abscissa of P is x.

Hence, by Art. 111,

$$x = \frac{\int_0^a \pi y^2 \delta x . x}{\int_0^a \pi y^2 \delta . x} = \frac{\int_0^a x(a^2 - x^2)\,\delta x}{\int_0^a (a^2 - x^2)\,\delta x}$$

$$= \frac{\left[\frac{a^2 x^2}{2} - \frac{x^4}{4}\right]_0^a}{\left[a^2 x - \frac{x^3}{3}\right]_0^a}$$

$$= \frac{\frac{a^4}{2} - \frac{a^4}{4}}{a^3 - \frac{a^3}{3}} = \frac{3}{8}\,a.$$

Plane of the paper, and let OA be the radius of the hemisphere which is perpendicular to its plane base.

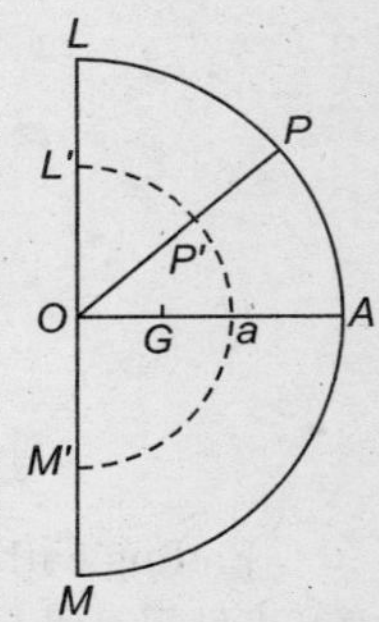

Take any point P on the hemisphere and consider an exceedingly small element of the surface at P. The centre of gravity of the very thin pyramid, whose base is this small element and whose vertex is O, is at a point P' on OP, such that $OP' = \frac{3}{4} OP$. (Art. 107.)

The weight of this very thin pyramid may therefore be considered concentrated at P'.

Let the external surface of the hemisphere be entirely divided up into very small portions and the corresponding pyramids drawn. Their centres of gravity all lie on the hemisphere $L'\,P'\,aM'$ whose centre is O and whose radius is $Oa\left(-\frac{3}{4}OA\right)$.

Hence the centre of gravity of the solid hemisphere is the same as that of the hemispherical shell $L'\,P'\,aM'$, *i.e.*, it is at G, where

$$OG - \frac{1}{2} Oa = \frac{3}{8} OA.$$

231. In a similar manner we may obtain the position of the centre of gravity of a spherical sector which is the figure formed by the revolution of a circular sector, such as the figure $OAQEBO$, in the figure of Art. 228, about the bisecting radius OE.

The distance of its centre of gravity from O is easily seen to be $\frac{3}{8}(OL + OE)$.

232. There are some points which are not quite satisfactory in the foregoing proofs. For a strict demonstration the use of the Calculus is required.

233. Virtual Work.

When we have a system of forces acting on a body in equilibrium and we suppose that the body undergoes a slight displacement, *which is consistent with the geometrical conditions under which the system exists*, and if a point Q of the body, with this imagined displacement, goes to Q', then QQ' is called the Virtual Velocity, or Displacement, of the point Q.

The word Virtual is used to imply that the displacement is an imagined, and not an actual, displacement.

234. If a force R acts at a point Q of the body and QQ' is the virtual displacement of Q and if $Q'N$ be the perpendicular from Q' on the direction of R, then the product $R \cdot QN$ is called the Virtual Work or Virtual Moment of the force R. As in Art. 127 this work is positive, or negative, according as QN is in the same direction as R, or in the opposite direction.

235. *The virtual work of a force is equal to the sum of the virtual works of its components.*

Let the components of R in two directions at right angles be X and Y, R being inclined at an angle ϕ to the direction of X, so that

$$X = R\cos\phi \text{ and } Y = R\sin\phi.$$

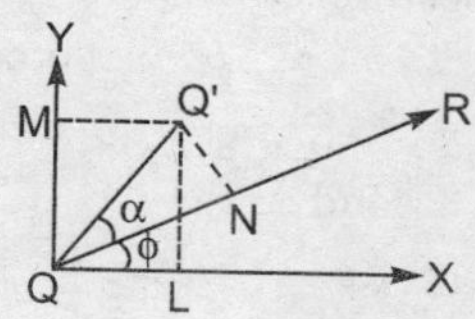

Let the point of application Q of R be removed, by a virtual displacement, to Q' and draw $Q'N$ perpendicular to R and let

$$\angle NQQ' = \alpha.$$

The sum of the virtual works of X and Y

$$= X \cdot OL + Y \cdot QM$$
$$= R\cos\phi \cdot QQ'\cos(\phi+\alpha) + R\sin\phi \cdot QQ'\sin(\phi+\alpha]$$
$$= R \cdot QQ'\,[\cos\phi\,(\cos(\phi+\alpha) + \sin\phi\sin(\phi+\alpha)]$$
$$= R \cdot QQ'\cos\alpha$$
$$= R \cdot QN$$
$$= \text{the virtual work of } R.$$

236. The principle of virtual work states that *If a system of forces acting on a body is in equilibrium and the body undergo a slight displacement consistent with the geometrical conditions of the system, the algebraic sum of the virtual works is zero; and conversely if this algebraic sum is zero the forces are in equilibrium. In other words, if each force R has a virtual displacement r in the direction of its line of action, then $\Sigma\,(R \cdot r) = 0$; also conversely if $\Sigma\,(R \cdot r)$ be zero, the forces are in equilibrium.*

In the next article we give a proof of this theorem for coplanar forces.

237. *Proof of the principle of virtual work for any system of forces in one plane.*

Take any two straight lines at right angles to one an other in the plane of the forces and let the body undergo a slight displacement. This can clearly be done by turning the body through a suitable small angle α radians about O and then moving it through suitable distances a and b parallel to the axis.

[The student may illustrate this by moving a book from any position on a table into any other position, the book throughout the motion being kept in contact with the table].

Let Q be the point of application of any force R, whose coordinates referred to O are x and y and whose polar coordinates are r and θ, so that $x = r\cos\theta$ and $y = r\sin\theta$, where $OQ = r$ and $XOQ = \theta$.

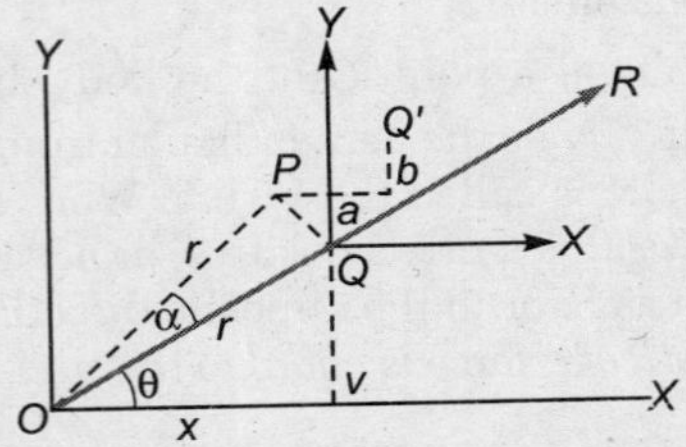

When the small displacement has been made the coordinates of the new position Q' of Q are

$$r\cos(\theta + \alpha) + a \text{ and } r\sin(\theta + \alpha) + b,$$

i.e.,
$$r\cos\theta\cos\alpha - r\sin\theta\sin\alpha + a$$

and
$$r\sin\theta\cos\alpha + r\cos\theta\sin\alpha + b,$$

i.e.,
$$r\cos\theta - \alpha\cdot r\sin\theta + a$$

and
$$r\sin\theta + \alpha\cdot r\cos\theta + b,$$

since a is very small.

The changes in the coordinates of Q are therefore

$$a - \alpha\cdot r\sin\theta \text{ and } b + \alpha\cdot r\cos\theta,$$

i.e.,
$$a - \alpha y \text{ and } b + \alpha x.$$

If then X and Y are the components of R, the virtual work of R, which is equal to the sum of the virtual works of X and Y, is

$$X(a - \alpha y) + Y(b - \alpha x),$$

i.e.,
$$a\cdot X + b\cdot Y + \alpha(Yx - Yy).$$

Similarly we have the virtual work of any other force of the system, a, b, and α being the same for each force.

The sum of the virtual works will therefore be zero if

$$a\,\Sigma(X) + b\,\Sigma(Y) + \alpha\Sigma(Yx - Xy) \text{be zero.}$$

If the forces are in equilibrium then $\Sigma(X)$ and $\Sigma(Y)$ are the sums of the components of the forces along the axes OX and OY and hence, by Art. 83, they are separately equal to zero.

Also $Yx - Xy$ = sum of the moments of X and Y about the origin O = moment of R about O. (Art. 62.)

Hence $\Sigma(Yx - Xy)$ = sum of the moments of all the forces about O, and this sum is zero, by Art. 83.

It follows that if the forces be in equilibrium the sum of their virtual works is zero.

238. Conversely, if the sum of the virtual works is zero for any displacement, the forces are in equilibrium.

With the same notation as in the last article, the sum of the virtual works is

$$a\Sigma(X) + b\Sigma(Y) + a\Sigma(Yx - Xy) \qquad ...(1),$$

and this is given to be zero *for all displacements.*

Choose a displacement such that the body is displaced only through a distance a parallel to the axis of x. For this displacement b and a vanish, and (1) then gives

$$a\Sigma(X) = 0,$$

so that $\Sigma(X) = 0$, *i.e.* the sum of the components parallel to OX is zero.

Similarly, choosing a displacement parallel to the axis of y, we have the sum of the components parallel to OY zero also.

Finally, let the displacement be one of simple rotation round the origin O. In this case a and b vanish and (1) gives

$$\Sigma(Yx - Xy) = 0,$$

so that the sum of the moments of the forces about O vanishes.

The three conditions of equilibrium given in Art. 83, therefore hold and the system of forces is therefore in equilibrium.

239. As an example of the application of the principle of virtual work we shall solve the following problem.

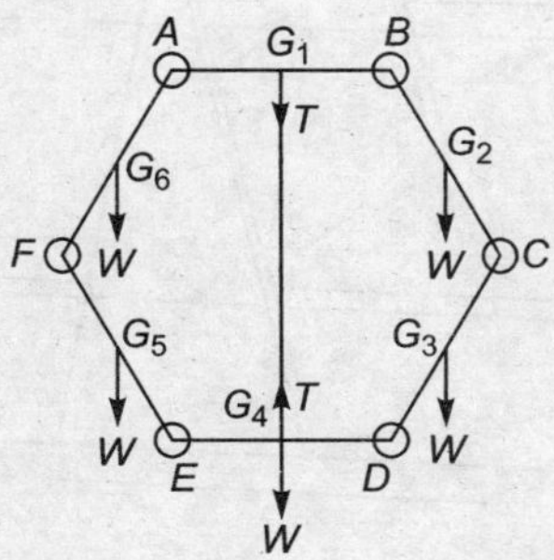

Six equal rods AB, BC, CD, DE, EF, and FA are each of weight W and are freely jointed at their extremities so as to form a hexagon; the rod AB is fixed in a horizontal position and the middle points of AB and DE are joined by a string; prove that its tension is 3W.

Let G_1, G_2, G_3, G_4, G_5, and G_6 be the middle points of the rods.

Since, by symmetry, BC and CD are equally inclined to the vertical the depths of the points C, G_3 and D below AB are respectively 2, 3, and 4 times as great as that of G_2.

Let the system undergo a displacement in the vertical plane of such a character that D and E are always in the vertical lines through B and A and DE is always horizontal.

If G_2 descend a vertical distance x, then G_3 will descend $3x$, G_4 will descend $4x$, whilst G_5 and G_6 will descend $3x$ and x respectively.

The sum of the virtual works done by the weights

$$= W \cdot x + W \cdot 3x + W \cdot 4x + W \cdot 3x + W \cdot x$$
$$= 12W \cdot x$$

If T be the tension of the string, the virtual work done by it will be

$$T \times (-4x)$$

For the displacement of G_4 is in a direction opposite to that in which T acts and hence the virtual work done by it is negative.

The principle of virtual work then gives

$$12W \cdot x + T(-4x) = 0,$$

i.e., $$T = 3W.$$

240. Roberval's Balance. This balance, which is a common form of letter-weigher, consists of four rods AB, BE, ED, and DA freely jointed at the corners A, B, E, and D, so as to form a parallelogram, whilst the middle points C and F, of AB and ED are attached to fixed points C and F which are in a vertical straight line. The rods AB and DE can freely turn about C and F.

To the rods AD and BE are attached scale-pans. In one of these is placed the substance W which is to be weighed and in the other the counterbalancing weight P.

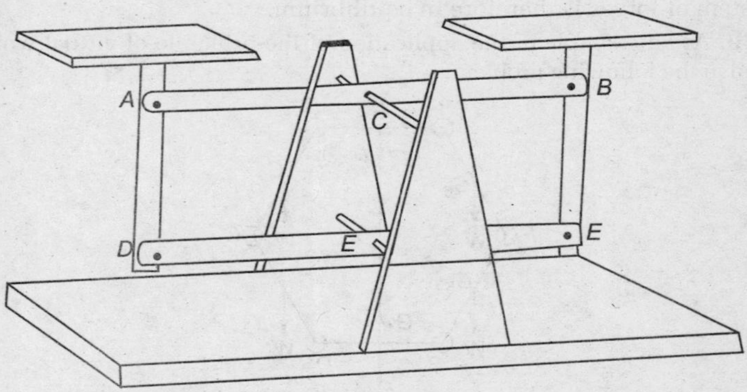

We shall apply the principle of virtual work to prove that it is immaterial on what part of the scale-pans the weights P and W are placed.

Since $CBEF$ and $CADF$ are parallelograms it follows that whatever be the angle through which the balance is turned, the rods BE and AD are always parallel to CF and therefore are always vertical.

If the rod AB is turned through a small angle the point B rises as much as the point A falls. The rod BE therefore rises as much as AD falls, and the right-hand scale-pan rises as much as the left-hand one falls. In such a displacement the virtual work of the weights of the rod BE and its scale-pan is therefore equal and opposite to the virtual work of the weights of AD and its scale-pan. These virtual works therefore cancel on another in the equation of virtual work.

Also if the displacement of the right-hand scale-pan is p upwards, that of the left-hand one is p downwards.

The equation of virtual work therefore gives

$$P \cdot p + W(-p) = 0,$$

i.e.,

$$P = W.$$

Hence if the machine balances in any position whatever, the weights P and W are equal, and this condition is independent of the position of the weights in the scale-pans. The weights therefore may have any position on the scale-pans.

It follows that the scale-pans need not have the same shape, nor be similarly attached to the machine, provided only that their weights are the same.

For example, in the above figure either scale-pan instead of pointing away from CF may point towards it, and no change would be requisite in the position of the other.

Examples XL

1. Four equal heavy uniform rods are freely jointed so as to form a rhombus which is freely suspended by one angular point and the middle points of the two upper rods are connected by a light rod so that the rhombus cannot collapse. Prove that the tension of this light rod is $4W \tan \alpha$, where W is the weight of each rod and 2α is the angle of the rhombus at the point of suspension.

2. A string, of length a, forms the shorter diagonal of a rhombus formed of four uniform rods, each of length b and weight W, which are hinged together.

If one of the rods is supported in a horizontal position prove that the tension of the string is

$$\frac{2W(2b^2 - a^2)}{b\sqrt{4b^2 - a^2}}.$$

3. A regular hexagon $ABCDEF$ consists of 6 equal rods which are each of weight W and are freely jointed together. The hexagon rests in a vertical plane and AB is in contact with a horizontal table; if C and F be connected by a light string, prove that its tension is $W\sqrt{3}$.

4. A tripod consists of three equal uniform bars, each of length a and weight w, which are freely jointed at one extremity, their middle points being joined by strings of length b. The tripod is placed with its free ends in contact with a smooth horizontal plane and a weight W is attached to the common joint; prove that the tension of each string is

$$\frac{2}{3}(2W + 3w)\frac{b}{\sqrt{9a^2 - 12b^2}}.$$

5. A square framework, formed of uniform heavy rods of equal weight W, jointed together, is hung up by one corner. A weight W is suspended from each of the three lower corners and the shape of the square is preserved by a light rod along the horizontal diagonal. Prove that its tension is $4W$.

6. Four equal rods, each of length a, are jointed to form a rhombus $ABCD$ and the angles B and D are joined by a string of length l. The system is placed in a vertical plane with A resting on a horizontal plane and AC is vertical. Prove that the tension of the string is

$$2W\frac{l}{\sqrt{4a^2 - l^2}},$$ where W is the weight of each rod.

7. A heavy elastic string, whose natural length is $2\pi a$, is placed round a smooth cone whose axis is vertical and whose semivertical angle is α. If W is the weight and λ the modulus of elasticity of the string, prove that it will be in equilibrium when in the form of a circle whose radius is $a\left(1 + \frac{W}{2\pi\lambda}\cot\alpha\right)$.

8. Two equal uniform rods AB and AC, each of length $2b$, are freely jointed at A and rest on a smooth vertical circle of radius a. Show, by the principle of virtual work, that, if 2θ is the angle between them, then

$$b\sin^3\theta = a\cos\theta.$$

9. Solve Ex. 13, page 229, by the application of the principle of virtual work.

18

Vectors

1. Pure numbers and physical quantities which are specified completely by their magnitude are called *scalar quantities*, or simply *scalars*. Examples of such quantities are mass, temperature, length and energy.

A *vector quantity* or simply a *vector*, is a quantity which needs for its complete specification both magnitude and direction. Examples of such quantities are velocity, momentum and force.

A vector may be represented graphically by an arrow drawn between two points. The distance between these points denotes the magnitude of the vector quantity. We shall represent vectors by letters in bold face type and scalars in light face italics.

Vectors may be *localised* or *free*. A localised vector is one which is confined to a particular line. In some cases it is necessary to consider a vector to be localised. For instance, when calculating the moment of a force, the line of action of the force is relevant. A vector is said to be free when it is completely specified by its magnitude and direction. Thus, it can be drawn in any convenient position.

2. Addition and subtraction of vectors.

By definition a vector behaves in the same way as the rectilinear displacement of a point. So vector addition is reduced to a composition of linear displacement.

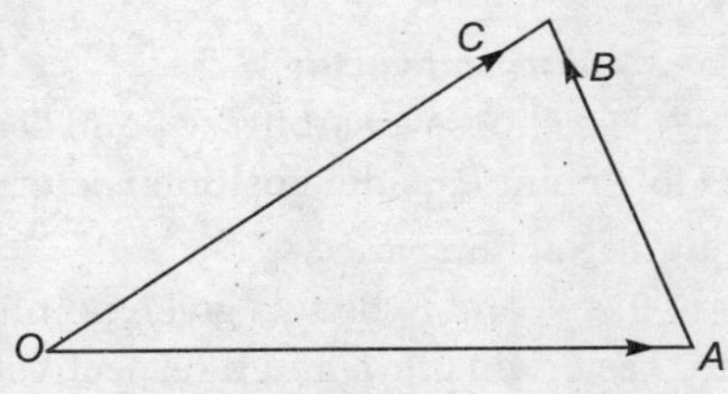

Fig. 1

Let us consider two vectors **A** and **B** as shown in Fig. 1. The vector **C** is obtained by moving a point along **A** and then along **B**. It is called the sum of the vectors **A** and **B** and is written as **C** = **A** + **B**. From the definition of vector addition.

$$\mathbf{A} + \mathbf{B} = \mathbf{B} + \mathbf{A}$$

and hence vector addition is commutative.

To add several vectors **A**, **B** and **C**, we first find the sum of **A** and **B** and then that of **A** + **B** and **C**. The result is easily seen to be the same as first finding the sum of **B** and **C** and then that of **B** + **C** and **A**. Thus vector addition is associative.

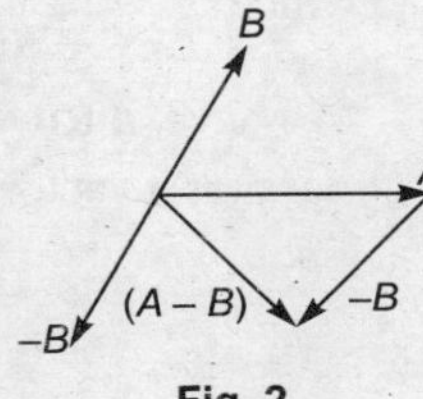

Fig. 2

The difference of two vectors **A** and **B**, which is written **A** – **B**, is obtained by adding –**B** to **A** as shown in Fig. 2.

3. Multiplication of a vector by a scalar.

Let us consider the product of a vector **A** by a scalar n which we write as n**A**. The result of such multiplication is a vector whose magnitude is the product of the magnitudes of n and **A** and whose direction is that of **A** or –**A**, depending on whether n is positive or negative.

4. Unit vectors and components of a vector.

A vector with unit magnitude is called a unit vector. A set of important unit vectors is that which has the direction of a right-handed cartesian co-ordinate system as shown in Fig. 3. The vectors **i**, **j**, **k** are unit vectors in the direction of x, y and z-axes respectively.

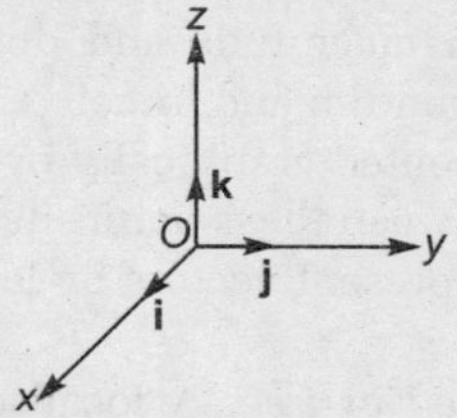

Fig. 3

We can use these units vectors to write a vectors **A** in term of its components along the axis of co-ordinates as $\mathbf{A} = \mathbf{i}A_x + \mathbf{j}A_y + \mathbf{k}A_z$, where A_x, A_y and A_z are the projections of **A** on the axes x, y, z respectively .

It can be seen from a diagram that the magnitude of the vector **A** is $\sqrt{A_x^2 + A_y^2 + A_z^2}$.

5. Position vector.

We choose an arbitrary point O as origin. Then the vector directed from O to a point P, is the position vector of P with reference to the origin O.

6. Section ratio.

Let A and B be two given points whose position vectors with reference to O as origin are **a** and **b** respectively. Let R be a point on AB, dividing it in the ratio $m : n$. The position vector of R is denoted by **r**.

Since $$\frac{AR}{RB} = \frac{m}{n}$$

We have, $n\,\vec{\mathbf{RB}} = m\,\vec{\mathbf{RB}}$ (the arrow mark denotes a vector)

i.e., $$n(\mathbf{r} - \mathbf{a}) = m(\mathbf{b} - \mathbf{r})$$

∴ $$\mathbf{r} = \frac{m\mathbf{b} + n\mathbf{a}}{m + n}$$

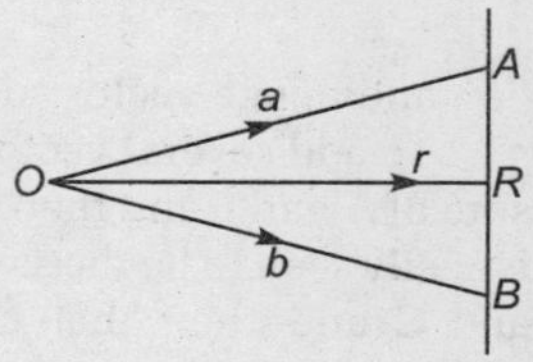

Fig. 4.

N.B. —When R is on AB produced, $\frac{m}{n}$ is negative.

7. Scalar product of two vectors.

The scalar product of two vectors **a** and **b** is defined as $ab \cos \theta$, where **a** and **b** are the magnitudes of **a** and **b** and θ is the angle included between **a** and **b**. It is denoted as **a** · **b**.

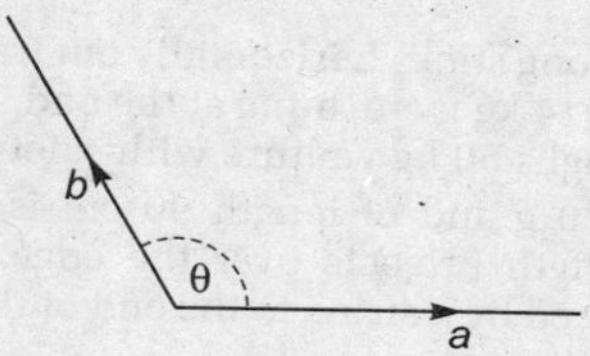

Fig. 5.

From the definition it follows that **a** · **b** = **b** · **a** and thus scalar product of two vectors is commutative.

8. Vector product of two vectors.

The *vector product* of two vectors **a** and **b** is defined by a vector whose magnitude is equal to the product of the magnitudes of **a** and **b** with the sine of the angle between them, and is perpendicular to **a** and **b**. It is denoted by **a** × **b**. The direction of this vector is given by the motion of a right-handed screw rotating from **a** to **b**.

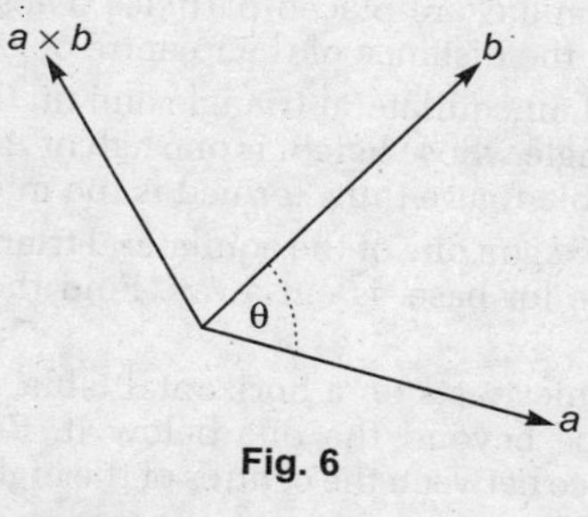

Fig. 6

It follows from the definition of **a** × **b** that

$$\mathbf{b} \times \mathbf{a} = -\,\mathbf{a} \times \mathbf{b}.$$

This meant that the vector product of two vectors is not commutative.

Easy Miscellaneous Examples

1. Find the resultant of two forces, equal to the weights of 13 and 14 kg respectively, acting at an obtuse angle whose sine is $\frac{12}{13}$.

2. Resolve a force of 100 kg weight into two equal forces acting at an angle of 60°.

3. *ABCD* is a square; forces of 1 kg wt, 6 kg wt and 9 kg wt act in the directions *AB*, *AC*, and *AD* respectively; find the magnitude of their resultant correct to two places of decimals.

4. The resultant of two forces, acting at an angle of 120°,is perpendicular to smaller component. The greater component is equal to 100 kg weight; find the other component and the resultant.
5. If E and F are the middle points of the diagonals AC and BD of the quadrilateral $ABCD$, and if EF be bisected in G, prove that the four forces represented in magnitude and direction by AG, BG, CG and DG, will be in equilibrium.
6. A stiff pole 3.60 m long sticks horizontally out from a vertical wall. It would break if a weight of 14 kg were hung at the end. How far out along the pole may a boy who weighs 50 kg venture with safety ?
7. A rod weighing 120 g and of length 90 cm is placed on a table so that one-third of its length projects over the edge. Find the greatest weight which can be attached by a string to the end of the rod without causing it to topple over.
8. A uniform beam of weight 30 kg, rests with its lover end on the ground, the upper end being attached to a weight by means of a horizontal string passing over a small pulley. If the beam is inclined at 60° to the vertical, prove that the pressure on the lower end is nearly 40 kg wt, and that the weight attached to the string is nearly 26 kg wt.
9. Find the centre of parallel forces which are equal respectively to 1, 2, 3, 4, 5 and 6 kg weight, the points of application of the forces being at distances 1, 2, 3, 4, 5 and 6 cm respectively measured from a given point A along a given line AB.
10. The angle B of a triangle ABC is a right angle, AB being 16 cm and BC 22 cm in length; at A, B and C are placed particles whose weights are 4, 5 and 6 respectively; find the distance of their centre of gravity from A.
11. On the side AB of an equilateral triangle and on the side remote from C is described a rectangle whose height is one half of AB; prove that the centre of gravity of the whole figure thus, formed is the middle point of AB.
12. From a regular hexagon one of the equilateral triangles with its vertex at the centre. and a side for base, is cut away. Find the centre of gravity of the remainder.
13. A pile of six pennies rests on a horizontal table, and each penny projects the same distance beyond the one below it. Find the greatest possible horizontal distance between the centres of the highest and lowest pennies.
14. The pressure on the fulcrum when two weights are suspended in equilibrium at the end of a straight level, 30 cm long, is 10 kg and the ration of the distances of the fulcrum from the ends is 3 : 2. Find the weights.
15. A straight lever of length 150 cm and weight 5 kg has its fulcrum at one end and weights of $1\frac{1}{2}$ and 3 kg are fastened to it at distances of 30 cm and 90 cm from the fulcrum; it is kept horizontal by a force at its other end; find the pressure on the fulcrum.
16. Find the relation between the effort P and the weight W in a system of 5 movable pulleys in which each pulley hangs by a separate string, the weight of each pulley being P.
17. In the system of 5 weightless pulleys in which each string is attached to a weightless bar from which the weights hang, if the strings are successively one inch apart, find to what point of the bar the weight must be attached, so that the bar may be always horizontal.

18. A body, of mass 5 kg, rests on a smooth plane which is inclined at 30° to the horizon and is acted on by a force equal to the weight of 2 kg acting parallel to the plane and upwards, and by a force equal to P lb weight acting at an angle of 30° to the plane. Find the value of P if the body is in equilibrium.

19. If one scale of an accurate balance be removed and no mass be placed in the other scale, prove that the inclination of the beam to the horizon is $\tan^{-1}\dfrac{Sa}{W'k + Sh}$, where $2a$ is the length of the beam, h and k are respectively the distances of the point of suspension from the beam and the centre of gravity of the balance, and S and W' are respectively the weight of the scale-pan and the remainder of the balance.

20. If the distance of the centre of gravity of the beam of a common steelyard from its fulcrum is 5 cm, the movable weight 120 g, and the weight of the beam 0.96 kg find the distance of the zero fo graduations from the centre of gravity. Also, if the distance between the fulcrum and the end at which the scale-pan is attached is 10 cm, find the distance between successive graduations.

21. If the circumference of a screw is 40 cm and the distance between successive threads 1.5 cm, find its mechanical advantage.

22. The height of a rough plane is to its base as 3 to 4 and it is found that a body is just supported on it by a horizontal force equal to half the weight of the body; find the coefficient of friction between the body and the plane.

23. A ladder, 9 m long, rests with one end against a smooth vertical wall and with the other on the ground, which is rough, the coefficient of friction being $\frac{1}{2}$; find how high a man whose weight is 4 times that of the ladder can ascend before it begins to slip, the foot of the ladder being 1.8 m from the wall.

24. A cylindrical shaft has to be sunk to a depth of 180 meters through chalk whose density is 2.3 times that of water; the diameter of the shaft being 3 m, what must be the H.P. of the engine that can light out the material in 12 working days of 8 hours each?

**Harder Miscellaenous Examples

1. If O is the centre of the circle circumscribing the triangle ABC, and if forces act along OA, OB and OC respectively proportional to BC, CA and AB, show that their resultant passes through the centre of the inscribed circle.

2. Three forces act along the sides of a triangle ABC, taken in order, and their resultant passes through the orthocentre and the centre of gravity of the triangle; show that the forces are in the ratio of

$$\sin 2A \sin(B - C) : \sin 2B \sin(C - A) : \sin 2C \sin(A - B).$$

Show also that their resultant acts along the line joining the centres of the inscribed and circumscribing circles, if the forces are in the ratio

$$\cos B - \cos C : \cos C - \cos A : \cos A - \cos B.$$

3. Three forces PA, PB and PC diverge from the point P and three others AQ, BQ and CQ converge to a point Q. Show that the resultant of the six is represented in magnitude and direction by $3PQ$ and that it passes through the centre of gravity of the triangle ABC.

4. T is the orthocentre, and O the circumcentre of a triangle ABC; show that the three forces AT, BT and CT have as resultant the force represented by twice OT.
5. Find the centre of gravity of three particles placed at the centres of the escribed circles of a triangle, if they are inversely proportional to the radii of these circles.
6. $ABCD$ is a rectangle; find a point P in AD such that, when the triangle PDC is taken away, the remaining trapezoid $ABCP$ may, when suspended from P, hang with its sides AP and BC horizontal.
7. A triangular lamina ABC, obtuse-angled at C, stands with the side AC in contact with a table. Show that the least weight, which suspended from B will overturn the triangle, is
$$\frac{1}{3}W\frac{a^2+3b^2-c^2}{c^2-a^2-b^2},$$
where W is the weight of the triangle. Interpret the above if $c^2 > a^2 + 3b^2$.
8. A pack of cards is laid on a table and each card projects in the direction of the length of the pack beyond the one below it; if each project as far as possible, show that the distances between the extremities of successive cards will form a harmonical progression.
9. If aA, bB, cC....represent n forces, whose points of application are a, b, c... and whose extremities are A, B, C....., show that their resultant is given in magnitude and direction by $n \cdot gG$, where g is the centre of inertia of n equal particles a, b, c...., and G the centre of inertia of n equal particles A, B, C....
What follows if g coincides with G?
10. From a body, of weight W, a portion, of weight w, is cut out and moved through a distance x; show that the line joining the two positions of the centre of gravity of the whole body is parallel to the line joining the two positions of the centre of gravity of the part moved.
11. Two uniform rods, AB and AC of the same material are rigidly connected at A, the angle BAC being 60° and the length of AB being double that of AC. If G is the centre of inertia of the rods, show that $BG = AC\sqrt{\frac{9}{12}}$, and, if the system is suspended freely from the end B of the rod AB, show that the action at A consists of a vertical force equal to one-third of the weight, W, of the system, and a couple whose moment is
$$\frac{2}{3}W\frac{AC}{\sqrt{19}}.$$
12. If the hinges of a gate are 1.20 m apart and the gate is 3.0 m wide and weights 250 kg, show that, on the assumption that all the weight is borne by the lower hinge, the stress on the upper hinge must be 312.5 kgf.
13. A step-ladder in the from of the letter A, with each of its legs inclined at an angle α to the vertical, is placed on a horizontal floor, and is held up by a cord connecting the middle points of its legs, there being no friction anywhere; show that, when a weight W is placed on one of the steps at a height from the floor equal to $\frac{1}{n}$ of the height of the ladder, the increase in the tension of the cord is $\frac{1}{n}W\tan\alpha$.

14. A cylinder, of radius r, whose axis is fixed horizontally, touches a vertical wall along a generating line. A flat beam of uniform material of length $2l$ and weight W, rests with its extremities in contact with the wall and the cylinder, making an angle of 45° with the vertical. Show that, in the absence of friction, $\frac{l}{r} = \frac{\sqrt{5}-1}{\sqrt{10}}$, that the pressure on the wall is $\frac{1}{2}W$ and that the reaction of the cylinder is $\frac{1}{2}\sqrt{5}\,W$.

15. A uniform rod, of length $32a$, rests partly within and partly without a smooth cylindrical cup of radius a. Show that in the position of equilibrium the rod makes an angle of 60° with the horizontal and prove also that the cylinder will topple over unless its weight is at least six times that of the rod.

16. A tipping basin, whose interior surface is spherical, is free to turn round an axis at a distance c below the centre of the sphere and at a distance a above the centre of gravity of the basin and a heavy ball is laid at the bottom of the basin; show that it will tip over if the weight of the ball exceeds the fraction $\frac{a}{c}$ of the weight of the basin.

17. A thin hemispherical shell, closed by a plane base, is filled with water and when suspended from a point on the rim of the base, it hangs with the base inclined at an angle α to the vertical. Show that the ratio of the weight of the water to that of the shell is $\tan\alpha - \frac{1}{3} : \frac{3}{8} - \tan\alpha$.

18. A hollow cylinder, composed of thin metal open at both ends of the radius a, is placed on a smooth *horizontal* plane. Inside it are placed two smooth spheres, of radius r, one above the other $2r$ being $> a$ and $< 2a$. If W is the weight of the cylinder and W the weight of one of the spheres, show that the cylinder will just stand upright without tumbling over, if

$$W \cdot a = 2W'(a-r).$$

19. An isosceles triangular lamina, with its plane vertical, rests, vertex downwards, between two smooth pegs in the same horizontal line : show that there will be equilibrium if the base make an angle $\sin^{-1}(\cos^2\alpha)$ with the vertical, 2α being the vertical angle of the lamina and the length of the base being three times the distance between the pegs.

20. A prism, whose cross section is an equilateral triangle, rests with two edges horizontal on smooth planes inclined at angles α and β to the horizon. If θ is the angle that the plane through these edges makes with the vertical, show that

$$\tan\theta = \frac{2\sqrt{3}\sin\alpha\sin\beta + \sin(\alpha+\beta)}{\sqrt{3}\sin(\alpha \sim \beta)}.$$

21. A thin board in the form of an equilateral triangle, of weight $\frac{1}{2}$ kg, has one-quarter of its base resting on the end of a horizontal table, and is kept from falling over by a string attached to its vertex and to a point on the table in the same vertical plane as the triangle. If the length of the string is double the height of the vertex of the triangle above the base, find its tension.

22. A solid cone of height h and semi-vertical angle α, is placed with its base against a smooth vertical wall and is supported by a string attached to its vertex and to a point in the wall; show that the greatest possible length of the string is $h\sqrt{1+\frac{16}{9}\tan^2\alpha}$.

23. The altitude of a cone is h and the radius of its base is r; a string is fastened to the vertex and to a point on the circumference of the circular base, and is then put over a smooth peg; show that, if the cone rests with its axis horizontal, the length of the string must be $\sqrt{h^2+4r^2}$.

24. Three equal smooth spheres on a smooth horizontal plane are in contact with one another, and are kept together by an endless string in the plane of their centres, just fitting them; if a fourth equal sphere is placed on them, show that the tension of the string is to the weight of either sphere as $1:3\sqrt{6}$.

25. A smooth rod, of length $2a$, has one end resting on a plane of inclination α to the horizon, and is supported by a horizontal rail which is parallel to the plane and at a distance c from it. Show that the inclination θ of the rod to the inclined plane is given by the equation $c \sin\alpha = a\sin^2\theta\cos(\theta-\alpha)$.

26. A square board is hung flat against a wall, by means of a string fastened to the two extremities of the upper edge and hung round a perfectly smooth rail; when the length of the string is less than the diagonal of the board, show that there are three positions of equilibrium.

27. A hemispherical bowl, of radius r, rests on a smooth horizontal table and partly inside it rests a rod, of length $2l$ and of weight equal to that of the bowl. Show that the position of equilibrium is given by the equation.

$$l\sin(\alpha+\beta) = r\sin\alpha = -2r\cos(\alpha+2\beta).$$

where α is the inclination of the base of the hemisphere to the horizontal and 2β is the angle subtended at the centre by the part of the rod within the bowl.

28. A uniform rod, of weight W, is suspended horizontally from two nails in a wall by means of two vertical strings, each of length l, attached to its ends. A smooth weightless wedge, of vertical angle 30°, is pressed down with a vertical force $\frac{W}{2}$ between the wall and the rod, without touching the strings, its lower edge being kept horizontal and one face touching the wall. Find the distance through which the rod is thrust from the wall.

29. AB is smooth plane inclined at the angle α to the horizontal and at A, the lower end, is a hinge about which there works, without friction, a heavy uniform smooth plank AC, of length $2a$. Between the plane and the plank is placed a smooth cylinder, of radius r, which is prevented from sliding down the plane by the pressure of the plank from above. If W is the weight of the plank, W' that of the cylinder and θ the angle between the plane and the plank, show that

$$\frac{W'r}{Wa} = \cos(\alpha+\theta)\frac{1-\cos\theta}{\sin\alpha}.$$

30. Two equal circular discs—of radius r –with smooth edges, are placed on their flat sides in the corner between two smooth vertical planes inclined at an angle 2α, and touch each other in the line bisecting the angle; prove that the radius of the least disc that can be pressed between them, without causing them to separate, is $r(\sec\alpha-1)$.

31. A rectangular frame *ABCD* consists of four freely jointed bars, of negligible weight, the bar *AD* being fixed in a vertical position. A weight is placed on the upper horizontal bar *AB* at a given point *P* and the frame is kept in a rectangular shape by a string *AC*. Find the tension of the string and show that it is unaltered if this weight is placed on the lower bar *CD* vertically under its former position.

32. A uniform rod *MN* has its ends in two fixed straight rough grooves *OA* and *OB*, in the same vertical plane, which make angles α and β with the horizon; show that, when the end *M* is on the point of slipping in the direction *AO*, the tangent of the angle of inclination of *MN* to the horizontal is $\dfrac{\sin(\alpha-\beta-2\varepsilon)}{2\sin(\beta+\varepsilon)\sin(\alpha-\varepsilon)}$, where ε is the angle of friction.

33. A rod, resting on a rough inclined plane, whose inclination α to the horizontal is greater than the angle of friction λ, is free to turn about one of its ends, which is attached to the plane; show that, for equilibrium, the greatest possible inclination of the rod to the line of greatest slope is $\sin^{-1}(\tan\lambda\cot\alpha)$.

34. Two equal uniform rods, of length $2a$, are jointed at one extremity by a hinge, and rest symmetrically upon a rough fixed sphere of radius c. Find the limiting position of equilibrium and show that, if the coefficient of friction is $c \div a$, the limiting inclination of each rod to the vertical is $\tan^{-1}\sqrt[3]{c \div a}$.

35. A uniform straight rod, of length $2c$, is placed in a horizontal position as high as possible within a hollow rough sphere, of radius a. Show that the line joining the middle point of the rod to the centre of the sphere makes with the vertical an angle $\tan^{-1}\dfrac{\mu a}{\sqrt{a^2-c^2}}$.

36. A rough rod is fixed in a horizontal position and, a rod, having one end freely jointed to a fixed point, is in equilibrium resting on the fixed rod; if the perpendicular from the fixed point upon the fixed rod is of length b and is inclined to the horizontal at an angle α, show that the portion of the fixed rod upon any point of which the movable rod may rest is of length

$$\frac{2\mu b\cos\alpha}{\sqrt{\sin^2\alpha-\mu^2\cos^2\alpha}},$$

where μ is the coefficient of friction.

37. A glass rod is balanced, partly in and partly out of a cylindrical tumbler, with the lower end resting against the vertical side of the tumbler. If α and β are the greatest and least angle which the rod can make with the vertical, show that the angle of friction is

$$\frac{1}{2}\tan^{-1}\frac{\sin^3\alpha-\sin^3\beta}{\sin^2\alpha\cos\alpha+\sin^2\beta\cos\beta}.$$

38. A rod rests partly within and partly without a box in the shape of a rectangular parallelopiped, and presses with one end against the rough vertical side of the box, and rests in contact with the opposite smooth edge. The weight of the box being four times that of the rod, show that if the rod is about to slip and the box is about to tumble at the same instant, the angle that the rod makes with the vertical is $\frac{1}{2}\lambda+\frac{1}{2}\cos^{-1}\left(\frac{1}{2}\cos\lambda\right)$, where λ is the angle of friction.

39. A uniform heavy rod lies on a rough horizontal table and is pulled perpendicularly to its length by a string attached to any point. About what point will it commence to turn ?
Show also that the ratio of the forces, required to move the rod, when applied at the centre and through the end of the rod perpendicular to the rod, is $\sqrt{2}+1:1$.

40. Two equal heavy particles are attached to a light rod at equal distances c, and two strings are attached to it at equal distances a from the middle point; the rod is then placed on a rough horizontal table and the strings are pulled in directions perpendicular to the rod and making the same angle θ with the vertical on opposite sides of the rod. Find the least tensions that will turn the rod and show that, if the coefficient of friction is $\frac{a}{c}$, the tension will be least when θ is 45°.

41. Two equal similar bodies, A and B each of weight W, are connected by a light string and rest on a rough horizontal plane, the coefficient of friction being μ. A force P, which is less than $2\mu W$, is applied at A in the direction BA, and its direction is gradually turned through an angle θ in the horizontal plane. Show that, if P is greater than $\sqrt{2}\,\mu W$, then both the weights will slip when $\cos\theta = \frac{P}{2\mu W}$, but, if P is less than $\sqrt{2}\mu W$ and is greater than μW, then A alone will slip when $\sin\theta = \frac{\mu W}{P}$.

42. A uniform rough beam AB lies horizontally upon two others at points A and C; show that the least horizontal force applied at B in a direction perpendicular to BA, which is able to move the beam, is the lesser of the two forces $\frac{1}{2}\mu W$ and $\mu W\frac{b-a}{2a-b}$, where AB is $2a$, AC is b, W is the weight of the beam, and μ the coefficient of friction.

43. A uniform rough beam AB, of length $2a$, is placed horizontally on two equal and equally rough balls, the distance between whose centres is b, touching them in C and D; show that, if b is not greater than $\frac{4a}{3}$, a position of the beam can be found in which a force P exerted at B perpendicular to the beam will cause it to be on the point of motion both at C and D at the same time.

44. A uniform heavy beam is placed, in a horizontal position, between two unequally rough fixed planes, inclined to the horizontal at given angles, in a vertical plane perpendicular to the planes. Find the condition that it may rest there.

45. A uniform rod is in limiting equilibrium, one end resting on a rough horizontal plane and the other on an equally rough plane inclined at an angle α to the horizon. If λ is the angle of friction, and the rod is in a vertical plane, show that the incrimination, θ, of the rod to the horizontal is given by

$$\tan\theta = \frac{\sin(\alpha - 2\lambda)}{2\sin\lambda\sin(\alpha-\lambda)}.$$

Find also the normal reactions of the planes.

46. If a pair of compasses rests across a smooth horizontal cylinder of radius c, show that the frictional couple at the joint to prevent the legs of the compasses from slipping must be

$$W(c\cot\alpha\operatorname{cosec}\alpha - a\sin\alpha),$$

where W is the weight of each leg, 2α angle between the legs, and a the distance of the centre of gravity of a leg from the joint.

47. The handles of a drawer are equidistant from the sides of the drawer and are distant c from each other; show that it will be impossible to pull the drawer out by pulling one handle, unless the length of the drawer from back to front exceeds μc.

48. If one cord of a sash-widow breaks, find the least coefficient of friction between the sash and the window-frame in order that the other weight may still support the window.

49. A circular hoop, of radius 30 cm, hangs on a horizontal bar and a man hangs by one hand from the hoop. If the coefficient of friction between the hoop and the bar is $1 \div \sqrt{3}$, find the shortest possible distance from the man's hand to the bar, the weight of the hoop being rejected.

50. A square, of side $2a$, is placed with its plane vertical between two smooth pegs, which are in the same horizontal line and at a distance c; show that it will be in equilibrium when the inclination of one of its edges to the horizontal is either 45° or $\frac{1}{2}\sin^{-1}\frac{a^2 - c^2}{c^2}$.

51. Three equal circular discs, A, B and C are placed in contact with each other upon a smooth horizontal plane, and in addition, B and C are in contact with a rough vertical wall. If the coefficient of friction between the circumferences of the discs and also between the discs and wall is $2 - \sqrt{3}$, show that no motion will ensue when A is pushed perpendicularly towards the wall with any force P.

52. If the centre of gravity of a wheel and axle is at a distance a from the axis, show that the wheel can rest with the plane through the axis and the centre of gravity inclined at an angle less than θ to the vertical, where $\sin\theta = \frac{b}{a}\sin\phi$, b being the radius of the axle, and ϕ the angle of friction.

53. A particle, of weight w, rests on a rough inclined plane, of weight W, whose base rests on a rough table, the coefficients of friction being the same. If a gradually increasing force is applied to the particle w along the surface of the inclined plane, find whether it will move up the plane before the plane slides on the table, the angle of inclination of the plane being α.

54. A rough cylinder, of weight W', lies with its axis horizontal upon a plane, whose inclination to the horizontal is α, whilst a man, of weight W (with his body vertical), stands upon the cylinder and keeps it at rest. If his feet are at A and a vertical section of the cylinder through A touches the plane at B, show that the angle, θ, subtended by AB at the centre of the section, the friction being sufficient to prevent any sliding, is given by the equation

$$W \sin(\theta + \alpha) = (W + W')\sin\alpha.$$

55. Two rough uniform spheres, of equal radii but unequal weights W_1 and W_2, rest in a spherical bowl, the line joining their centres being horizontal and subtending an angle 2α at the centre of the bowl; show that the coefficient of friction between them is not less than

$$\frac{W_1 - W_2}{W_1 + W_2}\tan\left(45^\circ - \frac{\alpha}{2}\right).$$

56. Two rigid weightless rods are firmly jointed, so as to be at right angles, a weight being fixed at their junction and are placed over two rough pegs in

the same horizontal plane, whose coefficients of friction are μ and μ', Show that they can be turned either way from their symmetrical position through an angle $\frac{1}{2}\tan^{-1}\frac{\mu+\mu'}{2}$, without slipping.

57. A sphere, of weight W, is placed on a rough plane, inclined to the horizontal at an angle α, which is less than the angle of friction show that a weight $W\frac{\sin\alpha}{\cos\alpha-\sin\alpha}$, fastened to the sphere at the upper end of the diameter which is parallel to the plane, will just prevent the sphere from rolling down the plane. What will be the effect of slightly decreasing or slightly increasing this weight ?

58. Two equal uniform rods are joined rigidly together at one extremity of each to form a V, with the angle at the vertex 2α, and are placed astride a rough vertical circle of such a radius that the centre of gravity of the V is in the circumference of the circle, the angle of friction being ε. Show that, if the V is just on the point of motion when the line joining its vertex with the centre of the circle is horizontal, then $\sin\epsilon = \sqrt{\sin\alpha}$.

If the rods are connected by a hinge and not rigidly connected and the free ends be joined by a string, show that the joining string will not meet the circle if $\sin\alpha$ is $< \frac{1}{3}$; if this condition satisfied, show that if the V is just on the point of slipping when the line joining its vertex to the centre is horizontal, the tension of the string will be $\frac{W}{2}\sqrt{1+\operatorname{cosec}\alpha}$, where W is the weight of either rod.

59. A vertical rectangular beam, of weight W, is constrained by guides to move only in its own direction, the lower end resting on a smooth floor. If a smooth inclined plane of given slope is pushed under it by a horizontal force acting at the back of the inclined plane, find the force required.

If there is friction between the floor and the inclined plane, but nowhere else, what must be the least value of μ so that the inclined plane may remain, when left in a given position under the beam, without being forced out ?

60. A circular disc, of weight W and radius a, is suspended horizontally by three equal verical strings of length b, attached symmetrically to its perimeter. show that the magnitude of horizontal couple required to keep it twisted through an angle θ is

$$Wa^2\frac{\sin\theta}{\sqrt{b^2-4a^2\sin^2\frac{\theta}{2}}}.$$

61. Two small rings, each of weight W, slide one upon each of two rods in a vertical plane, each inclined at an angle α to the vertical; the rings are connected by a fine elastic string of natural length $2a$, and whose modulus of elasticity is λ; the coefficient of friction for each rod and ring is $\tan\beta$; show that, if the string is horizontal, each ring will rest at any point of a segment of the rod whose length is

$$W\lambda^{-1}a\operatorname{cosec}\alpha\{\cot(\alpha-\beta)-\cot(\alpha+\beta)\}.$$

62. A wedge with angle 60°, is placed upon a smooth table, and a weight of 10 kg on the slant face is supported by a string lying on that face which after passing through a smooth ring at the top, supports a weight W hanging vertically ; find the magnitude of W.

Find also the horizontal force necessary to keep the wedge at rest
(1) when the ring is not attached to the wedge ,
(2) when it is so attached.
Solve the same question supposing the slant face of the wedge to be rough, the coefficient of friction being $\frac{1}{\sqrt{3}}$ and the 10 kg weight on the point of moving down.

63. Show that the power necessary to move a cylinder, of radius r and weight W, up a smooth plane inclined at an angle α to the horizontal by means of a crowbar of length l inclined at an angle β to the horizon is

$$\frac{Wr}{l}\,\frac{\sin\alpha}{1+\cos(\alpha+\beta)}.$$

64. A letter-weigher consists of a uniform plate in the form of a right-angled isosceles triangle ABC, of mass 90 g which is suspended by its right angle C from a fixed point to which a plumb-line is also attached. The letters are suspended from the angle A, and their weight read off by observing where the plumb-line intersects a scale engraved along AB, the divisions of which are marked 30 g, 60 g, 90 g, etc. Show that the distances from A of the divisions of the scale form a harmonic progression.

65. A ladder, of length l metres and weight W kg, and uniform in every respect throughout, is raised by two men A and B from a horizontal to a vertical position. A stands at one end and B, getting underneath the ladder , walks from the other end towards A holding successive points of the ladder above his head, at the height of d metres from the ground , the force he exerts being vertical. Find the force exerted by B when thus supporting a point n metres from A, and show that the work done by him in passing from the nth to the $(n-1)^{\text{th}}$ metre is $\frac{Wld}{2n(n-1)}$.

When must A press his feet *downwards* against his end of the ladder?

66. Prove that an ordinary drawer cannot be pushed in by a force applied to one handle until it has been pushed in a distance $a.\mu$ by forces applied in some other manner, where a is the distance between the handles and μ is the coefficient of friction .

67. Three equal uniform rods, each of weight W, have their ends hinged together so that they form an equilateral triangle ; the triangle rests in horizontal position with each rod in contact with a smooth cone of semivertical angle α whose axis is vertical ; prove that the action at each hinge is $\frac{W\cot\alpha}{\sqrt{3}}$.

68. A reel, consisting of a spindle of radius c with two circular ends of radius a, is placed on a rough inclined plane and has a thread wound on it which unwinds when the reel rolls downwards . If μ is the coefficient of friction and α is the inclination of the plane to the horizontal show that the reel can be drawn up the plane by means of the thread if

$$\mu \text{ be not less than } \frac{c\sin\alpha}{a-c\cos\alpha}.$$

69. Prove the following geometrical construction for the centre of gravity of any uniform plane quadrilateral $ABCD$; find the centres of gravity, X and Y, of the triangles *ABD,CBD*; let *XY* meet *BD* in *U*; then the required centre of gravity is a point *G* on *XY*, such that

$$YG = XU.$$

70. There is a small interval between the bottom of a door and the floor, and a wedge of no appreciable weight has been thrust into this interval, the coefficient of friction between its base and the floor being known. If the angle of the wedge is smaller than a certain amount, show that no force can open the door, the slant edge of the wedge being supposed smooth.

71. On the top of a fixed rough cylinder, of radius r, rests a thin uniform plank, and a man stands on the plank just above the point of contact. Show that he can walk slowly a distance $(n + 1)be$ along the plank without its slipping off the cylinder, if the weight of the plank is n times that of the man and e is the angle of friction between the plank and the cylinder.

72. A hoop stands in a vertical plane on a rough incline which the plane of the hoop cuts in a line of greatest slope. It is kept in equilibrium by a string fastened to a point in the circumference, wound round it, and fastened to a peg in the incline further up and in the same plane. If λ is the angle of friction, θ the angle the hoop subtends at the peg, and α that of the incline, show that there is limiting equilibrium when $\theta = \alpha + \cos^{-1}\left[\dfrac{\sin(\alpha - \lambda)}{\sin\lambda}\right]$.

What will happen if θ has a greater value?

73. Show that the least force which applied to the surface of a heavy uniform sphere will just maintain it in equilibrium against a rough vertical wall is

$$W \cos\varepsilon \text{ or } W \tan\varepsilon\,[\tan\varepsilon - \sqrt{\tan^2\varepsilon - 1}]$$

according as $\varepsilon <$ or $> \cos^{-1}\dfrac{\sqrt{5}-1}{2}$, where W is the weight and ε the angle of friction.

74. A uniform rod, of weight W, can true freely about a hinge at one end, and rests with the other against a rough vertical wall making an angle α with the wall. Show that this end may rest anywhere on an arc of a circle of angle $2\tan^{-1}[\mu \tan\alpha]$, and that in either of the extreme positions the pressure on the wall is $\frac{1}{2} W[\cot^2\alpha + \mu^2]^{-1/2}$, where μ is the coefficient of friction.

75. If the greatest possible cube is cut out of a solid hemisphere of uniform density, prove that the remainder can rest with its curved surface on a perfectly rough inclined plane with its base inclined to the horizon at an angle

$$\sin^{-1}\left[\frac{8(3\pi - \sqrt{6})}{9\pi - 8}\sin\alpha\right],$$

where α is the slope of the inclined plane.

76. A cylindrical cork, of length l and radius r, is slowly extracted from the neck of a bottle. If the normal pressure per unit of area between the bottle and the unextracted part of the cork at any instant is constant and equal to P, show that the work done in extracting it is $\pi\mu r l^2 P$ where μ is the coefficient of friction.

Answers To The Examples

I. (Pages 11-12.)

1. (i) 25; (ii) $3\sqrt{3}$; (iii) 13; (iv) $\sqrt{61}$; (v) 60°; (vi) 15 or $\sqrt{505}$; (vii) 3.
2. 20 gf; 4 gf.
3. $\sqrt{2}$ gf in a direction south-west.
4. 205 kgf.
5. P gwt at right angles to the first component.
6. 2 gf. **7.** 20 gf. **8.** 17 gf.
9. 60°. **10.** 3 kgf; 1 kgf.
11. (i) 120°; (ii) $\cos^{-1}\left(-\frac{7}{8}\right)$, *i.e.*, 151° 3′.
12. $\cos^{-1}\left(-\frac{1}{2}\frac{A^2+B^2}{A^2-B^2}\right)$.
13. In the direction of the resultant of the two given forces.
14. (i) 23.8; (ii) 6.64; (iii) 68° 12′; (iv) 2.56.

II. (Pages 14-15.)

1. $5\sqrt{3}$ and 5 kg wt. **2.** (i) $\frac{1}{2}P\sqrt{2}$; (ii) $\frac{12}{13}P$.
3. 50 kgf.
4. Each is $\frac{1}{3}100\sqrt{3}$, *i.e.*, 57.735 gf.
5. 36.603 and 44.83 gf nearly.
6. $P(\sqrt{3}-1)$ and $\frac{P}{2}(\sqrt{6}-\sqrt{2})$, *i.e.*, $P\times .732$ and $P\times 0.5176$.
8. $F\sqrt{3}$ and $2F$.
9. $F\sqrt{2}$ at 135° with the other component.
10. $10\sqrt{5}$ at an angle $\tan^{-1}\frac{1}{2}$ (*i.e.*, 22.36 at 26°34′) with the vertical.
11. 33.62 kgf; 51.8 kgf.

III. (Pages 20-21.)

1. $1:1:\sqrt{3}$. **2.** $\sqrt{3}:1:2$.
3. 120°.
4. 90°, 112° 37′ (= 180° − $\cos^{-1}\frac{5}{13}$), and 157° 23′.
9. $R_1 = 34.4$ kgf, $\alpha_1 = 81°$; $R_2 = 6.5$ kgf, $\alpha_2 = 169°$.
10. $101\frac{1}{2}$°; 57°. **11.** 52; 95°. **12.** 67.2 ; 101. **13.** 46;138°.
14. 29.6; 14°. **15.** 149 kgf.

IV. (Pages 21-23.)

1. 40.
2. $\cos^{-1}\left(-\frac{1}{4}\right)$ *i.e.* 104° 29′.
3. $2\sqrt{3}$ and $\sqrt{3}$ kgf. **4.** $15\sqrt{3}$ and 15 kgf.
5. 5 : 4.
6. 5 and 13. **9.** 12 kgf.
16. The straight line passes through C and the middle point of AB.
19. The required point basects the line joining the middle points of the diagonals.
20. Through B draw BL, parallel to AC, to meet CD in L; bisect DL in X ; the resultant is a force through X, parallel to AD, and equal to twice AD.

V. (Pages 27-29.)

1. 4 gf in the direction AQ.
2. $\sqrt{50 + 32\sqrt{2}}$ at an angle $\tan^{-1}\frac{7 + 4\sqrt{2}}{17}$, *i.e.* 9.76 kgf at 30°40′, with the first force.
3. $2P$ in the direction of the middle force.
4. $7P$ at $\cos^{-1}\frac{11}{14}$, *i.e.* 38° 13′, with the third force.
5. $\sqrt{3}P$ at 30° with the third force.
6. 12.31 making an angle $\tan^{-1} 5$, *i.e.* 78° 41′, with AB.
7. 14.24 kgf.
8. 5 kgf opposite the second force.
9. $\frac{1}{4}P(\sqrt{5} + 1)\sqrt{10 + 2\sqrt{5}}$ bisecting the angle between Q and R.
10. 10 kgf towards the opposite angular point.
11. $\sqrt{125 + 68\sqrt{3}}$ kgf at an angle $\tan^{-1}\frac{65 + 19\sqrt{3}}{23}$, *i.e.* 15.58 kgf at 76° 39′, with the first force.
13. $P \times 5.027$ towards the opposite angular point of the octagon.
14. 17.79 kgf at 66° 29′ with the fixed line.
15. 9.40 gf at 39° 45′ with the fixed line.
16. 39.50 kgf at 111°46′ with the fixed line.
17. 42.5 kgf at 30° with OA.

VI. (Pages 32-36.)

1. $\frac{W}{2}(\sqrt{6} - \sqrt{2})$; $W(\sqrt{3} - 1)$.
2. $2\frac{2}{3}$ and $3\frac{1}{3}$ kgf. **3.** 63 and 6 kgf.

4. 56 and 42 kgf. **5.** 48 and 36 kgf.
6. 4, 8, and 12 kgf. **7.** W.
8. 54 kgf.
9. The inclined portions of the string make 60° with the vertical and the thrust is $W\sqrt{3}$.
10. 7.23 kgf.
11. The weights are equal.
12. 4.0 cm. **13.** 1.4 and 4.8 kgf.
14. 14 kgf.
15. 1.82 m; 0.63 m.
16. They are each equal to the weight of the body.
18. $2P\cos\frac{\alpha}{2}$, where α is the angle at the bit between the two portions of the rein.
20. $\frac{W}{2}\sec\frac{C}{2}$. **22.** $W; W\sqrt{2}$.

VII. (Pages 38-40.)

1. 42.9 kg wt; 19.91 kg wt.
2. $1666\frac{2}{3}$ and $1333\frac{1}{3}$ kgf.
3. 37.8 and 85.1 kg wt.
4. 15.2 kg.
5. 169.9, 330, 183.4, 377.5, and 250 kgf respectively.
6. 160 kgf and 120 kgf; 128 and 72 kgf.
7. 100 kgf nearly and 30 kgf.
8. 244.84 and 561.34 kgf.
9. 2.73 and 0.93 metric ton wt.
10. (1) 3, $1\frac{1}{3}$ and 1 metric ton wt. (2) 2, $\frac{1}{3}$ and 1 metric ton wt.
11. A thrust of 5.01 metric ton wt in AC, and a pull of 1.79 metric ton wt in CD.

VIII. (Pages 46-49.)

1. (i) $R = 11$, $AC = 14$ cm; (ii) $R = 30$, $AC = 47.5$ cm; (iii) $R = 10$, $AC = 45$ cm.
2. (i) $R = 8$, $AC = 62.5$ cm; (ii) $R = 8$, $AC = -187.5$ cm; (iii) $R = 17$, $AC = -47\frac{11}{17}$ cm.
3. (i) $Q = 9$, $AB = 17$ cm; (ii) $P = 2\frac{3}{4}$, $R = 13\frac{3}{4}$; (iii) $Q = 6\frac{3}{4}$, $R = 12\frac{3}{4}$.
4. (i) $Q = 25$, $AB = 6\frac{3}{25}$ cm; (ii) $P = 24\frac{3}{4}$; $R = 13\frac{3}{4}$; (iii) $Q = 2\frac{4}{7}$, $R = 3\frac{3}{7}$.
5. 15 and 5 kgf. **6.** $43\frac{1}{3}$ and $13\frac{1}{3}$ kgf.

8. $43\frac{3}{4}$ and $31\frac{1}{4}$ kgf.
9. The block must be 2 metres from the stronger man.
10. 4 metres 25 cm.
11. 1 kgf.
12. 1 metre.
13. 20 kg; $33\frac{1}{3}$ cm; $66\frac{2}{3}$ cm.
14. Nearly 35.94 and 26.58 cm.
16. 16 and 14 kgf.
17. $\frac{1}{2}W$.
18. The force varies inversely as the distance between his hand and his shoulder.
19. (i) 100 and 150 kgf; (ii) 50 and 100 kgf; (iii) 25 and 75 kgf.
20. 1 kgf at 5 metres from the first.
21. 34.62 and 15.38 kgf approx.

IX. (Pages 60-63.)

1. 10.1.
2. $5\sqrt{3}$ metre - kg.
3. $75\sqrt{3} = 129.9$ kgf.
4. $3\frac{2}{3}$ metres from the 6 kgf.
5. At a point distant $6\frac{3}{5}$ metres from the 20 kg.
6. $2\frac{6}{7}$ metres from the end. 7. $2\frac{2}{3}$ kg.
8. $2\frac{1}{3}$ kg.
9. (1) 4 tonne wt each; (2) $4\frac{1}{3}$ and $3\frac{2}{3}$ tonne wt.
10. B is 3 cm from the peg.
11. $42\frac{6}{7}$ kgf.
12. One-quarter of the length of the beam.
13. 55 kg wt.
14. The weight is $3\frac{1}{2}$ kg and the point is $8\frac{1}{2}$ cm from the 5 kg wt.
15. 3 oz.
16. $42\frac{3}{4}$, $42\frac{3}{4}$, and 14.5 kgf.
17. 48, 48 and 23 kgf.
18. 4.5 cm from the axle.
19. $2\sqrt{2}$ kgf, parallel to CA, and cutting AD at P, where AP equals $\frac{9}{2}AD$.
20. $2P$ acting along DC.
21. The resultant is parallel to AC and cuts AD at P, where AP is 12 cm.
22. $20\sqrt{5}$ kgf cutting AB and AD in points distant from A 8 metres and 16 metres respectively.

23. $P\sqrt{3}$ perpendicular to BC and cutting it at Q where BQ is $\frac{3}{2}$ BC.

29. The required height is $\frac{1}{2} l\sqrt{2}$, where l is the length of the rope.

31. A straight line dividing the exterior angle between the two forces into two angles the inverse ratio of whose sines is equal to the ratio of the forces.

33. 112.5 kg.

X. (Pages 66-67.)

2. 9 metres-kg. **3.** 6.

4. A force equal, parallel, and opposite, to the force at C, and acting at a point C' in AC, such that CC' is $\frac{2}{5}$ AB.

XII. (Pages 81-84.)

2. 45°. **3.** $10\sqrt{2}$ and 10 kgf.

4. The length of the string is AC.

5. $\frac{2}{3} W\sqrt{3}; \frac{1}{3} W\sqrt{3}$. **8.** $\frac{a}{l}$ must be < 1 and $> \frac{1}{2}$.

12. $\frac{3}{5}\sqrt{5}$ and $\frac{6}{5}\sqrt{5}$ kgf.

14. W cosec α and $W \cot \alpha$. **15.** $\frac{1}{3} W\sqrt{3}$.

16. $30°; \frac{2}{3} W\sqrt{3}; \frac{1}{3} W\sqrt{3}$. **17.** $\sqrt{7} : 2\sqrt{3}$.

18. $\frac{40}{3}\sqrt{3}$ kg wt. **19.** $3\frac{1}{3}$ kgf.

21. $h\sqrt{h^2 + a^2 \sin^2 \alpha} / (h + a \cos \alpha)$, where $2a$ is the height of the picture.

22. The reactions are $\frac{b}{a+b} \frac{r}{\sqrt{r^2 - ab}} W$ and $\frac{a}{a+b} \frac{r}{\sqrt{r^2 - ab}} W$.

28. 3.16 metres; 133 and 118.8 kgf.

29. 15.5 kgf. **30.** 3.38 and 8.3 kgf.

31. 141.4 and 180.3 kgf. **32.** 13.4 and 16.1 kgf.

XIII. (Pages 89-92.)

1. $\frac{1}{4} W\sqrt{3}$. **2.** $\frac{1}{6} W\sqrt{3}$. **4.** $\frac{1}{2} W \cot \alpha ; \frac{5}{6} W \cot \alpha$.

6. $\frac{W \sin \beta}{\sin(\alpha + \beta)}; \frac{W \sin \alpha}{\sin(\alpha + \beta)}; \tan^{-1}\left(\frac{\cot \beta - \cot \alpha}{2}\right)$.

8. $\frac{3}{5}$ kgf. **11.** $AC = a$; the tension $= 2W\sqrt{3}$.

14. The reactions at the edge and the base are respectively 8.6 and 12.8 g nearly.

15. $W \cdot \frac{r}{2}\sqrt{R^2 - r^2}$. 18. $W\frac{a}{b}$. 23. $\frac{1}{8}W\sqrt{6}$.

24. $133\frac{1}{3}$ and $166\frac{2}{3}$ kgf. 26. Nearly 8.65 and 0.35 kgf.

27. 20 kgf.

XIV. (Page 94.)

1. The force is $4\sqrt{2}$ kgf inclined at 45° to the third force, and the moment of the couple is $10a$, where a is the side of the square.
2. The force is $5P\sqrt{2}$, parallel to DB, and the moment of the couple is $3Pa$, where a is the side of the square.
3. The force is 6 kgf, parallel to CB, and the moment of the couple is $\frac{21\sqrt{3}a}{2}$, where a is the side of the hexagon.

XV. (Pages 97-98.)

1. The side makes an angle $\tan^{-1} 2$ with the horizon.
2. $15a$. 3. $(n+2)\sqrt{b^2+c^2}$.
4. A weight equal to the weight of the table.
6. 10 kg.
7. On the line joining the centre to the leg which is opposite the missing leg, and at a distance from the centre equal to one-third of the diagonal of the square.
8. 120 kg. 9. $\sin^{-1}\frac{p}{p+w}$.
11. The pressure on A is $W\frac{\cos A}{2\sin B\sin C}$.

XVI. (Pages 105-106.)

1. $1\frac{1}{3}, 1\frac{3}{5}$, and $1\frac{3}{5}$ cm. 2. $2, 2\frac{2}{3}$, and $1\frac{3}{5}$ cm.
3. $2\sqrt{5}$, 3, and 3 cm.
6. The pressure at the point A of the triangle is
$$\frac{w}{3} + W\frac{a}{c\sin B},$$
where a is the perpendicular distance of the weight W from the side BC.
10. 60°. 12. $\cos^{-1}\frac{7}{25}$, *i.e.* 73° 44′.

XVII. (Page 108.)

1. $11\frac{2}{3}$ cm from the end.
2. $37\frac{1}{2}$ cm from the end.
3. $2\frac{5}{9}$ decimetres.
4. $\frac{20}{21}$ cm from the middle.
6. It divides the distance between the two extreme weights in the ratio of 7 : 2.
7. 5 : 1.
8. 40.0 cm nearly,
9. $\frac{5n}{3}$ cm.
10. 12 kg; the middle point of the rod.

XVIII. (Pages 113-115.)

1. One-fifth of the side of the square.
2. $\frac{3a}{4}$ from *AB*; $\frac{a}{4}$ from *AD*.
3. At a point whose distances from *AB* and *AD* are 16 and 15 cm respectively.
4. $14\frac{2}{3}$ and $16\frac{2}{3}$ cm.
5. $\frac{a}{6}\sqrt{19}$; $\frac{a}{30}\sqrt{283}$.
7. At the centre of gravity of the lamina.
8. $8\frac{1}{3}$ and $11\frac{1}{3}$ cm. **10.** 2 : 1 : 1.
12. At a point whose distances from *BC* and *CA* are respectively $\frac{3}{13}$ ths and $\frac{4}{13}$ ths of the distances of *A* and *B* from the same two lines.
14. It divides the line joining the centre of the fifth weight in the ratio of 5 : 9.
18. One-quarter of the side of the square.
20. $8\frac{2}{3}$ cm from *A*.
21. It passes through the centre of the circle inscribed in the triangle.

XIX. (Pages 118-119.)

1. $4\frac{1}{12}$ cm from the joint.
2. $5\frac{7}{8}$ cm from the lower end of the figure.
3. It divides the beam in the ratio of 5 : 11.
4. At the centre of the base of the triangle.
5. $7\frac{3}{5}$ cm.

7. One cm from the centre of the larger sphere.
8. Its distance from the centre of the parallelogram is one-ninth of a side.
9. The distance from the centre is one-twelfth of the diagonal.
10. The distance from the centre is $\frac{1}{21}$th of the diagonal of the square.
11. It divides the line joining the middle points of the opposite parallel sides in the ratio of 5 : 7.
12. $\frac{1}{3}\sqrt{3}$ cm from O. 14. $\frac{5a}{18}$.
15. A' bisects AD, where D is the middle point of BC.
16. It divides GA in the ratio $\sqrt{m} - 1 : m\sqrt{m} - 3\sqrt{m} + 1$.
17. The height of the triangle is $\frac{3 - \sqrt{3}}{2}$, *i.e.* 0.634, of the side of the square.
18. $\frac{15}{194}$ cm from the centre.
19. The centre of the hole must be $1\frac{1}{3}$ metre from the centre of the disc.
20. It is at a distance $\frac{b^3}{a^2 + ab + b^2}$ from the centre of the larger sphere.
21. $\frac{45}{56}h$, where h is the height of the cone.
22. 27.06 cm nearly.
23. The height, x, of the part scooped out is one-third of the height of the cone.
24. 4928 km nearly.

XX. (Pages 121-123.)

1. By 7, 8, and 9 kgf respectively.
2. $3\frac{2}{5}$ cm. **6.** 5 : 4.
10. At the centre of gravity of the triangle.
14. $2\sin^{-1}\frac{1}{3}$. **15.** $\sqrt{6} : 1$.
16. The height of the cone must be to the height of the cylinder as $2 - \sqrt{2} : 1$, *i.e.* as $0.5858 : 1$.
19. It divides the axis of the original cone is the ratio 3 : 5.

XXI. (Pages 131-132.)

1. $16\frac{2}{3}$ cm. **2.** $\frac{6}{\sqrt[3]{\pi}}$ cm **4.** $\frac{W}{6}$.
7. 120; $\frac{1}{120}$ th.

8. 18 if they overlap in the direction of their lengths, and 8 if in the direction of their breadths.

11. $\sqrt{3}$ times the radius of the hemisphere.

12. $1 : \sqrt{2}$. **14.** $4r$.

18. The string makes an angle $\cos^{-1}\left(\frac{W \sin\alpha}{P}\right)$ with the plane where α is its inclination to the horizon; the equilibrium is stable.

19. The line from the fixed point to the centre is inclined at an angle $\sin^{-1}\left(\frac{W - w}{p + W + w} \cdot \frac{r}{c}\right)$ to the vertical; the equilibrium is stable.

XXII. (Pages 144-145.)

1. (1) 63000 m-kgf; 48000 m-kgf. **2.** 600 m.
3. 432×10^6 m-kgf.
4. 612 cu-m nearly.
5. 8.84 hours nearly.
6. 8.32 nearly.
7. 45.4 hours.
9. 3.285.
10. 660,000 ft-lb; 30 H.P.
11. 114.8 metric ton wt.
13. 20 m-kgf; 0.174 H.P.
14. 28.45... J; $\frac{49}{1600} n(n+1)$ J.
16. 4.41 J.
18. 244.02 J.

XXIII. (Pages 151-152.)

1. 5 metres.
2. 4 metres from the first weight; toward the first weight.
3. 11 : 9.
4. 2.75 kgf.
6. 4 kg.
7. $9\frac{4}{5}$ kg.
8. 15 cm from the 756 g; $4\frac{2}{7}$ cm.
9. 30 cm. **10.** 2520 kgf. **11.** 10.5 kgf.
12. 15 kgf. **13.** $2\sqrt{2}$ at 45° to the lever.
14. 25 kgf.
15. The long arm makes an angle $\tan^{-1}\frac{7}{\sqrt{3}}$ with the horizon.
16. $4\frac{1}{4}$ kgf.
20. 20 kg.
20. The weight of 225 kgf.
21. $\frac{n}{6}(\sqrt{3} - 1)\, a$.

XXIV. (Pages 157-158.)

1. (i) 160; (ii) 4; (iii) 3.
2. (i) 3.5; (ii) $22\frac{3}{4}$; (iii) 3.5; (iv) 6.

3. 290 kg. 4. $10\frac{3}{4}$ kg. 5. 5 kg.

7. 5 kg. 9. 40 kg; 1 kg each.

10. $4w; 21w$. 12. $4\frac{16}{17}$ kgf. 13. 18 kgf.

XXV. (Page 159.)

1. 6 kg. 2. 4 strings; 2 kg.
3. $23\frac{1}{2}$ kg ; 6 pulleys.
4. 7 strings; 14 kg.
5. $\frac{W}{n+1}$, where n is the number of strings; $\frac{W}{n-1}$.
6. 63 kgf.
7. The cable would support $2\frac{1}{4}$ tonnes
8. n.
9. $37\frac{1}{2}$ kg; $83\frac{1}{2}$ kg. 10. $63\frac{7}{11}$ kg.

XXVI. (Pages 164-165.)

1. (i) 30 kg; (ii) 4 kg; (iii) 4.
2. (i) 161 kgf; (ii) 16 kgf; (iii) $\frac{1}{2}$ kg; (iv) 5.
3. 5 kgf; the point required divides the distance between the first two strings in the ratio of 23 : 5.
4. $\frac{11}{18}$ cm from the end 5. $18\frac{6}{53}$.
6. $\frac{4}{7}$ cm from the end.
8. $W = 7P + 4w; 200\,g; \frac{1}{2}$ kgf.
9. 4; 1050 kg. 10. 4.
12. $W = P(2^n - 1) + W'(2^{n-1} - 1)$.

XXVII. (Pages 169-170.)

1. 12 kg wt; 20 kg wt. 2. 30°; $W\frac{\sqrt{3}}{2}$.
3. 51.96 kgf. 5. $3:4; 2P$.
6. $\sqrt{3}:1$ 7. $\cos^{-1}\frac{11}{18}$; $\sin^{-1}\frac{1}{4}$ to the plane.
8. $\frac{1}{\sqrt{3}}$ kgf; $\frac{7}{\sqrt{3}}$ kgf. 9. 6 kg wt.

11. $8\frac{1}{4}$ kg. **12.** $\frac{\sin\alpha}{\sin\beta - \sin\alpha}$ tonnes.

14. The point divides the string in the ratio $1 : \sin\alpha$.

16. 8.687 kgf; 23.442 kgf.

17. 5.159 kgf; 6.104 kgf.

18. 8.06 kgf; 17.028 kgf.

XXVIII. (Pages 174-175.)

1. $3\frac{1}{2}$ kgf.

2. 60 kgf; 35 kgf on each ; $55\frac{5}{11}$ kgf.

3. 50 cm. **4.** 210 cm.

5. 4256 kg. **6.** $1\frac{1}{2}$ kgf.

7. $27\frac{1}{2}$ kg. **8.** $11\frac{2}{3}$ kgf.

9. $1\frac{1}{6}$ kgf. **10.** 180 kg.

11. 60 kg. **12.** 225 kg-m.

13. 47040 ft-lb; 2 cwt; 210 feet.

14. $\frac{2b}{c-a}$; $\frac{2R}{R-r}$.

XXIX. (Pages 180-181.)

1. 11 kg. **2.** $13\frac{1}{8}$ kg.

3. 50 g. **4.** 2 : 3; 6 kg.

5. 12.247 kg. **6.** $5 : \sqrt{26}$.

7. $\frac{6}{5}\sqrt{110}$ inches ; $\frac{\sqrt{110}}{2}$ kg.

9. Rs. 4.50 P; Rs. $3\frac{5}{9}$.

10. He will lose $22\frac{1}{2}$ P.

12. $10 : \sqrt{101}$; $\sqrt{101} : 10$.

13. $\frac{P-Q}{2}$; $\frac{P+Q}{2}$.

14. $w - P : P - w'$; $\frac{ww' - P^2}{P - w'}$.

15. $R - \frac{(Q-R)^2}{P-Q}$. **16.** 8 kg.

XXX. (Pages 184-186.)

1. $69\frac{2}{3}$ cm from the fulcrum.
2. 4 cm from the end; 2 cm.
3. 64 cm from the fulcrum.
4. $1\frac{1}{3}$ cm; $2\frac{1}{4}$ kg.
5. 10 cm.
6. 8 kg; 20 cm beyond the point of attachment of the weight.
7. $\frac{4}{9}$ kg; $1\frac{17}{19}$ kg.
8. 13 kg; 7.5 kg; 25 cm from the fulcrum.
9. 1.5 kg.
10. $7\frac{15}{16}$ kg; $3\frac{7}{16}$ kg; 10 cm.
11. It is 20 cm from the point at which the weight is attached.
12. 75 g.
13. 60 cm.
15. The machine being graduated to show kg the weights indicated must each be increased by $\frac{1}{6}$th of a kg.
16. The numbers marked on the machine must each be increased by $\frac{x}{y}\frac{W}{10}$, where x and y are respectively the distances of the centre of gravity of the machine and its end from the fulcrum, and W is the weight of the machine.
17. He cheats his customers, or himself, according as he decreases, or increases, the movable weight.

XXXI. (Pages 190-191.)

(*In the following examples π is taken to be $\frac{22}{7}$.*)

1. 2200 kg.
2. $11\frac{5}{11}$ cm.
3. $\frac{23}{54}$ kgf.
4. $\frac{245}{352}$ kgf.
5. $2\frac{47}{99}$ kgf.
6. $150\frac{6}{7}$ quintals.
7. 70.4 quintals.
8. $25\frac{5}{11}$ kgf.
9. $11\frac{11}{35}$ cm.
10. $4523\frac{5}{7}$.
11. $5430\frac{6}{7}$.
12. $\frac{5}{8}$ kg-m.

XXXII. (Pages 201-202.)

1. 10 kgf; $12\frac{1}{2}$ kgf; $10\sqrt{17}$ and $\frac{15}{2}\sqrt{17}$ kgf respectively, inclined at an angle $\tan^{-1} 4$ with the horizontal.
2. $\frac{P}{W} = \frac{\sqrt{2}}{3} = 0.4714.$
3. $10\sqrt{10}$ kg wt at an angle $\tan^{-1} 3$ with the horizon.
6. $\frac{1}{4}$.
7. $\frac{4}{3}\sqrt{3}$ lb wt.
9. $\frac{\sqrt{3}}{15}$.
10. $\sin\beta = \sin\alpha + \mu\cos\alpha$.
11. $\tan^{-1}\left(\mu\frac{W_1 + W_2}{W_1 - W_2}\right)$, where W_1 and W_2 are the two weights.
14. $a \times 0.134$.
15. At an angle equal to the angle of friction.
16. 122.64 kg. 17. 39.85 kgf; .32.

XXXIII. (Pages 211-212.)

1. 571.2 kg-m.
2. 990,000 kg-m; 7.19 H.P. nearly
3. 31,242, 240 J; $5\frac{9}{11}$ H.P.
4. 209.682 cu. m.
6. 0.446.
7. 0.11, 0.34, and 0.47 nearly.
8. $a = 4.125$; $b = 0.01125$.

(The answers to the following four questions will be only approximations.)

9. $a = 5.3; b = 0.097$.
10. $P = 7.3 + 0.236\,W;\ E = \frac{W}{36.5 + 1.18\,W};\ M = \frac{W}{7.3 + 0.236\,W}$.
11. $P = 4.3 + 4.7\,W$; 0.36 and 0.39 nearly.
12. $P = 18.5 + 5.5\,W$; 0.26 and 0.35 nearly.

XXXIV. (Pages 214-215.)

1. $5\frac{5}{6}$ kgf.
2. 45°.
5. It can be ascended as far as the centre.
8. 15 m; one-quarter of the weight of the ladder.
9. $w\frac{2\mu - \tan\alpha}{\tan\alpha - \mu}$; if $\tan\alpha > 2\mu$, the weight is negative, *i.e.* the ladder would have to be *held up* in order that there should be equilibrium; if $\tan\alpha < \mu$, the weight is again negative, and we should then only get limiting equilibrium if the ladder were held up, and in this case the feet would be on the point of moving *towards* one another.

XXXV. (Pages 217-218.)

1. $\tan^{-1}\frac{1}{2}$; height = twice diameter.

4. 45°.

6. $2\tan^{-1}\frac{\sqrt{3}}{2} = 2\tan^{-1}(0.1443) = 16°26'$.

8. Unity.

XXXVI. (Pages 221-225.)

11. $\frac{\sqrt{3}}{30} = 0.0577$.

15. $\mu\left(\frac{W}{w}+1\right)\sqrt{b^2-a^2}$.

18. $\frac{7}{9}$.

20. The required force is $\frac{2}{5}W$ at an angle $\cos^{-1}\frac{11}{14}$ with the line of greatest slope.

21. In a direction making an angle $\cos^{-1}\frac{5\sqrt{3}}{9}(-15°48')$ with the line of greatest slope.

24. If $\mu\cot\alpha$ is greater than unity, there is no *limiting* position of equilibrium, *i.e.*, the particle will rest in any position.

28. 60°.

XXXVII. (Pages 228-229.)

1. At P, where BP equals $\frac{1}{3}BC$; $\frac{3W}{2}$.

5. $\frac{W}{2}\tan\frac{ACB}{2}$.

7. $\frac{3W}{\sqrt{5}}$; $\frac{W}{5}\sqrt{10}$ at $\tan^{-1}\frac{1}{3}$ to the horizontal.

8. $\frac{W}{2}$; $\frac{3W}{2}$; $\frac{\sqrt{3}\,W}{4}$.

10. Half the weight of the middle rod.

12. One-eighth of the total weight of the rods, acting in a horizontal direction.

XXXVIII. (Pages 234-235.)

6. 0.105 kg-m.

7. 0.075 kg-m.

XXXIX. (Pages 240-243.)

1. 39 kg wt; 25.8 kg wt at 1° 40' to the horizon.

2. 76.15 and 133.98 kgf.

3. 0.41.

4. 124°, 103°, 133°.
5. 13.45 kgf.
6. 74 kg wt; 12.7 kg wt.
7. A force 2.6 kg along a line which cuts BC and AC produced in points K and L such that $CK = 38.5$ cm and $CL = 35.2$ cm.
8. (1) 37.5 cm; (2) 2.25 m in the direction opposite to AB.
9. 1.17 m from the end.
10. 3.575 kgf and 3.425 kgf.
11. 75, 79.06, (nearly) and 25 kgf.
13. Each equals the wt of 560 kgf.
14. 0.46; 91.2 and 57.2 kgf.
15. 29.05, 32.9, 18.7, 16.6, and 14.5 kgf respectively.
20. $T_1 = 730.8$; $T_2 = 548.24$; $T_3 = 182.56$; $T_4 = 469.84$; $T_5 = 280$ kg. T_4 and T_5 are ties; the others are struts.
21. $T_1 = 469.84$; $T_2 = 670.88$; $T_3 = 538.72$. T_2 is a strut; T_1 and T_3 are ties.
22. 20.832, 26.6 and 24.136 quintals.
23. 6 tonnes and 2 tonnes; 5.77, 1.155, 1.155 and 3.464; of these last four the first, third and fourth are struts and the second is a tie.
24. The tensions of AB, BC, CD, DA are 16.2, 18.2, 8.4 and 12.75 kgf; the thrust of BD is 18.35 kgf.

Easy Miscellaneous Examples.

(Pages 261-263.)

1. 15 kgf at an angle $\tan^{-1}\frac{4}{3}$ with the second force.
2. Each component is 57.735...kgf.
3. 14.24 kgf.
4. 50 and 86.6025...kgf.
6. 90 cm.
7. 60 g.
9. $4\frac{1}{3}$ cm from A.
10. $14\frac{2}{3}$ cm.
12. It divides the line joining the centre to the middle point of the opposite side in the ratio 2 : 13.
13. $\frac{5}{6}$ ths of the diameter of a penny.
14. 4 and 6 kgf.
15. 4.9 kgf.
16. $W = P$.
17. The required point divides the distance between the two extreme strings in the ratio 13 : 49.
18. $\frac{1}{3}\sqrt{3}$ kg wt.
20. 45 cm; 10 cm.
21. $26\frac{2}{3}$.
22. $\frac{2}{11}$.
23. He can ascend the whole length.
24. 10.02 H.P. nearly.

Harder Miscellaneous Examples

(Pages 263-272.)

5. The centre of the inscribed circle.
6. P divides AD in the ratio $1 : \sqrt{3}$.
9. The forces are in equilibrium.
21. $\frac{1}{5}$ kgf.
28. $\frac{l}{2}$.
31. $W\frac{x\sqrt{a^2+b^2}}{ab}$, where a and b are the lengths of the sides of the frame and AP is x.
39. At a point distant $\sqrt{c^2+a^2} - a$ from the centre of the rod, where $2c$ is the length of the rod, and a is the distance from the centre of the given point.
40. $\frac{\mu c W}{a\sin\theta + \mu c\cos\theta}$, where W is the weight of each particle.
44. The difference between the angles of inclination of the planes to the horizon must be not greater than the sum of the angles of friction.
45. $W\cos\lambda\sin(\alpha-\lambda)$ cosec α, and $W\cos\lambda\sin\lambda$ cosec α, where W is the weight of the rod.
48. The ratio of the depth to the width of the sash.
49. $\sqrt{3}$ feet.
53. The particle will move first, if $\mu W > (1+\mu^2)w\cos\alpha\sin\alpha$, where α is the inclination of the face of the plane.
57. The equilibrium will be broken.
59. $W\tan i$; $\frac{W}{W+W'}\tan i$, where W' is the weight of the inclined plane.
62. $W = 5\sqrt{3}$; the force is (i) $\frac{5}{2}\sqrt{3}$ kg weight, and (ii) zero.

    $W = \frac{10\sqrt{3}}{3}$; the force is (i) $\frac{5}{\sqrt{3}}$ kgf, and (ii) zero.
65. He must press downwards when B has raised more than half the ladder.

NOTES